Investigating Patterns of Change

Middle School Science & Technology

Level A

Second Edition

KENDALL/HUNT PUBLISHING COMPANY
4050 Westmark Drive Dubuque, Iowa 52002

BSCS

BSCS Development Team

These titles and dates indicate the primary area of responsibility for each person and the years they worked on the project. Everyone on the project team contributed in numerous ways to create this curriculum.

Rodger W. Bybee, *Principal Investigator (1988–92)*
Janet Carlson Powell, *Project Director (1988–92)*
Kathrine A. Backe, *Staff Associate, Implementation (1991–92)*
Wilbur C. Bergquist, *Staff Associate, Evaluation (1991–92)*
Deirdre Binkley-Jones, *Project Secretary (1992)*
Jan Chatlain Girard, *Art Coordinator (1989–92)*
Sariya Jarasviroj, *Production Assistant (1992)*
Terri Johnston, *Project Secretary (1991–92)*
Donald E. Maxwell, *Staff Associate, Staff Development (1990–92)*
Mary E. McMillan, *Staff Associate, Curriculum Development (1991–92)*
Josina Romero-O'Connell, *Staff Associate, Curriculum Development (1991–92)*
Teresa Powell, *Project Secretary (1989–92)*
Judith Martin Rhode, *Research Assistant, (1989–91), Staff Associate, Curriculum Development (1992)*
Joe Ramsey, *Production Assistant (1992)*
William C. Robertson, *Staff Associate, Curriculum Development (1989–91)*
Nancy Smalls, *Project Secretary, Graphics (1990–92)*
Jenny Stricker, *Staff Associate, Curriculum Development (1992)*
Pamela Van Scotter, *Staff Associate, Editing (1990–92)*
Lee B. Welsh, *Production Coordinator (1989–92)*
Yvonne Wise, *Project Secretary (1989–92)*

BSCS Revision Team

Pamela Van Scotter, *Project Director*
Sariya Jarasviroj, *Coordinator for Art and Educational Technology*
Karen Bertollini, *Production Assistant and Art Production Assistant*
Teresa Powell, *Production Assistant*
Louis Jarasviroj, *Art Production Assistant*

BSCS Administrative Staff

Timothy Goldsmith, *Chair, Board of Directors*
Joseph D. McInerney, *Executive Director*
Michael J. Dougherty, *Assistant Director*
Lynda B. Micikas, *Assistant Director*
Larry Satkowiak, *Chief Financial Officer*

Advisory Team for the Second Edition

Janet Carlson Powell, *Spectrum Science Education, Boulder, Colorado*
Sam Milazzo, *University of Colorado, Colorado Springs, Colorado*
Josina Romero-O'Connell, *Eagleview Middle School, Colorado Springs, Colorado*
Charlotte Schartz, *Kingman Elementary School, Kingman, Kansas*
Dick Sevits, *Panorama Middle School, Colorado Springs, Colorado*

continued on page 457

Library of Congress Catalog Card Number: 97-68461

ISBN 0-7872-5375-8

This material is based on work supported by the National Science Foundation under Grant No. MDR 8855657. Any opinions, findings, conclusions, or recommendations expressed in this publication are those of the authors and do not necessarily reflect the views of the granting agency.

Printed in the United States of America
10 9 8 7 6 5 4 3 2 1

Table of Contents LEVEL A

UNIT 3

UNIT 4

Preface

Welcome to *Middle School Science & Technology*, second edition. We hope you enjoy your learning journey. We developed this science program specifically for middle school students like you. In the process, we considered middle school students, their teachers, and schools. We communicated with more than 20,000 students and teachers across the United States and in South America.

Our program has been a great success with students, teachers, and parents. Students are enjoying science as a way of learning about their world. Teachers, although working harder in this program than in other science programs, know it is worth it when they see their students truly thinking and understanding. Parents are pleased because their children are enjoying science and are successful at it.

There are, however, always ways to make things better, and during the past five years there also have been advances in science and technology that we want to share with you. In this second edition, there are some new investigations, readings, connections, and sidelights. These activities provide you with opportunities to explore in more depth some of the science content. These changes also reflect the most current understanding of various concepts in science. We also added more artwork to enhance the book and to better explain some ideas that need more than words alone. PC&F, Inc., a design firm in New Hampshire, has created an exciting and fun design, and Kendall/Hunt, the publishing company in Iowa, has worked hard to bring you the highest quality book.

If you have comments or questions about the program, please write to us at the following address. We would enjoy hearing from you.

BSCS
Attention: The Middle School Project
5415 Mark Dabling Boulevard
Colorado Springs, CO 80918

Sincerely,

Pam Van Scotter
Project Director

Program Overview

Middle School Science & Technology is probably unlike other science programs you have used in school. This overview briefly describes some of the key features. You will learn more about these special features when you complete Chapters 1 and 2 in the Introduction.

Themes

The organization of information in this program might be different from other science programs that you have seen or used. This is because we have organized each level around a unifying theme. One way of describing a unifying theme is as a common idea that is repeated to tie other ideas together. Writers use a unifying theme, called a story line, when they write novels. Often music has a unifying theme that you hear over and over in the piece of music; Beethoven's Fifth Symphony is a famous example of this.

We used a different unifying theme at each level, but each theme has the same purpose: to provide a thread that ties together many scientific and technological ideas. In Level A, the unifying theme is patterns of change; in Level B, the theme is diversity and limits; and in Level C, the theme is systems and change. To help keep the unifying theme from becoming repetitive or boring, we use a different curriculum emphasis and focus question for each unit.

The Five Es

As you begin using your textbook, you will notice that each investigation, reading, or connections has a word that begins with an E to introduce it: *Engage, Explore, Explain, Elaborate,* or *Evaluate.* These words make up five phases that you will use as you learn an idea. These phases describe what you are doing as a learner and what your teacher is doing as a teacher. Generally you will go through this cycle once in each chapter. For example, when you are doing an **engage** activity, you will be thinking about a new idea. Then you will **explore**

SCOPE AND SEQUENCE

Level A: Patterns of Change

UNIT	1	2	3	4
Curriculum Emphasis	Personal Dimensions of science and technology	The nature of scientific explanations	Technological problem solving	Science and technology in society
Focus Questions	How does my world change?	How do we explain patterns of change?	How do we adjust to patterns of change?	How can we change certain patterns?

Level B: Diversity and Limits

UNIT	1	2	3	4
Curriculum Emphasis	Personal Dimensions of science and technology	The nature of scientific explanations	Science and technology in society	Technological problem solving and society
Focus Questions	How much diversity is there?	Why are things different?	Why are we different?	How does technology affect people in society?

Level C: Systems and Change

UNIT	1	2	3	4
Curriculum Emphasis	Personal Dimensions of science and technology	The nature of scientific explanations	Technological problem solving	Science and technology in society
Focus Questions	How much can things change and still stay the same?	How do things change through time?	How can we adapt our use of energy?	What are the limits to growth?

that idea in one or several activities. Next you will begin to **explain** the idea by constructing an explanation for the idea. Then you will **elaborate** your understanding of the idea, usually by doing another activity. Finally you and your teacher will **evaluate** your understanding of the idea. If your evaluation shows that you are successful in understanding the idea, it is time to be engaged in a new idea and to go through these phases for that idea. You will learn more about these words in Chapter 1, *A Learning Journey.*

Cooperative Learning

We have incorporated cooperative learning strategies into the program for a variety of reasons. One reason is that cooperative learning gives you a chance to learn and practice how to work successfully with others. The skills you gain will become more important to you in many different aspects of school and life. In addition, by using cooperative learning strategies, you will be working in a way that is most similar to the way professional scientists and engineers work. Also researchers have shown that cooperative learning can increase the success of students in science class. Cooperative learning also cuts down on the materials needed for each investigation. Your school then can afford to buy other materials so that you can do more investigations.

The Characters

We use four characters in this book. Al, Marie, Isaac, and Rosalind are in the book for three main reasons:

1. To provide a concrete method for demonstrating the value of different learning styles and ways of being smart,
2. To teach some of the history of science, and
3. To provide a positive role model for cooperative learning and doing science.

The characters are introduced and thoroughly described in Chapter 1, *A Learning Journey,* of the Introduction. This information identifies the strengths of each character's learning style, the historical reference for the character's name, and a bit about the character's personality. In the text, the characters provide examples of why science is something everyone can do, because they are a diverse group of learners and each contributes something positive to the group.

Questions

The two primary places you will find questions in this book are in readings as Stop and Think questions, and at the end of investigations as Wrap Ups. At first some of the questions may seem hard to answer because you have to carefully think about your answer—you cannot just copy the answer out of the book. One of our goals for this program is just that—to increase your ability to think critically. You will notice that many of the questions in the book have more than one answer that can be considered correct. This is because we tried to write questions that you can answer in a variety of ways as long as you provide support for your answer. If this is a new way of answering questions for you, you might feel frustrated at first, but eventually you might find that you enjoy learning this way. Using this questioning method places you more in charge of your own learning.

In addition to questions that we ask you, there are many opportunities for you to ask the questions. Science often begins with a question and as you have more practice thinking like a scientist, you will have more questions of your own. Keep track of these questions and share them with your teacher and classmates. Although there are some questions in science that we cannot answer (at least not yet), your teacher will help you to discover ways of finding answers to some of your questions.

Assessment

Because the topics, themes, and questions in this book are different from most other science programs, it makes sense to include different ways of assessing your success and progress. In many programs, you are assessed only by your performance on quizzes and tests at the end of a chapter or unit. In this program, we recommend that teachers use a variety of assessment strategies. These include ongoing techniques such as daily notebooks, checklists, performance tests, and class discussions as well as short-answer tests, and portfolios to measure how much you have learned and improved and to identify areas to focus on for future improvement. This type of assessment provides you, your teacher, and your parents with a much more realistic and broader understanding of your progress in science class. So don't be surprised if the "tests" don't remind you of tests you are used to taking.

Safety

As in any science program, safety is a concern for everyone who uses *Middle School Science & Technology*. Chapter 2, *For Safety Sake,* in the Introduction will introduce you to the important safety rules that you will need to follow while in the science classroom. We have made every effort to alert you, the learner, to potentially dangerous situations or materials. We have marked these places with the following symbol:

CAUTION:

In addition your teacher should tell you about the safe behaviors that you should use in a science classroom. It is your responsibility to follow all safety warnings, rules, and procedures to avoid possible injury to yourself or others.

INTRODUCTION

What Will This Program Be Like?

You are about to begin a learning journey in science and technology. Your year will be filled with activity and discovery as you learn about the nature of the world around you. Before you begin your journey, we want to prepare you for the road ahead. If you know what to expect, then you can make the most of it. That's what this Introductory Unit is all about. If you keep an open mind and ask the best of yourself, you might experience a learning journey that will last a lifetime.

Chapter 1: *A Learning Journey*

Chapter 2: *For Safety Sake*

FLIGHT DIRECTOR
PAYLOADS
Mission Control Center

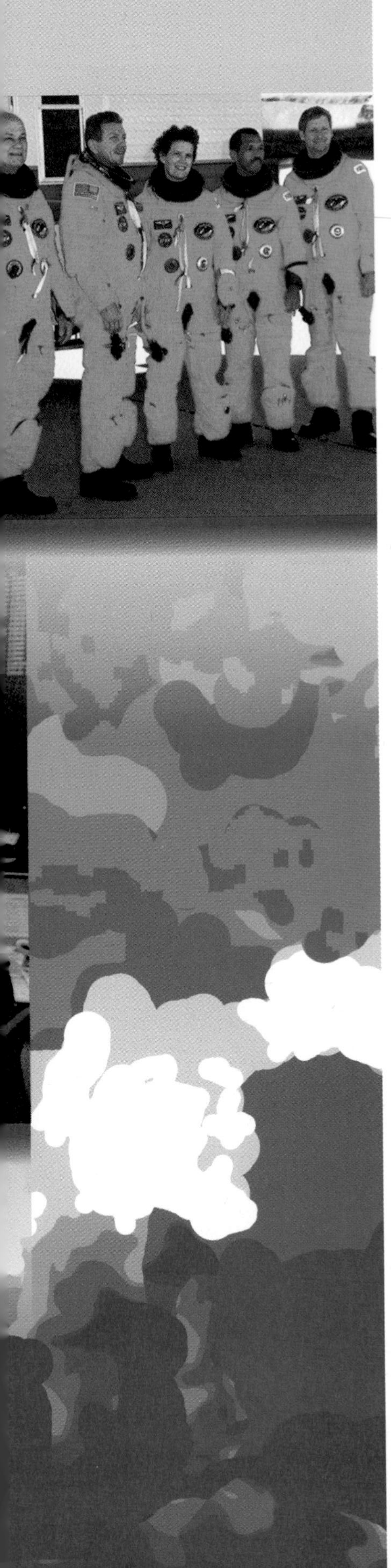

A Learning Journey

Do you like to work alone or in small groups? Do you like to work with people who are similar to or different from you? Why? In this chapter, you will explore what it means to work in cooperative teams with a variety of different people just as these NASA teams do every day. During the year, you will have opportunities to work both with others and independently.

engage

Investigation: Your Winning Ways

explore

Investigation: Finding Your Way Around
Investigation: Meet Marie, Al, Rosalind, and Isaac

explain

Reading: Learning and Working Cooperatively

elaborate / evaluate

Connections: What's in Here?

NASA/CUKJATI DESIGN

Investigation: Your Winning Ways

What have you won lately? A spelling bee? A game of monopoly? A costume contest at Halloween? What is the difference between winning at these and winning a baseball game or a regatta? In this investigation, you will see how your science classroom can be the playing field for a great team of players.

Working Cooperatively

You will work in two teams during this investigation and you will practice using your classmates' names.

Materials for Each Team:

- several pieces of chalk

Process and Procedure

1. Observe the tic-tac-toe game that two of your classmates play.
2. Join one of two teams as your teacher directs and review the rules in Figure 1.1 for a group game of tic-tac-toe.
3. Play the game according to these rules.
4. As a class, briefly discuss the following questions.
   a. Do we have a team of winners and a team of losers? Why or why not?
   b. Could you change the rules and setting of the game so that there would be no losers?

▶ **FIGURE 1.1**

As you play the group game of tic-tac-toe follow these rules.

RULES FOR TIC-TAC-TOE

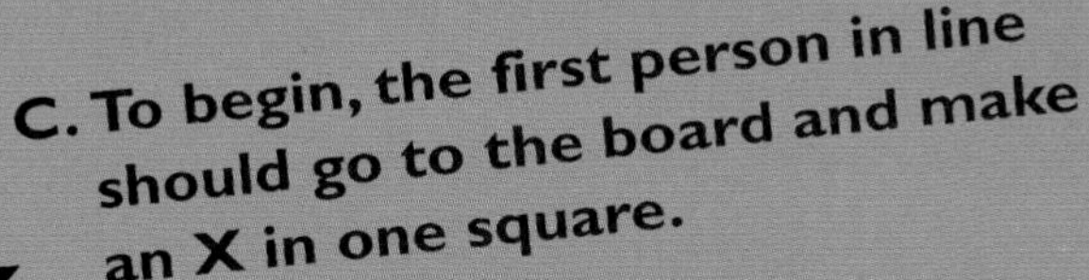

A. DO NOT TALK to anyone else.

B. Each team should form a straight line facing the chalk board.

C. To begin, the first person in line should go to the board and make an X in one square.

D. BE PREPARED for your turn, and when you are finished, move quickly to the BACK of the line.

E. The team that completes the most rows of Xs in either a vertical, horizontal, or diagonal pattern wins.

F. You have 30 SECONDS to complete this task.

5. With your team, develop a new plan of action for playing the game that might result in a different outcome.

   Introduce yourself to your teammates and try to use each other's names.

6. When you have developed a new team plan for playing the game, demonstrate your plan as you play the game again.

Wrap Up

Compare and contrast the results of the second game with the results of the first game.

1. How were the results the same?
2. How were the results different? Why do you think this was so?
3. How did your team's plan encourage cooperation?

explore

Investigation: Finding Your Way Around

Have you ever found yourself in a completely new location with unfamiliar people and surroundings? How did you find your way around? In this investigation, you will work together as a team of four to complete an obstacle course in your science classroom. Because you will be working in this classroom for the rest of the year, it will be important to familiarize yourself with your surroundings and get to know your classmates.

Working Cooperatively

You will work in a team of four in this activity. As you complete the investigation, use your teammates' names.

Materials for Each Team of Four:

- 4 blindfolds

Process and Procedure

1. Follow your teacher's instructions for dividing into teams of four.
2. Record the first and last names of your teammates in your science notebook.
3. Discuss the following challenge and related rules with your teammates:

   Your team's goal is to complete an obstacle course in your science classroom as safely as possible. To do this, you must stick to the following rules:

   a. During this activity, you will be a Guide at certain times and an Explorer at other times. The Guide will lead the three Explorers while they are wearing blindfolds.

   b. The Guide is responsible for helping the blindfolded Explorers accomplish specific tasks along the obstacle course, but the Guide cannot do the tasks for the Explorers.

   c. All team members may talk to one another unless specifically instructed not to.

   d. The team must stay on the course.

▶ FIGURE 1.2

A dressage event is very much like an obstacle course for a horse and its rider. There are challenges and rules to follow.

4. Listen as your teacher describes the following things:
   - how the obstacle course is set up around your classroom,
   - how the teams will rotate through each station of the obstacle course, and
   - how you will take turns being the Guide for your team.

5. With the other members of your team, discuss the following questions.
   a. What does it mean to be a member of a team?
   b. In what ways is the Guide responsible to the team?
   c. In what ways are the Explorers responsible to the team?
   d. When you are the Guide, how might you ensure the safety of your teammates?
   e. When you are an Explorer, what might you do if you have trouble on the obstacle course?
   f. Why might it be important to know your teammates' names for this investigation?

6. Proceed through the obstacle course as a team after the Explorers have their blindfolds in place.

   Each team member should have his or her own blindfold; team members should not trade blindfolds. During the time that you are the Guide, you should store your blindfold in a pocket or other safe place.

▶ FIGURE 1.3

As you complete the obstacle course, the Explorers will be blindfolded. What will the Explorers and Guides need to do to be successful?

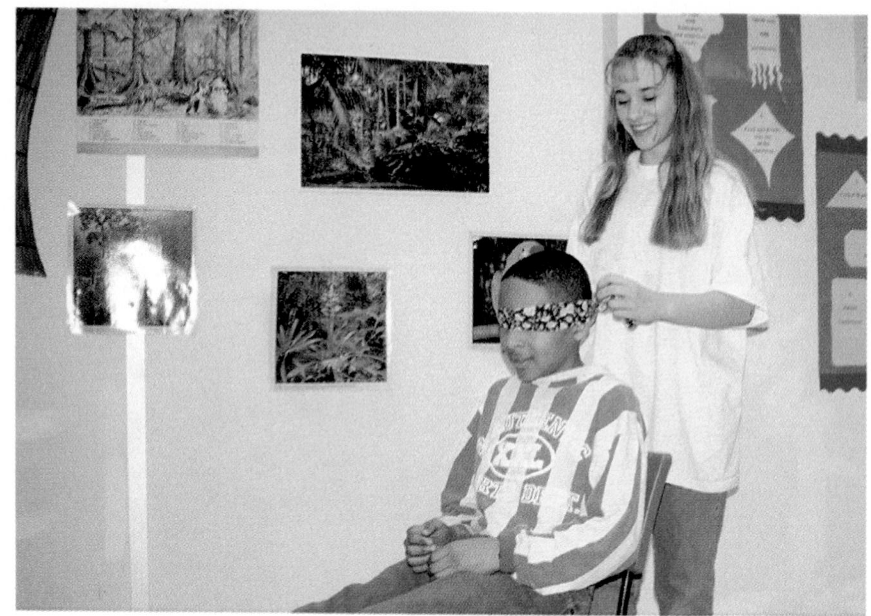

Remember that the goal of your team is to complete the course in as safe a manner as possible.

DO NOT rush through the obstacles to try to be the first team to finish.

7. When your team has completed all four stations of the obstacle course, remove your blindfolds and review your answers to the six questions listed in Step 5 (a through f) as a team.

   If you changed your mind about any of these answers, discuss why you did so.

8. Working with your teammates, create a list of the ways in which the obstacle course is similar to real experiences or situations that you might encounter in your science classroom.

Wrap Up

Discuss the questions with your classmates and write your own answers in your notebook.

1. What are some characteristics of a good team?
2. Describe some ways that your team solved problems?
3. How do you feel about how you and your teammates worked together as a team?
4. How might you improve how well you work within a team?

explore

Investigation: Meet Marie, Al, Rosalind, and Isaac

Take a moment to look in your book and see whether you can find all four characters who will be joining you in *Middle School Science & Technology: Investigating Patterns of Change.* In this investigation, you will learn about the scientists for whom these characters are named and about why we have included them in the program.

Working Cooperatively

In this activity, you will work in a team of four. As you are completing the activity, practice letting other people know your thoughts and ideas and continue to use your teammates' names.

Materials for the Class:

- poster board
- magazines
- glue
- scissors
- assorted art supplies

Process and Procedure

1. Write in your notebook today's date and the title and purpose of the investigation.
2. Participate in the count off.

   Notebook entry: Write down whether you are a one, two, three, or four.

3. Locate the reading *Getting to Know You* that follows this procedure. Each person on the team should read about one character. Divide the reading as follows:

   ones—read about Al

   twos—read about Marie

   threes—read about Isaac

   fours—read about Rosalind
4. When you have finished the reading, copy the chart in Figure 1.4 into your notebook and create teams of four members, each with a different number.

   You should be in a team that has a person who is a one, a person who is a two, and so on.
5. Take turns telling your teammates about the scientist and character you just read about. Fill in the chart as you learn about each scientist and character.
6. Study the chart in Figure 1.5 and think about the words that describe Type W, X, Y, and Z.
7. Think about which set of words best describes you.

   Although you may not identify with every entry in a column, think about which column best fits you.

   Notebook entry: Write down which set of words you chose—W, X, Y, or Z—and why.

► FIGURE 1.4
Copy this chart into your notebook and fill it in as your team discusses each character.

Character	Named After	Born	Died	Area of Science
Al				
Marie				
Isaac				
Rosalind				

Chart of Learning Styles

Type W	Type X	Type Y	Type Z
appreciates facts more than ideas	likes to learn by reading	likes to think about many things at once	likes to learn by experiment
likes to have exact directions	likes to think about what makes an idea important	likes to work without thinking about time limits	likes to discover new information
uses numbers effectively	knows self well	is perceptive about others' intentions and feelings	enjoys musical expression
likes to do one thing at a time	uses language effectively	appreciates ideas more than facts	likes to be independent and to compete
likes to find out how things are useful	likes to know what is happening next	enjoys working in a group	enjoys using tools or gadgets

▲ **FIGURE 1.5**

Think about each set of words. Which set best describes you?

8. Find three classmates who chose the same set of words that you did. Take time to learn everyone's name and find out what things you have in common.
9. In this team of four, use the materials that your teacher provides to create a collage to represent the traits and ideas that describe your group.

   In addition to images, you may want to use words or phrases.

Getting to Know You

We have developed four characters to join you as you explore ideas in science and technology this year. The characters are designed to show the different ways people learn, to show the various talents that people have, and to present some of the history of science. The characters do not represent actual animals or people, although they are named for real scientists.

Meet Al

Al is named after Alfred Wegener, a German geophysicist and meteorologist who was born on 1 November 1880. Dr. Wegener made many expeditions to Greenland to test his ideas about meteorology and geophysics. On his last expedition, Dr. Wegener and an Eskimo companion named Rasmus Villumien brought supplies to a science station in the center of Greenland. Without these supplies, the people at the station would not have been able to survive the winter. A few days later, on his fiftieth birthday, Dr. Wegener and Villumien left to return to the coast by crossing 250 miles of Greenland with two sleds and 17 dogs. As the two men left the science station, the other scientists noted that the dogs were worn out and the men were racing with death. Wegener and his colleague were never again seen alive. Six months later, Wegener's body was discovered carefully buried beside the trail, halfway between the science station and the west coast station, but Villumien was never found.

▲ **FIGURE 1.6**

Al would like you to know about Alfred Wegener, a German geophysicist and meteorologist.

Dr. Wegener is most noted for his work regarding the origins of the continents and oceans. He developed the theory of continental drift. Wegener believed that all of the continents originally had been one land mass. He also claimed that the movement of the continents caused great changes in climate. When Wegener proposed his ideas in 1912, other scientists scoffed at him. In the 1930s and 1940s, professors used Wegener's ideas as an example of scientific blundering. It was not until the 1950s that Wegener's ideas were reexamined and taken seriously. In the 1960s, a number of ecological discoveries completely supported his theory. Today his theory is commonly held in geology.

In *Middle School Science & Technology,* Al is someone who does science for the fun of it. He would rather learn by doing than by reading about things, and he enjoys doing lots of things at the same time. He likes knowing how science and technology connect to his life. He also likes using his imagination and being part of a group.

Meet Marie

Marie is named for Marie Curie. Dr. Curie was born in Poland in 1867. She moved from Poland to France in 1891 to study science at the Sorbonne because she could not find satisfying work in her homeland. It was at this university that she met the man who became her husband, Pierre Curie. He already was a well-known scientist. They worked together on many projects until Pierre was killed in an accident in 1906. After her husband's death, Dr. Curie continued the research on her own.

Marie Curie was quite a trendsetter for her time. She is most famous for her research on radioactivity. She won two Nobel prizes, one for physics and one for chemistry. Her first Nobel prize, in 1903, was credited to Marie, Pierre, and their colleague Antoine Becquerel. The second prize, which Dr. Curie won in 1911, was for her discovery of the new elements radium and polonium (named after her homeland of Poland), and for her study of the chemical properties of radium. She is the only person ever awarded Nobel prizes in both physics and chemistry. Although Dr. Curie made many scientific discoveries, earned two Nobel prizes, and taught at a prestigious university, she was never elected to the Academy of Sciences because at that time the academy did not elect women. Marie lived until 1934.

In this curriculum, Marie is the one who wants to understand. It is important for her to know how ideas connect and also to know what will happen next. She enjoys reading and writing and learns best that way. She always asks *why* and gets frustrated when her *why* questions can't be answered. She understands herself pretty well.

▲ **FIGURE 1.7**
Marie would like you to know about Marie Curie, a Polish physicist and chemist.

▲ **FIGURE 1.8**
Isaac would like you to know about Isaac Newton, an English physicist, astronomer, and mathematician.

Meet Isaac

Isaac is named after Sir Isaac Newton, an English physicist, astronomer, and mathematician who was born on 25 December 1642. He lived until he was 75 years old. During his long life, he caused a certain amount of trouble in the scientific community because he questioned some ideas that had been around for many years. For instance, his theory of gravity is well accepted today, but it was not 300 years ago. Newton developed the notion of gravity while living alone in the country where he had moved to avoid the outbreak of bubonic plague in Cambridge.

He also invented the branch of mathematics known as calculus. And he developed an explanation for the nature of light and color. Other scientists did not accept Newton's ideas at the time. Newton was a very sensitive person, and the criticism hurt him greatly. In fact he was so sensitive he did not always want to publish his ideas, and his friends had to plead with him to do so. In 1705 Queen Anne knighted him. Newton enjoyed exploring ideas in many areas, not just science and mathematics.

Isaac in *Middle School Science & Technology* likes to know facts, lots of them. But he does not particularly need to understand how the facts fit together. He also likes to understand how something is useful. Isaac has a good memory for factual information and enjoys working with numbers. Isaac is always on time and helps others stay on schedule.

Meet Rosalind

The character Rosalind is named after Rosalind Franklin, a British chemist and molecular biologist who lived from 1920 until 1958, when she died of cancer. Rosalind was born in London and attended St. Paul's Girls' School where she received an excellent background in physics and chemistry. She entered Cambridge University in 1938. Between 1947 and 1950, she worked in a lab in Paris. It was in this lab that she worked with Jecques Mering and learned x-ray diffraction techniques.

▲ **FIGURE 1.9**

Ros would like you to know about Rosalind Franklin, a British chemist and molecular biologist.

In 1951 she left France to begin a three-year research fellowship at King's College. Even though she had poor equipment to work with, Dr. Franklin was able to develop a system for taking high-resolution photographs of single fibers of DNA (deoxyribonucleic acid). This technique helped to determine what the shape of DNA was. Her work contributed greatly to the work of Watson and Crick who developed the idea that DNA is shaped like two spirals (a double helix). She also studied the structure of coal and the tobacco mosaic virus. These studies helped people understand the properties of each more thoroughly.

In this program, Rosalind loves computers and other technological gadgets as well as music and musical instruments. She enjoys doing experiments independently and trying to figure out how to do the most precise experiment possible. She would rather be doing science than talking about ideas in science.

Wrap Up

1. What are some similarities among the scientists listed in your chart?
2. What are some of the differences among the scientists listed in your chart?
3. Each character has a unique way he or she likes to learn. Write down the name of each character and two characteristics of that character's style.
4. Which character are you most similar to in terms of how you like to learn? Why?
5. When working in a group, why is it beneficial to have people with different talents?
6. Describe your success in expressing your thoughts and ideas.

Reading: Learning and Working Cooperatively

explain

Think about the differences in the characters that you just met. Also think about the differences in how they learn. Do you think they all learn the same way or in different ways? Understanding *how* you learn can make learning more fun. It also can help you be more successful. Scientists who study how people learn are called cognitive psychologists. When we wrote this program, we used some of their ideas because we wanted to develop a program that helped everyone learn better. As you continue the program, you will notice that each investigation, reading, or connection

▲ **Figure 1.10**

In what ways does each photograph in this reading represent a cooperative team?

has a word that begins with an E associated with it. There are five E words altogether: **Engage, Explore, Explain, Elaborate, and Evaluate**. This series of words describes a good way for students to learn, and it allows for different strengths.

For each big idea that we present, you will experience that idea in a series of ways. First you must be **Engaged** in an idea. To engage you, we might ask you some intriguing question to find out what you already know about an idea. Or we might provide you with a simple and fun activity to generate your interest. After you are interested in the idea, then you need to **Explore** the idea in more detail. In the explore activities, you will have an opportunity to investigate the idea more thoroughly and to ask more questions. After you have explored the idea and have had more experience with the idea, then you will begin to develop an **Explanation** for what you have been exploring. Sometimes these activities are readings and sometimes they are investigations. After you have an explanation, then you need time to **Elaborate** on that understanding. In the elaborate activities, you apply your understanding to new settings or learn more about some specific aspect of the idea. Finally, you are able to **Evaluate** what you have learned.

When we present another big idea, we will begin the cycle again. You will notice that in each chapter, we go through this cycle one time. Sometimes there are several explore, explain, or elaborate activities, for example, and sometimes we combine an engage and an explore activity or an elaborate and an evaluate activity. During the year as you learn, you will notice that rather than explaining things all the time, your teacher is there to help *you* do the learning and the explaining. Cognitive scientists know that this is an effective way for students to really understand science. This way of learning also accommodates the different strengths and styles of each student.

Stop & Think

1. What do you think is the difference between an Engage activity and an Evaluate activity?
2. What do you think is the difference between an Explore activity and an Elaborate activity?

3. Even though the entire cycle of activities is important for learning, which E activity do you think Marie would like the best? What about Al? What about you?

Notice that we often call the groups of students that you will work with "teams" and not "groups." That is because there is a big difference between team work and group work. You can work with a group, but still not need cooperation to accomplish a task. When you work as a team, however, you rely on each other to complete a certain task.

Consider a number of people in a gymnasium. Each person has on athletic shoes, workout clothing, and is holding a basketball. Each person then begins dribbling the ball and shooting baskets into the same hoop. You could say that this group of people is playing basketball. But you wouldn't call this group of people a basketball *team*.

Stop & Think

4. Why wouldn't you call the group of people shooting baskets a team?

Members of a team usually rely on each other for opinions, for help in understanding something, or for help in achieving a goal. A team usually accomplishes something that an individual alone might have a hard time accomplishing. When you work in a team and as a team to learn something like science, educators call that process cooperative learning.

Some of you might have used cooperative learning before, and for others it might be new. In either case, to complete many activities in science this year, you should know a few important things about cooperative learning. Some of the things that you should know about are social skills, roles, working environment, and being responsible as an individual for your learning.

Social Skills

A social skill is a specific skill that you practice to help you develop a more effective team. In this book, you will see and practice two types of social skills. One type of social skill is an activity skill. The other type of skill is a unit skill.

The activity skills that you will practice are mostly things that members of a team can do to make working with each other enjoyable. One activity skill that you already have begun to practice and that you will see in Unit 1 is *use your teammates' names*. The other activity

skills that you will practice in cooperative investigations are as follows:

- Move into your teams quickly and quietly,
- Speak softly so only your teammate can hear you,
- Stay with your team, and
- Treat others politely.

In addition to the activity skill, you will practice a unit skill in each cooperative activity within a unit. The section called Working Cooperatively always will include an activity skill for you to work on, but may not remind you to keep using the unit skill. You should try to use the unit skill in every cooperative activity. You already have tried the Unit 1 skill: *Express your thoughts and ideas aloud.* The other unit skills that you will work on are:

Unit 1: Listen to others.

Unit 2: Show caring and respect for others and their ideas.

Unit 3: Encourage others to participate.

Unit 4: Include everyone in discussions.

Stop & Think

5. What is the advantage of working cooperatively in the investigation, Meet Marie, Al, Rosalind, and Isaac?

6. Would you consider the investigation, Finding Your Way Around a cooperative activity? Explain your answer.
7. Look back at the sections called Working Cooperatively in the investigation, Meet Marie, Al, Rosalind, and Isaac and in Finding Your Way Around. What specific actions were you to practice as you worked?
8. Explain why the actions you listed in Question 7 might be important for people who are trying to work as a cooperative team.

Roles

When people work together to accomplish a certain goal, each person brings a certain strength to the team. Sometimes two people in a team are good at the same thing. Both people then might want to do the same thing or both might not want to do something else that needs to be done. This could be a problem for a team as people try to decide who is going to do what.

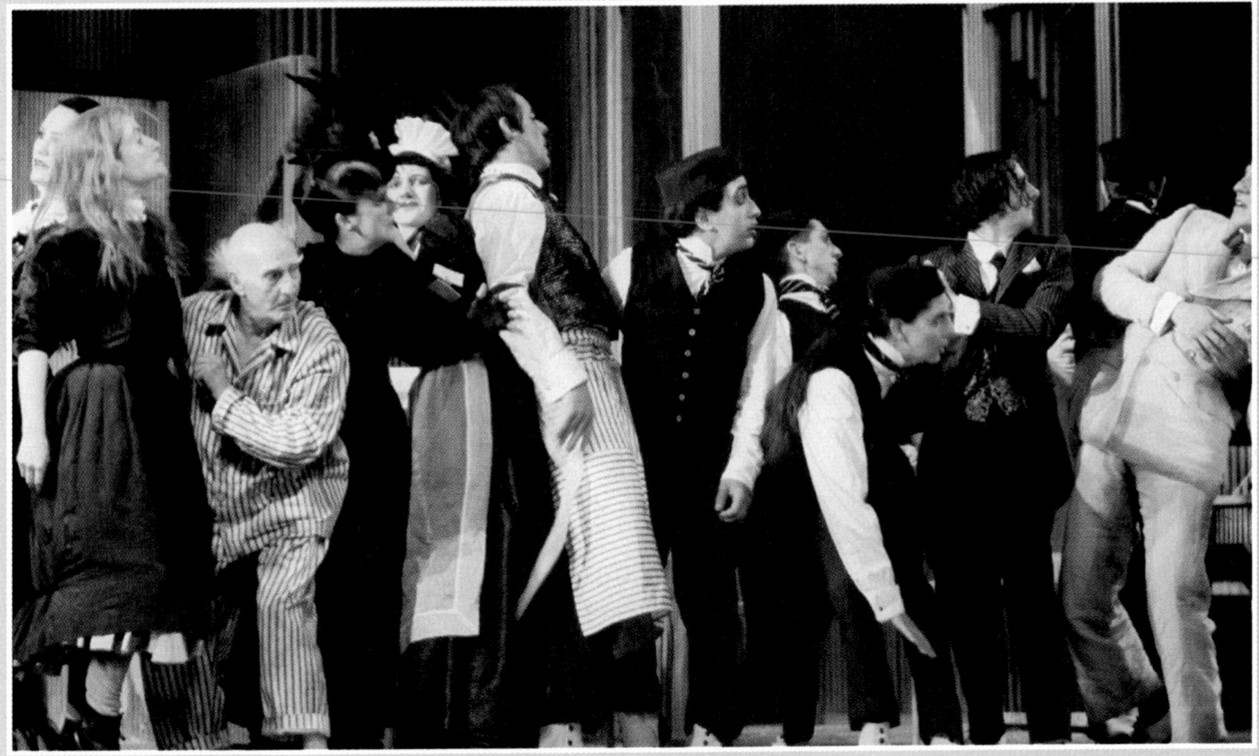

▲ **FIGURE 1.11**
Producing a school play can be a lot of work. How would it be similar to cooperative work in your science class? How would it be different?

Stop & Think

9. In the investigation, Meet Marie, Al, Rosalind, and Isaac, which team member obtained the art supplies? How did you decide who would do this?
10. Describe how the investigation, Finding Your Way Around, might be different without the specific jobs you used to complete the obstacle course.

The use of roles is an important part of cooperative learning. Using roles helps team members become more efficient as they work together. In this science program, you will use a combination of the roles listed in Figure 1.12 during each cooperative learning investigation.

Stop & Think

11. Try to use a single phrase or sentence to summarize what you think the major responsibility of each role is.
12. Do you think the investigations, Meet Marie, Al, Rosalind, and Isaac and Finding Your Way Around, required all four roles? Explain your answer.

▶ **FIGURE 1.12**
As you work in cooperative teams in science class this year, you will use these roles.

ROLES AND DUTIES

Manager:
- **Pick up, distribute, and return materials.**
- **Report shortages and damage of materials to the teacher.**
- **May leave the team to collect materials.**

Communicator:
- **Maintain communications with other teams.**
- **Seek help from other teams or the teacher.**
- **May leave the team to talk with other teams or the teacher.**

Tracker:
- **Help the team keep track of procedural steps, deadlines, and times.**
- **Make sure that each member is aware of the directions for an activity.**

Team Member:
- **Help in team clean up.**
- **Summarize the team's thoughts or activities.**
- **Act as spokesperson for a team.**
- **Help others remember their job descriptions.**

About Working Cooperatively
In each investigation in this book, you will encounter a section called Working Cooperatively. The Working Cooperatively section first tells you whether or not a particular activity is cooperative. If it is, this section will list the social skills that you are to practice for that investigation. This section also will tell you which roles are necessary during the investigation. Finally the Working Cooperatively section will describe what your working environment should be, that is, how to move your desks or where to sit during a particular activity.

Individual Responsibility
The idea of cooperative learning is not to make an activity quicker or easier. The idea of cooperative learning is to share your ideas with others so that you learn more than you would learn by yourself. You are

responsible to the team to help accomplish a certain task and to share your ideas and opinions. But a team is not a successful team until everyone on the team understands what happened in an investigation and understands the ideas related to that investigation. You are always a Team Member, no matter what other jobs you perform. It is the responsibility of the Team Member to be able to explain the team's actions and results.

You can be sure that everyone knows what is happening during an investigation by communicating during an activity, by being sure that everyone does his or her job, and by discussing the Wrap-Up questions for each investigation. These Wrap-Up questions not only will help you determine how much you understand, but also will help you determine how successful you were at cooperative learning.

As you proceed through this Introductory Unit and then into Unit 1, pay special attention to the appearance of the cooperative learning elements about which you just read. Before long, cooperative learning should be comfortable for you and will be an enjoyable way to learn.

elaborate / evaluate

Connections:
What's in Here?

We designed this science book to be different from many other science books. In this activity, we have designed a scavenger hunt to help you learn about the features of your science book. Work together according to your teacher's directions.

Welcome to the Scavenger Hunt
Complete the scavenger hunt according to your teacher's directions. Some of you will be working in teams and some of you will be working individually.

Directions for Teams
Work with your team and take 15 minutes to answer the following questions. You can divide the questions up any way the team feels is appropriate. You may talk to your teammates in soft voices, but do not talk to anyone else. Your team's goal is to answer every question.

Directions for Individuals

In 15 minutes, answer as many of the following questions as you can. Your goal is to answer every question. Do not talk to, or share answers with, any other students.

1. Where are the How To activities located?
2. What materials does each student need for the investigation, Getting Off on the Right Foot? What materials does each team need?
3. What are the parts of an investigation?
4. What is on the opening page of Unit 3?
5. On what page is the *Connections: Sorting Out the Patterns?*
6. What is the social skill listed in the Working Cooperatively section for the investigation, How Do You Know?
7. What is the name of the last reading in Unit 2?
8. How do you think readings and connections differ?
9. How do readings and investigations differ?

10. How many chapters are in your book?
11. What are the titles of the four units in your book?
12. What is the title of the Explore activity in Chapter 11?
13. What is the title of the Elaborate activity in Chapter 14?
14. How many Stop and Think questions are in the *Reading: Combining Ideas?*

Discuss the following questions as a class.

1. In general who was able to answer more of the questions, the students who worked alone, or the students who worked in teams?
2. Explain your answer for Question 1.
3. Which group of students learned more about their science book during this activity, those who worked alone or those who worked in teams?
4. Explain your answer to Question 3.
5. Do you think it would be fair for your teacher to grade everyone the same way on this activity?
6. What are the advantages of working as a team?
7. What might be some disadvantages of working as a team?

CHECKED
BY
RADAR

For Safety Sake

Caution. It means proceed with care. It means think about what you are doing. It means be aware of your working environment. Caution is an extremely important trait to display in a science classroom just as it is on city streets. In this chapter, you and your classmates will learn how to make your science classroom a safe place for everyone. A safe environment is a great environment for exploring concepts in science.

engage

Investigation: Science Is . . . Technology Is . . .

explore

Connections: Thinking for Safety

explain

Investigation: Classroom Safety

elaborate

Investigation: Fizzy Science

evaluate

Investigation: Science Safety Game

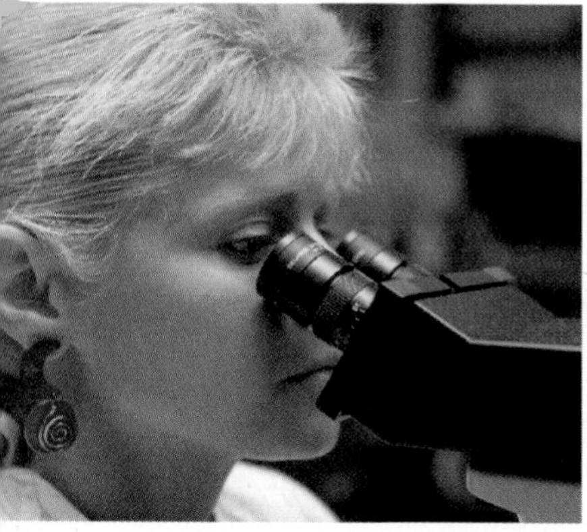

engage

Investigation:
Science Is . . . Technology Is . . .

Both of the words *science* and *technology* are in the title of this book. What do these words mean to you? What do these words mean to your teammates? In this investigation, you will begin to find answers to these questions.

Working Cooperatively

Work in combined teams of two. Your teacher will assign each of you a role so that each team will have a Tracker, a Manager, a Communicator, and a Team Member. Work on the social skill *Move into your teams quickly and quietly.* Arrange your desks in a circle.

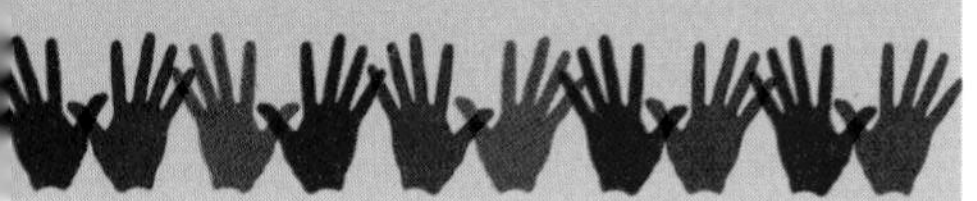

Process and Procedure

1. Record the date, your name, and the purpose of the investigation in your notebook. Also record who is on your team and what each person's job is for the day.
2. The Tracker should read the directions to the team. The Team Member should say the sentence "Science is ________." and fill in the blank.
3. The Communicator should repeat the sentence that the Team Member said and add something to the sentence. "Science is ________ and also is ________."
4. Continue in this fashion until each person has added two things to the sentence.

   The Tracker and Manager should go next. You may need to record some of the ideas in your notebook when the sentence begins to get long.
5. After everyone has added two things to the sentence, discuss the ideas that the team had about what science is.
6. Develop a summary sentence that everyone can agree with.

7. After you agree on a summary, the Communicator should visit two other teams, compare summaries, and report back to the team.
8. Repeat Steps 2–7 using the sentence "Technology is ________."

Wrap Up

Discuss these questions in your team. Be sure everyone is prepared to contribute to a class discussion.

1. How was your team's summary of science similar to other teams' summaries? How was it different?
2. How was your team's summary of technology similar to other teams' summaries? How was it different?
3. How easy was it to move into your team quickly and quietly?

Connections: Thinking for Safety

Have you done many science experiments in the past? Have you ever worked in a laboratory or with special science equipment?

In the scene below, Al, Marie, Isaac, and Ros are participating in a science laboratory activity. Study this scene carefully and then make a list of all of the things the characters are doing or are involved in that might not be safe in a science classroom. Along side each item on your list, explain why you think it is unsafe. Be ready to share your ideas when you have a class discussion.

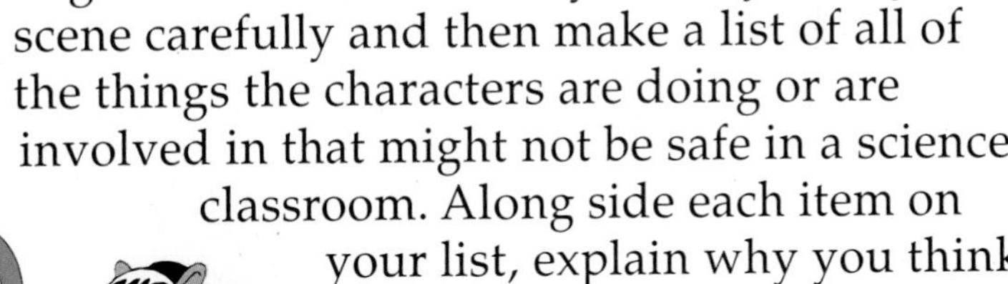

Investigation: Classroom Safety

explain

Look around your classroom. What are some possible safety hazards that you notice? What could you do to reduce the danger? In this investigation, you will participate in discussions about classroom safety and develop a list of classroom rules.

Working Cooperatively

You will work both as a class and in teams of four during this investigation. You will practice the skill *Express your thoughts and ideas.*

Process and Procedure

1. Participate in a class discussion about possible hazards in your school and in your science classroom. Also discuss procedures that people could follow to reduce those hazards.
2. With your classmates, generate a list of rules for safe behavior in your science classroom.
3. Discuss with your classmates the consequences that a student would face if he or she did not follow one of the rules.
4. Work in teams of four to create a poster, a slogan, or a collage that illustrates some aspect of safety that you have been discussing, perhaps one of the rules.
   Use the art supplies that your teacher provides.
5. Read the Student Safety Contract and Medical Letter that your teacher distributes. Take these forms home for your parent or guardian to read and sign.

Investigation:
Fizzy Science

elaborate

In this investigation, you will mix two chemicals and record your observations. As you do so, practice safe laboratory procedures and your cooperative learning roles.

Materials for Each Team of Two:

- 1 beaker (250 mL) containing 200 mL of chemical E
- 1 medicine cup (30 mL) of chemical F
- 1 beaker (250 mL) empty

Working Cooperatively

You will work with a partner. One will be a Tracker/Communicator and the other will be a Manager. You should practice the social skill *Express your thoughts and ideas* during this investigation.

Process and Procedure

1. In your science notebook, record the date, the title, and the purpose of the investigation, and your job for this investigation. Also, make a table or chart in which to list your team's observations.
2. Make sure that both team members have reviewed all of the directions for the activity and understand what they will be doing.

   This is the Tracker's job.
3. Collect the materials listed above.

   This is the Manager's job.
4. As a team, share your observations about the chemicals before you mix them.

Notebook entry: Record your observations.

5. Mix some of the two chemicals together in the empty beaker.

   Notebook entry: Record your observations.

6. As a team, discuss your observations.

   Add other observations to your list as you discuss them.

7. Think about what you could do differently in Step 5 to identify other patterns about these two chemicals.

8. Repeat Step 5 using different procedures.

9. Check with other teams periodically to see whether they are trying something your group did not think of.

   This is the Communicator's job.

10. Make sure the materials are cleaned up.

    This is the Manager's job.

Wrap Up

Discuss the wrap-up questions, then record one set of answers that everyone on the team is willing to sign. Your teacher will collect these.

1. Write one sentence that describes the pattern of how the two chemicals react.
2. What are some possible hazards or safety problems you might expect with this activity?
3. What safety problems might occur during Step 5?
4. How might you rewrite Step 5 of the procedure to make it safer?
5. What is the job of the Manager? Give one example of something that the Manager did during this activity that indicated he or she was doing the job appropriately.
6. What is the job of the Communicator? Give one example of something that the Communicator did during this activity that indicated he or she was doing the job appropriately.
7. What is the job of the Tracker? Give one example of something that the Tracker did during this activity that indicated he or she was doing the job appropriately.

8. What are the benefits of everyone doing his or her assigned job?
9. What might happen if people did not do their assigned jobs?

evaluate

Investigation: Science Safety Game

Cooperative learning! Safety! Are you ready for Unit 1? In this investigation, you will play a game that gives you the chance to use cooperative learning to review your understanding of safety. As you play the game, you will have the opportunity to look ahead and see what is coming.

Working Cooperatively

You will work cooperatively in teams of four. Push your desks together to form a table or work at a large space on a table or on the floor. All Team Members will need equal access to a game board. Use the roles of Manager, Communicator, Tracker, and Team Member. As you play, practice the social skill *Use your teammates' names.*

Materials for Each Team of Four:

- 1 die
- 1 game board
- 2 cups for tokens
- 100 tokens
- 4 player pieces

Process and Procedure

1. Get into your team of four.
2. Read all of the following procedures.

   Make sure everyone understands how to play the game. Whose job is this?
3. Place token cups on the game board in the marked location.
4. Select a playing piece and place it on "START."
5. Take one token and begin to play by rolling the die.
6. Move your piece the number of spaces indicated on the die.
7. Read and follow the directions on the space on which you land.

   If you land on a space that sends you to time out, you lose a turn. When your turn comes up again, you must return to the space that sent you to time out and roll the

die. You will collect and lose tokens as you move around the game board.

8. If you are the first person to reach the last square, "Completed the Science Investigation Safely," take five tokens.
9. Count the tokens that you have collected.

   The winner is the individual who collected the most tokens, not necessarily the player who completed the game first.

▲ **FIGURE 2.1**

These men are playing life-sized chess in a park in Austria. What kind of safety considerations might they be making?

Wrap Up

Discuss the following questions as a team. Record your responses in your science notebook. Be prepared to describe your team's process if the teacher calls on you.

1. On a scale of 1–10, rate your team on how well the Team Members understand safety in the science classroom.
2. List the activity that you previewed that looks the most interesting to you.
3. Describe your team's success in using each other's names.

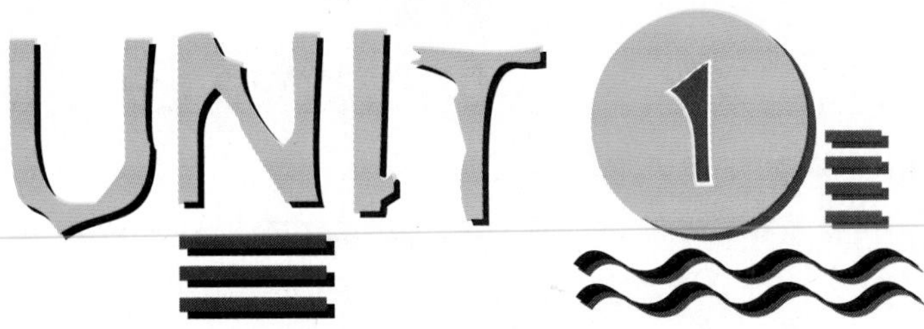

Patterns of Change

If you happen to live close to the seashore, or if you have spent any time in coastal areas, you are probably aware of some of the patterns that exist along the coast. The ocean itself shows different patterns of waves, sometimes low and gentle and sometimes big and powerful. There is also a continuous pattern of low tide and high tide.

You might not think that you know much about patterns, but you probably are more of a scientist than you realize. Science begins with keen observations that can help unravel mysteries. In this unit, you will have opportunities to do just that—to look at things carefully and to unravel mysteries.

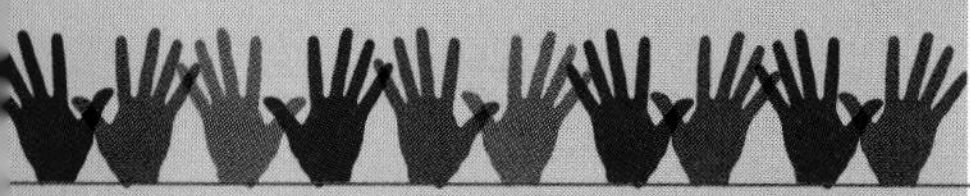

Cooperative Learning Overview

Throughout Unit 1, you will be practicing the following two social skills: *Express your thoughts and ideas aloud,* and *Listen politely to others.* As you think about them and practice them, you will see how well they fit together. When a Team Member is expressing his or her thoughts, the rest of the Team Members should listen politely.

Study the character scene on the next page. Some of you probably have had different experiences with cooperative learning; you might have had a lot of experience in previous grades, or this might be your first time. Throughout this book, you will have frequent opportunities to work in cooperative teams. Remember to refer to the cooperative job descriptions as often as necessary until you are sure about the duties of each job. Always take time to think about the new skill when we first introduce it.

Right now, as Al said, you need to create a T-chart for this social skill. Do so according to your teacher's directions. Keep this T-chart handy. Even though activities will mention other social skills, you need to keep practicing your unit skill through the entire unit.

Hi. I'm Isaac. The first time I ever worked in cooperative teams was in the cooperative learning unit we just finished in here. I'm not too sure about cooperative learning.
We did some cooperative learning last year, and I thought it was really fun.
By the way, she's Ros. I'm Marie. I remember doing lots of work in groups before. Is that the same thing? What are we supposed to do with social skills?
My name is Al. This is gonna be cool doing cooperative learning! This is a pretty big social skill though. I'm supposed to tell you guys that we need to make a T-chart for it.

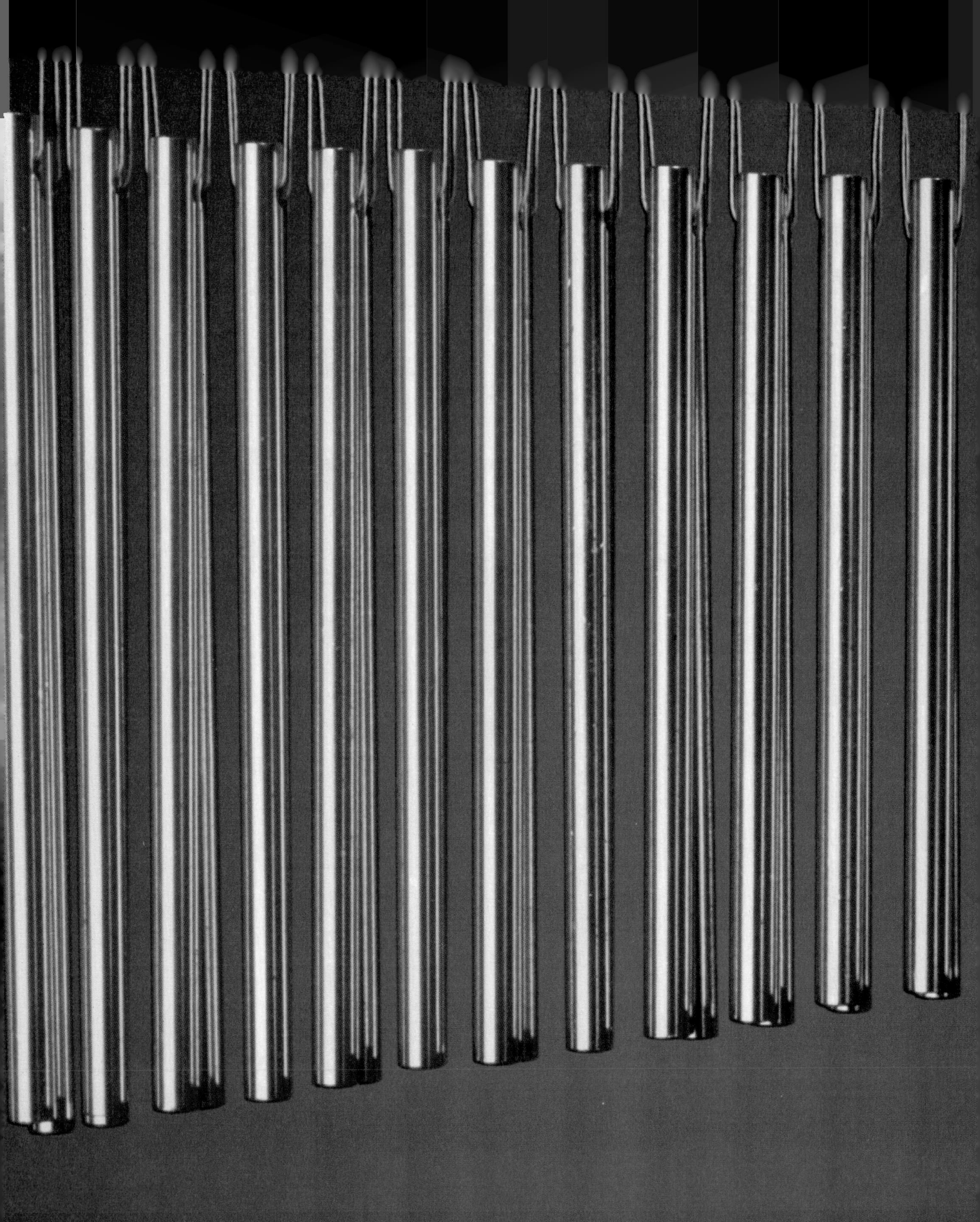

Uncovering Patterns

Do you know what the weather will be like tomorrow? Do you know what time the bus will drop you off at school? Do you know the next time you might see a rainbow? Do you know which chime will make the highest note and which will make the lowest note?

Sometimes you have a good idea about what is going to happen, and sometimes you can only guess. When you are familiar with something, you do not have to guess as much.

engage

Investigation: Puzzles

explore

Investigation: Driving Day
Investigation: Getting Off on the Right Foot

explain

Reading: Patterns and Predictions
Investigation: That's the Size of It
Investigation: In the Swing
Reading: Types of Patterns

elaborate

Connections: Patterns in Nature
Investigation: Moon Watch
Investigation: Making Music

evaluate

Connections: What Do You Know about Patterns?

Investigation:
Puzzles

engage

Many times scientists investigate nature the same way you might solve a puzzle. They look for clues to help them figure out what is happening. How good are you at solving puzzles? Have you ever used a code to communicate? In this activity, you will work to solve such a puzzle.

Materials for Each Team of Two:

- 2 copies of the Decoding Chart
- glue, stapler, or tape

Process and Procedure

Part A—The Social Skill

1. Get into your teams.
2. In your notebook, record the date and the name of the investigation. Also write the first and last name of your teammate.
3. By yourself make a list of two reasons why using each other's names is important in teamwork.
4. Share and discuss your lists.

Part B—Mystery Language Puzzle

1. Pick up two copies of the Decoding Chart.
   This is the Manager's job.
2. With your partner, look at the Mystery Language Puzzle in Figure 3.1.

Working Cooperatively

You will work in cooperative teams of two. Both people in the group should follow the Team Member role. In addition to that role, one of you will be the Manager and the other will be the Communicator, according to your teacher's directions. Check the job descriptions of each person. Move your desks side by side or sit together at a table. Work on the social skill *Use your teammate's name.*

A VERY STRANGE KING NAMED FAIN
RACED HIS ZEBRA WHILE IN PAIN.
JUST EXTREMELY POOR LUCK
CAUSED THE ZEBRA TO BUCK AND
QUICKLY PUT AN END TO HIS REIGN.

1 8*=9 7)=~3* ‡¢•3 •15O $1¢•
=1>O +¢7 <*X=1 #+¢£* ¢• 61¢•.
4(7) *⊙)=*5*£9 6--= £(>‡
>1(7O)+* <*X=1)- X(>‡ 1•2
C(¢>‡£9 6() ~ *•2)- +¢7 =*¢3•.

▶ **FIGURE 3.1**
Mystery Language Puzzle: This diagram shows the same words written in English and in the mystery language.

3. Read the decoded letters aloud from the Mystery Language Puzzle while your partner records them on the blank Decoding Chart.

   For example, the first symbol is the number 1, which stands for the letter A. Try having the Communicator read letters while the Manager records them.

4. Check your team's Decoding Chart.

   It should now show what the mystery language alphabet is.

5. Copy your partner's chart if you do not have one.

   Both partners should have a copy of a completed Decoding Chart. Check your chart to be sure you can find the symbol for each letter.

6. Put your chart into your notebook.

   Use tape, staples, or glue to attach the chart to a page in your notebook.

7. Ask the teacher for a new message to decode.

   This is the Communicator's job.

8. Record the decoded message in your notebook.

Part C—More Puzzles

1. Study Puzzles A through D in Figure 3.2 in your book.

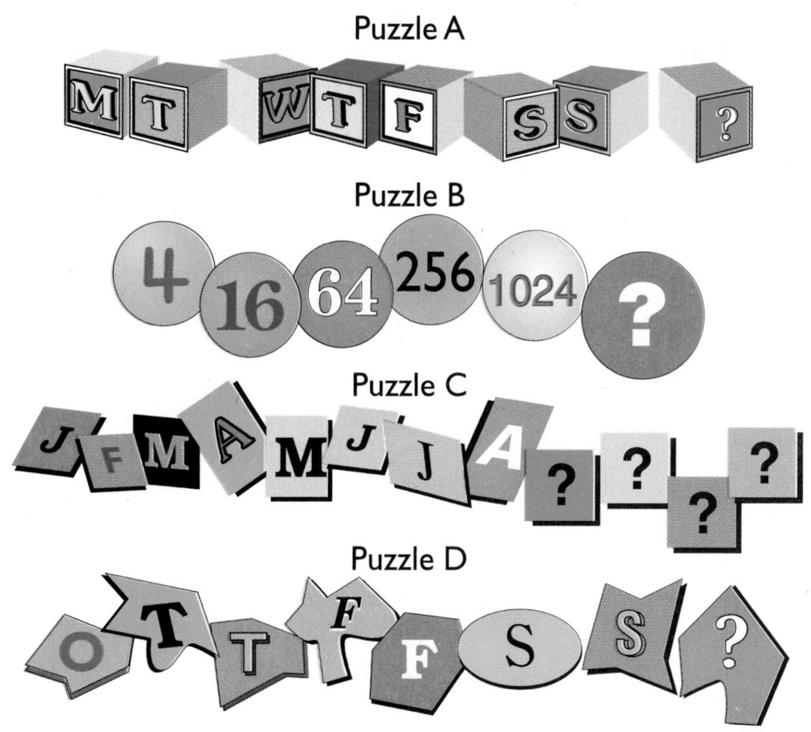

▶ **FIGURE 3.2**
Short puzzles A, B, C, D. See whether you can solve each one.

Puzzle E

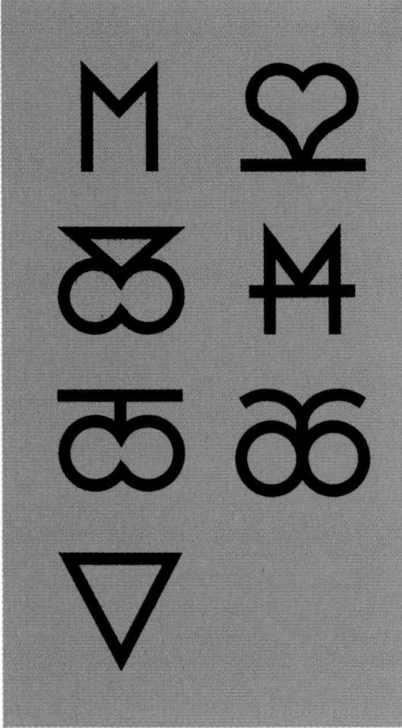

▲ **FIGURE 3.3**

Here is a puzzle that might be easier to solve if you could first cut the symbols in half.

2. As a team, decide what goes in each blank.
3. After you and your teammate have agreed on the missing pieces for Puzzles A through D, record the answers in your notebooks.

   STOP: Are you using each other's names? Are you listening politely to each other?
4. Look at Puzzle E in Figure 3.3.
5. Decide what the last symbol would look like and draw it in your notebook.

Wrap Up

Discuss the following questions with your partner and write your answer for each question in your notebook. Be sure each of you can explain your answers during a class discussion.

1. In the Mystery Language Puzzle from Part B, what was the first symbol you were able to decode?
2. When your team decoded the first set of symbols, how did you determine the answers?
3. Imagine that you meet a friend in the hall and that he or she wants to know what you just did in science class. What would you tell your friend?
4. What is your teammate's name?
5. How well did you use your teammate's name?
6. How did using names help you complete this investigation?

Investigation: Driving Day

explore

Every birthday is a special event, but one particular birthday is extra special. This is the day you become eligible for a driver's license. In this investigation, you will have a new puzzle to solve—figuring out on which day of the week you will turn 16 years old.

Working Cooperatively

You will work in the same cooperative teams of two. In addition to being Team Members, one will be a Communicator and the other a Tracker.

After procedural step 7, move your desks side by side or sit beside each other at a table so you can work together on the wrap-up section. Practice the social skill *Use your teammate's name.*

Materials for Each Student:

- monthly calendars

Process and Procedure

1. Make your notebook entry.
2. Find the calendar page that shows the year, month, and day of your birth.
3. Determine on which day of the week you were born.
4. Record in your notebook the day you were born.
   See Figure 3.4.
5. Determine the day of the week you turned 1 year old.
   Notebook entry: Record this day in your notebook.
6. Do the same for ages 2 and 3.
   Notebook entry.

My birthday

April 8, 1987 Wednesday the day I was born

*April 8, 1988 Friday 1 year old

April 8, 1989 Saturday 2 years old

April 8, 1990 Sunday 3 years old

▶ **FIGURE 3.4**
This is an example of what your notebook entry might look like.

7. Figure out on which day of the week you will be eligible to drive.

   This will not be as easy as the previous step because you do not have a calendar for that year. Figure out a way to tell without looking up the day.

Wrap Up

After moving your desk next to your partner's, share your thoughts and ideas with your partner. In your notebook, write your answer for each question. Be sure each of you can explain your answers during a class discussion.

1. On which day of the week will you be eligible to drive?
2. On which day of the week will your partner be eligible to drive?
3. Could you determine this day accurately without looking at any calendars? Explain your answer.
4. Describe how you were able to determine on which day of the week you will be eligible to drive.
5. As you discussed these questions, did you remember to use each other's names?

explore

Investigation:
Getting Off on the Right Foot

You probably know your shoe size, but how long do you think your foot is? Do you suppose that everyone in your class has the same foot length? In the previous two investigations, you predicted things based on puzzles and calendars. In this investigation, you will predict foot sizes based on measurements you make.

Materials for Each Student:

- 1 piece of light-colored construction paper

Materials for Each Team of Two:

- 1 metric ruler or tape measure
- masking tape, one 10-cm strip
- 1 wide, felt-tipped, nonpermanent marker

Working Cooperatively

You will work in cooperative teams of two. Each of you will be a Team Member. In addition one of you will be the Communicator, and the other will be the Manager and Tracker. Check the job descriptions to make sure you understand your roles. Work on the social skill *Move into your groups quickly and quietly.*

Process and Procedure

Part A—The Social Skill

1. Create a T-chart in your notebook.

   Title it, "Move into your groups quickly and quietly." Label the left column "Sounds Like" and the right column "Looks Like."

2. Fill in the columns according to the social skill.

   As you discuss with your teammate and fill in the columns, consider the following:

   - What kind of noise is appropriate as you move into groups?
   - What kind of noise is inappropriate as you move into groups?
   - How quickly is quick?
   - What kind of behavior is appropriate and inappropriate as you move into your groups?

3. When your teacher says "Go," see which team can move into its group the most quickly and quietly.

Part B—The Activity

1. Collect the necessary materials.

   Remember it is the Manager's job to collect the materials.

2. Take off your right shoe.

   Keep your sock on.

3. Have your partner trace your foot.

   Have one person stand with his or her right foot on one of the pieces of construction paper while the other person traces the outline of the foot. Your entire foot should be on the construction paper while your partner is tracing it.

4. Repeat Step 3 for your partner.

   Put your shoe back on.

5. Use a metric tape measure or ruler to measure the length of your foot tracing in centimeters.

   Figure 3.5 will show you how to measure your foot tracing.

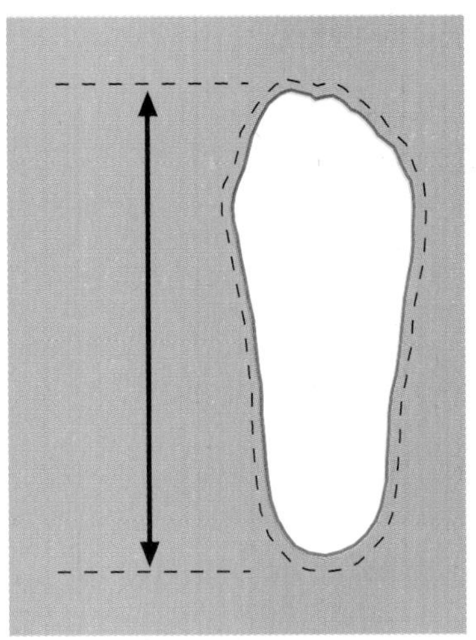

▲ **FIGURE 3.5**

Measure your foot tracing from your big toe to the end of your heel as shown.

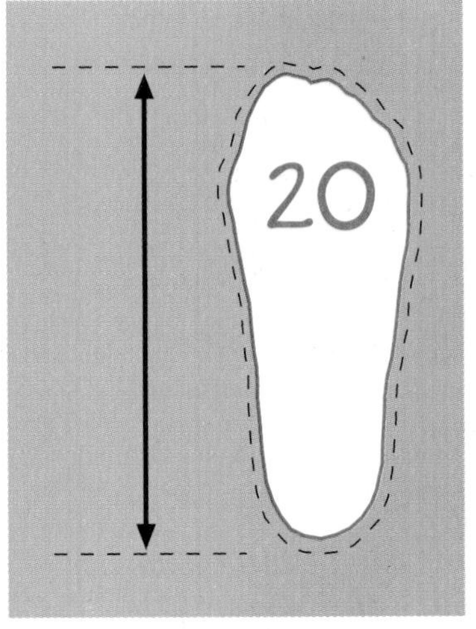

▲ **FIGURE 3.6**

Your finished tracing might look something like this.

6. Round off your measurement if it is not a whole number.

   If you do not know how to round off, go to How to Round Off Numbers (How To #1) at the end of your book.

   STOP: Now is a good time to help each other round off numbers by expressing your thoughts and ideas aloud to your partner.
7. Write this number in the center of your tracing.

   Figure 3.6 shows you what your tracing should look like now.
8. Take your foot tracing to the graph that your teacher has on the wall or chalkboard and tape it above the number that corresponds to your foot length.
9. Draw a picture in your notebook that shows the shape of your class graph and its two labeled axes.

   If you want to know more about graphs, read How to Identify the Parts of a Graph (How To #2).

Wrap Up

Discuss the following questions with your partner and write your answer to each question in your notebook. Be sure you could explain your answers if your teacher called on you.

1. Look at the graph and describe where your tracing is, compared with where the rest of the tracings are.
2. How many students have foot sizes of 20 cm?
3. How many students have foot sizes of 25 cm?
4. Write a summary of this graph. Be sure your summary includes
   a. how many people were included,
   b. the smallest and largest foot size,
   c. the most common foot size, and
   d. a description of the shape of the graph.
5. If another class of middle school students constructed a graph of their foot sizes, would the graph have the same shape?
6. Imagine that you invited a professional football team into your classroom. Suppose the football players took off their shoes, outlined their feet, and added their tracings to your class graph. Would the shape of the graph change? If so, how?

7. How might the shape of your original class graph change if you measured a group of preschool children's feet and added their foot measurements to the graph instead of the football team's measurements?
8. How could you and your partner improve how quickly and quietly you move into your group?
9. When were you the best at moving quickly and quietly—at the beginning of the investigation or at the end?

explain

Reading: Patterns and Predictions

In the three previous investigations, you solved puzzles, discovered on which day of the week you would be eligible to drive, and studied the shape of a graph. You might have wondered what these activities had in common with each other. To answer the questions in each investigation, you had to uncover a pattern. A **pattern** is a collection of things or events that repeat themselves. Because the pattern repeats itself, we know what to expect and can make predictions.

There are many kinds of patterns in the world. For example, most of us know that to cross a street safely, we must watch for cars. Traffic lights cause the pattern to change. You might notice a rush of cars, then no cars. If you want to cross safely, you wait until the right moment in the pattern.

Recall the sequence of letters O T T F F S S ? The sequence doesn't seem to make much sense until you suddenly see the pattern—what the letters represent. They are the first letters of the words for the numerals one through seven. Using this pattern, it is easy to predict what comes next.

Think back to another example. After you and your classmates taped your foot tracings on the board, your completed graph had a particular pattern: more foot tracings near the middle and fewer near the ends. Its general pattern was similar to the shape of the graph in Figure 3.7.

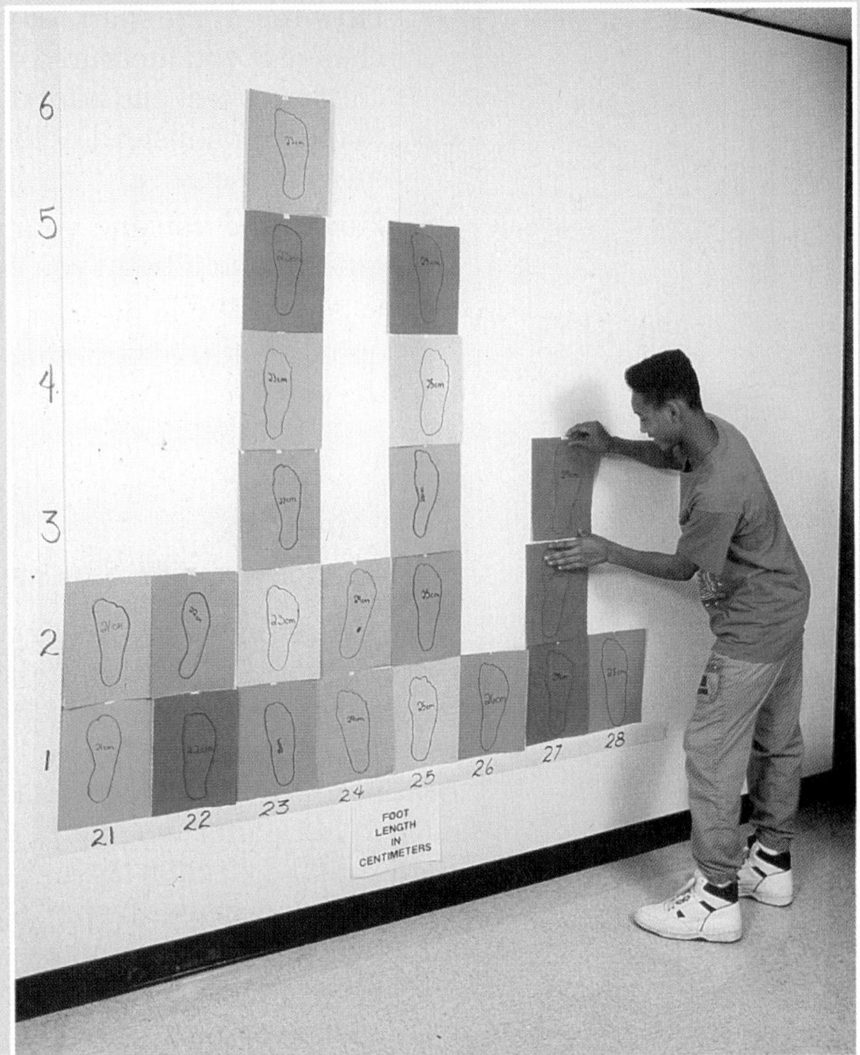

▶ **FIGURE 3.7**

Your class graph probably looked something like this. How might this graph change if a group of senior high students added their measurements?

Stop & Think

1. Now that you have seen several examples, describe ways we can use patterns.
2. Try making this prediction: What will most of your classmates be doing tomorrow at 4:00 a.m.?
3. What pattern did you use to make your prediction?

If you know a pattern, you can use it to make predictions. A **prediction** is a statement about the future, which is based on information gathered from past performances. Patterns provide one type of information. Throughout this year, you will study patterns of change and use them to help you make predictions.

The Corbis-Bettmann Archive

▲ **FIGURE 3.8**

The Rosetta stone is inscribed with three different languages. The top inscription is in hieroglyphics. The middle inscription is in demotic. Both of these are Egyptian languages. The bottom inscription is in Greek. Each inscription repeats the same phrases honoring a Greek king of Egypt called Ptolemy V. The Rosetta stone is kept at the British Museum.

We made up the puzzles that you solved here involving patterns, but there are also puzzles with patterns in the world around you. Some patterns are not familiar so we might not recognize them at first. In 1799, for example, a construction worker in the French army found a most unusual piece of stone near Rosetta, Egypt (see Figure 3.8). It had writing carved into it, so he knew there was a pattern involved. But he could not read the writing. He thought it was interesting, however, that there were three different patterns of writing on the same stone. Scholars recognized that one of the patterns was ancient Greek and the other two were ancient Egyptian forms of writing. Because these scholars could read the Greek, they were able to decode the Egyptian writings, which they never before had been able to do. The scholars realized that the two Egyptian forms were closely related. One form, called hieroglyphics, was the sacred form, and only religious officials used it. The word *hieroglyphics* comes from the Greek words meaning "sacred carvings." The other form, called demotic, was the common, everyday form. The scholars named this stone tablet the Rosetta stone.

Because the stone provided a relationship between the three languages, scholars were able to decode Egyptian carvings on other stones, in addition to this stone. As scholars decoded the writings, they unlocked years of history. None of this information would have been uncovered if someone had not noticed the pattern. The decoding of the Rosetta stone eventually provided the world with information about everything from the crowning of kings to medical history.

We can use patterns to predict rather than to guess. The ability to use patterns to make predictions is an

important skill. We expect doctors to recognize patterns of illness so that they can predict methods of treatments. Auto mechanics make predictions about what is necessary to repair a car by recognizing patterns in the noises that an engine makes. You can predict how your parents will react to a particular piece of news because you know the pattern of how they have reacted in the past.

Of course recognizing patterns isn't always easy, and the predictions you make from patterns won't always be correct. But the more you look for patterns, the better you will be at recognizing them and putting them to use. The following activities will help you do just that.

explain

Investigation: That's the Size of It

In the previous reading, you learned about some everyday patterns such as traffic and some unusual patterns such as the Rosetta stone from Egypt. Sometimes patterns are familiar, and sometimes they are new to us. In the investigation that follows, your challenge will be to identify the patterns.

Working Cooperatively

You will work in cooperative teams of two at two different stations. When you arrive at a station, make a notebook entry that includes the station number. You both will be Team Members. In addition one of you will be the Communicator, and the other will be the Tracker. Continue to practice the skill *Move into your groups quickly and quietly.*

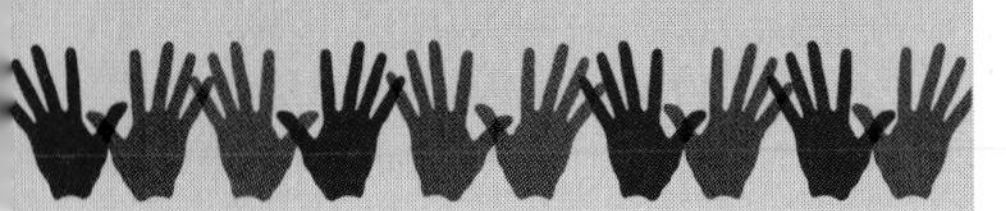

Materials for Each Team of Two:

For Station 1:

- 2 sheets of Graph Paper with Axes Set Up
- Foot Length Data Table
- 1 metric ruler

For Station 2:

- 1 metric measuring tape

Process and Procedure for Station 1

1. Copy the chart in Figure 3.9 into your notebook.
   Leave plenty of space (about half a page).
2. Fill in the chart you made by writing down foot length measurements.
   If someone's foot length is 14 cm and he or she is 3 years old, you would write down the foot length in the first row of the chart in the child category. See the examples in Figure 3.10.

▶ FIGURE 3.9

This is a sample of the chart you will use to record the foot measurements. Copy this into your notebook.

	AGE	FOOT LENGTH (cm)
Child	0-9	
Adolescent	10-17	
Adult	18+	

▶ FIGURE 3.10

As you fill in your chart, it will begin to look like this. The first person on your data table is 1 year old and has a foot length of 10 cm, so you would write 10 in the first row.

	AGE	FOOT LENGTH (cm)
Child	0-9	10,14,18
Adolescent	10-17	24,20,22
Adult	18+	26,29,26

3. Use Xs to graph the data on children's foot measurements.

   Use the top section of the prepared graph paper at this station and refer to How to Plot Data on a Graph (How To #3) if necessary.
4. Use Xs to graph the data on adolescent foot measurements.

   Use the middle section of the graph paper.
5. Use Xs to graph the data on adult foot measurements.

   Use the bottom section of the graph paper.
6. Compare the three graphs you have made.
7. Record in your notebook any pattern you notice about the graphs. Answer the wrap-up questions and then go to another station.

≋Wrap Up for Station 1

Discuss the wrap-up questions with your partner and record your answers in your notebook before you go on to another station.

1. Describe the difference between the foot measurement of a child and that of an adolescent.
2. Describe the difference between the foot measurement of an adolescent and that of an adult.
3. Compare the three graphs you have made and describe the patterns you see.
4. Based on the numbers you have, predict a common foot measurement for 70-year-old people. Explain your answer.

▼ **FIGURE 3.11**

To measure your height, stand with your back against the wall and have your partner place a book on your head. Measure to the bottom edge of the book. Stand up straight!

Process and Procedure for Station 2

1. With your partner, take and record the measurements listed below.

   If you are not certain how to do some of the measurements, see the accompanying illustrations. Remember to record the number and units for each measurement beside the list. For example, foot length = 24 cm.

   height
   ankle circumference
   thumb circumference
   length of forearm (elbow to wrist)
   length of ear
   foot length (if you don't already have it)
   length of little finger
   arm span

≋Wrap Up for Station 2

Discuss this question with your partner and record your answer in your notebook before going to the next station.

1. What patterns did you find in your measurements?

≋Wrap Up for the Social Skill

With your partner, complete this Wrap Up after you have completed the work at both stations. Record your answers.

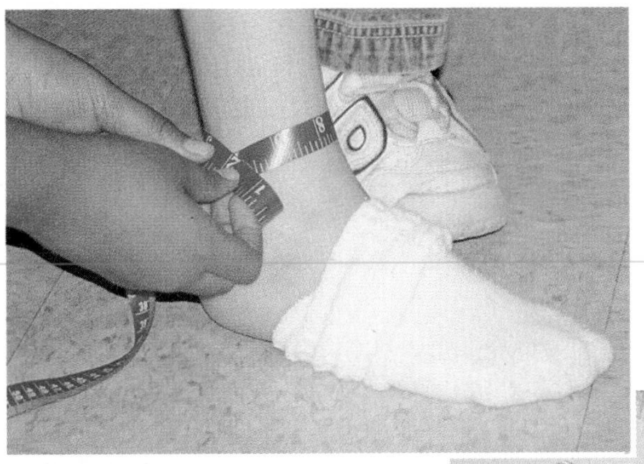

▼ **FIGURE 3.13**

Your partner will help you measure your arm span. Stand with your arms straight out at each side at shoulder height. Your partner should measure from the tip of your middle finger across your back to the tip of your other middle finger. You may need to ask another team for help.

▲ **FIGURE 3.12**

To measure your ankle circumference, roll your sock down and measure around the bony part–the largest part of your ankle.

◀ **FIGURE 3.14**

To measure your thumb circumference, measure around the knuckle of your thumb.

1. On a scale of 1–10, 10 being the best, rate your team for how well you are expressing thoughts and ideas and listening politely to each other.
2. On a scale of 1–10, rate your team for how quickly and quietly you moved between stations.

explain

Investigation: In the Swing

When you investigated sizes, you identified different types of patterns as you measured different parts of your body. In this investigation, you will uncover another type of pattern—a pattern of motion—of a simple system called a pendulum.

► **Figure 3.15**

Students at Eagle Rock School in Estes Park, Colorado built a 26-foot-long pendulum. This pendulum models the one Edgar Allen Poe wrote about in his story, "The Pit and the Pendulum." The Eagle Rock students did many experiments with pendulums so that they could make predictions about the one they built. The students thought it would be fun to use a classmate as the pendulum bob.

Working Cooperatively

In this investigation, you will work in teams of four. You each will have the role of a Team Member and one of you will be the Tracker. In addition this activity requires some special roles. Your teacher will help you assign these roles and explain how you will rotate these roles from time to time. Remember to practice the unit skill of *Expressing your thoughts and ideas aloud.*

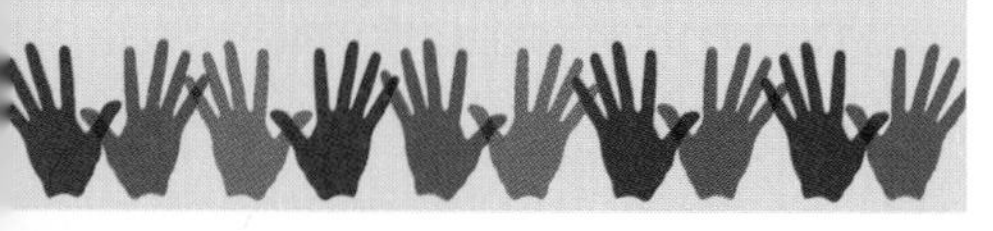

Materials for Each Team of Four:

- 1 wooden dowel, 1 M
- 1 small ball of string
- 2 chairs
- 1 pair of scissors
- 1 pendulum bob, (one of several choices)
- stop watch
- metric stick
- tape

Process and Procedure

Part A—Making General Observations

1. In your team of four, collect the materials you will need and set up the pendulum according to your teacher's instructions.

   It should look something like the diagram in Figure 3.16. You may use tape or string to attach the dowel to the chairs and the pendulum string to the dowel. The length of the pendulum string should be about 60 cm to begin with. Each team will have a different type of pendulum bob.

2. Take turns holding the pendulum bob to one side and releasing it. Watch it for a few minutes each time.

   Record your observations in your journal. Also record any questions that you have about the pendulum system so far.

▶ **FIGURE 3.16**

Before you begin, your pendulum set up should look something like this.

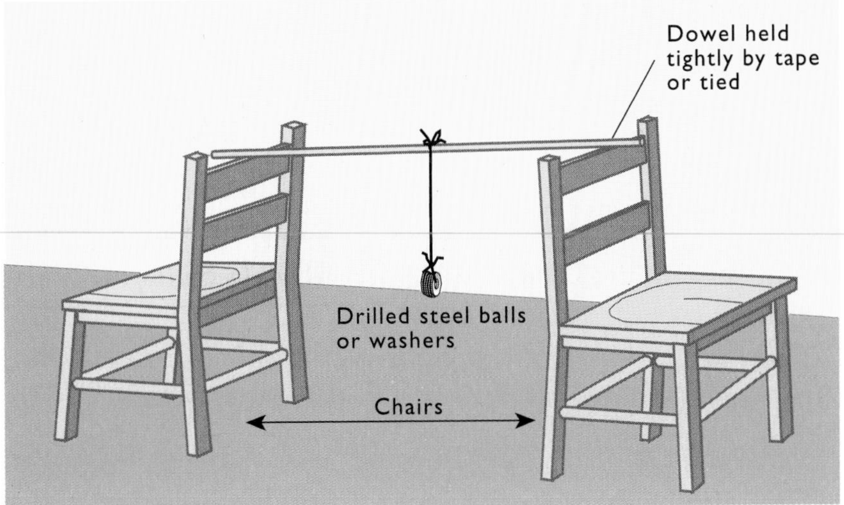

3. Again take turns releasing the pendulum and this time as you watch closely, record answers to the following questions in your notebook.
   a. How high is the bob at each end of the swing?
   b. How high is the bob in the bottom of the swing?
   c. Do you think it is moving faster at the ends or the bottom of each swing?
   d. Does each swing take the same amount of time?
   e. Do you think the pendulum will ever stop swinging?
4. Think about what would happen if you cut the string when the bob was at the bottom of the swing.

   Think about what would happen if you cut the string when the bob was at one end of the swing.

   Discuss your ideas with your teammates.

Consult the teacher before trying this.

Part B—Making More Specific Observations

Before you begin this part of the investigation, read all of the procedures. The Tracker should make certain that all Team Members understand the steps. You will need a Communicator to say "GO" and "STOP," an Operator to swing the pendulum, a Timer to time each swing, and a Recorder to record the data. Your teacher will assign and help you rotate these roles.

▶ FIGURE 3.17

A data table like this one will help you organize your data.

NAME: ____________

DATA TABLE FOR IN THE SWING

Time of 1 Complete Swing (Single Swing)	Time of 1 Complete Swing (while swinging continuously)
1.	1.
2.	2.
3.	3.
4.	4.
	5.
	6.
	7.
	8.
	9.
	10.

Time of 10 complete swings {long string}
prediction:
actual time:

Time of 10 complete swings {short string}
prediction:
actual time:

1. In your notebook, create a data table like the one in Figure 3.17.

   Each team member should create a data table.

2. Agree on the height of a start position for each swing.

   Determine a start position by measuring up from the floor.

3. When the Communicator says "GO," the Operator should release the pendulum from the agreed upon start position and the Timer should begin timing the swing.
4. When the pendulum returns to its start position, the Communicator should say "STOP," and the Timer

should announce the time. This is called the period of the swing. The Recorder should record this time in his or her data table.

5. Repeat Steps 3–4 three more times.
6. Now when the Communicator says "GO," release the pendulum from the start position and let it continue swinging. While the pendulum is swinging, record the period for ten different swings.

   You do not need to time consecutive swings. You may allow several swings in between the swings that you time. Record the period for each swing in your data table.
7. Together with your teammates, study the data that you have collected so far and see whether you can uncover any patterns.

   If you do not have all of the data recorded in your own table, do so now.
8. After you have studied the data and discussed any patterns with your teammates, make a team prediction about how long it will take the pendulum to complete ten full swings. Record this prediction in your notebook.
9. Test this prediction as a team and record your results in your data table.

   Remember what roles you need and remember to let the pendulum continue swinging for ten complete swings.
10. You can determine the average period by dividing the total time by ten. Record the average time in your notebook.
11. Measure the length of the pendulum's string and record this in your notebook along with the data from Step 10.

    Measure the string from its point of attachment to the middle of the pendulum bob.
12. Shorten the length of this string by one-half and then repeat Steps 8–10.

    Use tape to attach the string to the wooden dowel at the halfway point. You do not need to cut the string and reattach it.

SIDELIGHT on History

Measuring Time

Imagine that you are trying to make plans with a friend to see a movie. How do you describe the time when you should meet? What if you could not mention the day or the time? Perhaps you could tell your friend to count the number of sunrises and, on the day of the fourth sunrise, wait until the bats fly from their cave in the evening and meet you then. Sure sounds complicated, doesn't it?

Before calendars people measured time by watching motion—the motion of the earth, moon, sun, and stars. Ancient people based their system of time keeping on some regularly occurring event, such as the time from one full moon to the next or the time from one sunrise to the next.

You probably take for granted the yearly calendars you just used in the investigation Driving Day. It might surprise you to know that this calendar has gone through many changes. People based the first calendars on the pattern of change in the shape of the moon and divided the year into 12 months of 30 days each, or 360 days. Because it actually takes 365 and one-quarter days to get from one spring to the next, these early calendars became less accurate each year. To keep things from getting totally out of step, people had to keep adding extra days. The process of tracking time became very complicated.

Eventually the Egyptians stopped looking to the moon and chose Sirius, the Dog Star, to mark their year. Once a year, Sirius rose in the morning in direct line with the rising sun. The Egyptians also found that 12 months of 30 days provided a useful calendar of the seasons

Wrap Up

Study the results you have recorded in your notebook and look for patterns. Participate in a class discussion and then write your own answers in your notebook.

1. In Part A, what types of patterns did you begin to see?
2. In Part B, what patterns did you see in your team's data?
3. What patterns did you see in other teams' data? Did using different pendulum bobs make a difference in the data? Explain your answer.
4. What patterns, if any, surprised you?
5. In Part B, how did your team come up with its prediction in Step 8 each time?

if they added another five days at the end to make a year of 365 days. They also added an extra day to every fourth year. This time the difference between the calendar year and the solar year was so small that it took many years—far longer than any one person's lifetime—for the error to disturb daily life. So this was the calendar that Julius Caesar adopted—it was called the Julian calendar.

We would probably be using the Julian calendar today if it were not for the actions of Pope Gregory XIII in 1582. Even though the Julian calendar was closer to the solar year than the Egyptian calendar, the calendar was still falling behind. The difference between the Julian calendar and an actual solar year is only 11 minutes and 14 seconds per year. But, that adds up to eight days every 1,000 years. By 1582 the calendar did not match with the seasons and seasonal celebrations, such as Easter. Pope Gregory XIII decided to change the calendar so that it reflected true solar years. The Pope based the changes on the ideas of several astronomers.

First the Pope decreed that the day following 4 October 1582, would be 15 October. He also declared that people would skip leap year once every 128 years. For the years that end a century, only those that are divisible by 400 should be leap years. So the years 1800, 1900, and 2100 have no extra day, but the year 2000 does have the extra day. This shortened the calendar year and made it almost exactly the same length as the solar year. In fact, the difference is less than one-half a minute per year. This calendar will get out of step only one day every 3,000 years.

What did they do about people's birthdays during those lost 10 days? Did they just skip 'em?

6. Did you answer any of the questions that you had about pendulums? If so, which ones? What other questions do you have now?

explain

Reading:
Types of Patterns

In the investigation That's the Size of It, you found different kinds of patterns. At Station 1, you identified a pattern in the way people's feet grow. People's feet get longer until their feet stop growing. A **trend** is a type of pattern that goes in a particular direction for a certain length of time. For example, if you examine the pattern of human growth across time, you would see these three

▲ **FIGURE 3.18**
What trends can you identify in these two photographs?

trends: height increases from birth until about age 20, height stays the same from age 20 to about age 50, and then height gradually decreases. Figure 3.18 shows another type of trend.

Stop & Think

1. Identify a trend in your school.
2. What other trends are you aware of?

At Station 2, you found patterns between the sizes of different body parts. In human beings, the length of a person's forearm is about the same as the length of his or her foot. You could say that certain measurements go with certain other measurements. Patterns that involve connections like these are called **correlations**. When you are aware of certain correlations, you can make predictions. For example, if you know the circumference of your head, you can predict your height because there is a correlation between those two measurements.

There are other correlations in addition to those that involve body parts. For example, there is a correlation between the amount of exercise you get and how long you will live. In some areas of the country, birds fly south at the same time that the leaves on trees change color. Because these two events occur at the same time, we say there is a correlation between them.

Stop & Think

3. Identify a correlation in your school.
4. What other correlations are you aware of?

In the investigation In the Swing, you saw a pattern that might have seemed very different from puzzles and body measurements. You probably noticed that there was always a pull toward the bottom of the swing—first from one direction and then from the other, over and over. This type of repeating pattern is called a **cycle**. Also when you looked at a single swing, first there was a decrease in height and an increase in speed. Then there was an increase in height and a decrease in speed. This pattern repeating itself over and over represents another cycle.

In addition to these cycles, there is a cycle of energy that is going on at the same time. The pendulum bob is temporarily stopped at the top of the swing. Then it moves with maximum speed as it passes through the bottom of the swing. Scientists say that there is an increase in its **energy of motion,** or kinetic energy. The word "kinetic" comes from the Greek word that means "to move." As the pendulum bob leaves its initial position, its height decreases and so does the amount of stored energy that it has available. This type of energy is called **energy of position,** or potential energy. In fact the increase in the energy of motion is exactly equal to the decrease in the energy of position. On the upward half of the swing, the process is just the reverse. Now the decrease in the energy of motion is equal to the increase in the energy of position. It is this cycle of energy—the conservation of energy—that allows the pendulum to continue swinging.

Stop & Think

5. Recall from your observations that the pendulum did not continue to swing. It seems that the energy gradually decreased instead of staying the same. Why do you think this happened?

You have experienced other cycles in your life as well. For example, every day you can expect daylight and darkness. This pattern repeats day after day. In addition unless you live near the equator, you can expect seasons to change every year. Even the years are a cycle, as you found in the investigation Driving Day. On our calendar, a particular date (such as January 2) will shift forward one day per year until seven years later, when January 2 will be on the same day again. As long as we keep the same type of calendar, this cycle will repeat over and over.

Stop & Think

6. Identify a cycle in your school.
7. What other cycles are you aware of ?

SIDELIGHT *on History*

The Pendulum Clock

In the investigation In the Swing, you learned about the period of a pendulum, that is, the time it takes for a pendulum to make one complete swing. This periodic motion of a simple pendulum has been useful in the past in the design of a dependable timepiece—the pendulum clock. When the support for the pendulum bob is 24.8 cm long, the period will be one second. Each complete swing of the pendulum then can be connected through a system of gears to advance the hands of a clock so that the clock reads the correct time. The loss of energy through friction can be compensated for by storing energy in a spring or a system of weights. Even so this stored energy sometimes must be replenished.

Today most pendulum clocks have been replaced by electric clocks. These electric clocks can be smaller and are constantly energized by electricity.

Wristwatches make use of the periodic vibration of a spring and recent models of watches make use of the periodic behavior of a quartz crystal.

Now you know more than just what a pattern is. You know about three kinds of patterns: trends, correlations, and cycles. You will have more opportunities to identify and use these types of patterns throughout the rest of the unit.

Stop & Think

8. How are trends, correlations, and cycles similar?
9. How are trends, correlations, and cycles different?

elaborate

Connections:
Patterns in Nature

Many patterns exist in nature. Look at the following photographs and at the objects your teacher provides. In your notebook, list as many patterns as you can identify in these photographs and objects. What type of pattern is each one?

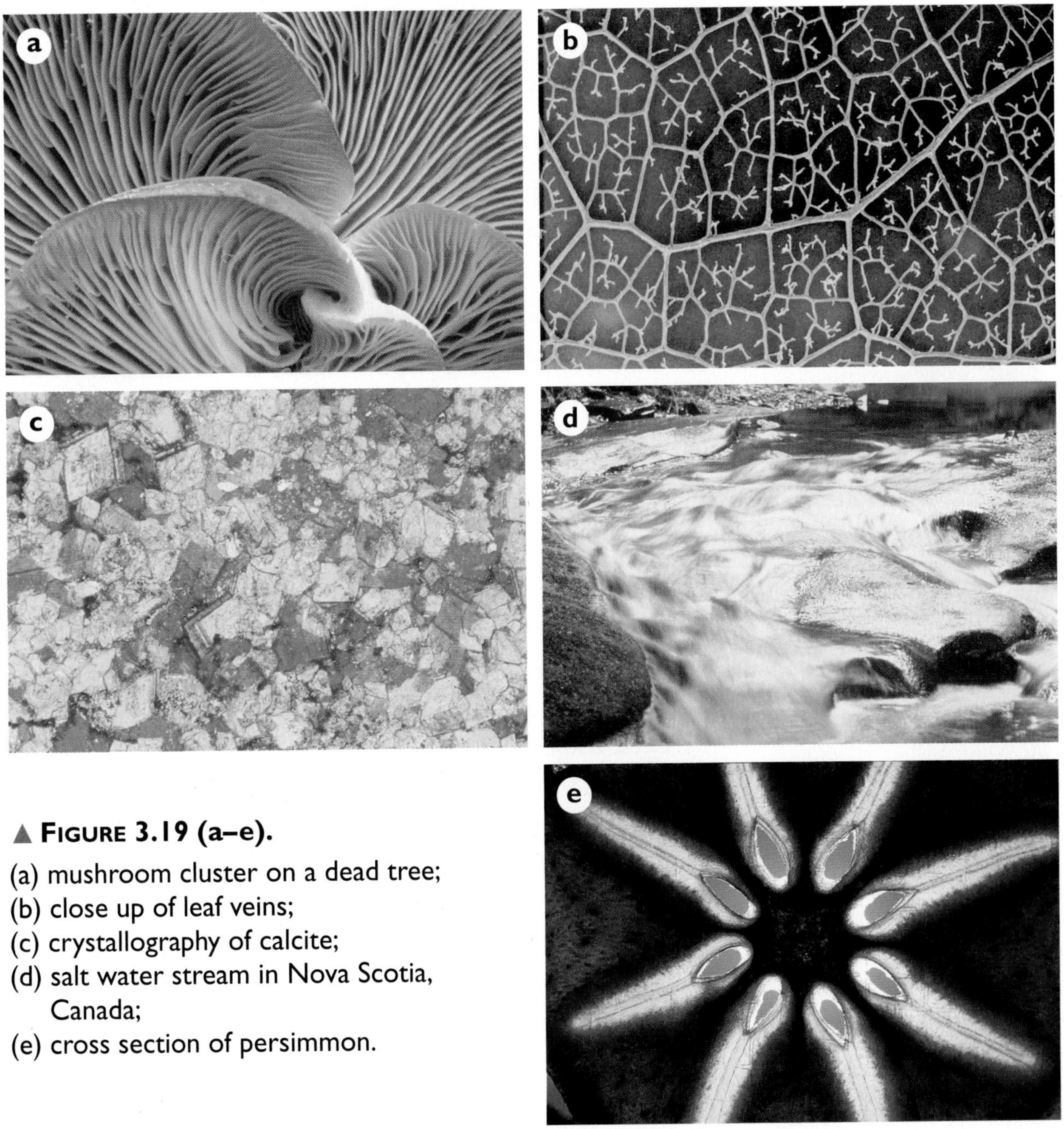

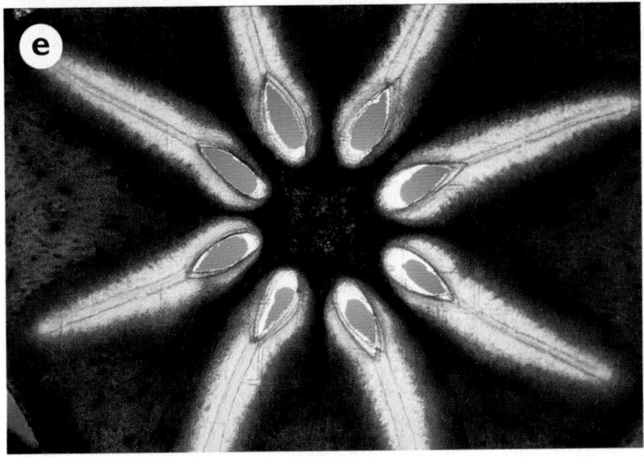

▲ **FIGURE 3.19 (a–e).**
(a) mushroom cluster on a dead tree;
(b) close up of leaf veins;
(c) crystallography of calcite;
(d) salt water stream in Nova Scotia, Canada;
(e) cross section of persimmon.

Investigation:
Moon Watch

Now that you know more about patterns of change, you will be observing a very familiar pattern: the changing phases of the moon. In this investigation, your challenge is to keep track of the pattern. In Chapter 4, you will be using the data you gather to explain the whole pattern.

Materials for the Entire Class:

- 1 calendar
- small box with dated slips of paper

Materials for Each Student:

- 1 Moon Watch Chart
- 1 Parent/Guardian Letter
- tape, glue, or stapler

Process and Procedure

1. Take a copy of the Moon Watch Chart and a copy of the Parent/Guardian Letter.

   Notebook entry: Be sure to include today's date and the investigation title.

2. Place your Moon Watch Chart into your notebook.

   Use tape, glue, or staples.

3. Fill out the first square of your chart based on your teacher's moon watch report.
4. Draw your moon watch assignment from the small box.

   Each Team Member should draw a date.

5. Record your date and your partner's date.

   Notebook entry: This also will go on the class calendar.

6. Fill in the blanks of your Parent/Guardian Letter.

   Remember to get your letter signed.

7. With your partner, work out a strategy for remembering your dates. Record your strategy.

   Notebook entry: When it is your turn to do the moon watch report, have one partner draw on the chalkboard and one partner describe the moon. You will do two moon watch reports.

Working Cooperatively

You will work in your cooperative teams of two. In addition to the role of Team Member, you will need a Communicator and a Tracker. Move your desks together or sit somewhere so that you face each other. Practice the social skill *Move into your groups quickly and quietly.*

Wrap Up

1. Since the first time you practiced moving into your groups quickly and quietly, how much has your team improved: not at all, some, or a lot?
2. On your Moon Watch Chart, record the moon watch report that other students give each day.

elaborate

Investigation: Making Music

What do foot measurements and music have in common? Both have patterns. In this investigation, you will see how you can use patterns to make music. Try to identify the types of patterns you hear. If you cannot remember the differences among trends, correlations, and cycles, refer back to the reading Types of Patterns.

Working Cooperatively

You will stay in your team of two, but this time your teacher will ask you to join another team and work in a team of four. Practice the social skill *Use your teammates' names*. In addition to the job of Team Member for everyone, there will be a Manager, a Communicator, and a Tracker. Check the job descriptions to make sure you understand your roles.

Materials for Each Team of Four:

- 2 rulers (15-cm) or metric tapes
- 4 glass bottles of the same size and shape (one per Team Member)
- 4 beakers or small cups filled with water
- 1 bowl (size of 1-qt margarine tub, 800 mL) (for waste water)
- 4 pieces of masking tape (each about 10-cm long)
- 1 tuning fork (1000/sec)

Process and Procedure

1. Pick up the materials you will need for this investigation.

   This is the Manager's job; the Tracker may help if needed.

Glass containers can break easily. If water spills occur, be careful not to slip. Clean up water immediately.

2. Use a piece of masking tape to label your bottle with your name. Put on your goggles.

   Each Team Member should have a bottle and a piece of masking tape.

3. Hold the empty bottle and blow over the top of it.
4. Use your beaker or cup to add a small amount of water to your bottle.

   The water level should be approximately 1 cm deep.
5. Again hold the bottle and blow over the top of it. Describe any changes in what you hear.

   Notebook entry: Record your observations.
6. Determine how the pattern of sounds changes when you vary the amount of water in the bottle.

   Try to use small amounts of water each time.
7. Now blow across the bottle while it is resting on the table without anyone holding it. Use different amounts of water to try to determine the patterns.
8. Next try gently tapping your bottle to uncover another pattern.

   Use your pen or pencil.
9. Describe the types of patterns you observed.

   Notebook entry: Record your observations.
10. While the bottle is resting on the table, hold a vibrating tuning fork about 1 cm above the bottle.
11. Add small amounts of water until the sound is the loudest. (See Figure 3.20.)

▶ FIGURE 3.20

Hold the tuning fork over the bottle as you slowly add water. What happens?

Think back to the pendulum that you built in the investigation In the Swing. You learned that the period was the number of seconds it took for one complete swing—or cycle. When the vibrations are much faster than they were in your pendulum, scientists usually talk about the number of cycles per second. This number is the frequency. For example, if the period were one-half second, the frequency would be two cycles per second.

12. With the water at this same level, blow across the bottle while it is resting freely on the table.
13. Repeat this while holding the bottle in your hand.

    This is resonance. The natural frequency of the air column in the bottle is exactly equal to that of the tuning fork.

Wrap Up

Discuss the following questions with your team and record your own answer for each question in your notebook. Be sure each of you can explain your answers in a class discussion.

1. Did you notice any difference in the pattern when you tapped on your bottle, compared with when you blew over the top of it?
2. Describe the correlation between the height of water in the bottle and the sound you heard.
3. When you strike a tuning fork against a table so that it is vibrating, you can hear it. Could you hear your pendulum? Why not?
4. Were you able to remember and use your teammates' names?

Connections: What Do You Know about Patterns?

evaluate

The focus question for this unit is How does my world change? Recognizing patterns of change can help you answer that question. In this chapter, you have been exploring patterns of change. First you solved puzzles by uncovering patterns. Then you learned about three types of patterns and how to recognize them. Part of that skill is seeing patterns on graphs. Another part is recognizing patterns in descriptions, events, or pictures. Use the information from this chapter to answer the following questions.

1. Look at the graph in Figure 3.21, People's Pattern of Eating Vegetables, and answer these questions.
   a. According to the graph, how has the people's pattern of eating fresh vegetables changed?
   b. What type of pattern is visible in the graph (a trend, cycle, or correlation)? Explain your answer.
2. Read the following and answer the questions. Isaac decided to go rowing every day. Each day he went out at 4:00 p.m. Each day he came back at 6:00 p.m. He repeated this activity each day for three months.
   a. What kind of pattern is this? Explain your answer.
   b. If Isaac exercised every day and grew stronger, what kind of pattern occurred? Explain your answer.
3. Describe a pattern that is a cycle. What other questions do you have about this cycle or another cycle that you know of. Ask your teacher for ideas about exploring answers to your questions.

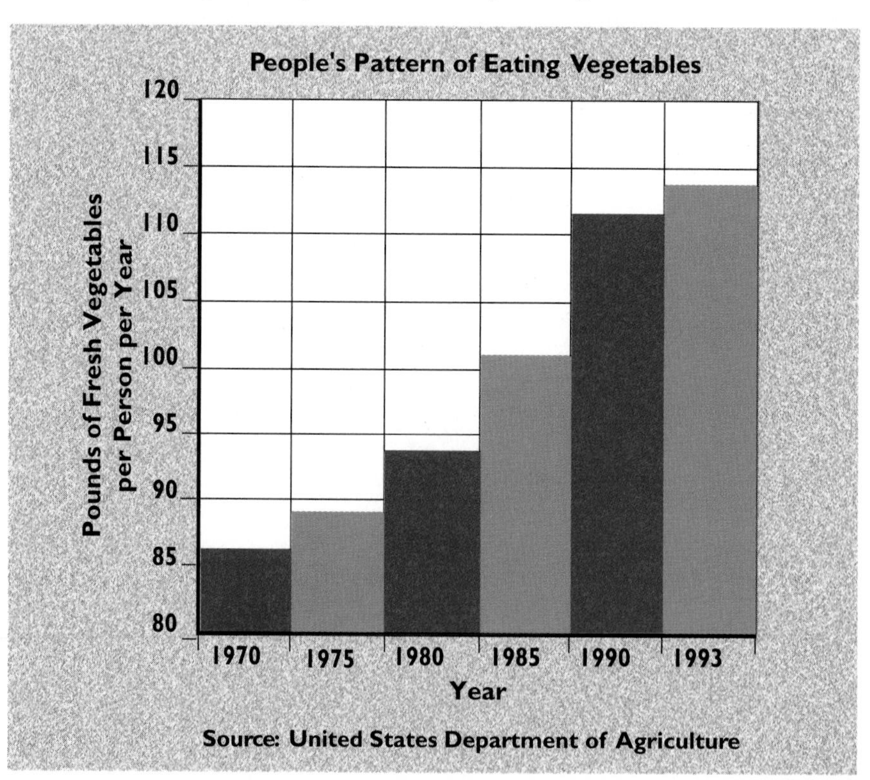

▶ FIGURE 3.21

This graph shows how people's pattern of eating fresh vegetables changed between 1970 and 1993. What changes do you notice?

SIDELIGHT on History

Footprints from the Past

In the 1950s and early 1960s, Louis and Mary Leakey, along with other scientists in Africa, were just beginning to unearth a puzzle dating from a time long before recorded history. They found some humanlike skeletons they were curious about. By the shape of the bones, they could tell that these humanlike animals were not apes. They also could tell that these animals walked upright as we do. Scientists named these animals *Australopithecines*. Many of the skeletons were not complete, so the scientists could not tell how tall these creatures had been.

Then in 1978, scientists working with Mary Leakey revisited the site and made another discovery. In rock that had once been soft, damp, volcanic ash, they found trails of footprints from long ago that appeared to be made by humanlike creatures. First the scientists measured these footprints. Then they were able to estimate the height of these creatures by using a correlation that exists in humans between height and foot length. That is, the foot length of a person is generally about 15 percent of that person's height. The scientists concluded that one of the travelers was about 1.4 meters (about 4 feet, 6 inches) tall, and the other was about 1.2 meters (about 4 feet) tall.

The Leakey family—Mary, Louis, and their son Richard—have been important in piecing together the puzzle of early humans in Africa. Recognizing patterns is one way they have been able to help determine some of these pieces. Louis died in 1972, and Mary died in 1996. Richard is carrying on their work.

4. Use the following scale to rate your understanding of patterns:

1 = I can't explain anything about patterns.
2 = I can give an example of one type of pattern.
3 = I can define all three types of patterns.
4 = I can explain all three patterns to myself.
5 = I could teach others about all three patterns.

Patterns That Grow

By now you probably realize that you have been seeing patterns all your life—patterns like the one shown here in a leaf. Now that you are better at recognizing patterns, consider these questions: Do patterns always stay the same? If not, what makes them change? How can you discover how patterns can change? In this chapter, you will have a chance to answer these questions.

engage

Connections: Growing, Growing, Grown

explore

Investigation: Beanstalk I

explain

Reading: What Affects Patterns?
Reading: Controlled Experiments

elaborate

Investigation: Beanstalk II
Reading: Cause and Effect in My Life
Connections: Captain Sneezy's Cold Cure

evaluate

Investigation: Radishes on the Rise
Connections: Your Green Thumb

▶ FIGURE 4.1
What do you think this rosebush or this tree needs in order to grow?

engage

Connections:
Growing, Growing, Grown

Move your desks side by side to work with your partner on this Think-Pair-Share activity.

Think: Imagine what it would be like to be a flowering plant such as a rosebush or a green, leafy tree such as those in Figure 4.1. What do you think you would need in order to grow?

Pair: With your partner, discuss your ideas about plant growth. Record all your ideas on one list in one of your notebooks.

Share: Contribute your ideas to a class discussion. You will create a large list on the board.

explore

Investigation:
Beanstalk I

In the connections activity Growing, Growing, Grown, you and your classmates generated ideas about what plants need in order to grow. In this investigation, you will begin testing your ideas by planting seeds and observing what happens.

Materials for Each Team of Two:

- 3 bean seeds
- 1 paper cup
- potting soil

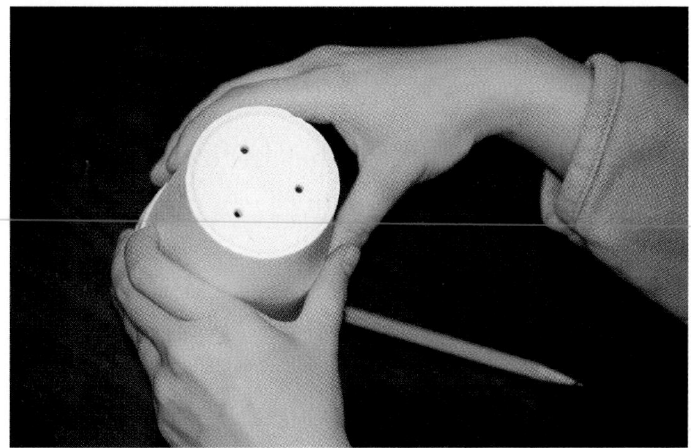

- water supply
- ½ paper towel
- beaker or cup for water
- 1 metric ruler
- masking tape—a strip long enough to label your team's cup
- 1 small tray with gravel or one large tray with gravel for several teams
- 2 pencils

Working Cooperatively

You will work in your same cooperative teams of two. Besides Team Members, additional roles you need are Communicator/Tracker and Manager. Work at a table or push your desks together to form a table. Practice the social skill *Move quickly and quietly into your groups.*

Process and Procedure

1. Read through the list of materials and the procedure.
2. Collect the materials.
3. Label the paper cup "C" for control. Put your initials and your teammate's initials on your cup.
4. Poke three holes into the bottom of the cup.
   Use a pencil or a pen to do this.
5. Cover the inside bottom of the cup with the wet, folded paper towel.
   Use a half-sheet of a paper towel and moisten it with water.
6. Fill the cup ⅔ full with potting soil.
   Hold the cup over a tray. Do this at the location your teacher designates.
7. Pour water into the cup until the soil is soaked.
   Let any extra water drip onto the tray.
8. Measure 2 centimeters down the side of a pencil by beginning at the tip of the eraser. Mark this place on the pencil, using a marker, to create a measuring stick (See Figure 4.2).
9. Poke three holes that are 2 centimeters deep in the soil.
   Use the measuring stick you created in step 8 for this.
10. Put one bean seed into each hole. Cover the seeds with soil.
11. Describe the contents of your control cup.
    Notebook entry: Record this description in your notebook. If you have followed the procedure, your control cup should have three bean seeds each planted 2 centimeters deep.

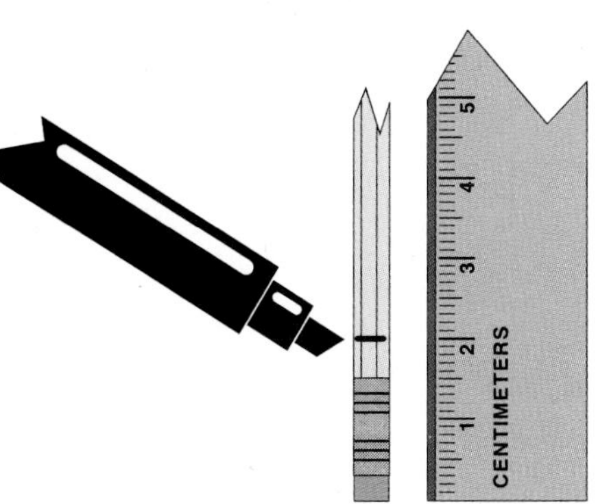

▲ **FIGURE 4.2**
Mark off 2 centimeters on your pencil like this.

12. Decide on the best location for the control cups and place your cups there.
    Do this as a class.
13. Clean up materials as your teacher indicates.
    Practice moving quickly and quietly as you clean up.

Wrap Up

In your own notebook, write today's date. Draw a chart like the one in Figure 4.3 and fill in Day 1 with "No growth yet." Now discuss the following as a team and record your answers.

1. If you are doing well moving quickly and quietly into your groups, write one thing you can do to further improve your use of this skill.
2. If you are not doing well moving quickly and quietly into your groups, list three things you could do to improve this skill.

▶ **FIGURE 4.3**

By using a chart like this one, you will be able to keep track of your plant's growth.

		Control plants (Beanstalk I)	Experimental plants (Beanstalk II)
Date planted			
Date sprouted			
Number of sprouts Number of days for sprouting to occur			
		Observations	
Day	1	no growth yet	
	2		
	3		
	4		
	5		
	6		
	7		
	8		
	9		
	10		
	11		
	12		
	13		
	14		

▶ FIGURE 4.4

In this photograph, you can see the pattern of tree rings. Each year as the tree grows upward and outward, a new layer of living material is added around the older layers.

explain

Reading:
What Affects Patterns?

At the beginning of this chapter, we asked you to imagine what a flowering plant or tree needs in order to grow. You might have thought about other trees you have seen and realized that all growing plants need many of the same things. Based on what you studied about patterns in Chapter 3, you might recognize that plants grow in patterns.

For example, some trees show a cycle. Every spring they grow new leaves, and every autumn the leaves change color and fall. With the passing of winter and the beginning of another spring, the cycle begins again.

If you look at the stump of a tree that has been cut down, you will see rings. These tree rings are also a pattern of growth that people can observe. Every ring represents one year of growth for each year of the tree's life (see Figure 4.4). Every year the tree grows outward, as well as upward, creating a new layer of living material surrounding the older layers. These layers appear as rings. Notice that some of the rings are wider than others. This is because the same tree can grow at a different rate from one year to the next. In years that the tree grows quickly, the rings are wider than those it forms when it grows slowly. We can say that there is a correlation between how quickly trees grow and how wide their rings are.

Not only can a particular tree grow at different rates, but similar trees in different environments will grow at different rates. For example, pine trees in Louisiana's warm, moist climate grow much faster than pine trees in Colorado's cold, dry climate. In the same environment, different types of trees will grow at different rates. For example, spruce trees growing in the same forest as lodgepole pines grow more slowly than the lodgepole pines.

As you can see, many things influence the pattern of plant growth. The things that influence patterns are called factors. This reading describes several factors that influence the pattern of plant growth.

Stop & Think

1. Describe the factors you read about that affect the pattern of plant growth.
2. What additional factors might affect the pattern of plant growth?

explain

Reading:
Controlled Experiments

Sometimes it is difficult to single out what factors are influencing a pattern. But usually there is a way to determine whether or not a factor is affecting something.

For example, suppose you are raising fish in a pond. One day you decide to cut in half the amount of food you give them and move them to a different pond. If the fish stopped growing, which factor would you say was causing the change—the reduction in food or the change to a new pond? You might guess that it was the food, but it would be only a guess. To be certain, you would have to change only one thing at a time.

To see whether the change in food caused the fish to stop growing, you would have to cut in half the amount of food but leave them in the same pond. To see whether a new pond caused the fish to stop growing, you would have to move the fish to a new pond but continue feeding them the same amount of food.

Let's say that Rosalind was doing an experiment with fish. She wanted to find a factor that would affect their pattern of growth. She found two identical fish tanks and placed the same number and same type of fish in both tanks. She kept the water in both tanks at the same temperature and fed them all the same type of food. The only factor Ros varied was the amount of food she fed them. When you change only one factor and leave all the other factors the same, the experiment is called a **controlled experiment**.

Rosalind varied only the amount of food in her two tanks and therefore could observe whether or not the amount of food affected the pattern of growth.

Marie and Isaac also were interested in factors that might affect the growth of fish. Marie wanted to know whether or not water temperature affected fish growth. Isaac wanted to know whether or not the size of the fish tank affected fish growth.

Marie decided to set up a controlled experiment using two fish tanks. She bought the same type of fish, food, and tanks that Rosalind bought. She kept the conditions the same for both fish tanks except that she varied the water temperature. In one tank she kept the water at room temperature, in the other tank she kept the water 10 degrees warmer.

Isaac also set up a controlled experiment using two tanks. He kept the number of fish, the type and amount of food, and the water temperature the same. The factor that Isaac decided to test was the size of the tank. He used one small tank and one large tank.

One day Al stopped by to look at what they were doing. He saw six fish tanks. Ros had two, Marie had two, and Isaac had two. They described their results to Al. Ros found that the fish that received more food were larger. Marie found that the fish in the cooler water were larger than the fish in the warmer water. And Isaac found that the fish in the larger tank had grown more than the fish in the smaller tank. Because Isaac, Marie, and Rosalind had done controlled experiments, their results meant something. When they each observed a difference in their fish, they were better able to explain what factors affected the pattern of fish growth.

As you may know already, fish can take a long time to grow. Some plants, however, can grow very quickly. In the next investigation, you will conduct a controlled experiment to determine what factors affect plant growth.

Investigation:
Beanstalk II

elaborate

In the last investigation, you and your classmates used the same procedure for planting bean seeds. Every team used the same type of seeds, cups, and soil. Then you all put your cups in the same place.

Now you and your partner will have a chance to do something different from other teams. Can you think of different factors that you might want to vary as you grow new plants?

Materials for Each Team of Two:

- 3 bean or 3 radish seeds
- 1 paper cup
- potting soil
- water supply

Working Cooperatively

Establish your environment as you did in Beanstalk I. Trade roles, but practice the same social skill *Move into your teams quickly and quietly.*

- ½ paper towel
- masking tape
- 1 metric ruler
- pencil

Process and Procedure

Part A—The Social Skill

1. Move into your team quickly and quietly.
2. When you are settled in your team, let your teacher know as quietly as you can that you are ready.

Part B—The Activity

1. With your partner, discuss and choose one factor that you will test. Make sure both of you have a chance to express your thoughts and ideas aloud.

   This factor should make the seeds you plant today grow differently from the seeds in your control cup that you planted several days ago. For some ideas, look at the list on the board.

2. Decide what one change you can make in your second cup—your experimental cup—to test that factor.

   Notebook entry: Record the factor you chose and the change you will make.
3. Predict how this change will affect your plants.

   Notebook entry: Record your predictions.
4. Tell your teacher what factor you chose.

   This is the Communicator's role.
5. Plant the seeds in your experimental cup according to your decisions.
6. Label your experimental cup.

   You may label it with a name, letter, or number and also both Team Members' initials.
7. Put your experimental cup on a tray in the appropriate location.

   Your location might be different from that of your control cup.
8. Clean up the materials.

▶ FIGURE 4.5

If you were able to see beneath the soil at different stages as your plants grow, you would see something like this.

Wrap Up

Discuss the following questions with your partner and write your answers in your notebook. Make sure each Team Member can explain your answers in a class discussion.

1. Predict how many days your plants will take to sprout and which of your two cups will show more growth. Figure 4.5 shows bean plants at four different stages of growth.
2. Each day for the next week, look for correlations between your plants' growth and the factor you are testing. For example, if one of your plants is getting more water, does getting more water correlate with the seeds sprouting sooner or the plants growing faster?
3. From your observations, would you say that you and your partner are expressing thoughts and ideas better now than you were in the last investigation?

elaborate

Reading:
Cause and Effect in My Life

One morning as you ride the bus to school, an accident occurs on the highway. Traffic is delayed for 15 minutes. Fortunately no one is hurt. Unfortunately as a result of the delay, you are late to your first class. Your teacher listens as you explain what happened.

Think about this situation for a moment. When one thing makes another thing happen, you say the first thing caused the second thing, the effect. You explained that you were late—**the effect**—because an accident delayed your bus—**the cause**. A cause is any event, circumstance, or condition that brings about a certain result or effect. Because you understood the relationship between cause and effect, you could explain to your teacher why you were late.

Stop & Think

1. Think of two examples of cause and effect in your life and share them with your classmates if your teacher asks.

Scientists often investigate cause-and-effect relationships. What causes the common cold? What causes bean plants to grow at different rates? What causes the changes we observe in the shape of the moon? All of these questions seek explanations (causes) for patterns (effects) we see in nature.

Yet two things can be related and still not have a cause-and-effect relationship. Here is one example: In North America, certain birds fly south at the same time that maple leaves change color. Does this mean that the birds cause the maple leaves to change color? Or do the changing leaves cause the birds to fly south? The answer to each question is no—neither event causes the other event to happen.

When two things are related but not cause and effect, we say they are **correlated.** The following are two examples of things that are correlated but not necessarily cause and effect. Read these examples and then answer the questions with your teammate.

Example 1
A local track team has been training vigorously for over a month. One student's mother works for Disgusto Cereal Company, and the student brought a case of free samples to the track team. The next day all the students who ate Disgusto Cereal for breakfast had the fastest times in the track meet.

Stop & Think

2. Did Disgusto Cereal cause the fast times?
3. How could you explain the relationship between Disgusto Cereal and fast times at the track meet?

Example 2

A scientist studied a group of people to determine their patterns of watching television. She found a correlation between watching TV and health: People who watched TV were healthier than people who didn't. This correlation puzzled scientists. Could watching TV cause good health? Further investigation showed that many people in this study rode exercise bikes while watching TV.

Stop & Think

4. What might explain the correlation between watching TV and good health?
5. Is the relationship between watching TV and good health cause and effect?
6. What are some examples of things in your life that are correlated but are not cause and effect?

elaborate

Connections:
Captain Sneezy's Cold Cure

Work on this section in your cooperative team of two. Each of you should work as a Team Member to accomplish the goal of this section.

Captain Sneezy's is a famous cold medicine. In fact the people who make Captain Sneezy's say that it will cure the common cold for all people. This type of amazing claim is common in advertising. Can you use what you know about controlled experiments to find out whether this amazing claim is true?

The following are experiments designed to find out whether the Captain Sneezy's claim is true. Take turns reading each of them aloud.

1. The first experiment, which includes two groups of people, tests both the regular and the extra-strength

Captain Sneezy's. Half of the people are in Arizona and half are in Kansas. The group in Arizona gets the extra-strength medicine, and the group in Kansas gets the regular strength. The group in Arizona got better faster.

2. The second experiment uses people of all ages in the same location. The people are divided into two groupings: children and adults. Children are divided into two more groups. Half of the children get a fake capsule that has no medicine. The other half gets Captain Sneezy's children's medicine. The adults all stay in one group, and they all get regular Captain Sneezy's. The children got worse after taking Captain Sneezy's, and all the adults stayed the same.
3. The third study also tests regular and extra-strength Captain Sneezy's. The people are all in the same location. In this group, some of the people are well and some are sick. Some of them get the regular medicine, and some get the extra-strength medicine. All of the people who got the regular dose felt good at the end of the experiment.

Discuss these questions with your partner and record your own answers in your notebook:

1. Which experiments were controlled experiments?
2. Why do you think so?
3. Design your own controlled experiment to test the effectiveness of Captain Sneezy's. Be sure you and your partner are prepared to participate in a class discussion.
4. After the discussion as a class, list three factors that companies should consider when designing a controlled experiment of Captain Sneezy's medicine.
5. Look at the company's updated graph in Figure 4.6.
6. Using the information in the graph, describe the changes that occurred. Answer these questions.
   a. What problems do you see in doing a controlled experiment on humans?
   b. Decide how you feel about whether scientists should use people in experiments.
   c. Now discuss how your feelings affect how you would design a controlled experiment.

▶ **FIGURE 4.6**

This graph shows what happened to people after they took Captain Sneezy's medicine. Compare the number and ages of the people who stayed the same with the number and ages of those who got better and those who got worse. What did you find out?

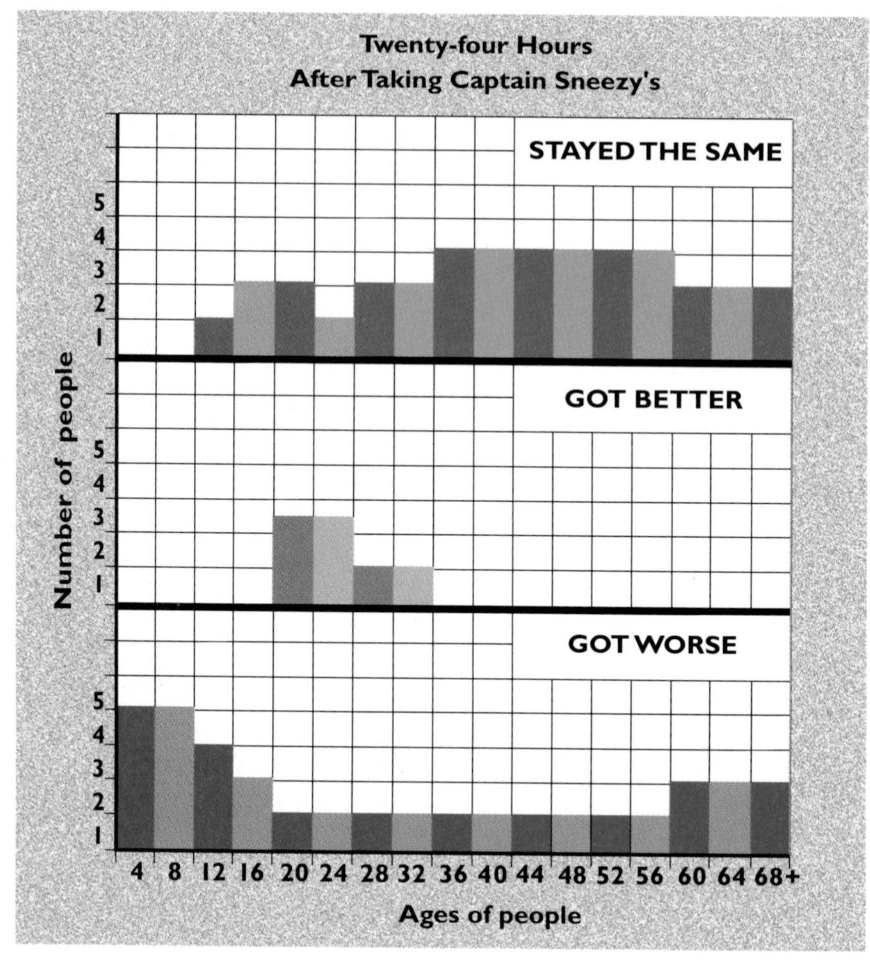

evaluate

Investigation:
Radishes on the Rise

By now you have made several observations of your team's plants. Recall that before you planted your bean or radish seeds, you made a prediction about what would affect their growth. Then you designed an experiment to test your prediction. What have you observed so far about the growth patterns of your plants? Do your observations match your prediction?

Materials for Each Team of Two:

- team plants
- one 250-mL beaker or cup, filled with water
- 1 metric ruler

Working Cooperatively

Set up the working environment as you did in Beanstalk I and Beanstalk II. Trade roles. The same person who was Communicator/Tracker in Beanstalk I should be the Communicator/Tracker again. The other person will be the Manager. You need the same type of work space, and you will continue to improve your use of the skill *Move into your groups quickly and quietly.*

Process and Procedure

1. Pick up your team's plants and bring them to your table or desks.
2. Observe whether or not any of your plants have sprouted yet.

   Notebook entry: Record or draw your observations.
3. Look for any differences between your control cup (from Beanstalk I) and your experimental cup (from Beanstalk II).

   Things to look for include:

   whether or not the seeds in the cups have sprouted,

   how much the plants have grown, and

   how healthy the plants look.
4. Water your plants if they are scheduled for watering today.
5. Return the cups to their locations.

Wrap Up

Discuss the following questions with your partner and write your answer to each question in your notebook. Make sure each of you can explain your answers if your teacher asks.

1. Were your predictions accurate about how long it would take the plants to sprout?
2. If your plants have sprouted, which ones are bigger?
3. Do the predictions you made during Beanstalk II seem to be accurate?
4. Write a prediction about how much you think your plants will grow during the next week. (You might measure growth by counting the number of new leaves or measuring the height, for example.)
5. What are you doing that will allow your class to make accurate predictions about plant growth?
6. Do your predictions change when you have data from the entire class rather than just from your team? If so, how?
7. Rate yourselves on a scale from 1 to 10 (10 being the best) for your progress in practicing the unit social skill and the social skill for this activity.

evaluate

Connections:
Your Green Thumb

Get into your teams of two. Discuss the following questions and be prepared to contribute to a class discussion.

1. Summarize the results of your plant growth experiments. Use a few sentences to describe the most important or interesting things that happened during the experiment.
2. How did the control plants and the experimental plants differ?
3. Knowing what you know now, what helpful hints could you make for other people who wanted to grow bean or radish plants?
4. Identify three patterns of plant growth. (You might need to listen to the class discussion first.)
5. How is this Evaluate activity different from the Engage activity at the beginning of the chapter?
6. Describe your experience with the 5E cycle of activities.

SIDELIGHT on Health

Human Growth Hormone

We have looked at how patterns of growth may change in plants. But is it possible to change the pattern of growth of humans? The hormone called growth hormone, or GH, greatly affects the patterns of growth in humans. We all need growth hormone to grow to our adult heights. Some people produce less of this hormone than other people, and these people are shorter. Some people produce a large amount and they grow taller. When people's bodies produce too much growth hormone, they are susceptible to serious diseases such as diabetes and heart disease, and they often die young.

Today human growth hormone can be manufactured artificially and then prescribed by doctors for people whose bodies do not produce enough of it. The problem today, however, lies in the potential abuse of growth hormone. Some athletes who want to grow bigger and stronger are willing to buy illegal supplies of this hormone. If they use too much, however, they could do a great deal of harm to their bodies.

SIDELIGHT *on Careers*

How Green Is Your Thumb ?

Does your city have flower beds in parks and other places? A greenhouse technician designs, plants, and maintains these flowers and shrubs. A greenhouse is a glass-walled building with a glass roof to let in light. It is typically kept very warm. The greenhouse worker starts new plants by planting seeds, bulbs, and leaf or stem cuttings. If the plants seem to be doing well in the greenhouse, the technician might later transplant them outside. When designing flower beds, the greenhouse technician must select flowers and shrubs that are appropriate for the particular environment. This requires knowledge about plant characteristics and growing requirements. The greenhouse technician also needs to know about soil types, plant disease, and insect problems and treatments. Greenhouse technicians have at least a high school diploma and some experience with plants.

Floral designers put together arrangements of flowers, leaves, and other ornamental things. They usually work in florist shops or in the floral department of a supermarket. A floral designer must be familiar with the names of plants and with the characteristics and requirements of different plants. A career in floral design requires at least a high school diploma. Many community colleges offer courses in floral design. If you are interested in owning your own business or managing a floral shop, a business degree would be helpful as well.

Scientists who study plants are called botanists. Some botanists do research to develop new varieties of flowers, fruits, or vegetables, or new methods of pest and disease control. This career requires a bachelor's degree or often a master's or doctorate degree in biology or botany.

Predictions Are More Than Just a Guess

When you play a card game with your friends, sometimes you can use your knowledge of the patterns in a deck of cards to make predictions. Sometimes those predictions can increase your chances of winning the game.

In Chapter 3, you solved puzzles such as a coded language and determined on which day of the week you would be eligible to drive. In Chapter 4, you identified factors that can change the patterns in plant growth. In this chapter, you will explore another way to use patterns. You will learn to use patterns to make predictions.

engage/explore

Investigation: Finney's Funny Food

explore

Investigation: The Power of Attraction

explain

Reading: Making Accurate Predictions
Investigation: What Is Density All About?

elaborate

Investigation: Will It Sink or Float?

evaluate

Connections: Minding Your Ps (Predictions) and Qs (Quality and Quantity) engage/explore

Investigation:
Finney's Funny Food

Spicy tacos, pizza with lots of cheese, ice-cold soft drinks, hamburgers, and foot-long subs! Some of these foods might be your favorites, while others don't interest you in the least. If you like the food at a particular restaurant, you probably will return. You may establish a pattern of eating at the same restaurant several times a month. To stay in business, restaurant owners depend on the return of their customers. In this investigation, you will have the opportunity to look at a pattern and to predict what lies ahead for Finney's Funny Food.

Working Cooperatively

You will work cooperatively in your same teams of two. The roles you need are Team Members, Manager, and Communicator. Work with your desks pushed together or sit side by side at a table. Continue to practice the social skill *Speak softly so only your teammate can hear you.*

Materials for Each Student:

- 1 copy of Sales Results for the Second Six Months at Finney's

Process and Procedure

Part A—The Social Skill

1. Move into your groups.
2. Construct in your notebook a T-chart labeled "Speak softly so only your teammate can hear you."

   It should have a "Sounds like" column and a "Looks like" column.
3. As you discuss the social skill, record in your chart your team's ideas about how this skill would look and sound when you practice it properly.
4. As you work through Part B of this investigation, try to be the most soft-spoken team.

Part B—The Activity

1. Read the following paragraph:

   From the beginning, Finney's was known for its big food. Finney's Food offers the largest food in town: Mammoth French Fries, Colossal Hamburgers, Gargantuan Ice Cream Cones, and Cosmic Pepperoni Pizza. People flocked to Finney's for the first six months after its grand opening. Being a smart businessperson, the manager of

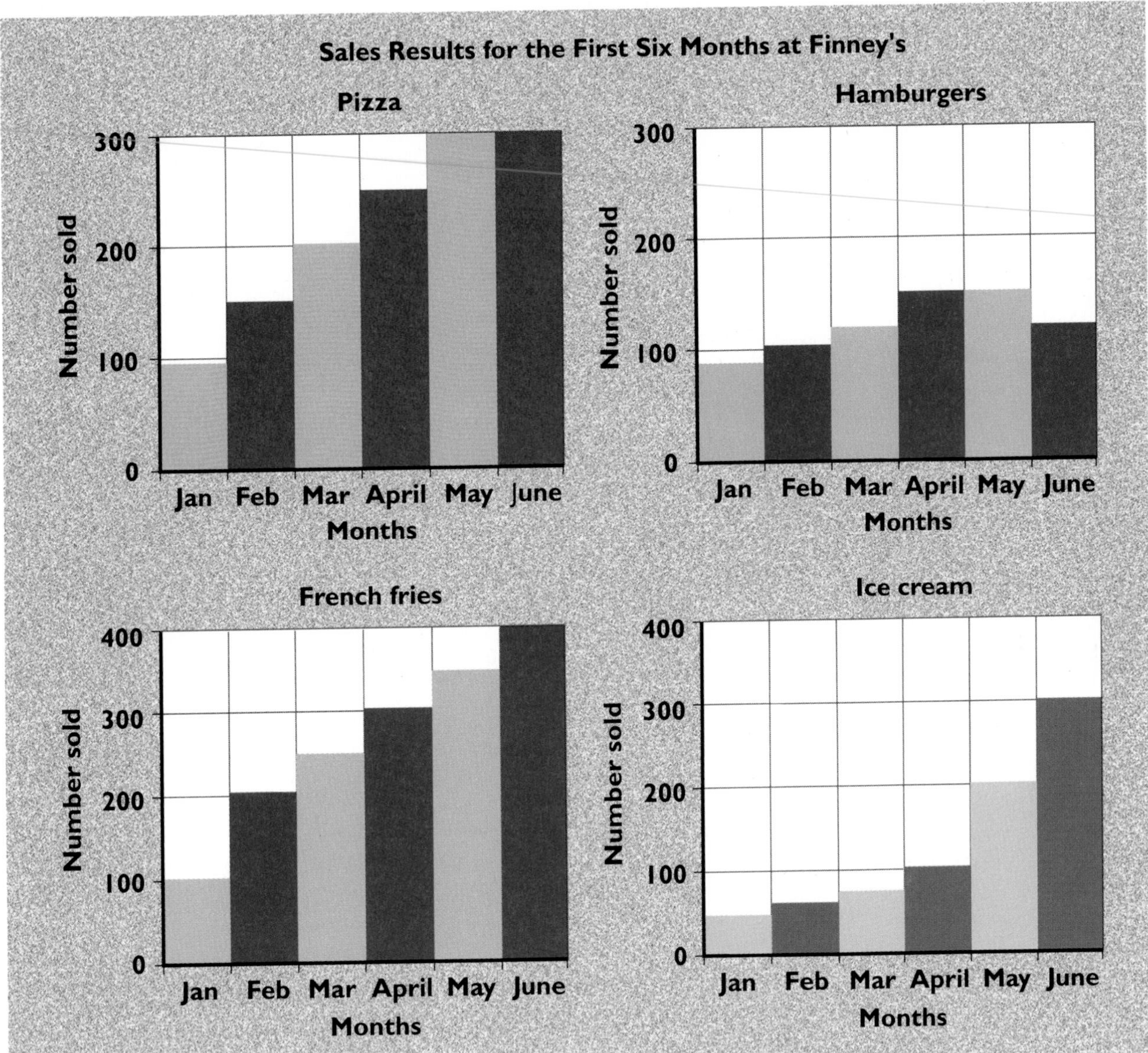

▲ **FIGURE 5.1**

These graphs show the sales results of certain foods at Finney's from January through June.

Finney's decided to keep track of the sales data. She organized the data into several graphs.

2. Study Figure 5.1, Sales Results for the First Six Months at Finney's.

   The graphs show sales data for January through June.

3. Discuss the patterns of sales results with your partner.

   Notebook entry: Write a comment about the pattern on each graph. Be sure to mention whether you see a trend, a cycle, or a correlation. If you don't remember the differences among these concepts, review Chapter 4.

4. Predict what patterns the graphs might show for the next six months.

   These graphs will show sales for July through December. Think about these questions: What items will sell well in cold weather? What items will sell well in hot weather? What items sold well before?

   Notebook entry: Record your predictions. You could draw a graph or write a sentence.

5. Participate in the class discussion.

   Be prepared to present your predictions to the rest of the class.

6. Study the graphs your teacher hands out.

   These graphs show the actual sales results of the second six months at Finney's.

   Notebook entry: Write a comment about the pattern you see in each graph.

Wrap Up

Think about each of the following questions and write your answer to each question in your notebook. Be sure each of you can explain your answers in a class discussion.

1. What was the best-selling food at Finney's during June?
2. Explain how you made your predictions of future sales.
3. How did your predictions for sales during the second six months compare with actual sales?
4. Now that you have twelve months of data, what type of sales would you predict for the next year?
5. As a class, decide which groups were the most soft-spoken during the investigation.

explore

Investigation:
The Power of Attraction

Sometimes patterns are surprising. Think back to the sales results from Finney's. Did you accurately predict the sales for the second six months? Understanding a pattern can help you make better predictions. And making better predictions can help you in many different situations.

How much do you know about magnets? You probably know that some magnets are stronger than others. But is there a pattern as to which ones are stronger? In this investigation, you will have the opportunity to test your knowledge about magnets by making some predictions. See whether you encounter any surprises!

Working Cooperatively

You will work cooperatively in your same teams of two. The roles you need are Team Members, Manager, and Communicator. Work with your desks pushed together or sit side by side at a table. Continue to practice the social skill *Speak softly so only your teammate can hear you.*

Materials for Each Team of Two:

- 1 small-sized magnet
- 1 medium-sized magnet
- 1 large-sized magnet
- 1 box of small metal paper clips
- transparent tape (four 1-cm strips)

Process and Procedure

1. Draw a chart in your notebook like the one in Figure 5.2.

   Notebook entry: Be sure your entry also includes the title of the investigation and today's date.

▶ FIGURE 5.2

This chart will help you record your predictions and the results during this investigation. Copy this chart into your notebook.

PREDICTION CHART

	PREDICTION	RESULTS
Magnet size	(# of paper clips I think the magnet will hold)	(# of paper clips the magnet actually held)
small		
medium		
large		

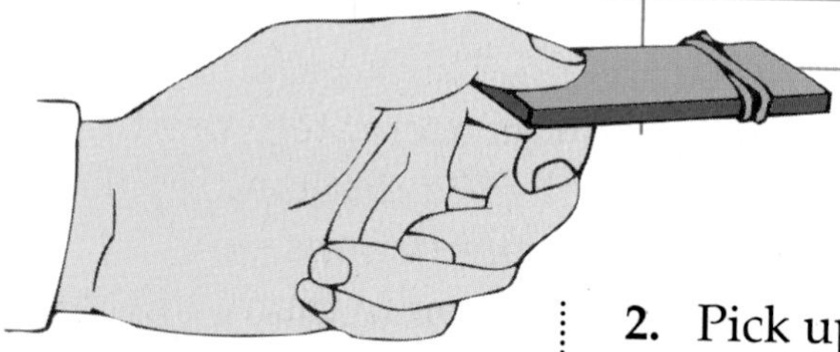

▲ FIGURE 5.3

The Manager should hold the magnet like this, between the thumb and index finger.

2. Pick up all the materials except the large magnet.
3. Holding the small magnet, add seven paper clips, one at a time. Stop adding paper clips.

   Have the Manager hold the magnet as shown in Figure 5.3 while the Communicator adds the paper clips.
4. Predict the total number of paper clips that you think the small magnet will hold.

   Notebook entry: Record this prediction in your chart.
5. Continue adding and counting the paper clips until some paper clips begin to slip off.

   You may put them on in any way, as long as they are in front of the band marked on the magnet. Stop when one paper clip has slipped off at least three times.
6. Record the total number of paper clips that the small magnet held.

   Notebook entry: Write this in your chart.
7. Pull the paper clips off the small magnet and set them aside.

   Do not use these clips again.
8. Predict how many paper clips the medium-sized magnet will hold.

Notebook entry: Record this prediction in your chart.

9. Hold the medium-sized magnet just as you held the small magnet. Use the medium-sized magnet and repeat Steps 3 through 7.

   Remember to use new paper clips and to add them only in front of the band marked on the magnet.

10. Ask your teacher for the large-sized magnet.

    This is the Manager's job. Do not test the magnet yet.

11. Use the pattern you have seen to predict how many paper clips the large magnet will hold.

    Notebook entry: Record this prediction in your chart.

    STOP: Are you remembering to practice the unit social skill: Express your thoughts and ideas aloud and listen politely to others?

12. Begin adding paper clips to the large magnet.

    Use new paper clips and hold the magnet as before. If you want to change your prediction during the investigation, enter your second prediction in the appropriate place in your chart.

13. Record the final number of paper clips the large magnet held.

    Notebook entry: Record this in your chart.

14. Clean up the materials.

    Keep the paper clips that you used separate from those you did not use.

Wrap Up

Discuss the following questions with your partner and write your answers in your notebook. Be sure to include your partner's ideas in your answers.

1. What information did you use to make your predictions?
2. How accurate was your prediction for the medium-sized magnet?
3. Did the strength of the large magnet surprise you? Why?
4. If you revised a prediction, explain what caused you to change your mind.

5. Describe any patterns you observed while using the magnets. Be sure to identify any trends, cycles, or correlations.
6. Use your own rating system to rate your team on how well you are practicing the social skill, *Speak softly so only your teammate can hear you.*
7. What specific things can you do to improve your rating?

Reading:
Making Accurate Predictions

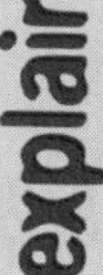

explain

So far in this chapter, you have used patterns to try to predict fast-food sales and how many paper clips a magnet would hold. Now think about the accuracy of your predictions. What happened to Finney's sales, compared with your prediction? What happened with the magnets?

Sometimes a pattern seems very clear and the outcome seems obvious. But the expected result does not always happen! When unexpected results occur, it is sometimes because the people making the predictions needed more information. To make an accurate prediction, you need a sufficient quantity of information. People cannot make accurate predictions without enough information. To be sure that their information is useful, people also must make careful observations and take accurate measurements. This provides information of good quality. Accurate predictions require information of both **sufficient quantity** and **good quality**.

After testing the small- and medium-sized magnets, you attempted to predict how many paper clips the large-sized magnet would hold. It is possible, however, that you based your prediction on too little information. After trying the first two magnets, maybe you thought you saw a pattern: the larger the magnet, the stronger its power of attraction. If you had been able to test several large magnets before making your prediction, you might have discovered that large magnets can be very weak. In other words, you had good information—you just didn't have enough (or sufficient) information to make an accurate prediction.

▲ **FIGURE 5.4**

The stock market rises and falls for a number of reasons. Sometimes it follows a pattern that stockbrokers can use to make predictions if they have both the quantity and the quality of information they need.

Now reconsider your predictions about sales at Finney's Foods. You might have predicted that sales would continue to increase because the graphs indicated a steady upward trend in total sales. By gathering more information on total sales, you might have revised your predictions for the following year. Yet you still would not know from total sales whether customers liked Finney's Foods and whether they will keep returning year after year. In this case, you could make better predictions if you had a different type of information. Sometimes you need to combine several types of information to make better predictions. When people have the types of information they need, we say that they have information of better quality.

Stop & Think

1. Describe a time when you made a prediction based on too little information.
2. How would more information have changed the prediction you mentioned in question 1?
3. Imagine that another fast-food restaurant similar to Finney's went out of business. Its owners had good information about sales for the first year. What other information could they have used to help them predict future sales accurately and perhaps have avoided going out of business?
4. If they had wanted responses from customers, what questions might they have asked?

We can try to make predictions about many things in our lives: the outcome of sports events, grades in school, the success of a restaurant, and even the weather. You might take weather predictions for granted. Turn on the news and there is the forecast.

More accurate weather predictions are now possible because we have satellites that orbit the earth and send back photographs of clouds and weather patterns. This technology has improved both the quality and quantity of data that help scientists predict the weather. In the past, hurricanes were difficult for scientists to predict. People have known about such storms for thousands of years. But predicting them accurately has been possible only recently. Now these predictions save many thousands of lives because people have enough warning about the storm to evacuate to a safe place.

In 1938 the United States Weather Service monitored hurricanes and tropical storms by using

▼ Figure 5.5

New computer and satellite technology has improved both the quality and quantity of information that scientists use to predict the weather. This graphic readout generated from satellite photos charts the pattern of cloud cover around the world. By being able to study this pattern, scientists can better predict the weather for certain areas.

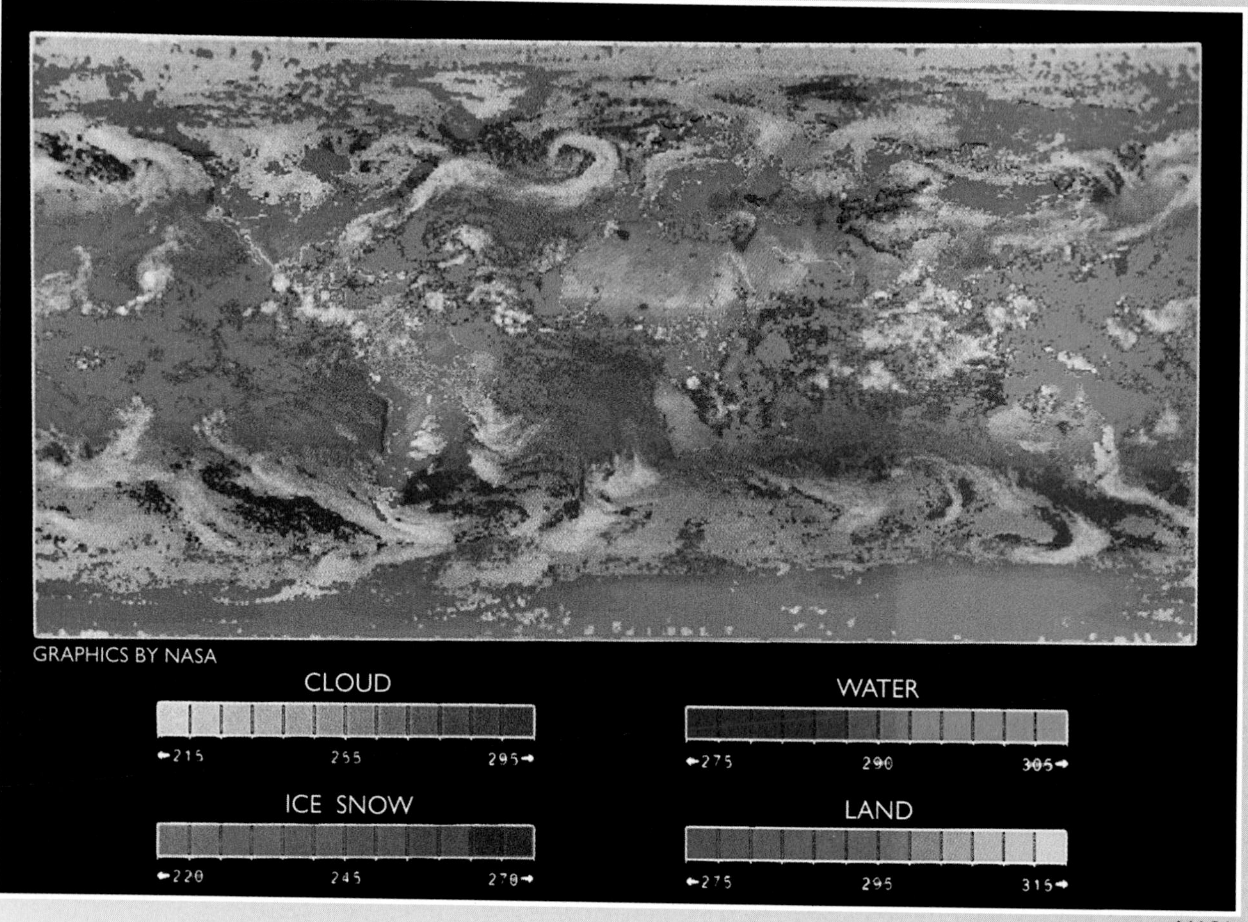

NASA

reports from ships at sea. In mid-September of 1938, the weather service received word about a tropical storm off the coast of Florida. This storm easily might have become a hurricane, so they broadcast warnings, and people in Florida prepared for the storm. The ships monitoring the storm then came back to port. But no storm hit the coast of Florida. Weather forecasters thought that the storm probably had turned back out to sea where it would eventually die out.

The storm, however, had not died out. Unknown to everyone, the storm was moving directly northward. Instead of curving east and back out to sea, the storm bore down on New England. The wave of floodwater was so high (40 feet) that people first thought it was fog. In order to escape, they literally had to swim for their lives. Within a few hours after the storm hit land, 600 people were dead and 60,000 homes were destroyed.

▼ FIGURE 5.6

This photograph shows the force of Hurricane Dora on 9 September 1964. In the past, hurricanes have been difficult to predict and to track. Advances in technology, however, provide scientists with better quality and quantity of information. Now predictions and tracking are more accurate.

The Corbis-Bettmann Archive

Stop & Think

5. How might the scientists have improved the accuracy of their prediction?
6. What would have happened if the scientists had been able to predict this storm more accurately?

Another tragedy occurred during World War II because of an inaccurate prediction. The Island of Malta, which lies in the Mediterranean Sea, was important to the British and their allies. The British had to find a way to defend the island. They dispatched, to Malta, an aircraft carrier with fourteen planes aboard. Due to enemy air patrols, the aircraft carrier could not get very close to the island, so the pilots had to fly the rest of the way there. The planes, called Hurricanes, had a listed flying range of 521 miles, so when the aircraft carrier reached a point about 420 miles from Malta, the planes took off. But no one had calculated for a change in wind direction. Flying into the wind, the planes' range was even less than 420 miles. Miraculously five planes did reach the island, but the other nine crashed into the sea.

Stop & Think

7. How do the examples above show the importance of accurate predictions?
8. What are the characteristics of accurate predictions?

▶ FIGURE 5.7

These planes were used by the U.S. Navy during World War II. In order to make accurate predictions about the flying range of a plane, you need information about the wind conditions, as well as about the plane.

SIDELIGHT *on History*

Lodestone

Have you ever tried to find your way around in a strange place? Without familiar landmarks or signs, or particularly if you are traveling after dark, it can be very difficult. For hundreds of years, people puzzled over the question of how to determine their location without the help of landmarks. They did not know that a simple tool could have helped them. That tool was a magnet.

Since at least the seventh century B.C., people have understood that magnets attracted metal objects. We have records of an ancient Greek legend that describes a magnetic island. According to the legend, if a ship sailed too close, the force of the island would pull out the ship's nails. But it was not until much later that people learned how to make use of magnets.

Using a magnet as a navigation tool was first recorded by the Chinese in the twelfth century A.D. They constructed a compass. A compass is an instrument that shows which direction a person is facing: north, south, east, or west.

Early compasses were very simple. A person would place a magnetic stone (a piece of magnetic iron ore) into a pan of liquid and watch to see which direction the stone turned. One end of the magnet would always point north. With this information, a person could then determine which way was south, east, and west. By doing this, sailors could navigate without the help of the stars as guides. Modern compasses are not set in a pan of liquid, but they make use of the same phenomenon to show which way is north.

When you align the point of the needle with the label "North"on the compass, you know which direction is north. Then by reading the other labels on the compass, you can tell which direction is south, east, and west.

By the seventeenth century, news of the compass had reached England. The English named the magnetic stones lodestones, meaning "leading stones." English scientists began to study these magnetic stones to determine how they worked. One scientist, William Gilbert, thought that the earth itself was a giant magnet and that objects such as lodestones became oriented in a particular direction because of the influence of the earth.

Today we know that many different materials can be magnetized, but the strongest magnets usually have iron in them. Lodestones, for example, contain the mineral magnetite, which has iron in it. Iron is a unique metal because of the way the particles in it can line up. When the particles line up in a certain way, this creates magnetism.

Scientists now understand that the earth does act as a giant magnet just as Gilbert thought. If you place a tiny magnet, a "tester," near a large magnet, the tester is attracted to or repelled by the large magnet. If you place this tester at different locations near the large magnet, it will be strongly attracted to or repelled by the large magnet. The entire region in which the large magnet influences the tester is called the field of the large magnet. In the example of the compass, the earth plays the role of the large magnet whose magnetic field influences the compass.

You can map magnetic fields by using a small magnet or a compass as a tester. Not only will the tester be attracted to or repelled by the magnetic field, but if you place the tester at a number of different locations near the magnet, you can map the strength of the attraction or repulsion, as well as the direction of the tester's orientation. You can use this map to predict the behavior of other magnetic materials placed near the magnet.

Human beings cannot detect magnetic fields without the aid of tools such as the compass. But some other organisms are capable of detecting magnetic fields. For example pigeons contain an internal compass that they use for long-distance navigation. And certain bacteria have internal compasses that appear to help them find a suitable living environment.

The Corbis-Bettmann Archive

▲ *Although the Chinese were using magnets as a tool for navigation as early as the twelfth century A.D., news of the compass did not reach England until the seventeenth century.*

Magnetic compass

► *The needle of a compass is really a bar magnet. The needle is attached to the middle of the circle but turns freely so that the needle always points north.*

Investigation:
What Is Density All About?

explain

Now that you have explored the importance of making predictions, let's use predictions to discover more about an important scientific concept—density. What is it and why is it important?

Working Cooperatively

In this activity, you will work with a partner. To make sure you and your partner understand the concepts in this activity, practice the skill *Express your thoughts and ideas aloud.*

Materials for Each Team of Two:

- 1 solid aluminum cube (2.5 cm per side)
- 1 solid wooden cube (2.5 cm per side)
- 1 hollow plastic cube with one face removed, (2.5 cm per side)
- 1 balance (may share with another team of two)
- metric ruler
- source of water

Process and Procedure

1. Collect the materials that you will need for this investigation.
2. Together with your partner, study the two solid cubes and record your observations in your notebook.

   Pick them up and hold them in your hand as you think about the following:

   a. How are the cubes the same?

   b. How are the cubes different?

   c. Which cube feels the heaviest?
3. Share your ideas with your classmates.
4. Use the spring scale to compare the weight of each of the solid cubes with the mass of an object that is a standard.

   Mass *is what we use to compare the weight of one object to a standard. The standard unit of mass is called a* ***gram.***

   Record your data in your notebook. Use a data table like the one in Figure 5.8
5. Now weigh the amount of water that fills the plastic cube.

   a. Weigh the plastic cube by itself.

   b. Fill the plastic cube with water and weigh it again.

▶ **FIGURE 5.8**

Use a data table like this one to record your data.

WHAT IS DENSITY ALL ABOUT?

	(gm) mass	(cm) length	(cm) width	(cm) height	(cm^2) area	(cm^3) volume	(gm/cm^3) density
wooden cube							
aluminum cube							
water in plastic cube							

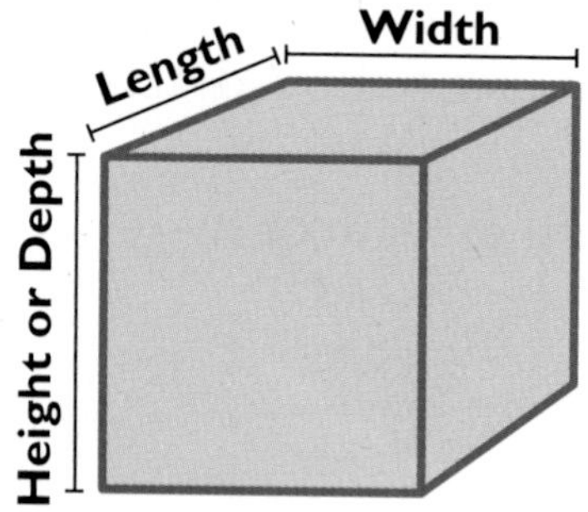

▲ **FIGURE 5.9**

Measure your cube this way.

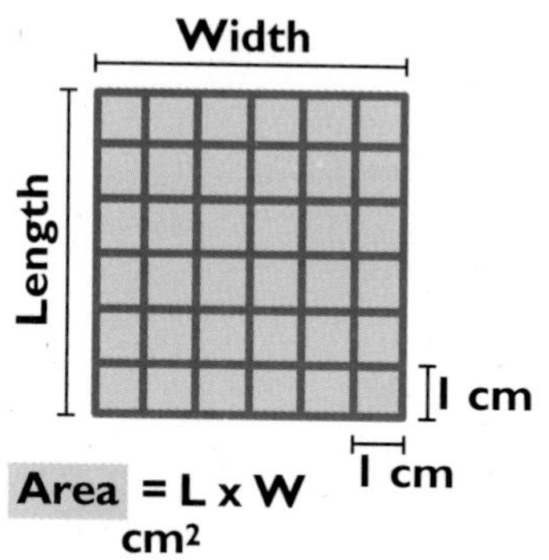

▲ **FIGURE 5.10a**

The area of this square is everything that is colored in. The area is determined by multiplying the length times the width. If you counted each square centimeter of this square, what would the area turn out to be?

c. *Subtract the weight of the plastic cube by itself from the weight of the plastic cube with the water.*

Record this weight in your notebook.

6. Use a ruler to measure in centimeters the length, width, and height of the aluminum cube as shown in Figure 5.9.

   Record this information in your notebook.

7. Measure in centimeters the length, width, and height of the wood cube in the same way.
8. Measure the length, width, and height of the plastic cube in the same way.
9. Calculate the area of one face of each cube.

   To calculate the area of a surface, multiply the length times the width. Your answer will be in cm^2 (See Figure 5.10a).

   Record this information in your data table.

10. Calculate the volume of each cube.

    To calculate the volume of a cube, multiply the length times the width times the height. Your answer will be in cm^3 (See Figure 5.10b).

    Record this information in your data table.

11. For each cube, divide its mass by its volume.

    We call this value its ***density****. It has units of gm/cm^3.*

    Record this information in your data table.

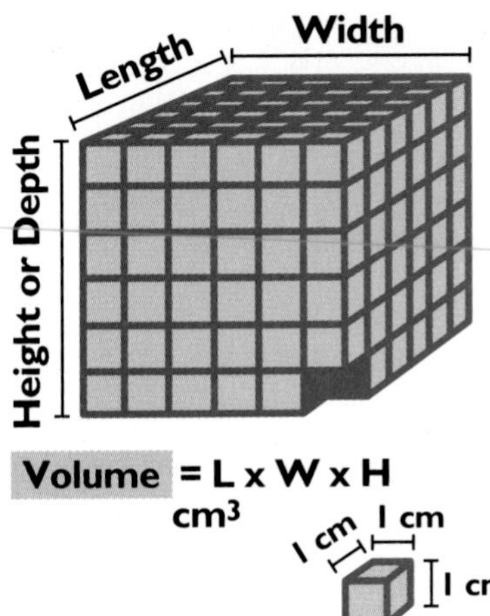

▲ **FIGURE 5.10b**

The volume of this cube is everything that is colored in. The volume is determined by multiplying the length times the width times the height. If you counted each cubic centimeter of this cube, what would the volume equal?

12. Compare the densities that you just calculated for each cube and, with your teammate, discuss what patterns you see.
13. Now obtain a different size aluminum cube from your teacher. Predict whether its density will be greater than, less than, or the same as the first aluminum cube that you studied.

    Record this prediction in your notebook.
14. Repeat Step 6 and Steps 9–11 to calculate the density of this new cube.

    Record this information in your data table.
15. Compare the density of the second aluminum cube with the density you recorded for your first aluminum cube. Was your prediction accurate?

Wrap Up

Think about the concepts of area, volume, mass, and density and discuss them with your teammate. Then write the answers to the following questions in your notebook.

1. What information did you use to make your prediction about the density of the second aluminum cube? Why?
2. Did the results surprise you? If so, how?
3. Based on the new information that you now have, what would you predict about the density of a second, larger wooden cube? Do you think its density would be greater than, less than, or the same as the first wooden cube? Explain your answer.

elaborate

Investigation:
Will It Sink or Float?

So far in this chapter, you have used patterns to make predictions. In addition you have learned that you can be more accurate in your predictions if you have enough information of good quality. In this investigation, your challenge is to observe what happens when certain liquids are placed in water. Then you will use the patterns you see to make predictions.

SIDELIGHT on Inquiry

Let's Think about It

Let's do a thought experiment with an automobile. (A real experiment might be dangerous!)

Imagine that you are standing in front of a parked car. Now think about trying to lift it. If you could lift it, you would be using the force of your muscles against the force of gravity instead of letting the surface of the parking lot handle this force. You could say that the car has a lot of weight. Now imagine that the car is sitting on this level surface and the brakes are off. Imagine that you are behind the car and that you are trying to push the car to make it roll. It would be difficult. But now imagine trying to stop the car from continuing to roll. This would be difficult too—and dangerous! Eventually because of friction, the car would stop on its own. We can say that the car has **inertia**. Inertia is the tendency of matter to remain at rest (a parked car) or in motion (a rolling car) unless acted upon by some outside force.

Working Cooperatively

You will work in the same cooperative teams of two. Use the following jobs: Team Members, Manager, and Communicator/Tracker. Work at a table or form a table with your desks. Practice the social skill *Move into your groups quickly and quietly.*

Materials for Each Team of Two:

- large container of water
- overflow tray
- 2 solid wooden cubes (one large—5cm; one small—2.5 cm; from What Is Density All About?)
- 2 solid aluminum cubes (one large—5 cm; one small—2.5 cm; from What Is Density All About?)
- 1 small plastic bag of oil with penny (closed with twist tie)
- 1 small plastic bag of salt water with penny (closed with twist tie)

Process and Procedure

1. Pick up the materials.

   Whose job is this?

2. Read through the procedures so that you and your teammate understand what you will be doing.
3. Create a data table in your notebook in which to record your predictions and results.

   Your chart might look something like the one in Figure 5.11.

WILL IT SINK OR FLOAT?		
	Prediction	Result
small wooden cube		
large wooden cube		
small aluminum cube		
large aluminum cube		
small bag of oil		
small bag of salt water		

▲ **FIGURE 5.11**

Use a chart like this one for recording your predictions and the results.

4. With your partner, review your findings about the density of some of the materials from the previous investigation. This information may help you develop a general rule for whether something will sink or float. Discuss whether you think each of the cubes will sink or float when you place them in water and why.
5. After you share your ideas, record your predictions in your data table.

   You do not have to have the same predictions as your teammate.
6. Test your predictions for each of the cubes.

   Gently place each cube into the water.

   Water spills can cause floors to be slippery.
7. Record the results for each cube.

   Notebook entry: Write "sinks" or "floats" in the Results column.
8. Predict whether each small bag will sink or float when you place it in water.

   You may want to discuss your ideas with your teammate first. Then record your predictions in your chart.
9. Test your predictions and record your results.
10. Return all materials.

Wrap Up

Discuss the following questions with your partner and write your answer to each question in your notebook. Be sure both you and your partner can explain the answers during a class discussion.

1. How accurate were your predictions for each item?
2. You had specific information about the cubes because you studied them in the previous investigation. Did this information help you when you made your predictions? Why or why not?
3. You also have information about the density of water from the previous investigation. When you compare the density of water with the density of aluminum what do you find? What happened to the aluminum cube in the water?
4. When you compare the density of water with the density of wood what do you find? What happened to the wooden cube in the water?
5. What pattern do you see about density and whether or not something sinks or floats?
6. How does this pattern help you make sense of the results you obtained with the bags of oil and salt water?
   a. Do you think that the density of oil is greater than, less than, or the same as the density of water?
   b. Do you think that the density of salt water is greater than, less than, or the same as the density of tap water?
7. If you had an aluminum cube that measured 8 cm on each side, do you think it would sink or float in water? Why?

Connections:

Minding Your Ps (Predictions) and Qs (Quality and Quantity)

evaluate

Work individually during this connections activity.

In the investigations in this chapter, you made predictions based on the information available to you. You might have found that some of your predictions were more accurate than others. What made the difference? When your predictions were inaccurate, was it because you did not have enough information or because you did not have the type of information you needed?

Read the questions below and then review Finney's Funny Food, The Power of Attraction, and Will It Sink or Float? Look at the type of information and the amount of information you had in each investigation. Write the answers to the following questions in your notebook and be prepared to discuss your answers with your classmates.

1. Which investigations do you think had quality information but not a sufficient quantity of information?
2. Which investigations do you think had a sufficient quantity of information but not the appropriate quality of information?
3. Which of the investigations do you think had both sufficient quantity and quality of information?
4. How did different types of information help you make predictions?

The Moon and Scientific Explanations

For thousands of years, people have been curious about the cycle of the moon and the changes in its shape. In cultures all around the world, people often gathered in the evenings to tell stories. On some evenings, they told their tales by the light of the moon. And when the moon mysteriously grew thin and disappeared, they told their stories to fill the darkness. They asked the same questions you might have asked: How did the moon get there? Why does it move across the sky? Where does it go when it disappears?

engage/explore

Reading: Moon Legends—Another Way of Explaining Patterns

explore

Connections: And So a Legend Begins
Investigation: Moon Movies
Connections: Moon Movies and Predictions

explain

Reading: What Makes an Explanation Scientific?

elaborate

Investigation: Explaining Phases

evaluate

Connections: The View from Earth

engage/explore

Reading:
Moon Legends—Another Way of Explaining Patterns

The stories people told long ago were important to them and to their way of life. The stories were so important that they were told over and over, and they were so powerful that they were passed from one generation to the next.

The people who told the stories were trying to explain things they observed in the world around them. They felt the power of the sun and the moon in their lives in many direct ways. Storytellers in some cultures gave the moon a personality: it was attractive, stubborn, and changeable; in some it was frightening, angry, and jealous. And in others, the moon was portrayed as hopeful and happy. Sometimes the stories portrayed the moon as mysterious with superhuman power. Regardless of the type of personality, the stories always depicted the moon as having an important place in the lives of men, women, and children.

Many stories explained why the whole face of the moon did not shine all the time. An old African folktale tells of the keeper of the "great shining stone" (the moon). In this tale, some special people, called sky people, are in charge of bringing food to the keeper of the great shining

The moon is like a fire in a hogon. When the door opens the fire glows and it is a full moon. When the moon is getting new, the blanket doorway is shutting.

Harley D. Ruiz
Tso Ho Tso Middle School
Ft. Defiance AZ

Once long ago somewhere in the sky a person sleeps in the daytime and at night he wakes up and gets his weapons. His weapons are a bow and arrow. His bow is really bright. That makes the cresent of the moon. Sometimes he sleeps for a long time and that's a new moon. The arrow is the stars. When he shoots it, the stars come out.

Patrick Begay
Marlene Scott
Tso Ho Tso Middle School
Ft. Defiance AZ

stone. Sometimes the sky people get tired of bringing food, however. When this happens, the keeper gradually covers the box that contains the stone. When fresh supplies of food come again, he gradually opens the box so that the stone can send its light down to earth.

explore

Connections:
And So a Legend Begins

For several weeks now, you have been studying patterns in the natural world. You probably have been looking at the world around you in a slightly different way; suddenly patterns are everywhere. Now you will have the opportunity to create a legend to explain a pattern that interests you. You may use any pattern you have seen or read about. If you cannot think of a pattern to write about, your teacher will offer some suggestions. Before you write your legend, create a list of ideas, an outline, or a concept map of your legend in your notebook.

As you write your legend, be imaginative but make sure you explain everything you observed or read about the pattern you chose. When you are finished writing, create a picture to go along with your legend.

Take turns sharing your legends with each other in the manner your teacher describes.

Investigation:
Moon Movies

explore

No matter how many times we have watched a full moon rise at sunset, it is always a moving experience. Even though we know the pattern, we still have a sense of wonder about the moon in the night sky.

Materials for Each Team of Two:

- moon charts from the moon watch
- 2 pairs of scissors
- 1 glue stick or bottle of school glue
- 16 index cards, 3-by-5-in.
- 2 Moon Movie Flip Pages
- 1 metric ruler

Materials for the Entire Class:

- at least one stapler

Process and Procedure

1. In your notebook, write the date and the title of the investigation.
2. Study the moon watch charts that you drew during the moon watch reports.
   The charts should be in your notebook.
3. Discuss with your teammates how the moon changes from a new moon to a full moon and identify three key stages that fall between the new moon and the full moon.
4. Fill in five pictures of the moon, including a new moon, the three key stages, and a full moon.
   Do this on your own Moon Movie Flip Page.
5. As a team, decide on three key stages of the moon that occur between the full moon and the next new moon.
   Notebook entry: Record your key stages.

   STOP: Review your unit skill.
6. On your Moon Movie Flip Pages, draw those three key stages that occur between the full moon and a new moon.

Working Cooperatively

You will work in cooperative teams of two. You will need a Tracker and a Manager. Push your desks together to form a table or sit together at a table. Practice the social skill *Use your teammates' names.*

Again work individually on your Moon Movie Flip Page.

7. Cut out all the moon pictures.

   These are the pictures you drew in Steps 4 and 6.

8. Glue each picture of the moon in the center of an index card.

9. Sort your cards so that the changes in the moon are in order, beginning with a new moon and ending just before the next new moon.

10. Check your partner's stack to be certain that you both agree on the order of the cards.

11. Staple the cards in your stack together.

    Measure the thickness of your stack of cards and record the thickness in your notebook.

12. Use your thumb and forefinger to flip through the index cards and watch the moon movie.

13. After you have watched your moon movie a few times, read the following Background Information.

Background Information

Each of the different pictures that you drew in this investigation was a picture of a phase of the moon. The word phase comes from the Greek word phaino, which means "to appear or to bring to light." As the phase of the moon changes, more (or less) of the moon is "brought to light." If you begin with a dark moon, the phase is called the new moon.

The next phase is a thin sliver of light in the shape of a crescent. This moon is called a crescent moon. When the moon appears as a shining half-circle, this phase is called the first quarter moon. The phase when the bright portion of the moon is larger than a half-circle is called the gibbous moon. Finally, when a full circle of the moon is bright, the phase is known as the full moon.

Wait a second...
I don't get it. If the moon is in the shape of a half-circle, why is it called a quarter moon?

There appear to be two trends to the changing shape of the moon: One is a change toward a full moon, and the other is toward the next new moon. The moon completes a full cycle from new moon to full moon and back to new moon every 29.5 days, or roughly every month.

If you do not watch the changes in the shape of the moon long enough, you might think that the pattern of change is simply a trend. By watching the phases for more than one month, you are able to see the full cycle of change.

Wrap Up

Discuss the following with your classmates and write your own answers in your notebook.

1. Describe what you saw when watching the moon movie.
2. Describe the pattern of change that occurs in the moon's shape.
3. Why is the moon's pattern of change called a cycle?

Connections:
Moon Movies and Predictions

explore

Work in your cooperative team of two in this connections section.

1. Imagine a whole year of moon movies. Approximately how many times would the cycle repeat?
2. Look back in your notebook and see how thick your moon movie stack was. How thick would your moon movie stack have been if you had made a movie that covered an entire year?
3. Explain why your information on the phases of the moon is of good quality and sufficient quantity.
4. What predictions can you make about the phases of the moon next year?
5. Create a poster for your classroom that depicts some of your ideas about the phases of the moon. Include both what you have learned and what you enjoy most about watching the moon in the night sky.

explain

Reading:

What Makes an Explanation Scientific?

Why do people invent legends and stories? If you think about the legends you read in this chapter, you probably realize that the legends explained a pattern of change. As you told your legend, you were providing explanations for a pattern as well. Perhaps your story explained why we have day and night or why water moves downhill. In order to tell such a story, you must have observed a pattern and then developed an explanation for it.

The explanations that you develop and learn about in your science classroom do not sound like legends or stories. In these explanations, the moon is not a person and white horses do not pull the moon across the sky. In science we explain many of the patterns in nature by gathering information and making predictions. Such explanations are called **scientific explanations**. People base these explanations on information—that is, something they can hear, see, or experience.

People then use this information to make predictions. If they have sufficient quality and quantity of data, people often can make an accurate prediction about a pattern. This prediction, then, helps them develop an explanation for that pattern. In Chapter 5, you learned how to make accurate predictions by using data of good quality and sufficient quantity. Now you will see how you can strengthen your predictions by using scientific explanations.

Stop & Think

1. What are the characteristics of a scientific explanation?
2. How is a scientific explanation different from a story or legend?

3. In which of the investigations that you have completed in this unit did you develop a scientific explanation?
4. Evaluate the following story. How is it like a legend? How is it like a scientific explanation?

   An invisible elf put a spell on a dairy cow that caused her milk to taste very sweet. All of her milk was made into ice cream and delivered to Finney's. This particular ice cream was very popular with the customers.

elaborate

Investigation:
Explaining Phases

The moon is a familiar part of your surroundings. Even so, many people don't know how or why the appearance of the moon changes from day to day. In this investigation, you will gather evidence that will help explain the relationships among the earth, moon, and sun. You will use this evidence to explain the patterns of change in the moon's appearance.

Working Cooperatively

You will be working individually and as an entire class. The skill to practice in this investigation is *Express your thoughts and ideas aloud and listen politely to others.*

Materials for the Entire Class:

- 2 floodlights or light bulbs in fixtures

Materials for Each Student:

- 1 Styrofoam™ ball, with an X marked on it, mounted on a pencil

Process and Procedure

1. Read through this procedure.
2. Stand in your assigned place.

   The teacher will tell you where to stand. Take your Styrofoam™ ball with you.
3. Hold your Styrofoam™ ball out away from you and above your head, with the X facing you.

   The Styrofoam ball represents the moon, and you represent the earth. (See Figure 6.1).

▶ **FIGURE 6.1**

Hold the ball with the X facing you. The ball represents the moon and you represent the earth. The light represents the sun. Make one-quarter of a turn as you stand in one spot. Then stop and look at the ball. Notice what phase of the moon the ball resembles.

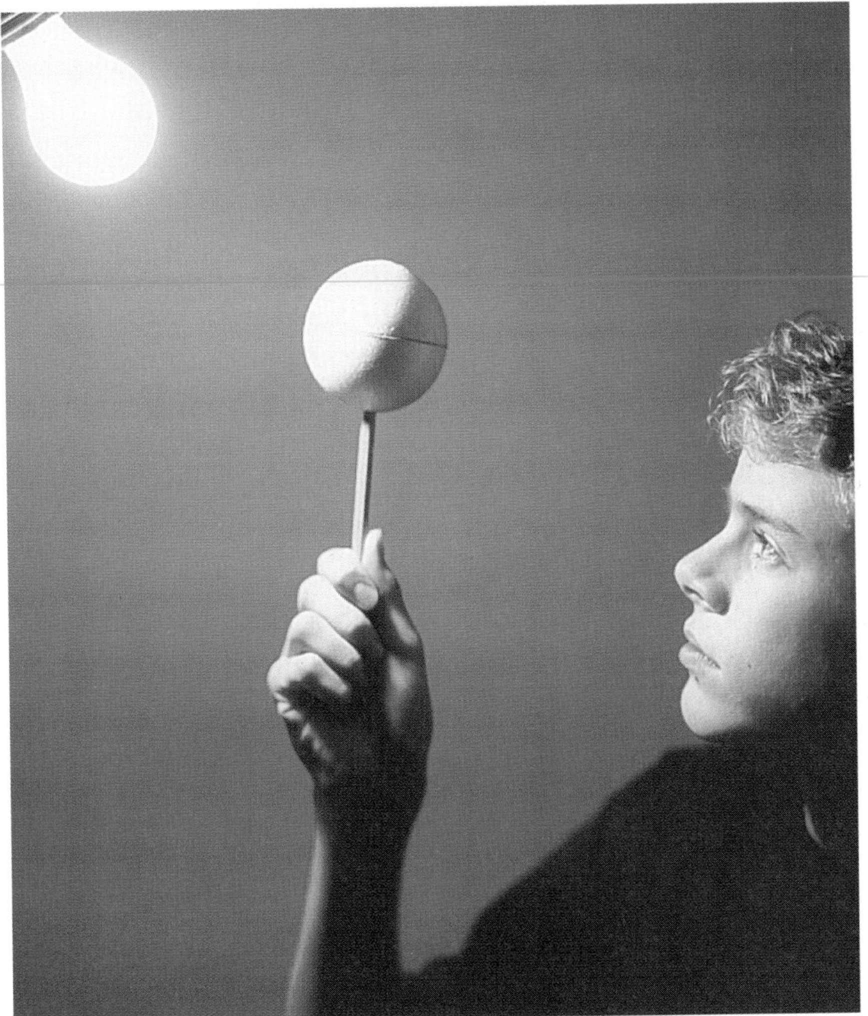

4. Stay in one spot and slowly rotate yourself one-quarter of a turn to your right. Now look at the ball.

   Hold the ball at arm's length, higher than your head. As you turn and look at the ball, notice how the light falls on it.

5. Rotate another quarter of a turn to the right and look at the ball again.

   Again compare the ball with what you know about the moon.

6. Repeat Step 5 two more times.

   You will have made one complete turn while standing in the same place.

7. Make another full turn while holding the ball out, but this time make only one-eighth of a turn at a time.

   You will be turning only half as far each time as you did before. You will make eight little turns to make one complete turn. After each little turn, look at the ball and compare it with the moon.

8. As you turn in a circle again, this time find the exact location to demonstrate each of the following:

   a. a full moon

   b. a gibbous moon

   c. a quarter moon

   d. a crescent moon

   e. a new moon

   Be certain that you know how to demonstrate each phase of the moon. If you do not, ask questions!

9. When you are finished, put away your materials.

Wrap Up

Discuss the following questions with your classmates and write your own answers in your notebook.

1. What approximate length of time does it take for the moon to complete all the phases? (Think back to the moon watch you have been doing.)
2. Explain why we see different phases of the moon from the earth.
3. What do you think is the source of the moonlight you see?
4. Look at the diagrams your teacher shows you on the overhead transparency. Describe how the phases of the moon are different from before.

5. Explain how these different shapes of the moon phases might occur.
6. Come up with a class rating for how well you practiced the social skill, *Express your thoughts and ideas aloud and listen politely to others.* Use a scale from 1 through 10. Discuss how you could improve your rating.

evaluate

Connections:
The View from Earth

In this chapter, you have read and learned about the moon and about scientific explanations. The investigation you just did demonstrated a model for the apparent changes in the shape of the moon.

Part A

Individually read through the following explanation and decide whether or not it is a scientific explanation. Record and justify your decision in your notebook.

We see phases of the moon because the earth and the moon do not sit still in space. They are both moving around the sun, which is a constant source of light. The sun shines on both the earth and the moon. When we see moonlight, we really are seeing the sunlight that is reflecting off the surface of the moon. When we see the lighted side of the moon, we are seeing its "daylight" side. When we see phases of the moon, we are seeing parts of the moon's daylight side.

The phases of the moon have the shape they do because the moon is a sphere (like a globe) and because of our location on earth when we view the moon. Half of the moon is always lit, but we cannot always see all that is lit because this part is not always directly facing the earth. When the moon is almost between the earth and the sun, we see the light that is reflected off the moon as the light comes around the curved side of the moon. Look at Figure 6.2 for examples of how the moon appears at different times in its cycle.

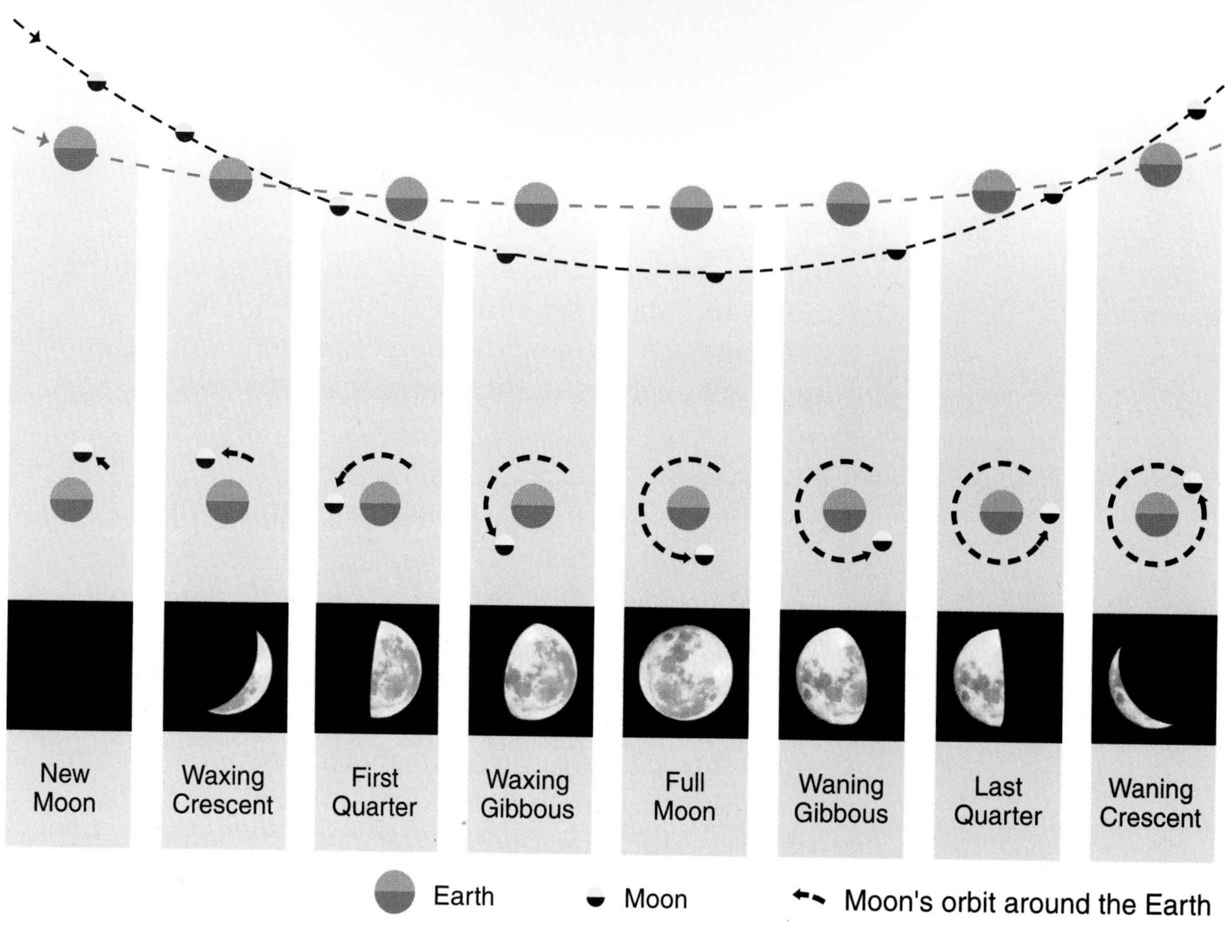

▲ **FIGURE 6.2**

These are the eight major views we see of the moon. This illustration shows where the moon is, compared with the sun and the earth, for each phase.

Part B

Draw a picture of the positions of the sun, the earth, and the moon when we see a new moon.

Once you understand the scientific explanation for the phases of the moon, your predictions about what the moon will look like at a certain time will be more accurate. For example if you know the exact relationship of the earth, the sun, and the moon as they move, you can predict exactly when eclipses will occur. An eclipse of the moon occurs when the moon passes through the earth's shadow. A total eclipse of the moon happens

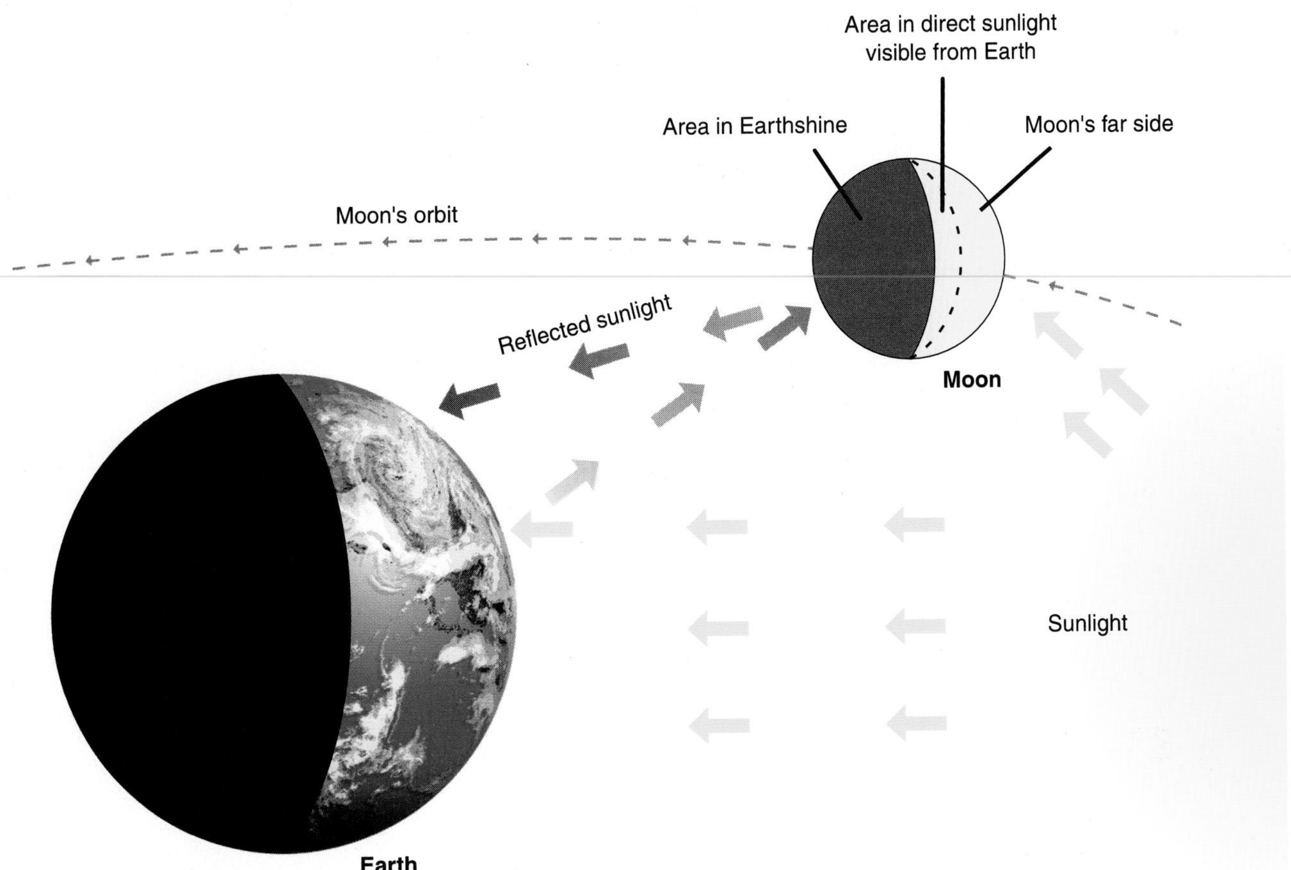

▲ FIGURE 6.3

The moon appears bright to us because it reflects light from the sun. This illustration shows the paths of reflected sunlight. As the moon orbits the earth, different amounts of its surface receive sunlight. This is why we can see the moon's many phases. The area of the moon in earthshine represents the part of the moon that we sometimes can see faintly while another part of it appears very bright.

about once a year, and partial eclipses happen about twice a year. If you didn't have a scientific explanation of the moon's phases, you would have to observe the moon for a long time to figure out the pattern of eclipses. Now you know how explanations that are scientific can help you make predictions about patterns. Furthermore you can improve the accuracy of your predictions each time you improve your scientific explanations.

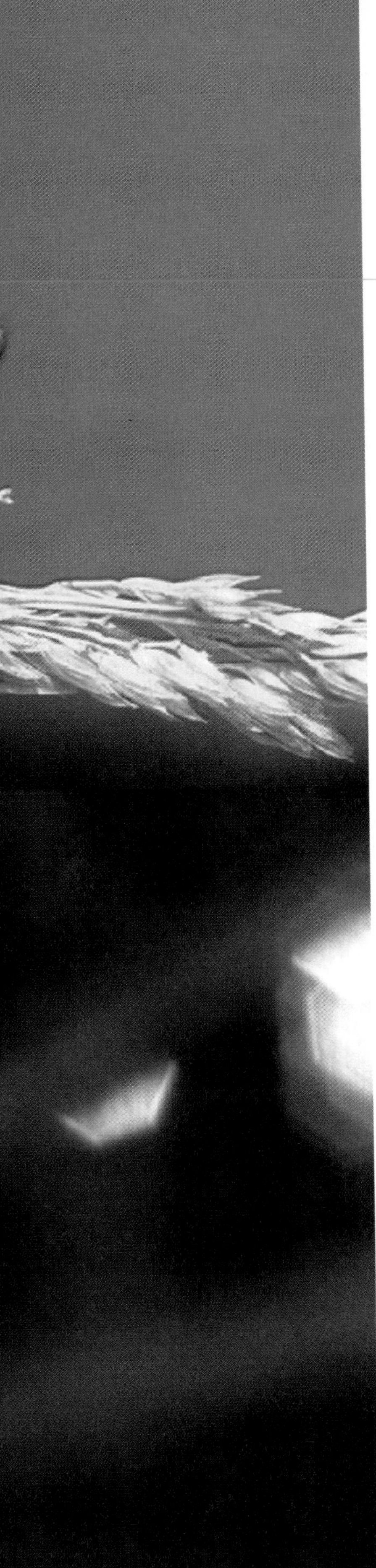

Recognizing Patterns of Change

Look at the changes in the dragonfly in these photographs. What patterns do you recognize? How could you explain these patterns to someone else? The world is full of patterns and many patterns help scientists explain changes that we all experience. Use the questions in this chapter to evaluate your understanding of patterns of change.

engage / explore

Investigation: What's Going on Here?

explain / elaborate

Reading: The Value of Patterns and Scientific Explanations

evaluate

Connections: Sorting Out the Patterns

engage / explore

Working Cooperatively

You and your partner will join with another team of two to work in a cooperative team of four. You will all be Team Members, and you will need a Tracker and a Communicator. Push your desks together to form a table or sit close together at a table. Practice the social skill *Speak softly so only your teammates can hear you.*

Investigation: What's Going on Here?

Several hundred years ago, people died from diseases that people rarely die from today. Often people faced serious illnesses with little hope of a cure. In this investigation, see whether you can use your knowledge of patterns to make predictions. Maybe you can discover what would have kept some people from getting sick.

Process and Procedure

1. Get into your teams.
2. Listen to your teacher read the guided imagery.
3. Read aloud the descriptions of people in the village of Rainy Corner.

   Each Team Member should read one description. Then the Communicator and Tracker each might read one more. Listen politely as your teammates are reading.

Descriptions

Colin Smith—Blacksmith and Farmer

Colin is 28 years old and has five children. He always has been strong and healthy. He enjoys working outdoors but also works in his blacksmith shop making horseshoes and plow blades.

Ann Howard—Seamstress

Ann Howard is a fine seamstress and travels to London from time to time. She sews gowns, curtains, and everyday items for the women of the village. She is 30 years old, has three children, and is married to James Howard. Unlike most people in the village, she does not keep a garden because she does not enjoy being out in the cold, damp climate.

Ellen Throckmorton—Milkmaid

Ellen is 20 years old and works for the Smith family. Her duties include cleaning the house, watching the children, and milking the cows. Ellen milks the cows twice a day. She is quite fond of the cows and calls them by name when she takes them to pasture.

James Howard—Farmer

James Howard is 35 years old and farms the land next to Colin Smith's. He enjoys farming, even in the damp climate of England. He is married to Ann Howard, and they often visit the Smith family on Sundays. James has always had good health, except for a childhood injury to his leg. He now walks with a slight limp. He enjoys his work and takes care of the cows, chickens, and pigs, as well as his fields.

Sarah Wesley—Hired Girl

Sarah Wesley, age 19, works for the Howard family and is a friend of Ellen Throckmorton. She often visits Ellen when Ellen is taking care of the Smith children. Sarah prefers to be indoors most of the time, and she enjoys working for the Howard family. She is glad that she does not have to do the outdoor chores that Ellen has to do.

Richard Cooke—Baker

Richard Cooke, age 26, sees all the people of the village. He is famous for the good bread he bakes—even visitors from London stop to buy it. He enjoys being a baker because he dislikes working outdoors in the cold. He does not yet have a family, but sometimes visits Ellen Throckmorton while she works at the Smiths. He dislikes the barns, but he occasionally helps Ellen with the farm chores anyway.

▶ FIGURE 7.1

Use a data table like this one to record your predictions about who will or will not get sick. Copy this data table into your notebook.

PREDICTIONS

Person's Name	Will Get Sick	Won't Get Sick	Reason

4. Compare the descriptions.

   To compare descriptions, discuss the following: What do the people have in common? How are their situations different?

5. Create a data table in your notebook that looks like Figure 7.1.

6. Record each person's name in the first column of your data table.

   We described six people, so you should have six names.

7. Discuss with your teammates who you think will and will not get sick. Then record your predictions for each person.

   Place a check mark in the appropriate column. Your predictions do not have to be the same as your teammates' predictions.

8. Write a reason for each of your predictions in the last column.

9. Participate in the class discussion and listen as your teacher reads you the rest of the story.

Wrap Up

After participating in the class discussion, record your own answers to the following questions in your notebook.

1. How accurate were your predictions?
2. What patterns did you use to make your predictions?
3. Describe what people could have done to keep from getting sick.
4. How did you express your thoughts and ideas within your team and during the class discussion?
5. In teams of two, you have been practicing the social skill *Speak softly so only your teammates can hear you.* What did you have to do differently when working in teams of four?

explain / elaborate

Reading: The Value of Patterns and Scientific Explanations

Throughout history people have faced situations as puzzling as the one you just encountered. After you learned that the milkmaids never got sick, you had a clue—an important piece of the puzzle. But this clue was not the whole story. You needed information of a different type to discover the fact that the cows often had a milder form of smallpox called cowpox.

This discovery gave you a second piece of the puzzle. If you were able to link these two pieces of the puzzle, you might have concluded that milkmaids got this mild form of the disease by touching the cow's udder as they milked them.

This new clue eventually might have led you to the realization that catching cowpox was good because it made people immune to smallpox. After you understood this, then you would have to figure out how everybody could catch cowpox so that they would not get smallpox. It took more than 160 years from the time when people first realized that milkmaids never got smallpox to the time when people figured out how to protect the whole world from smallpox.

The fact that milkmaids got cowpox but not smallpox was a pattern. Based on this pattern, you could make a prediction that milkmaids would not get smallpox. Determining the cause behind the pattern, however, is an important part of developing a scientific explanation.

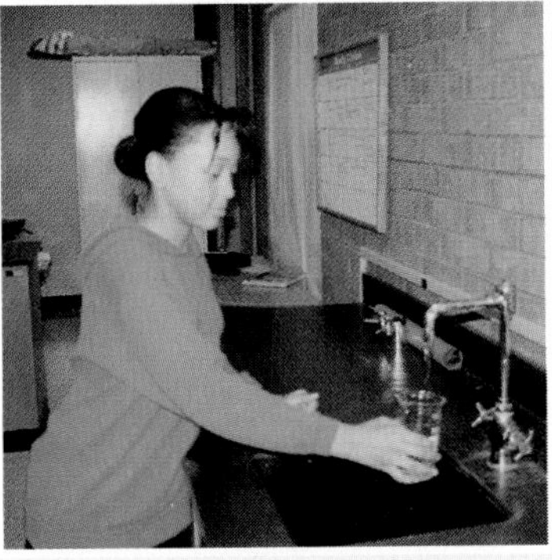

▲ **FIGURE 7.2**

Clean tap water helps you to continue to explore and explain patterns you observe. When we build on other scientists' evidence and explanations, sometimes we can elaborate on them with our own work.

▼ Figure 7.3

These photos are from a water treatment plant much like the one you have in your city. Because people like William Farr and Dr. Snow carefully observed patterns and came up with explanations about the need for clean water, we now clean our drinking water before it is distributed to our homes.

Once someone develops a scientific explanation, then that person or others could make an even more powerful prediction. In this case, scientists were able to determine how to prevent the disease in everyone. The scientific explanation was that cowpox prevented people from getting smallpox—if a person got cowpox, for some reason, he or she would not get smallpox.

Using scientific explanations, people have been able to eliminate or control other medical problems. A good example comes from England in the 1830s. Many people lived in very poor conditions. They lived in the streets and drank water contaminated with sewage. Water purification systems were unknown, and few sewers existed. During the summer of 1831, an epidemic of cholera (**KAH** ler uh) swept through England. Cholera caused people to have a very high fever and severe diarrhea; many died within a few days. At that time, no one knew how to prevent it. No one knew what caused cholera or how it was transmitted. It struck rich neighborhoods as well as poor. Three people who observed and recognized patterns were responsible for saving thousands of lives.

William Farr began a study of all the afflicted neighborhoods in London. But he could see no pattern. Then after nearly five years, he saw a pattern that no one else had been able to see. Neighborhoods that were closest in elevation to the Thames River had the highest percentage of death due to cholera. Neighborhoods up on hills higher than the river had fewer deaths due to cholera.

Farr believed that cholera was linked somehow to the smell from the polluted river. Nearly twenty years later, a doctor named John Snow looked at the same pattern in a slightly different way. Dr. Snow thought that cholera was transmitted by polluted water. The pattern Dr. Snow observed was that the death rate was ten times greater in areas where people obtained their water directly from the Thames than in areas that had a different water supply. He also observed that in a previously healthy district, 600 people suddenly died when a cesspit overflowed into the district well. This evidence supported Snow's explanation: Water polluted with sewage was causing cholera. Snow then could predict that if a neighborhood had clean water, the people probably would not get cholera.

A medical officer in London named John Simon worked hard to pass laws that required the city of London to clean up its water supply. Finally in 1858, city sewers were constructed and the cholera epidemic disappeared from England.

Today we tend to take many scientific explanations for granted. We expect scientists of all types to identify the causes and to make powerful predictions. These powerful predictions are based on a lot of work. First people must make careful observations of patterns, just as William Farr and John Snow did. Second they must develop explanations for the patterns they observe. After people have observed and explained patterns, their ability to make accurate predictions increases greatly.

▼ **FIGURE 7.4**

This is the Ganges River in North India. Rivers all over the world are an important source of water for people living near them. A river that becomes polluted may affect thousands of people as well as other living organisms in the environment.

Connections:
Sorting Out the Patterns

evaluate

Record your answers to the following in your notebook.

1. Look at the graph in Figure 7.5 showing the percentages of recycled aluminum in the United States.
   a. What percentage of aluminum was recycled in 1980? What percentage was recycled in 1994?
   b. Do you think the pattern is a trend, a cycle, or a correlation? Explain your answer.
2. Look at the graph in Figure 7.6 on tobacco harvesting.
   a. Describe how the number of acres harvested in 1995 was different from what it was in 1980.
   b. Make a prediction about tobacco harvesting in 2010.
   c. Explain your prediction and why it is or is not likely to be accurate.

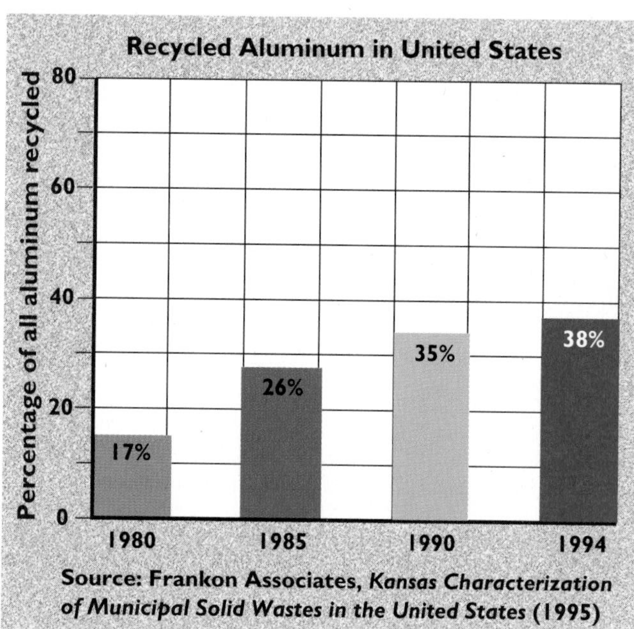

▲ **FIGURE 7.5**

This graph shows the percentages of aluminum that was recycled in the United States from 1980–1999.

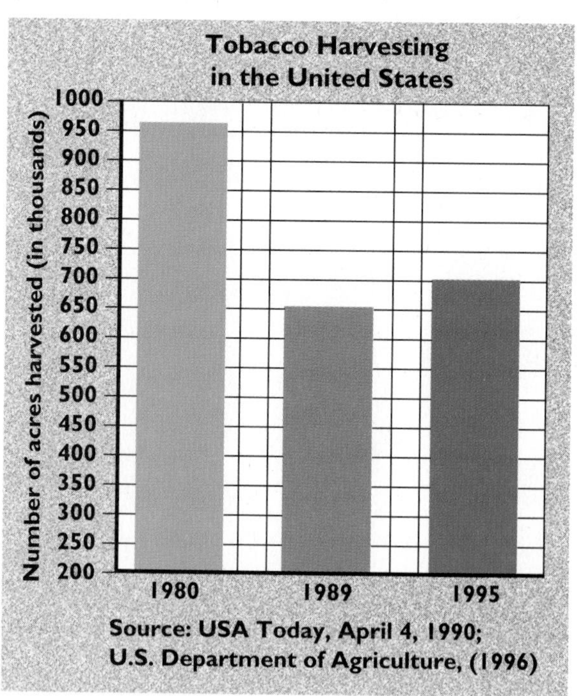

► **FIGURE 7.6**

This graph shows the number of acres of tobacco that were harvested in the United States from 1980–1995.

3. The makers of Fizzy Cola have found a correlation: Everyone in the audience who drank Fizzy Cola at a basketball game last night stayed for the entire game. The people who design advertisements for Fizzy Cola want to start an ad campaign in a sports magazine. They plan to say:

   "Sell Fizzy Cola to make sure your fans stay for all of your game!"

   a. The makers of Fizzy Cola have definitely found a correlation. But have they found the true cause behind the effect? (The effect is that people stayed for the entire game, but what other causes could there be?)

   b. Design a controlled experiment that will test whether or not drinking Fizzy Cola causes people in the audience to stay for the entire game. Write a description of your experiment in your notebook.

4. Students at Central Valley Middle School studied bean plants. They watched more than forty plants grow. The conditions for all the plants were exactly the same with the exception of the amount of fertilizer they received. Half of the plants received a specific amount of fertilizer, and the other half received none. The students observed that the fertilized plants were bigger and healthier looking.

   a. What is the pattern in this experiment?

   b. What predictions might you make, based on this experiment?

5. Using any trends that you observed during the Beanstalk experiment, predict what would happen to your plants if you continued the experiment for another six weeks.

6. Think of another pattern that exists in nature (it might have to do with plants, insects, or the weather). Make a prediction based on this pattern and design an experiment to test this prediction. (If it is a practical experiment that you could do in the classroom, ask your teacher for permission to complete it.)

North America
EQUATOR
South America
Panthalasa Ocean

UNIT 2

Explanations for the Patterns of Change on Earth and Beyond

The earth is a planet of great beauty and contrast. In the contrasting layers of the earth, we see patterns emerge. These patterns tell an experienced geologist like Alfred Wegener much about the history of the planet and how it has changed across time. This map represents one explanation that scientists have developed about the history of the planet. What interests you about this explanation?

Throughout time people in cultures around the world have developed legends about how various land features came to be, and others looked for scientific explanations for their existence. We will explore some of those scientific explanations and you will learn how people have recognized and used patterns to develop explanations for some of the earth's features.

Cooperative Learning Overview

In this unit, you will continue to work cooperatively with others. You and your partner will have another unit skill to practice—*show respect for others and their ideas.* Practice this skill in all cooperative activities, whether or not it is mentioned in the Working Cooperatively section. Some of the investigations will have additional social skills that you should practice. And remember to use the skills from Unit 1. You should continue to build you cooperative skills throughout the year.

Create a class T-chart for your new unit skill as the characters are doing. When you have completed your chart, review it with your partner and then refer to it from time to time as you continue the unit.

SOUNDS LIKE
GOOD IDEA
YEAH!
LOOKS LIKE
LOOKING AT THE PERSON AS HE OR SHE TALKS

PRESS-EWING VERTICAL UP
To=15 SEC, Tg=30 SEC DOWN

Scientific Explanations Begin with a Question

Scientists begin their work by asking questions about the world around them. They make observations and then formulate explanations based on their observations. In Unit 1, you worked the way scientists work. You asked questions and made observations. Sometimes scientists use tools that help them make more precise measurements. This seismograph, for example, helps scientists measure and record movements of the earth. Sometimes your observations were in the form of measurements, such as measuring feet and plants. Then you looked at the patterns in your measurements. When you observed the moon, you kept a record of what you saw and then looked for patterns in the pictures you recorded.

But what if you want to explain something that you cannot see? How will you know whether your explanation is correct? In this chapter, you will experience how scientists formulate and test explanations even when they cannot observe directly what they are studying.

engage / explore

Investigation: How Do You Know?

explore

Investigation: Numbers, Names, and Cubes

explain

Reading: Science Is a Way of Explaining

elaborate

Investigation: The If–Then Box

evaluate

Connections: What Did We Do?

The Corbis-Bettmann Archive/Davis Creative

Investigation:
How Do You Know?

engage/explore

Have you ever stumbled around a dark room, trying to find something you can't see? Have you ever tried to make your way through a maze garden? Often because you can see only a small part of the pattern at a time, you keep running into dead ends. In this investigation, you and your classmates will try to describe another type of maze without being able to look at it.

Materials for the Entire Class:

- 10–15 assorted common objects
- 1 large paper bag
- 10 or more blindfolds (optional)
- clock with a second hand

Materials for Each Team of Two:

- 1 maze puzzle

Process and Procedure

Part A—Objects You Cannot See

1. Think about what you do to identify objects when you cannot see them.

Working Cooperatively

In the first part of this investigation, the entire class will work together. Then you will work cooperatively with your teammate for the rest of the investigation. In addition to being Team Members, one of you will be the Tracker, and the other will be the Manager/Communicator. Practice the social skill *Use your teammate's name.*

▶ **FIGURE 8.1**

You can find this maze garden in Chatsworth, England. What strategies would you use to find your way through it?

▶ FIGURE 8.2

This is a section of a maze garden in Villandry, France. If you couldn't see above these walls of shrubbery, how would you decide to turn left or right?

2. If your teacher calls on you, go to the front of the room.
3. Keep your eyes closed and try to identify the object.

   Notebook entry: If you are not called on, watch and record what the student does to identify the object.

Part B—The Social Skill

1. Move your desks together or sit at a table so that you and your teammate are facing each other.
2. Talk with your teammate for about two minutes. Discuss these questions:
   a. What are your feelings and thoughts about working cooperatively?
   b. What can you and your teammate do to make working in this new cooperative team a good learning experience?
   c. What are some specific strategies you will use to practice the unit skill?

Part C—Maze Puzzles

1. Pick up one maze puzzle.

   Each puzzle contains a small marble and a series of walls (a maze) that restrict the marble's movement.

▲ **FIGURE 8.3**

People who explore caves often have the sense of being in a maze or a life-size puzzle. Archeologists work through different types of puzzles as they piece together artifacts and make predictions about a culture. Pottery such as this was used by cliff dwellers who lived in the southwest United States hundreds of years ago.

2. Keep the puzzle closed and try to figure out the shape of the walls inside the puzzle.

   Do not share your ideas with your partner yet. Begin with the Manager. Use any method, except opening the puzzle box, to figure out the shape of the maze.

3. Stop after one minute.

   The Tracker should keep track of time.

4. Trade jobs.

   The Tracker should be holding the puzzle, and the Manager should keep track of time for another minute.

5. Pass the puzzle back and forth three times or until you have an idea of the shape of the walls inside .

   They may be a circle, a square, a zig-zag line, or one of many other shapes.

6. In your notebook, draw what you think the maze inside your puzzle looks like.

7. Share your ideas about the inside of the puzzle with your partner.

   If you and your partner disagree about the shape of the maze, decide on tests that you can perform to resolve these differences. Remember opening the puzzle is not one of the tests you can do.

8. Test your ideas about the inside of the puzzle.

   Notebook entry: Record your results.

9. Trade your puzzle with a nearby team.

   Do not share your ideas about your puzzle with the other teams.

10. Try to figure out the shape of the maze in the new puzzle.

    Repeat Steps 2 through 8.

Wrap Up

Discuss the following questions with your teammate, then write your own answers in your science notebook. Be sure each of you can explain your answers in a class discussion.

1. What was your first step when you (or someone you watched) tried to identify an object that you held but could not see?
2. How did you determine the shape of the walls in the maze puzzles?
3. How certain were you of your answers?
4. What could you have done to be more certain of your answers?
5. How did you feel when you realized you could never test your answer by looking inside the puzzles?
6. What are some things that scientists study that they will never see?
7. Why do you think scientists study things they cannot see?

Investigation:
Numbers, Names, and Cubes

explore

In this investigation, you will observe and think about patterns in order to answer a question. This activity shows you how scientists gather information in order to answer questions that they have. Observing carefully and thinking clearly are just as important as the answer you come up with.

Working Cooperatively

Work cooperatively with your teammate and with one other team to which your teacher will assign you. Move your desks together to form a table or sit together at a table. The roles you need are Communicator, Tracker, and Manager. Remember that you are always a Team Member as well. Continue to practice the skill *Use your teammates' names.*

Materials for Each Team of Four:

- 1 Number Cube
- 1 Name Cube
- 1 Challenge Cube (optional)

Process and Procedure

Part A—The Number Cube

1. Pick up a Number Cube and the paper plate to which it is attached.
2. Sit so that you can see only the top and one side of the cube.

   The Tracker, Communicator, and other Team Members should each sit facing another side of the cube.
3. DO NOT LOOK AT THE BOTTOM OF THE CUBE.
4. Try to solve the number puzzle in two minutes.

   Keeping track of the time is the Tracker's job.
5. Think about the following questions.

   The Communicator should read them aloud and a Team Member should write down the responses.

   a. Look at the cube. What do you want to know about the cube?

   b. What do you propose as the answer to your question?

▶ Figure 8.4

Stonehenge is the ruins of a Stone Age monument that is situated on a plain in southern England. Because of the patterns and arrangement of the stones, scientists think that ancient people used these stones to make predictions about the natural world. What predictions do you think ancient people might have made using the stones at Stonehenge?

   c. What observations did you make that will help support your answer?

6. Return the cube to the designated location and pick up a Name Cube along with the paper plate to which it is attached.

   REMEMBER NOT TO LET ANYONE SEE THE BOTTOM OF THE CUBE.

Part B—The Name Cube

1. Place the Name Cube in the center of your table.
2. Again sit so that you can see only the top and one side of the cube.
3. Solve the name puzzle.

   You will have 10 minutes.
4. Read aloud the questions that follow.

   This is the Communicator's job. The Team Member who has no other job should write the answers.

   a. Look at the cube. What question or questions do you want to answer about the cube?

   b. What do you propose as the answer to the question?

   c. What observations did you make that might support your answer?
5. Return the cube to its designated location.
6. Check your notebook. Make sure it contains enough information about the cubes to answer the questions in the Wrap Up.

   Share information with your teammates.

From: The Three Cube Method of Introducing Inquiry by Joe P. Buckingham. Copyright © 1973. Adapted with permission.

Wrap Up

Discuss these questions with your teammates. Each of you should record your own answers in your notebook. Work with your teammates to be sure that each of you is prepared to contribute to a class discussion.

1. What questions did you try to answer about the cubes?

2. If you could turn over each cube, what would you expect to see?
3. How can you support your proposed answers to convince others that your explanations are correct?
4. How sure are you that your answer is correct?
5. Use a scale of 1 to 10 (10 being the best) to rank your team on how well Team Members used each other's names. Share this ranking with the class.

explain

Reading:
Science Is a Way of Explaining

It might seem to you that science is only about answers. For example people often turn to scientific experts to solve disagreements or problems. News correspondents interview scientists who confidently explain their answers and support them with long lists of evidence.

Actually science has as much to do with questions as with answers. Science begins when a person has a general curiosity about something, such as the ocean or the stars. This curiosity often suggests specific questions, such as, How did the ocean come to be? Or, What are stars really made up of? These questions are the crucial first steps of a scientist.

What are the characteristics of a scientific question? Scientific questions can be simple or complex. They can be questions about who, what, where, when, how, or why. Yet one thing that all scientific questions share is their usefulness. They should engage your mind in a way of thinking that will help you find the answers.

Think about what you did in the investigation Numbers, Names, and Cubes. At first you solved the Number Cube. Perhaps you were successful with the Number Cube, but became frustrated with the Name Cube, and maybe you even asked yourself the question, Why are we doing this, anyway? Then you and your teammates discussed specific questions about the cube. These questions gave you a clear purpose. Once you recognized certain patterns, you could answer the questions you had about the cube. But because you

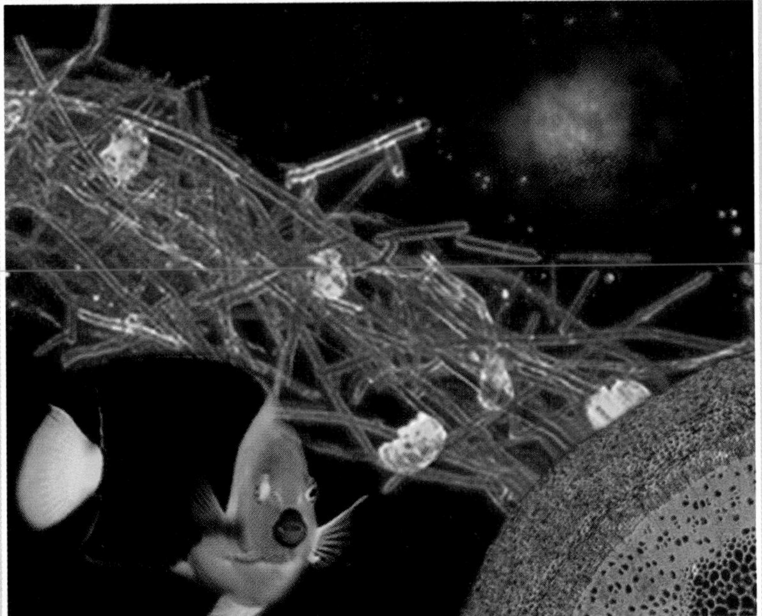

▲ **Figure 8.5**
What questions do you have about the things in this photocollage?

observed patterns, you had more than just an answer about what was on the bottom of the cube. You also could explain why you thought what you did and how you came up with your answer.

Stop & Think

1. What are examples of scientific questions that you have asked in this chapter?

After asking a question, scientists gather evidence that will help them find answers. Evidence is information that you obtain through your five senses. Anything you can see, hear, feel, taste, or smell can count as evidence. Scientists gather evidence by observing and measuring things in natural or artificial settings (for example, a laboratory). They also may use instruments such as a microscope, telescope, or magnet that extend their senses. Scientists then can use the evidence to develop and explain their answers.

Stop & Think

2. What are examples of evidence that you have collected in this chapter?

Now consider the role of evidence in the following situation.

Al stepped outside early one morning and saw a melted ice cream cone on the sidewalk.

The following ideas went through Al's mind:

a. Yuck, the ice cream is melted.

b. It must have been warm last night because the ice cream isn't frozen.

c. Maybe the person who dropped it got spooked by something and dropped it by accident.

d. Whoever dropped it was probably really bummed afterward.

e. Man this ice cream really smells like mint!

f. Whoever dropped it probably bought it at the Sugar Shack Ice Cream Shop.

g. The Sugar Shack closes at 10 o'clock at night.

h. The person was probably here before 10:30 p.m.

Stop & Think

3. Which of Al's ideas represent evidence? In your notebook, write the letters *a* through *h* to represent each of Al's ideas. Put an *E* beside the letter if that idea represents evidence. Think about your answers so that you can justify them in a class discussion.
4. How would you describe Al's other ideas? What do they represent?

The evidence that scientists gather helps them propose explanations. An explanation is more than just a yes or no answer to a question. When someone proposes an explanation, he or she not only has an answer in mind but also can justify why he or she feels it is probably accurate. The word "propose" indicates that scientific explanations are not permanent; they can and do change. Scientists base their explanations on evidence as well as their own creativity and thinking. In addition they often work with other scientists to form their explanations.

Stop & Think

5. Give an example of an explanation that you have proposed in this chapter.
6. Describe how you formed this explanation.

Now think back to the maze puzzle. Perhaps you feel a lingering dissatisfaction. Although you based your

explanation of the puzzle on evidence, how can you be sure that your explanation was correct? Chances are you will never be sure—unless, of course, you open the puzzle.

Scientists face the same dilemma. How can they be sure that their explanations are correct? The answer lies in careful tests. Contrary to what you might think, tests can be very useful. Through careful testing, scientists can find out whether their explanation is not accurate, partly accurate, or almost entirely accurate.

One way to test an explanation is to use an if–then statement. An if–then statement predicts what would happen if your explanation were correct. For example a scientist might say, "If my explanation is accurate, then such-and-such will happen." Other examples of if–then statements are:

- **a.** If plants need sunlight to grow, then plants that do not get sunlight will not grow.
- **b.** If cigarette smoking causes cancer, then smokers will get cancer more often than nonsmokers.

Although you might not understand how if–then statements work at this point, you will have many opportunities to increase your understanding in the next investigation.

To summarize we have talked about the methods of science. Science is a way of explaining that uses the following activities:

- **a.** asking questions,
- **b.** gathering evidence,
- **c.** proposing explanations, and
- **d.** testing explanations.

Scientists rarely do these activities in this exact order and usually go back and forth between activities. For example, you might not ask a question until you have gathered a lot of evidence about a problem. Or after gathering evidence, you might decide to ask a new question. Or after testing an explanation, you might want to revise your explanation and test it again. As a scientist, you are free to combine these activities in any order you wish; your main goal is to practice using science to explain your world.

elaborate

Investigation: The If–Then Box

Think about the last time you heard a doorbell, a school bell, or an alarm clock. You probably know that these objects often depend on electricity to make them work. In this investigation, you will have an opportunity to use electricity as you gather evidence. Once you have gathered enough evidence, you will be able to explain what you see and to test your explanation with if–then statements.

Working Cooperatively

You will be working cooperatively in a team of two. Sit together at a table or push your desks together to form a table. Work on the new skill *Stay with your group.* This investigation is also a good opportunity for you to practice your unit social skill. Review the T-chart for your unit skill now.

Materials for Each Team of Two:

- 1 component bag
- 1 circuit tester
- 1 If–Then Box
- 1 pair of scissors
- strong tape

Process and Procedure

1. Pick up a component bag and a circuit tester.

   The circuit tester will look similar to the one shown in Figure 8.6.

2. Touch the black alligator clip to the red alligator clip of your circuit tester.

   If the bulb glows, then you have a complete circuit. If the bulb does not glow, tell your teacher. You do not need to worry about being shocked by the electricity in this experiment because the battery puts out a very low current.

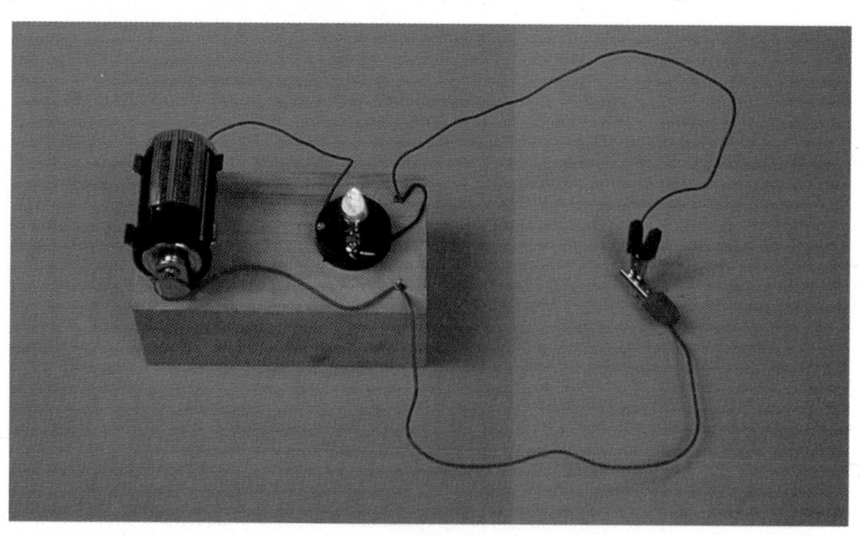

▶ Figure 8.6
Your circuit tester will have a battery, a very small light bulb, and two plastic-coated wires with alligator clips on the end.

3. Test the materials in your component bag, such as the string, plastic, paper, and metal wire.

   *If the bulb glows, we say the material is a **conductor** of electricity. If the bulb does not glow, we say the material is an **insulator.** Record your results in your notebook.*

4. Use your results from Step 3 to make as many complete circuits in as many ways as you can, using materials that conduct electricity.

The screws on the base of the lamp socket can become hot. Avoid touching them.

5. Record the different complete circuits you made by writing the information in a data table.

   If you do not know how to set up a data table, refer to How To #4, How to Construct a Data Table.

6. Pick up an If–Then Box.

   See Figure 8.7.

7. Use your circuit tester to touch two brads on the If–Then Box.

   Hold one alligator clip in each hand.

8. Look for patterns that will make the bulb light.

   Try every possible combination of brads.

9. Write if–then statements that predict what the inside of the box looks like.

10. Draw a diagram showing what you think the inside of your If–Then Box looks like.

    Draw this in your notebook.

11. Use the objects from your component bag to build a model that will work exactly as your If–Then Box works.

12. Test your new model to see whether it works the same way.

    Use the circuit tester to test different pairs of brads as you did in Step 7.

13. Pick up the scissors and several strips of tape.

14. Open your original If–Then Box.

    Cut away the tape from three sides of your If–Then Box.

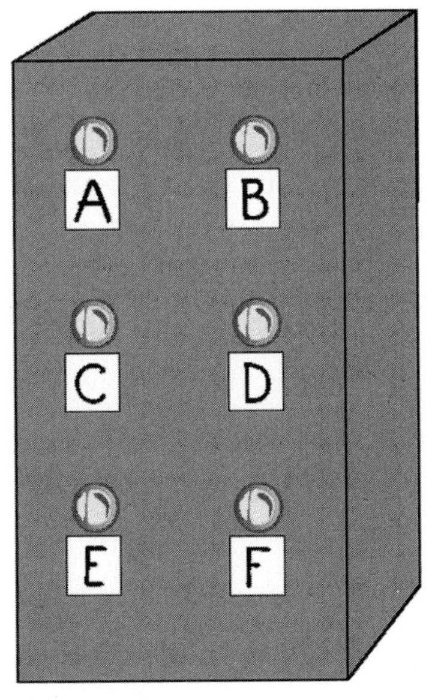

▲ **FIGURE 8.7**

This If–Then Box has brass brads mounted on a cardboard box.

Notebook entry: Record any differences between your model and the original If–Then Box.

15. Tape your original If–Then Box closed.
16. Return all materials.

Wrap Up

Discuss the following questions with your teammate and write your own answers in your notebook.

1. What did you have to do to make a complete circuit?
2. Did your If–Then Box have the same pieces that were in your component bag? Explain any differences you saw.
3. Describe any differences between your If–Then Box and the model you built. How do you account for these differences?
4. How did you test the diagram you drew to see whether or not it was accurate?
5. Use your own system to rate your team on how well you stayed together and made use of the unit skill.

evaluate

Connections: What Did We Do?

1. Copy the chart from Figure 8.8 into your notebook.
2. Think about what you did in each investigation. Make check marks in the columns that apply. For example, in which investigations were you unable to see inside what you were studying?
3. Now fill in the rest of the chart.
4. Be ready to justify to the rest of the class the way you completed your chart.

WHAT DID WE DO?

	How do you know?	Think like a cube!	The if-then box
Could not see inside what we were studying			
Could look but not touch			
Made observations			
Asked questions			
Had to use hearing to gather evidence			
Gathered evidence			
Proposed explanations			
Wrote if-then statements (tested ideas)			

▲ **FIGURE 8.8**

This chart lists some of the actions you took during the investigations in this chapter. Which actions did you take in each investigation?

Volcanoes, Earthquakes, and Explanations

Sometimes events in nature are dramatic. Think about earthquakes and volcanic eruptions. Both can strike suddenly, can cause a lot of damage, and may kill thousands of people. An earthquake flattened Lisbon, Portugal, in 1755 and killed more than 60,000 people. Volcanoes also can destroy. In the South Pacific in 1815, the volcanic mountain Tambora (tam BOR uh) erupted and at least 92,000 people died. In June of 1991, Mt. Pinatubo (pin ah Tu bo) in the Philippines erupted. This mountain had been dormant for 635 years, and this was the largest eruption in the twentieth century. Scientists, however, had been able to predict this eruption, and many thousands of lives were saved.

As you proceed through this chapter, see whether you can discover people's different ideas about why volcanoes erupt and earthquakes happen.

engage

Connections: Can You Imagine?

explore

Investigation: And Along the Way They Met . . .

explain

Reading: Evaluating Explanations

elaborate

Investigation: Patterns on the Earth

evaluate

Connections: Can You Explain the Observations?

engage

Connections:
Can You Imagine?

In this activity, these are your tasks.

1. Watch a demonstration and look at the video or photographs that your teacher shows you.
2. Join in the class discussion. Share what you observe in the video or photographs or share any other news item or experiences that relate to volcanoes and earthquakes.
3. Prepare for the class discussion by writing answers to the following questions in your notebook:
   a. What might you see, hear, or feel if you were near an erupting volcano?
   b. What might you see, hear, or feel if you were near an earthquake?
   c. What do you think might cause earthquakes? What might cause volcanoes to erupt?

Investigation:
And Along the Way They Met . . .

Marie recently watched a television program that showed earthquakes and volcanic eruptions. Now she is wondering what it was like to experience earthquakes and volcanic eruptions in ancient times. What did people think about these extraordinary events long ago?

In this investigation, you will take part in a play that will answer Marie's question. Along with Marie, Al, Isaac, and Ros, you will journey back in time to interview people who tried to explain the causes of earthquakes and volcanic eruptions.

Materials for the Entire Class:

- props (such as notebook, pencil, bag, and flashlight for Ros; several sheets of computer printout paper; setting cards)
- 1 large world map with political boundaries
- 1 package of self-stick removable dots or notes

Working Cooperatively

Everyone in the class will work together for this activity. All of you will join in the first reading of the play. Then some of you will be actors, and some of you will work behind the scenes to design and arrange the settings and props. For this investigation, *Show respect for others and their ideas.*

Process and Procedure

1. Read the play aloud with your classmates.
2. Join in the class discussion of the questions within the play.
3. Record answers to the questions from Audience Participation, Intermission, and Curtain Call in your notebook.
4. Think about which roles you would enjoy performing during the production of the play.

   There are three general types of roles: speaking roles, walk-on roles, and stage crew. People with speaking roles will have lines to learn in the script. Walk-on roles are actors who add to a scene but do not speak. People on the stage crew have the behind-the-scene jobs that make a play fun to watch.
5. Follow your teacher's instructions for choosing your roles in the play.
6. Make a list in your notebook of things you must do to prepare for the play.
7. Rehearse with your classmates and participate in the presentation of the play.

THINGS TO DO TO PREPARE FOR THE PLAY

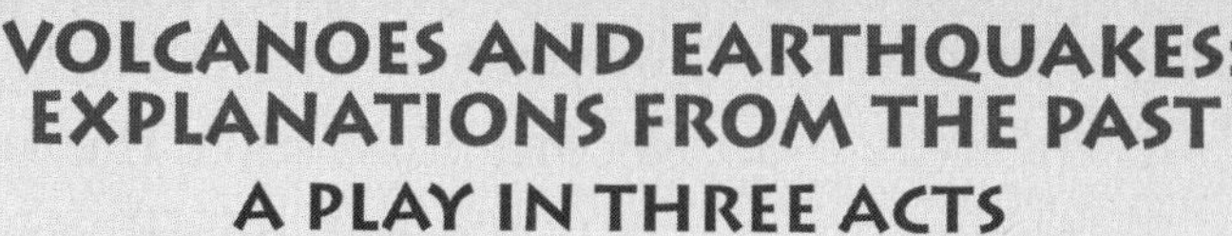

VOLCANOES AND EARTHQUAKES: EXPLANATIONS FROM THE PAST

A PLAY IN THREE ACTS

Cast of Characters

Act I

Narrator
Marie
Isaac
Al
Rosalind
Travel Agent
Farmer 1, Farmer 2,
Farmer 3, Farmer 4
Thales
Student 1, Student 2,
Student 3
Aristotle
Strabo

Act II

Narrator
Servant
Chang Heng
Al-Biruni
Student 4
Mystery Character
Anton-Lazzaro Moro
Friend
Isaac
Rosalind
Marie

Act III

Joseph Black
James Hutton
John Playfair
Antonio Snider
Alfred Wegener
Narrator
Rosalind
Isaac
Marie
Al

ACT I

HOW IT ALL BEGAN

Scene 1: It's Our Lucky Day

Narrator: Marie, Isaac, Rosalind, and Al are walking along a downtown street. They pass a new business called Time Travel.

Marie: Hey—I wonder what this place is. It wasn't here last week.

Isaac: Looks like a travel agency to me.

Al: I love the posters in those places. Let's go in!

Rosalind: Okay, as long as they don't expect us to have any money, because I don't.

Al: Nah. We'll just look at the posters and then go home.

The four of them walk in, moving toward a travel agent seated at a desk.

Marie (*moving ahead of the others and looking around with curiosity*): Excuse me, ma'am. Could you tell me why your business is called Time Travel?

Agent: Yes of course. We're called Time Travel because—(she stops and then says excitedly) is this ever your lucky day!

Marie: What?

Agent (*standing up and reaching out to shake Marie's hand*): Congratulations! You're our 50th customer, and you've just won a Time Travel trip—all expenses paid.

Marie: Me? I did? Oh boy! But what does that mean?

By this time Al, Isaac, and Rosalind have walked up beside Marie.

Agent: You can take a trip through time, and Time Travel will pay your way. You also can bring along three friends. You should feel lucky to have won it.

Al: Too convenient! Cool!

Rosalind: You want some company on a trip, Marie?

Isaac (*looking doubtful*): I'm not sure I want to go . . .

Marie: I know what I want to do! We've just been studying scientific explanations in science class. I want to talk to people and find out how they used to explain things like volcanoes and earthquakes!

Agent: Sure. Why not? I think I can put together a pretty exciting trip for you. When would you like to leave?

Marie and the others turn to each other in a huddle and whisper for a few seconds.

Marie: We'd like to go tomorrow.

Agent: All right, I'll make the arrangements for you. Do you want to know exactly where you are going, or do you want some surprises?

Rosalind: Let's have some surprises, Marie!

Agent: Okay. Your computer printout will tell you what year it is, and sometimes it even will tell you the place. Most often though, you'll have to ask questions to find out where you are.

Isaac: We'll be here tomorrow at 10:00 a.m.—I guess I'm going after all!

All the actors walk off the stage.

Narrator: The next morning Isaac, Marie, and Rosalind meet at the travel agency. Al is late again, but they hope that he will catch up. As soon as Marie picks up the printout, something strange begins to happen. In a whirlwind, they feel themselves suspended as they disappear and reappear in another time and place. When they regain their composure, they find themselves standing outdoors in a very different place.

▲ **FIGURE 9.1** This is a photograph of the ruin of the Ancient Greek Theatre of Miletus.

Scene 2: The Earliest Ideas about the Earth

Narrator: This is the city of Miletus (my LEE tus), a city-state in Asia Minor, in about 600 B.C. There are grassy plains and high cliffs beside the sea. A man is sitting on one of these cliffs. On the grassy plain, several farmers are harvesting grain.

The narrator should hold up a setting card that has the words: "Asia Minor, 600 B.C." Another student should stand beside a world map and point to Asia Minor (Turkey). Then the narrator, the student with the setting card, and the student who marks locations on the map should exit the stage. Each of these students should come back on stage during each scene to make the setting and location clear.

Farmer 1: Tell me again how Thales (THAY leez) made all that money harvesting grain. I'd like to have time to sit on a hillside and think.

Farmer 2: They say that he carefully bought up all the machinery farmers needed for the harvest. Then he charged the farmers to use the equipment.

Farmer 1: Okay, so he's clever. But I'm still not sure I believe in all those ideas he has.

Isaac, Marie, and Rosalind walk up behind the farmers and start looking around curiously. Farmer 2 turns around.

Farmer 2: Say, who are you three?

Marie: Hi! I'm Marie, and these are my friends Isaac and Rosalind.

Farmer 3: So you came to see Thales, did you?

Isaac: No we don't even know who Thales is. If you must know, we just came because Marie was curious.

Farmer 1: Yes lots of people are. Thales is supposed to be a great thinker. He has been to Egypt and has studied astronomy and mathematics.

Marie (*excitedly*): I wonder whether he has any ideas about earthquakes.

Farmer 1 (*laughing a little*): Yes he certainly does!

Farmer 2 (*annoyed*): Don't mind him. I think Thales has good ideas.

Farmer 3: Yes but if you'll excuse us, we're in the middle of a grain harvest. If you want to, just head up that hill and go visit with him. We've got to get back to work.

Rosalind: We will, thanks.

Isaac, Marie, and Rosalind walk up to Thales.

Marie: Hello sir. We're Marie, Isaac, and Rosalind. Those farmers told us that you're a great thinker. What are you doing?

Thales: I am watching the waves.

Marie: What can you learn by watching the waves?

Thales: You can see that as the waves crash onto the shore, the rocks

are broken into pieces, and you can feel the ground shake as the water pounds the shore. Water is the source of all things living and nonliving.

Marie: What do you mean?

Thales: For one thing, water can shake the land hard enough to cause an earthquake.

Rosalind (*taking out her notebook*): Okay, that's idea number one about earthquakes. Water is shaking the earth.

Marie: I'm not sure I believe that. What's your evidence?

Thales: You are wasting my time. It is clear to me that water is the main reason for what we see. Can you doubt what is right in front of your eyes?

Marie: Of course not, sir. It's just that your idea might need more evidence to support it.

Thales: Ho-ho—need more evidence? That makes no sense. I have other things to think of. Please leave me to my work.

Marie: Uh, okay. Well thanks for your time.

Audience Participation

1. How did Thales come up with his explanation and what was his evidence?
2. Because you will read about quite a few ideas in this play, start keeping track of them now. Copy into your notebook the chart shown in Figure 9.2. On the first line, write "Thales" and record his ideas.
3. So far this year, you have read about the four parts of a scientific explanation. You might already have an opinion about whether or not Thales' explanation of earthquakes has each part that a scientific explanation requires. Record your opinions on the chart you have created. (Y = yes, N = no, C = can't tell)

   Did Thales
   - ask questions?
   - gather evidence?
   - propose explanations?
   - test explanations?

Scientist's name and ideas	Asked questions	Gathered evidence	Proposed explanations	Tested explanations
Thales - Water causes earthquakes				

label these boxes Y, N or C

▲ **FIGURE 9.2** Use a full page of paper when you copy this chart into your notebook.

Scene 3: Aristotle's Ideas

Narrator: It is approximately 360 B.C. in Athens, Greece. The weather is mild, and a short man in white flowing robes is wandering down a garden path. A half-dozen students are following him and are trying desperately to write notes on wooden tablets covered with blackened beeswax.

The map person should point out Greece, and the setting card should read "Greece, 360 B.C."

Isaac: Hey, check out those notebooks. Who would have thought of scratching in wax to take notes?

Student 1 (*who has been trailing behind the others*): Thank you. We make these ourselves, you know, just to keep track of what Aristotle (AIR ih stah tul) says. But excuse me, I am behind again.

Marie: Aristotle! This means we must be in ancient Greece!

Isaac: Aris who?

Marie quickly follows the student. Isaac and Rosalind look at each other and then walk fast to catch up with the students and Marie.

GREECE

▲ **Figure 9.3** This is a photo of the famous ruins of the Acropolis in Athens, Greece.

Student 2: Don't you know about Aristotle, the greatest teacher of our time? Where are you from? It must be far away.

Rosalind: It's kind of hard to explain. We're from the future.

Student 2: Well at least that explains your clothing. Excuse me please, I need to get notes from one of my friends.

Isaac (*looking at the printout*): So we're in Athens, Greece? Where's that?

Rosalind points it out to him, and the map person points it out on the large map for the audience.

Isaac: Marie if you talk to Aristotle, be sure you don't offend him.

Marie: Do you think I made Thales mad? I just asked him for a little evidence for his idea.

Isaac: He did seem to get a little angry. Maybe that's because he had thought about it carefully. I've heard that for people in ancient times, it was enough to test a theory by thinking and talking about it.

Rosalind: Who is this guy Aristotle, anyway? Why did we end up here?

Isaac: Let's find that guy with the notepad. It looks like some of them are resting over there.

Student 1: So you did catch up with us. You really don't know who Aristotle is?

Isaac and Rosalind: Really.

Student 1: When he was 17, his father died. I heard that his father had been a wealthy doctor. But when Aristotle came to Athens at age 18, he started spending all of the money he had inherited.

Student 2 : But before he spent all of his money, he bought $3,500 worth of scrolls, and then he studied them for three years.

The student holds up a roll of paper that could be a scroll.

Student 3: Anyway Aristotle came to Athens to study with an older teacher named Plato. But Plato was away when Aristotle first arrived. Plato didn't return for three years, so that's why Aristotle had all that time to study those scrolls.

Student 1: He studied with Plato for seventeen years! Then he moved to Asia Minor for a short time before he went to tutor a prince named Alexander.

Student 2: This was where Aristotle's schooling really paid off. He helped Prince Alexander with his plans, and Alexander has become Alexander the Great! We've heard that Aristotle was paid millions of dollars for the advice he gave Alexander.

Student 3 (*speaking to other students*): Oh he's started again. Let's go!

Aristotle: . . . and so you see students, the earth is a sphere smaller than the stars yet at the very center of the universe. The land stays in place while the seas rise around it. Volcanoes give us evidence that the interior of the earth is very hot. The surface of the earth also is affected by earthquakes.

Marie: What causes those earthquakes?

Aristotle: Ah, a new student who asks an excellent question. Earthquakes are caused by wind.

Rosalind (*writing*): Okay—that's the second idea about earthquakes—they're caused by wind.

Marie: Gosh how can wind cause earthquakes?

Aristotle: It may appear to be a complex idea if one is not well educated, but the idea is quite simple. Strong winds cause great destruction on the surface of the earth. Also, if you have visited a cave, you know that winds flow in and out of the earth. When

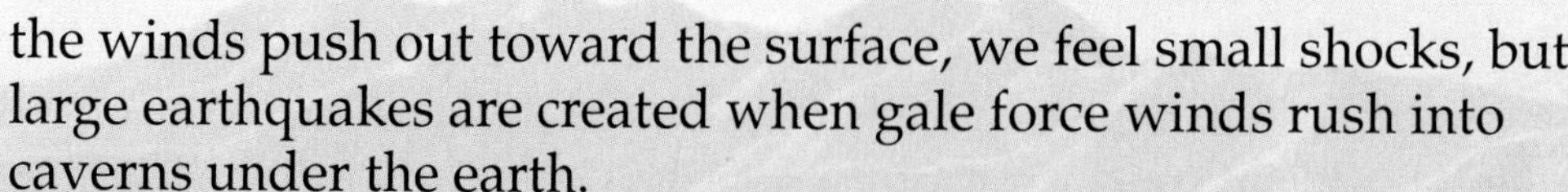

the winds push out toward the surface, we feel small shocks, but large earthquakes are created when gale force winds rush into caverns under the earth.

Marie: Hmm . . . I see. But is there a way to test this idea?

Aristotle: Of course not. But that is not necessary, because I have thought about it very carefully.

Marie: Thanks for letting us join you.

Aristotle: Of course.

Audience Participation

4. What was Aristotle's explanation for what he observed? What evidence did he give?
5. Make your notebook entry on your chart. Mark your opinions about what Aristotle said and again use Y, N, or C.

Scene 4: Strabo's Thoughts

Narrator: It is about A.D. 10 in the lands between Greece and Asia. There is a small field with trees around it. A farmer is working in the field, and another person is sleeping beneath a tree.

Person with a setting card should hold it up for the audience to read. The map person should point to Turkey.

Isaac: Hey is this someplace else? It looks somewhat similar. (*He looks at the printout.*) Hmm. We went from 360 to 10. Are we going backward in time?

Rosalind: No, Isaac. The 360 was B.C., and now the numbers are A.D. We're going forward in time.

Marie: Right. So when the years were B.C., the smaller numbers were closer to the present. Now that it is A.D., the numbers should start getting bigger.

Isaac: Okay. I'll figure it out at our next stop. Maybe that person over there can help us find whomever it is we are supposed to visit here.

Farmer 4: Hello there strangers. Have you come to see Strabo (STRAY boh)?

Isaac: Maybe. Who is Strabo?

Farmer 4: Strabo is the author of a geography book for our rulers.

He was born here between Greece and Asia. In order to write the book, he studied and traveled a lot. He is well known around here for his observations about the earth. (*He laughs.*) Why don't you ask him to explain his ideas about the earth to you?

Marie (*tapping a sleeping Strabo on the shoulder*): Excuse me sir, could I bother you for a few minutes?

Strabo (*rubbing his eyes*): No problem. I meant to get up a while ago anyway. How can I help you?

Marie: I was hoping you could tell me why volcanoes erupt and why earthquakes happen.

Strabo: Of course. You know Aristotle thought the land stayed in place while the seas rose and sank around it. But, personally, my observations have led me to believe that the ground is lifted up from the inside.

Marie: How?

Strabo: Internal fires cause the land to be uplifted. Aristotle was right about earthquakes—they are the result of underground winds. You can see these two forces working together in volcanoes. The winds of the earthquakes bring the internal fires out through the tops of the volcanoes.

Marie: Hmm . . . I'd never thought of that. Could you describe your evidence?

Strabo: Think about this. When a volcano erupts, ash and rocks often are thrown for many miles. What else could push these things besides a great wind?

Rosalind: That's idea number three—volcanoes, earthquakes, and wind are related. If you'll excuse us, sir, we need to leave.

Strabo: Of course. Goodbye.

Marie: So far I don't know about some of these ideas—water, wind, and fire inside the earth? Well, maybe they'll make more sense later.

Audience Participation

6. What events did Strabo explain, and what evidence did he give?
7. Make your notebook entry on your chart.

Intermission

Think about the first three scenes. Answer these questions in complete sentences in your notebook.

8. How were the scientists' ideas similar?
9. How were they different?
10. What tools do you think these people had for gathering and recording information?

ACT II
A NEW INVENTION

Scene 1: More Ideas about the Earth

Narrator: The time is A.D. 132 in an area near Beijing, China. There are steep mountain peaks in the distance. A beautiful wooden house is in the foreground, and a servant is standing near the door.

Person with setting card should hold it up for the audience to read. The map person should point to Beijing, China.

Isaac: This place looks different. Look at those mountains with the pointed peaks! I wonder where we are? Do you have the printout, Ros?

Rosalind: Hmm . . . let's see. It says the time is A.D. 132, so we have gone a little bit forward in time, but it doesn't say where we are. (*She looks up.*) You know, it looks as if it's about to rain.

Marie: Maybe they'll let us in that house over there. It looks like it has some kind of special garden. Maybe we're in Asia somewhere.

Marie, Ros, and Isaac knock on the door of the house.

Servant (*steps out of the house to see who they are*): May I help you? Oh, more strangers. No we don't know about the next earthquake. Chang Heng's (JANG HENG) device only tells us where they happen. It does not predict when the next one will occur.

Marie (*very interested*): Oh we must have come to the right place! May we please come in before the rain starts?

▶ **FIGURE 9.4** This traditional style of Chinese building has proven to be quite resistant to earthquake damage.

Servant: Very well. I will tell Chang Heng that he has more visitors.

Chang Heng (*coming into the room*): Ah, more visitors. Well I suppose I can tell a few more people about my invention before I show it to the emperor.

Marie: That would be great!

Chang Heng: You may know that we have many earthquakes here in China.

Isaac: No I didn't.

Chang Heng: Oh yes, and once an earthquake happens, communication is very bad. It is hard for us to send help unless we know exactly where the earthquake has happened. So I have built a device that will tell us in which direction an earthquake has happened.

Rosalind (*writing down what she has heard*): Device tells which direction earthquake is from us. How does it work?

Chang Heng: You see it is like a big bowl, nearly 2 meters across, and dragon heads are built all around the rim of the bowl. Each dragon head has a chunk of bronze in its mouth. If an earthquake occurs, one chunk of bronze falls to the floor. We find which dragon has dropped its chunk of bronze, and it is pointing in the direction of the earthquake! We have found it to be very accurate.

▲ **FIGURE 9.5** These two views show the (a) outside and (b) the inside of Chang Heng's earthquake detector. Historical records show that it was so sensitive it could detect earthquakes very far away that otherwise would not have been known about.

Marie: What a useful invention! But do you have any ideas about what causes earthquakes?

Chang Heng: No I really don't. I would need to gather more information about that before I could discuss ideas with you.

Marie (*turning aside to Rosalind and Isaac*): Finally someone who wants more evidence! (*Turns again to Chang Heng*) Thank you. This has been a really interesting visit. Look! The rain has stopped. We need to be moving along. Goodbye.

Chang Heng: Goodbye.

Audience Participation

11. Explain how Chang Heng's bowl worked.

12. Make a notebook entry on your chart for Chang Heng.

Scene 2: Back in North America

Narrator: This is the southwestern part of North America, in the area we know as California. The time is A.D. 574. The area is dry and dusty, with only a few trees on distant hills. Marie, Isaac, and Ros find themselves standing alone with no one else in sight.

Person with setting card should hold it up for the audience to read. The map person should point to California.

Isaac: Hey I know this place! It looks like we are in California! But I don't see any buildings.

Rosalind: The printout says it is A.D. 574.

Isaac: It looks as though there must have been volcanoes or earthquakes around here. I wonder what the people thought about them.

Rosalind: It says on the printout that people's explanations from this part of the world have survived by oral tradition, like storytelling, I guess. Apparently some of the people believed that when an earthquake occurred, the earth got larger.

Isaac: Look on that ridge.

Audience Participation

13. Who do you think the people who lived in this area were?
14. Record on your chart any ideas about earthquakes that you read in Scene 2.

Scene 3: Al-Biruni and His Maps

Narrator: This is a small town in Arabia in A.D. 1021. A man, hunched over a desk, is writing. Several of his students are seated nearby.

Person with setting card should hold it up for the audience to read.
The map person should point to Saudi Arabia.

Rosalind: Hey we've skipped a lot of years of history. Did you notice that?

Marie: Yeah! I wonder what's been happening?

Isaac: I know about this! (*He begins reading the printout.*) Much of the time period that we skipped is called the Dark Ages. It was a very tough time for people in Europe. Kings and invaders fought for power, and many people were hurt or killed.

Rosalind (*reaching out for the printout from Isaac and continuing to read*): May I have a turn? Medical services and sanitation facilities disappeared. Plagues and epidemics wiped out thousands of people. Many people were so busy fighting that they had no interest in learning. All across Europe books disappeared. Few people thought about science, art, or literature.

Narrator: The man who was at his desk now steps forward.

Al-Biruni: But some of the manuscripts from Greece were taken to Asia and Africa and studied by people there. Many Arabs, like me, study mathematics, chemistry, astronomy, literature, physics, and other areas of interest. Not too many people spend much time studying the earth; it is considered too "earthly" to devote much time to—except by me!

Marie: Oh hi! Who are you?

Al-Biruni: My name is Al-Biruni (al bih ROO nee). I am one of the wise men with whom the sultan speaks. I have made many observations of the earth during my travels. Like Al-Khwarizmi (al kwah REEZ mee), another of our mapmakers, I record my observations on maps.

Isaac: Huh. How do you know that your maps are accurate?

Al-Biruni: I'll tell you. On the longest day of the year, we measure how long the daylight lasts in a certain place. Then we compare it with our own location near the equator. On the day of the summer solstice, the earth's Northern Hemisphere is tilted toward the sun. The farther north one goes in the summer, the longer the day is. In the winter, the north part of the earth is tilted away from the sun, so the days there are shorter.

Marie and Isaac: I don't get it.

Al-Biruni (*gesturing to some of his students*): Would several of you come here? We need to show these new students about the sun and the earth—the way I explained it to the sultan. But we don't have a torch!

Rosalind (*writing again in her notebook*): Maps. (*Then speaking to Al-Biruni*). I have a flashlight. (*She pulls it out of a bag she's been carrying.*)

Student 4 (*looks in amazement at the flashlight*): My! What an amazing torch! Let's say that this light is the sun. (*He has one of his friends hold the flashlight while he holds a small sphere.*) It takes one full day for the earth to spin completely around. If the northern part of the earth is tipped toward the sun, that top part of the earth will

always be in the light. And in the summer, it is. But in the winter, the northern part of the earth is tipped away from the sun. Then the place that was always light during the summer always will be dark during the winter.

Marie: Let's see. You know how long the sun shines on the longest day here, near the equator.

Al-Biruni: Yes.

Isaac: And the farther north you are on that particular day, the longer the sun shines that same day?

Student 4: Yes.

Marie: So let's say it's the longest day of the year, and you have traveled to a new place. You measure how much longer the daylight lasts at the new place than it does near the equator. And the longer the daylight lasts, the farther north you are from the equator!

Al-Biruni: Yes! You've got it.

Isaac: So why do you make maps?

Al-Biruni: We are interested in making maps to help the people who sail our ships. We have traders who travel all over the world, and our maps help them find their way. We make the most accurate maps that the world has seen.

Marie: These are very interesting maps, sir. Thank you for your time.

Rosalind: Goodbye!

The three characters begin to walk away.

▲ **FIGURE 9.6** This is a photo of a volcanic harbor in Thera, Greece. Maps such as those created by Al-Biruni would help early sailors navigate through these areas.

Isaac: What do maps have to do with earthquakes and volcanoes? Why would the travel agent have sent us here?

Marie: Good question! I don't know. Maybe we'll figure it out soon.

Audience Participation

15. Explain how Al-Biruni's assistants knew how far north they were.
16. Fill in the chart in your notebook for Al-Biruni.

Scene 4: Moro and Volcanoes

Narrator: We are now in a small city in Italy during the early 1700s. A man and his friend are talking, and Marie, Rosalind, and Isaac are listening to the conversation. They do not have time to introduce themselves; they simply listen.

Person with setting card should hold it up for the audience to read.
The map person should point to Italy.

Rosalind: This is a quick visit. The printout says we will listen to Abbe Anton-Lazzaro Moro. (Abee AN tohn Luh ZAH ruh MOH ruh) We have a name, but we do not have much else.

Moro: I have collected much information, as Aristotle urges all observers of the earth to do.

▲ **FIGURE 9.7** Venice was built in an area of Italy that has a lot of water that rises high above the land surface. Instead of building roads, people traveled by boats on canals such as this one. They still do today.

Friend: What do your data show?

Moro: I have collected the records of sixteen islands formed by volcanic eruptions, and it is clear to me now how islands and their mountains are formed.

Friend: What is your evidence?

Moro: After the eruptions, all of the islands were bigger.

Friend: Then how are the mountains on the mainland formed?

Moro: A mountain is a mountain, so they all must be the result of volcanic action.

Marie: Hmm. How can he be so sure of his ideas?

Isaac: I guess it's my turn with the notebook. (*Rosalind hands it to him, and he talks aloud as he writes.*) Okay. We don't know why they erupt, but volcanoes form islands and mountains. Hey—this is our first idea that is just about volcanoes!

Audience Participation

17. What things did Anton-Lazzaro Moro explain, and what was his evidence?
18. Fill in your chart for Anton-Lazzaro Moro.

Intermission

19. How were the actions of Chang Heng and Al-Biruni different from the actions of the scientists in Act I? Which scientist in Act II sounded most like the scientists from Act I?
20. In the play, what do California, China, and Italy have in common?
21. What tools did the scientists have in Act II?

ACT III
THE BEGINNING OF MODERN GEOLOGY

Scene 1: Hutton's Ideas

Narrator: The time is A.D. 1795. Three friends are gathered at a dinner table in Edinburgh, Scotland.

Person with setting card should hold it up for the audience to read. The map person should point to Scotland.

Rosalind: This time the printout has more details. It says we are going to spend some time with James Hutton, a Scot born in 1726. Hutton's father died when James was young, and his mother decided that James should become a lawyer instead of a businessman like his father. (*Rosalind passes the printout to Isaac.*)

Isaac (*reading*): Hutton was not very interested in law and spent much of his time in the back of the law office doing chemistry experiments for his colleagues. When the odors from his experiments reached the front office, his employer asked Hutton to leave. Marie you should read this part.

Marie (*reading*): In 1744 it was not possible to study chemistry as a profession. After several years, Hutton ended up running the family farm.

▲ **FIGURE 9.8** This is a photo of the Loch of the Lowes in Scotland. Scotland is famous for its many lochs, which are like deep, large, connected lakes. Lochs can be found across the Scotish countryside. What do you think caused the formation of these lochs?

Joseph Black has noticed the visitors. He gets up from the table, walks toward them, and begins to speak.

Joseph (*speaking, not reading*): It was this experience on the farm that led him to geology. As the farm became profitable, Hutton spent more time studying science and eventually moved to Edinburgh. *He pauses.* I assume you are students. Won't you please join us? I'm Joseph Black—this is John Playfair, and this is James Hutton. And who are you?

Marie: I'm Marie, and these are my friends, Isaac and Rosalind.

Joseph: Welcome. Please join us.

John: So James, what new idea do you have to tell us tonight?

James: I believe that volcanoes are building the earth's crust! There are heat and pressure within the earth, and volcanoes allow some to be released!

Marie: Could you explain your evidence?

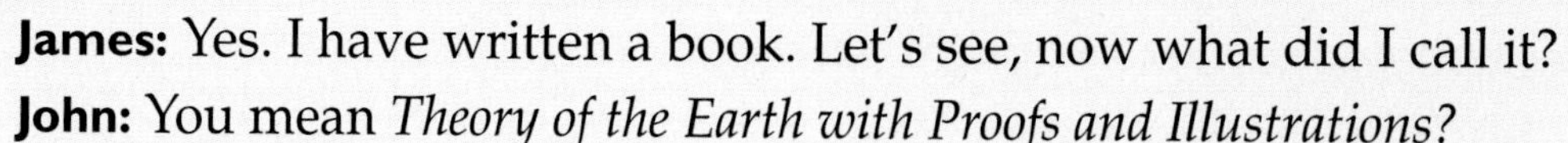

James: Yes. I have written a book. Let's see, now what did I call it?

John: You mean *Theory of the Earth with Proofs and Illustrations?*

James: Yes that's it. Anyway, in the book I described the idea that the processes that formed the earth are still taking place today. Volcanoes are still erupting, and they have erupted many times before. They are an example of molten rock breaking through the surface. This molten rock has cooled and has formed the hard surface of the earth. This process is still going on. But I think that if we could go inside the earth, we would find molten rock.

Marie: What do people say about your ideas?

James: Some say I am an atheist because I suggest there are forces at the center of the earth that have caused these changes.

Marie: Do you get tired of being criticized?

James: Yes and no. A healthy exchange of ideas helps strengthen the original idea or, if it cannot stand up to the challenge, causes the original idea to be tossed aside. But I do tire of people attacking me personally. If only they would stick to the ideas.

Marie: Do you have any ideas about how the rocks that you study could be related to earthquakes?

James: I do not have any evidence of that. I would have to gather more information. Good question though.

Marie: Thank you for your time. Enjoy the rest of your dinner.

Rosalind: So we have learned that sometimes the rock we find has cooled—and maybe there is hot and melted rock inside the earth.

Isaac: Even if we didn't get any more ideas about earthquakes, at least we know he was interested in gathering more data. He must have gotten accurate information, because the printout says his ideas are still important in geology. *(Isaac points to the printout)*

The characters exit the stage.

Audience Participation

22. What did James Hutton explain? What was his evidence?
23. Notebook entry: Fill out the chart for James Hutton.

Scene 2: Snider's Observation

Narrator: The time is A.D. 1858. This is a city park in Paris, France. Several people are walking here, and one person is sitting on a bench.

Person with setting card should hold it up for the audience to read. The map person should point to Paris, France.

Rosalind: The printout says that it is 1858. It also says, "Look for Antonio Snider (An TOH nee oh SNY der), an American living in Paris. Mr. Snider has a new idea."

Marie: Do you suppose he is that person over there on the bench?

As Isaac is looking around, Marie and Rosalind begin walking over to the man on the bench.

Isaac (*running after the others*): Hey Marie, Ros, wait!

Rosalind: Excuse me sir. Are you Mr. Snider?

Antonio: Yes I am. But how do you know that?

Isaac (*who has just caught up*): We are visitors from the future.

Antonio: Hmm. I haven't heard that joke before. But anyway, what is it you strangers would like to know?

Marie: Mr. Snider, could you tell me more about your latest idea?

Antonio: It is simple and elegant! Just study the map and maybe it will become clear!

Marie: But could you explain your evidence for this idea?

Antonio: The evidence is on the map!

Rosalind (*writing down the idea*): Maps.

Marie: Okay. I guess we'll study more maps. We have to be on our way now. Bye!

Scene 3: Wegener's Theory

Narrator: It is March 1930. This is Eismitte (EYE smit) Station, Greenland. Marie, Isaac, and Rosalind find themselves on a snowfield. A dog sled is sitting nearby, and someone is leaning on it. The three friends discover that the person is Al.

Person with setting card should hold it up for the audience to read. The map person should point to Greenland.

Marie: Brrr! It's cold here!

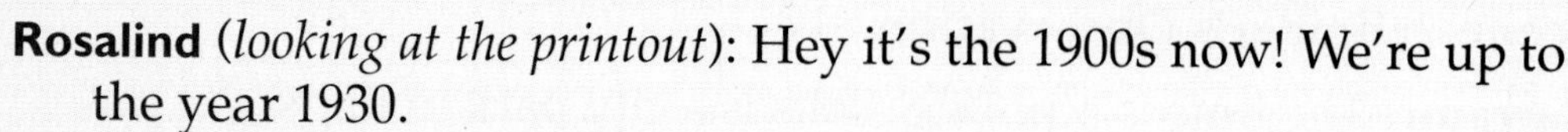

Rosalind (*looking at the printout*): Hey it's the 1900s now! We're up to the year 1930.

Isaac: Hey look! It's Al! Okay, where were you?

Al (*walking up to the group*): Sorry but I slept in too long. But hey I guessed right—you guys are in the twentieth century now. So who do we meet here?

Rosalind: Al, nice to see you, even if you are 2,000 years late. But who do you think we are going to meet?

Marie: Well the printout says it will be . . .

Al: I've got it. There's only one name you would expect me to guess, Ros. It's that Alfred Wegener guy that I'm named after, isn't it?

Rosalind: Look Al, why don't you just tell us about this guy.

Al: Okay. In the early 1900s, Alfred Wegener spent some time looking at maps of the world. Then he got this idea that he called continental drift. He was . . .

Alfred Wegener (*joins the group*): What do you mean *was?*

Marie: Wow! Dr. Wegener, could you tell us about your idea?

Alfred Wegener: Well I have to find more evidence for my idea, and there is very little time before winter sets in. Perhaps we could talk several months from now. By then I should have more evidence to share with you.

Marie: But . . .

Alfred Wegener: If you have time to study a map for a longer period of time, some of my ideas might become more evident! Goodbye!

Dr. Wegener leaves, with his dog sled in front of him.

Marie: Hmm. Let's go home and sort out some of these ideas.

Al: Yeah and maybe drink some hot chocolate! Brrr . . . it's cold.

The four friends leave the stage.

Audience Participation

24. What tool were Antonio Snider and Alfred Wegener both relying on for at least part of their evidence?

25. Make your final notebook entries, for Antonio Snider and Alfred Wegener.

Curtain Call

Look over the chart that you filled out as you wrote answers to the audience participation and intermission questions. Then write an answer to the following question.

26. You read about the ideas of at least ten scientists during this play. What trends did you see in their explanations? (Remember that a scientific explanation has a question, evidence, proposed explanation, and test.)

Reading:
Evaluating Explanations

explain

When you hear different explanations for the same type of event (such as an earthquake), you might not know whose explanation to accept. One way to solve your dilemma is to use the methods of science.

If you want to decide whether or not to agree with an explanation, you can ask yourself several questions:

- What questions were the people trying to answer?
- What explanation did the people give?
- What evidence did the people give?
- Was their evidence the kind and amount that the people needed? That is, did they keep the quantity and quality of evidence in mind?
- Have the people tested their explanations?

Think back to the play. Thales proposed a scientific explanation. He started with a question: What causes earthquakes? He observed different things that happened on the earth, such as the force that water could exert especially during strong storms. Because his observations were things he saw and heard, we would count them as evidence. His proposed answer, as you might remember, was that water caused earthquakes.

Now if Thales were to complete another step in the methods of science, he would test his proposed answer. It turns out that scientists in Thales's time did not test proposed answers. The accepted method during that time was to think about the proposed answer to see whether it made sense. This is still an important part of deciding whether or not to pursue a particular explanation and line of thinking.

If you decide that the evidence makes sense, you still might want to take the step of testing the explanation. The test would give you something to look for that would support or weaken the explanation. An if–then statement that you could use for Thales' explanation might read like this: *If* water causes earthquakes, *then* no earthquakes should occur in deserts. If you found out that earthquakes can indeed happen in very dry places, you might find yourself doubting Thales' explanation.

Stop & Think

Read the following information and answer the questions.

You have gone to watch a parade. Someone standing nearby says, "Look at those dark clouds in the sky, and listen to that thunder. I'm sure it's going to rain on the parade."

1. Do you agree with the person's conclusion? Explain why or why not.
2. How could you test the conclusion?

As you read the play, you probably noticed that the types of explanations that scientists offered changed throughout history. For example Strabo thought that winds were pushing rocks and ash out of volcanoes. A little more than 2,000 years later, James Hutton thought that heat was trapped beneath the earth's surface and that volcanoes were a way of releasing that heat and pressure. Hutton's idea is closer to what we accept today, but ideas continue to change.

Why do scientists' explanations change so much? There are many reasons, but an important one is new evidence. One reason that scientists acquire new evidence is because they have new tools. Tools can be anything from an earthquake device like Chang Heng's to a map like Al-Biruni's. Such tools help us find or organize our evidence.

Al-Biruni probably shows best how a new tool can help us recognize new evidence. When people in Arabia began making maps, the shape of the African continent was unknown. Making maps was a long and difficult process. But by 850 years later, virtually all of the coastlines of places where people lived had been mapped. Then it was possible for someone like Antonio Snider to look at a world map and come up with a new idea. The evidence had been put together in a new way—on an accurate world map. Antonio Snider was one of the first people to report that he had seen a pattern on the world map.

The scientists in the play could not have known the future. Today scientists have drawn even more conclusions from the evidence plotted on maps. Their evidence changed somewhat as different maps allowed the pattern to show up better. The following investigation encourages you to look at world maps and historical records to find patterns for earthquakes, volcanoes, and continents. And as you uncover more patterns (and evidence), you may develop an explanation of your own.

elaborate

Investigation:
Patterns on the Earth

In the last investigation, you learned about the earth by listening to other people's observations. In this investigation, you will use maps to look at a number of features of the earth and see whether you can find any patterns. You will look at the locations of volcanoes and earthquakes, the ages of rocks, and the surface features of the ocean floor. The evidence you gather will help you develop your own explanation for earthquakes and volcanoes. During each part of this investigation, you will be exploring the question: What patterns can we observe on the earth?

Working Cooperatively

Work cooperatively in your combined teams of four. You will need a Manager, a Communicator, and a Tracker. Your skill to practice for this investigation is *Stay with your group.*

Materials for the Entire Class:

- 1 or more large sheets of light-colored newsprint or butcher paper
- wide-tipped felt markers, assorted colors
- 1 large world map showing political boundaries
- 1 clock

Process and Procedure

1. Move your desks so that you are sitting with your teammates.
2. Review the definition for pattern that you have been using all year and write this definition in your notebook.

   Look at Chapter 3 if you need to.
3. Look at each of the three maps (Figures 9.9, 9.10, and 9.11). Follow these directions.

- Do not mark or draw on any of the maps in your book.
- Make a list of unfamiliar words and phrases that you see.
- Study each map for 15 minutes and answer the questions for each map.
- The Tracker will keep track of time.

Questions for Map A—Ocean Floor

a. Locate the Atlantic Ocean and the Pacific Ocean on Figure 9.9. Be sure you could point them out on a blank map if you were asked to.

b. People used to think that the ocean floor was flat. After looking at this map, would you agree or disagree with that? Explain your answer.

c. Find the features on the map that represent undersea mountain ranges. Describe where these mountains are in the Atlantic Ocean.

d. There are mountain ranges beneath the Pacific and the Atlantic Oceans. How are the locations of the mountain ranges different in each ocean? That is,

▼ **FIGURE 9.9 MAP A**

When this map of the ocean floor was completed, it revealed patterns that no one had guessed.

World Ocean Floor by Bruce C. Heezen and Marie Tharp, 1977. Copyright ©1977 by Marie Tharp. Reproduced by permission of Marie Tharp, 1 Washington Ave, South Nyack, NY 10960.

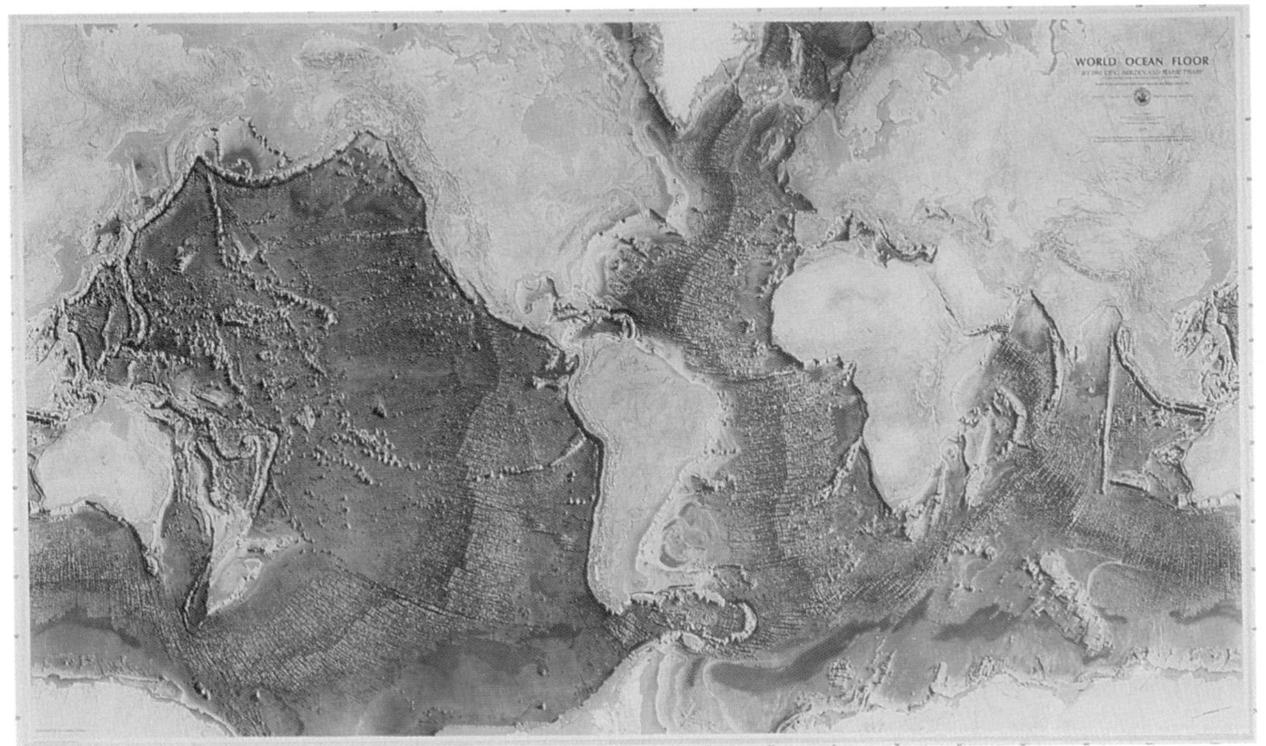

where are the mountains in the Atlantic Ocean? Where are the mountains in the Pacific Ocean?

e. The mountain ranges beneath the oceans are the longest in the world. Draw a circle in your notebook to represent the earth. Show where the mountain ranges begin and end. Then write in your notebook why these mountain ranges are longer than the ones on the continents.

f. Undersea mountain ranges also are called oceanic ridges. What large island has formed directly on the North Atlantic Oceanic Ridge?

Questions for Map B—Volcanoes (BLM 9.2)

a. What type of information is shown on the map in Figure 9.10?

b. As you answer the following questions, make sure you first find the locations listed. Use the world political map if you need to.

(1) Where would you be least likely to find a volcano if you had to choose from Japan, New Zealand, or the middle of Australia?

▼ **FIGURE 9.10 MAP B**

The pattern of volcanoes and earthquakes on the earth had puzzled geologists for many years. On this map, the black dots represent the location of volcanoes and earthquakes. To answer questions for this map, use the two handouts that your teacher provides.

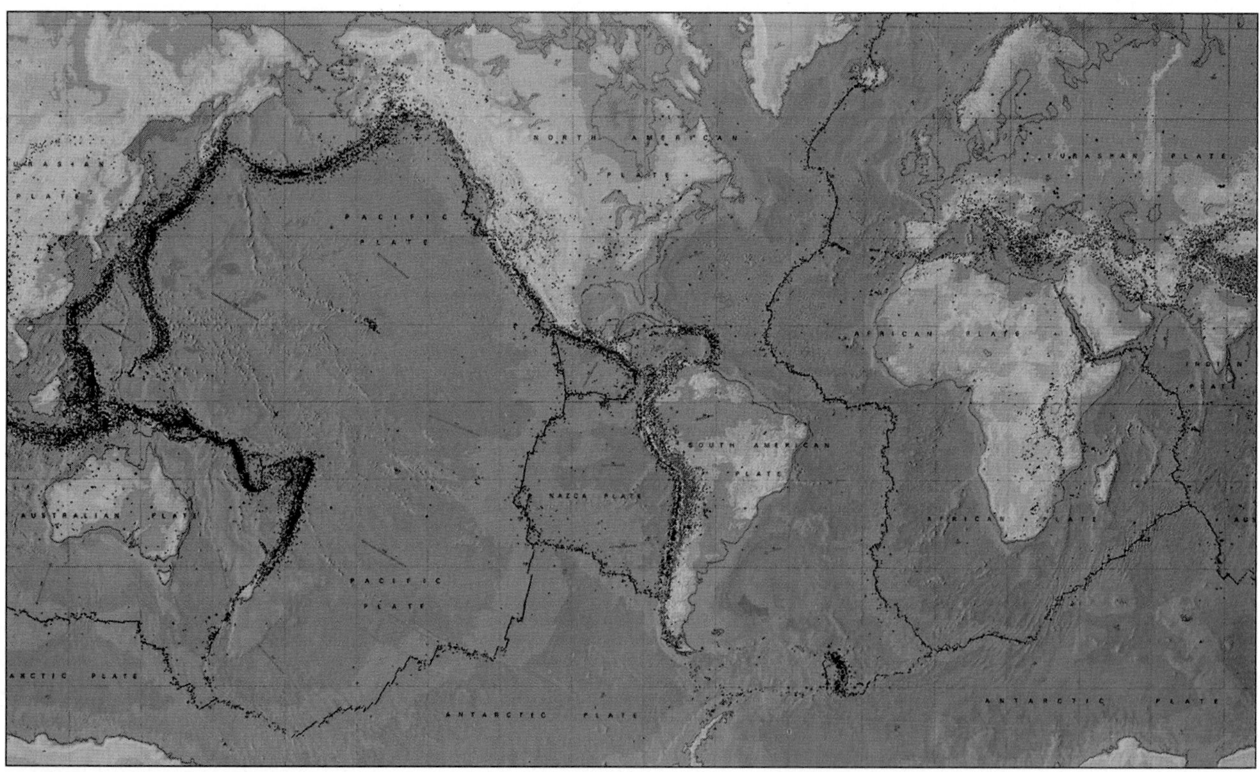

United States Geological Survey

(2) Where would you be least likely to find a volcano if you had to choose from the west coast of South America, the middle of the Atlantic Ocean, or central Asia?

(3) Where would you be least likely to find a volcano—Alaska, Mexico, or Norway?

c. Describe in general where volcanoes are located on the earth. Write it in your notebook after discussing this with your team.

Questions for Map B—Earthquakes (BLM 9.3)

a. Find each of the locations listed below. Use the world political map if you have questions. Then write down whether or not that location has had many, few, or no recorded earthquakes.

- mid-Atlantic Ocean
- southern Europe (for example Italy)
- Japan
- the east coast of South America
- Central America

b. Describe in general where earthquakes occur on the earth. Discuss your answer with your team and then write the description in your notebook.

Questions for Map C—Ages of Rocks

a. What does the map in Figure 9.11 show?

b. Which rocks are younger, the ones shown in red or the ones shown in blue?

c. Where are the youngest rocks in the Atlantic Ocean?

d. The white spaces on this map show places where geologists have not yet studied the ages of rocks. But there is a pattern among the rocks that already have been studied. Describe the pattern.

4. After you have studied all three maps, add your observations to the class's combined list.

Let the Tracker do this. Follow your teacher's instructions for this step.

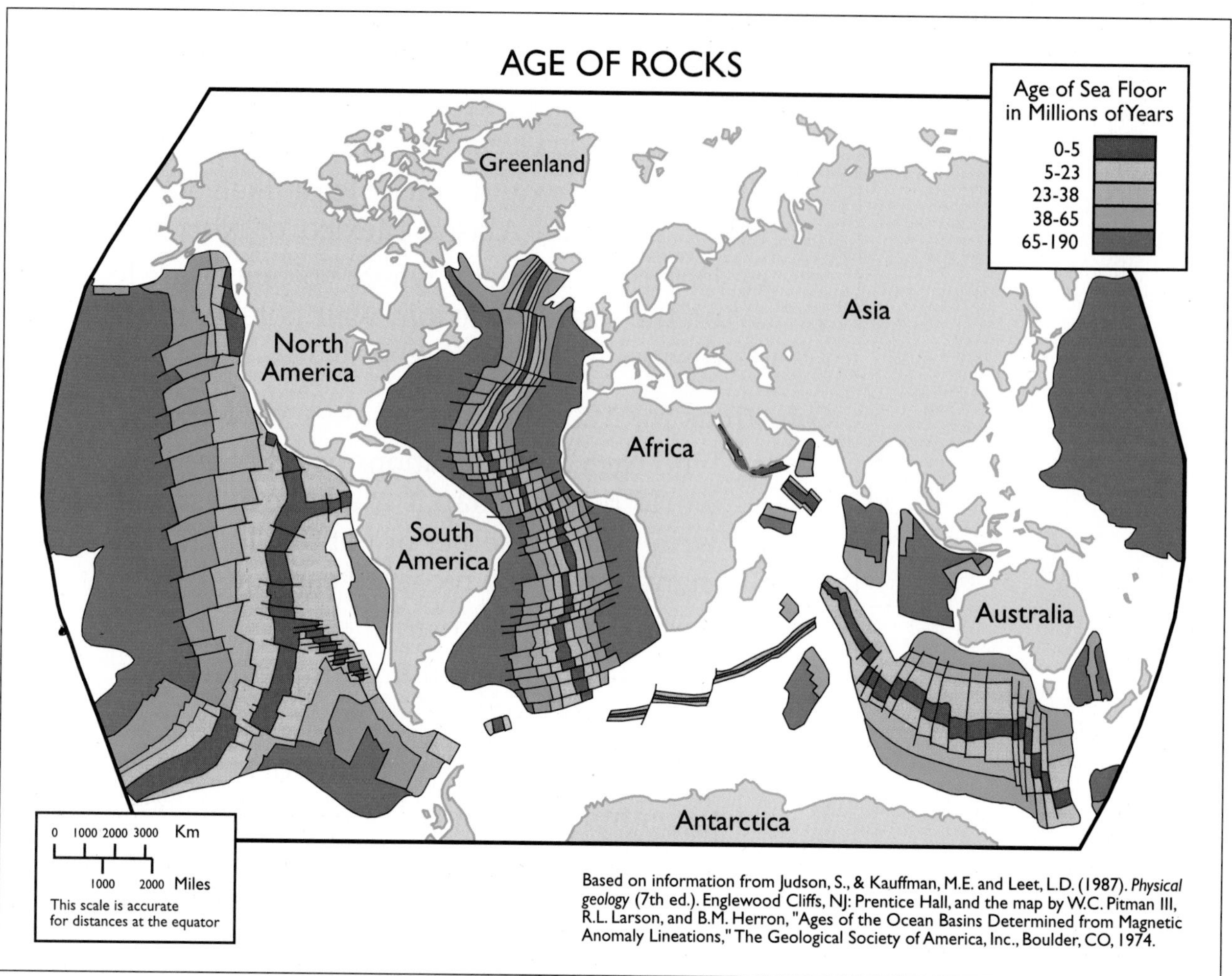

▲ **FIGURE 9.11 MAP C**

When scientists began to record the ages of rocks on the ocean floor, they were surprised to discover that the oldest rocks on the ocean floor were much younger than the oldest rocks on the continents. The oldest rocks on the continents are about 4.6 billion years old, and the oldest rocks on the ocean floor are only millions of years old.

Wrap Up

After you have finished all three maps, review each one and answer these questions:

1. How are Maps A and B similar?
2. How are Maps B and C similar?
3. How are Maps A and C similar?
4. Combine the information from all three maps of the earth that you have studied. What general patterns do you see?

5. Why do you think the youngest rocks are near earthquakes?
6. Do you think you could have accomplished more or less by working alone? Explain your answer.
7. Tell your teacher how you would rate your team at staying together: excellent, good, or fair.

evaluate

Connections:
Can You Explain the Observations?

In Chapter 8, you read about the methods of science. One point you should remember is that scientists do not always do things in a set order. After scientists ask a question and gather evidence, they often ask a new question. Scientists often ask new questions because they have more information and can improve the original question or can see things in a new way.

As a class, have a brainstorming session about questions that come to mind when you look at the patterns identified in the investigation Patterns on the Earth. If your class has not had a brainstorming session before, read How to Brainstorm (How To #5). As you participate in a brainstorming session, write down the ideas and questions. Post this list somewhere in the classroom so that you can refer to it periodically throughout the rest of the unit.

Now that you have identified several patterns on the surface of the earth, you can give an explanation for the patterns. You will be using a think-pair-share strategy to develop this explanation.

THINK Look over the list of questions you and your classmates just developed. Also ask yourself, What do all the patterns have in common?

PAIR Pair up with your teammate and discuss what you each thought about the patterns. How did the patterns form? Between the two of you, try to explain the locations of the patterns on the earth.

SHARE Share your explanation with the rest of the class. Be sure to list the evidence you needed to develop your explanation.

SIDELIGHT on History

The World Map

How long did it take to get an accurate map of the earth? It took more than 800 years! Al-Biruni, whom you read about in the play, was able to add map measurements to his maps only once a year, on the summer solstice (the longest day of the year). His mapmakers knew that the longer this day was, the farther north they were. They then could compare it with the length of the day at their own home near the equator. Al-Biruni's assistants worked to improve maps that had been drawn several hundred years earlier. Four hundred years later, in the 1400s, the Europeans learned about the North American and South American continents, so the world map changed again—mapmakers had more work to do. When the entire earth had to be mapped from the ground, mapmaking took a very long time.

Today advances in technology have made mapmaking easier and more accurate. Two advances that have been of particular benefit to mapmaking are remote sensing and the use of computers. Remote sensing is the ability to see or "sense" land surfaces from a great distance. Remote sensing involves the use of aerial photography, satellite imaging, and radar. These techniques provide mapmakers with much more accurate and detailed information about the world. Computers are able to do much of the detailed work that mapmakers used to have to do by hand.

In spite of the advances in technology, all mapmakers agree that most world maps include a lot of distortion. This distortion is due to the fact that mapmakers are trying to depict images from a sphere on a flat surface. Buckminster Fuller, who was one of America's most original thinkers, developed the Dymaxion Air-Ocean World Map as one way of responding to this concern (see next page). He began thinking about this idea for a map in 1934, but it took twenty more years of work and fine tuning to actually produce it. He used the form of the icosahedron, (ico sah HEE dron) which is a polyhedron with twenty triangular faces. Fuller's map was the first map in history to depict an accurate picture of the earth on a flat plane. It can be flat or folded and there is no upside down.

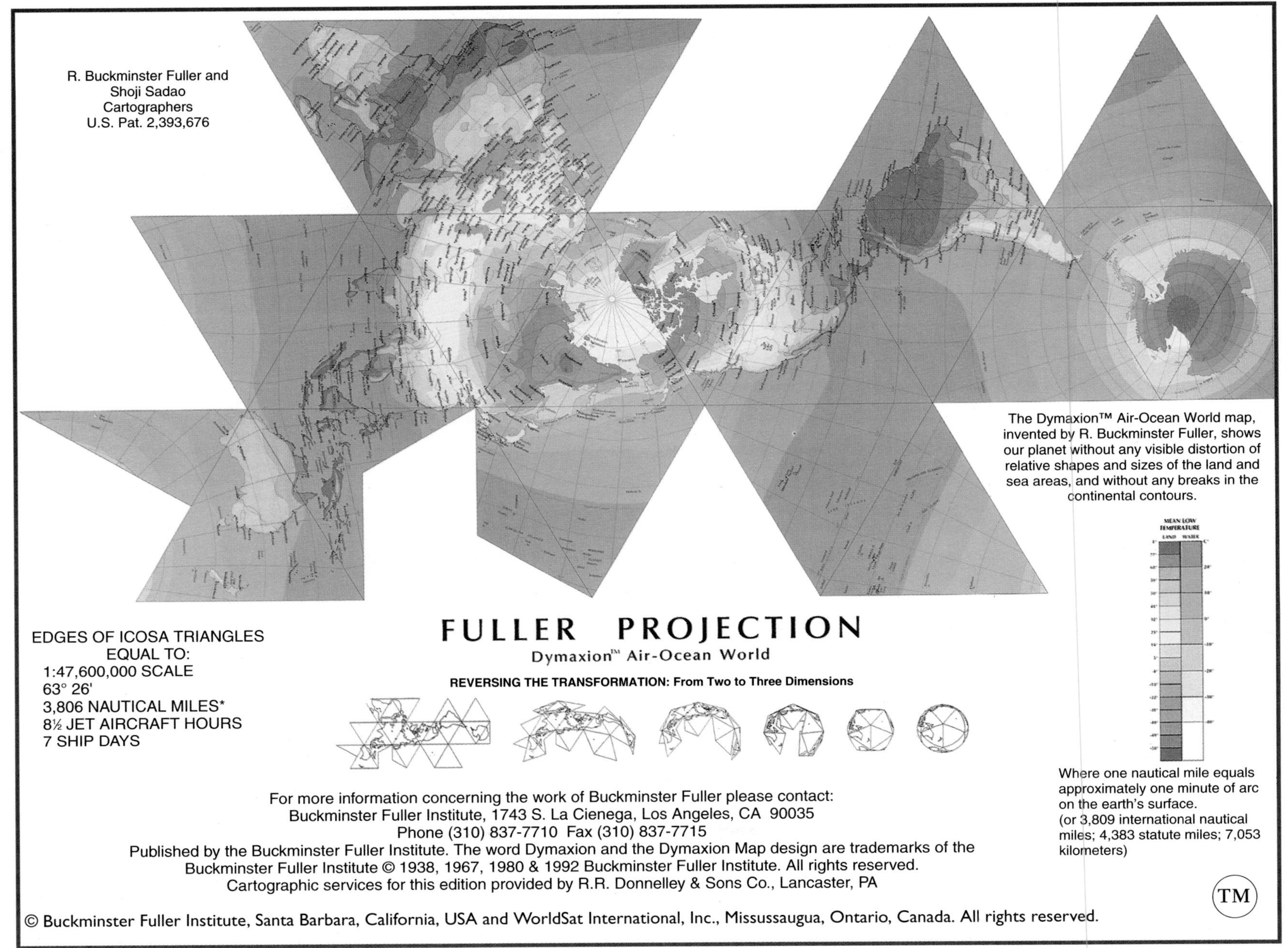

R. Buckminster Fuller and
Shoji Sadao
Cartographers
U.S. Pat. 2,393,676
The Dymaxion™ Air-Ocean World map, invented by R. Buckminster Fuller, shows our planet without any visible distortion of relative shapes and sizes of the land and sea areas, and without any breaks in the continental contours.
MEAN LOW TEMPERATURE
LAND WATER
EDGES OF ICOSA TRIANGLES
EQUAL TO:
1:47,600,000 SCALE
63° 26'
3,806 NAUTICAL MILES*
8½ JET AIRCRAFT HOURS
7 SHIP DAYS
FULLER PROJECTION
Dymaxion™ Air-Ocean World
REVERSING THE TRANSFORMATION: From Two to Three Dimensions
Where one nautical mile equals approximately one minute of arc on the earth's surface.
(or 3,809 international nautical miles; 4,383 statute miles; 7,053 kilometers)
For more information concerning the work of Buckminster Fuller please contact:
Buckminster Fuller Institute, 1743 S. La Cienega, Los Angeles, CA 90035
Phone (310) 837-7710 Fax (310) 837-7715
Published by the Buckminster Fuller Institute. The word Dymaxion and the Dymaxion Map design are trademarks of the Buckminster Fuller Institute © 1938, 1967, 1980 & 1992 Buckminster Fuller Institute. All rights reserved.
Cartographic services for this edition provided by R.R. Donnelley & Sons Co., Lancaster, PA
TM
© Buckminster Fuller Institute, Santa Barbara, California, USA and WorldSat International, Inc., Missussaugua, Ontario, Canada. All rights reserved.

Connecting the Evidence

You might have realized as you read Chapter 9, sometimes explanations do not occur to scientists immediately. They may ask the same questions as other scientists have been asking for many years before developing an explanation. When scientists cooperate and share their ideas, they often develop explanations that answer many questions at once. As you explore Chapter 10, you will see how certain questions and answers fit together.

This opening photograph is actually two photographs. The background is an aerial photograph of the San Fernando Valley in California. Superimposed on that photograph is one of the rescue effort after the 1994 earthquake in California.

engage

Investigation: Desks on the Move

explore

Investigation: Continents on the Move

explain

Reading: Combining Ideas

explain / elaborate

Connections: Putting It Together
Investigation: But Why Should They Move?

elaborate

Investigation: Near the Edges

elaborate / evaluate

Investigation: Plate Tectonics Research

evaluate

Connections: Looking Back
Connections: Listen to How They Say It

©Corbis-Bettmann Archive, NASA, Pizzazz Productions

engage

Investigation: Desks on the Move

Something mysterious has happened in your classroom. Do things look the way they did yesterday? What are the signs that something has occurred, and what puzzle needs to be solved?

A piece of the puzzle: Although it may seem impossible, your classroom has moving desks. Apparently for years, they have been moving during the night. Usually a teacher comes in early to straighten the desks and remove the evidence, but this morning your teacher left the evidence intact. What evidence can you find for how the desks were arranged last night?

Working Cooperatively

In this investigation, your entire class is to cooperate as you share information, so everyone is a Communicator. Also, you are all to function as Team Members collecting evidence. Practice the unit skill *Show respect for others and their ideas.*

Materials for the Entire Class:

- clues

Process and Procedure

1. Find out how the desks were arranged last night.
2. Tell the class recorder about clues you discover.
3. Decide how to interpret the evidence and then discuss it with your classmates.

   Examine the list of clues. You and your classmates might not agree on what the evidence means, so be sure to discuss different opinions as they arise.
4. After the class agrees on a method of arranging the desks, group the desks according to how you think they were arranged last night.
5. Sit at your desk or table in its new location.

Wrap Up

By yourself write answers to the following questions and then discuss your answers with your classmates.

1. Write several sentences to summarize the evidence you found.
2. What conclusions did you draw from the evidence?
3. Draw a picture of the way you think the desks were arranged last night.

4. Assign a class rating for using the social skill. Since the beginning of Unit 2, as a class our use of the unit skill is: much improved, improved, slightly improved, unimproved.

Investigation: Continents on the Move

explore

During the previous investigation, you probably realized that certain colors and shapes of paper gave you clues about which desks might have been situated near each other. (You also probably had a healthy skepticism about moving desks.) Believe it or not, your moving desks might help you develop an explanation for earthquakes and volcanoes.

Working Cooperatively

Work cooperatively in your teams of two. One of you will be the Manager, and one of you will be the Communicator. Review the role descriptions if you need to. Continue to practice the social skill *Stay with your group*. Move your desks together side by side or sit together at a table.

Materials for the Entire Class:

- 1 large world map

Materials for Each Team of Two:

- 2 pairs of scissors
- 1 copy of the Land Mass Worksheet
- 1 sheet of light-colored construction paper
- 10 cm of transparent tape or a glue stick
- 1 copy of Additional Information (for Part B)

Process and Procedure

Part A—Looking at the Land Masses

1. Read through all the steps of this procedure.
2. Pick up the materials.
3. Cut out the land masses from the team worksheet.

   Divide the cutting task fairly.
4. Arrange the land masses on a piece of construction paper in the way they are arranged on the large world map.

   Do not glue or tape them down yet!
5. Find as many patterns in the shapes of the continents as you can.

   Notebook entry: Record these patterns in your notebook.

6. Read this information.

   North and South America are moving away from Africa at a rate of 2.5 cm per year. In other words, ten years ago they were 25 cm closer to each other than they are now (2.5 cm per year x 10 years = 25 cm), and 100 years ago they were 250 cm (8 ft.) closer than they are now.

7. Think about these ideas.
   a. The continents have not always been as they are now.
   b. We can see patterns on the map of the world.
8. Arrange the continents in the way you think they were 200 million years ago. Draw this arrangement in your notebook.
9. Write down the evidence that led you to arrange the continents in the way you did.

   Notebook entry: Record this evidence.

Part B—Additional Information

1. Pick up the Additional Information Sheet and study it.
2. Change the arrangement of the continents from 200 million years ago as necessary to match the new evidence that you have from the Additional Information Sheet.

   If you have trouble deciding how to use the new information, think back to the investigation Desks on the Move.

3. Tape or glue your new arrangement onto the sheet of construction paper.
4. Draw in your notebook how you now think the continents were arranged 200 million years ago.

Wrap Up

Discuss the following questions with your teammate and record your own answers in your notebook.

1. In Chapter 9, both Antonio Snider and Alfred Wegener told the characters to look at a map. What pattern do you think each of them saw on a world map?

2. How did you use the new evidence in Part B to change the arrangement of the continents?
3. Do you think the continents really could have moved? Explain your answer.

explain

Reading:
Combining Ideas

You began this chapter by using evidence to figure out where your moving desks were the previous night. You just did something similar in the investigation Continents on the Move. You probably looked at the shapes of the continents and noticed that some of the edges matched. This evidence, along with the information that the continents presently are moving, might have helped you figure out what the continents looked like a long time ago.

After you cut out the continents and arranged them, you observed patterns. But you still might have had questions. Why would the continents have moved? A particular group of scientists, called geologists, have this same question. Geologists have studied maps, volcanoes, and fossils, and they have had questions after they observed certain patterns. But they could not explain the patterns. Each group of scientists had evidence, but they did not know how to pull the evidence together to develop an accurate explanation.

Alfred Wegener, a scientist whom the characters met during the play in Chapter 9, observed patterns and gathered evidence. Wegener thought that because the shapes of the continents fit together like a puzzle, it was likely that the continents had been together at one time and later moved to their present locations. Wegener called this theory **continental drift**. Other people supported Wegener's basic idea.

To test his theory of continental drift, Wegener used a very simple analogy. He pointed out that if a sheet of newspaper is torn in half leaving jagged edges, we should be able to fit it back together based on its shape as if it were a puzzle. Then to test our reconstruction, we should be able to read the newsprint across the tear and have it make sense. Wegener applied this idea to his

▶ **FIGURE 10.1**
Wegener used the newsprint model to help him explain his theory of continental drift.

theory of continental drift. He was able to collect evidence that supported his idea from sites all over the world. In addition to the continental shapes fitting back together, the geology across the pieces was continuous.

Wegener and other scientists found additional evidence that the continents might have been together at some time in the past. For example, geologists found **fossils** in Africa and Australia that were similar to fossils in South America and Antarctica. Fossils are the hardened remains or traces of animals or plants that lived long ago. Other geologists found that some fossils in North America and

Europe also were the same. This evidence suggested that the continents had been together but then moved apart.

Sometimes the types of animal and plant fossils that scientists found did not match the present-day climate of the continent. For example, scientists found tropical plant fossils on ice-covered Antarctica. This evidence indicated to some geologists that at one time the continents were much closer together and more similar.

But many scientists wondered how something as heavy as a continent could actually move. In other words, they had found a pattern on maps, as well as a pattern left by fossils, but they could not explain how the patterns occurred.

Another group of geologists identified other patterns on the earth. They knew the locations of earthquakes but did not know why they occurred where they did. They had noticed that earthquakes occurred in tight clusters in certain locations. Earthquakes were most common near mountain ranges and in certain locations in the ocean. Within the ocean, many of these earthquakes occurred in lines along the ridge tops of undersea mountains.

But geologists still had more patterns to explain. People who studied volcanoes had observed the locations of volcanic eruptions. They found that, like earthquakes, volcanoes occur in lines. They are common near mountains and along the ridge tops of undersea mountains. The pattern was evident, but geologists could not explain why it occurred.

Geologists finally shared their ideas, just as you shared your ideas in Desks on the Move. They combined their evidence to develop an explanation not only for earthquakes and volcanoes but also for other geologic events as well.

Geologists concluded that the surface of the earth is moving, but it is not just the continents that are moving. Geologists continued to explain that the continents sit on top of **plates** that make up the entire surface of the earth. It is these plates that move (see Figure 10.2). We call this explanation the **theory of plate tectonics**. According to this explanation, as the plates rub against each other, they cause earthquakes. Volcanoes occur where the plates move apart or where one plate pushes and melts

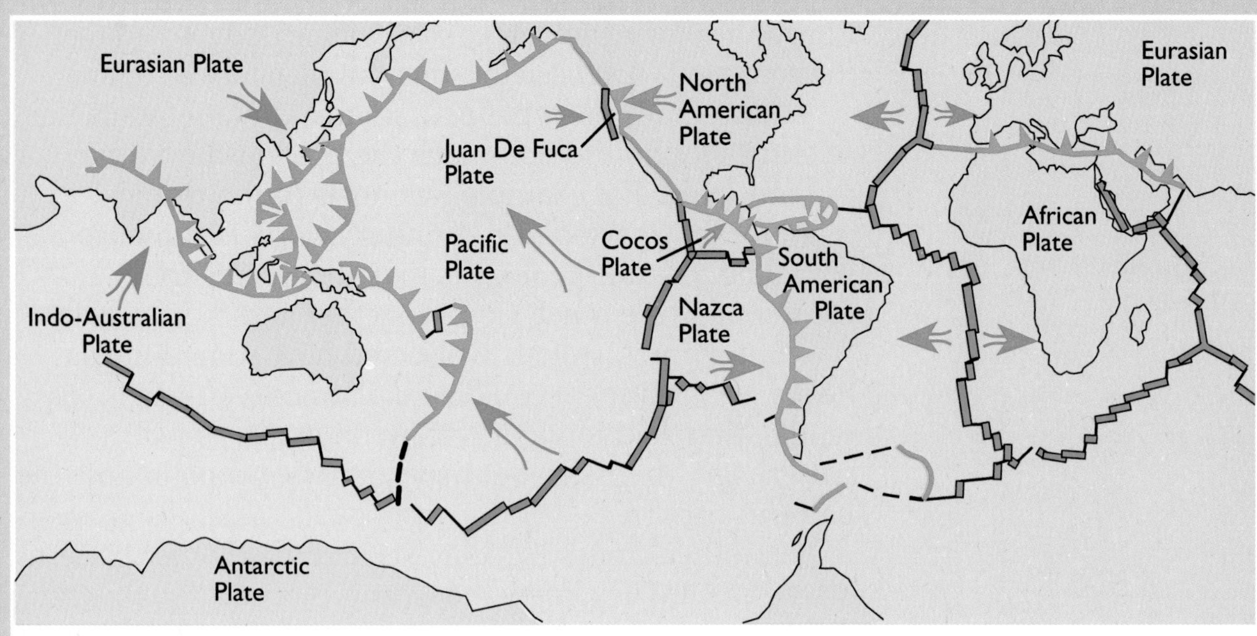

Legend

Plates moving apart

Plates moving side by side

One plate sinking beneath another
(Sinking plate is moving in direction of arrows)

Uncertain Boundary

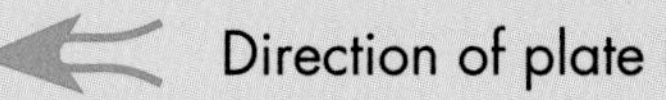
Direction of plate motion

Based on information from: Aylesworth, T.G. (1990). Moving continents: Our changing Earth. Hillside, NJ: Enslow. And information from: Montgomery, C.W., and Dathe, D. (1991). Earth: then and now. Dubuque, IA: Wm. C. Brown.

▲ **FIGURE 10.2**
Scientists have identified the major plates on the earth's surface. The continents move because they are part of these plates.

beneath another plate. This also explains why the rocks are youngest in the middle of the Atlantic Ocean. Along the Mid-Atlantic Ridge, two plates are pulling apart and new lava is rising up between them. As this lava cools, it forms the youngest rocks.

Stop & Think

1. List some of the patterns that scientists noticed but did not know how to explain.
2. How does the theory of plate tectonics explain earthquakes?
3. According to the theory of plate tectonics, why are the youngest rocks in the Atlantic Ocean in the middle of the ocean?

What makes the idea of moving plates a strong scientific explanation? If you remember from the play, Aristotle was a great thinker. He made careful observations, asked questions, and proposed that wind causes earthquakes. Today the idea that moving plates cause earthquakes is accepted more widely than Aristotle's explanation. Primarily this is because the evidence for plates is more convincing than the evidence for wind-caused earthquakes. The evidence for moving plates includes the locations of earthquakes and volcanoes, the ages of rocks, and the fossil evidence from the continents. Plate tectonics also connects many different events—the moving of continents, the locations of earthquakes, and the locations of volcanic eruptions.

In addition the theory of plate tectonics successfully predicts new observations. For example the theory of plate tectonics explains how earthquakes and volcanoes are related. If small earthquakes begin to happen in an area that also has volcanoes, then we can predict that a volcanic eruption will occur. The stronger the earthquakes, the more likely that an eruption will occur soon. We also can predict that places far from plate boundaries are much less likely to have earthquakes. Predictions of this sort have provided additional support for the theory of plate tectonics.

This theory is a strong scientific explanation because it uses all the components of a scientific explanation. It answers questions, it is based on evidence, and scientists have tested it. It also connects observations and allows for predictions. Moving continents, volcanoes, and earthquakes all make more sense when we explain them in relation to the idea that giant plates of rock move across the surface of the earth.

Before you go on, think for a minute about the explanations that you developed for earthquakes and volcanoes in Chapter 9. Do any parts of your explanations support the theory of plate tectonics? Do you think that you would have come up with the theory of plate tectonics if you had had all the evidence?

It is important to realize that just because plate tectonics is the currently accepted theory, this does not mean that it is completely correct. Maybe some of your ideas or someone else's could help improve the theory.

Stop & Think

4. How does the theory of plate tectonics explain why the continents are moving?
5. How does plate tectonic movement explain the formation of volcanoes?
6. Use the theory of plate tectonics to explain the correlations you saw between the locations of volcanoes and earthquakes.

Connections: Putting It Together

explain / elaborate

The previous reading provided you with a lot of information. One thing it said was that the continents moved because they are on top of moving plates. To see how the continents' pattern would have changed through time, assemble the flip book called Pangaea. Your teacher will hand out the scissors and copies of Pangaea. See how Pangaea's pattern has changed during the last 200 million years.

Investigation: But Why Should They Move?

explain / elaborate

It might seem that the theory of plate tectonics presents a complete explanation of earthquakes and volcanoes. But some questions are still unanswered. If the earth really has plates, what are they made of? What do they sit on? And most important, why would they move? Our explanation will be stronger if we can answer these questions. In this investigation, you will determine how solid plates might move.

Materials for the Entire Class:

- 1 clock

Working Cooperatively

Work cooperatively in your teams of two. One of you will need to be the Manager. As you work, practice the skill *Stay with your group*. Watch out for each other's safety because your working environment includes a heat source.

Materials for Each Team of Two:

- one 500-mL glass beaker
- 400 mL of water at room temperature
- 6 squares of card stock (2 cm square)
- 1 dropper bottle with food coloring
- 1 ring stand (or other apparatus to support the beaker)
- 1 heat source (Bunsen burner or votive candle)
- matches
- 2 pairs of goggles
- 1 pair of tongs

Process and Procedure

1. Collect the materials.
2. Fill the beaker about $\frac{2}{3}$ full of water and set up the materials as shown in Figure 10.3.
3. Put on your goggles and heat the water.

   If you use a Bunsen burner during this part, keep the flame very low. If you are not experienced with this equipment, see How to Use a Bunsen Burner (How To #7).

The heat source can cause burns.

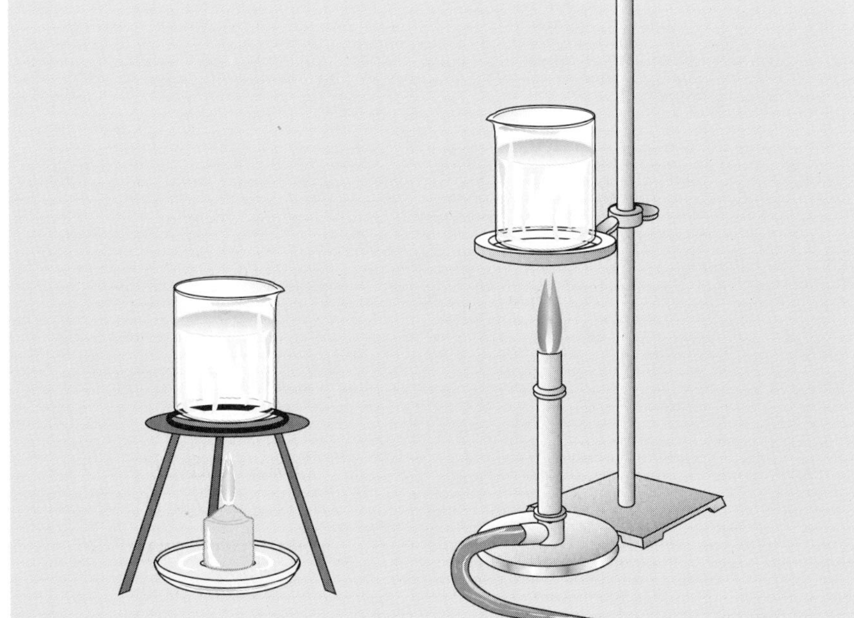

FIGURE 10.3
Use caution when you set up this equipment. Make sure things are steady before you add water to the beaker and before you light the heat source.

4. When the water begins to give off steam, add two drops of food coloring.

Hot liquids can cause burns.

5. Observe what happens for at least two minutes.
   Notebook entry: Record your observations.
6. Just as the water begins to boil, use the tongs to add the paper squares to the water.
7. Observe what happens as the water boils more strongly.
   Notebook entry: Record your observations.

Background Information

The earth consists of more than the rocky surface that we walk on. Scientists call this outside shell of mostly hard rock the **crust**. It covers both the land masses and the ocean floor. The crust is the top layer of the **upper mantle**. The upper mantle extends down to around 700 km. At about this point, the **lower mantle** begins; this is a solid layer with some molten areas. The inner mantle extends down to about 2900 km. To imagine what the mantle is like, think about a bowl of gelatin; it is not hard, but it is not fluid either. Scientists estimate that it is 10 percent molten and 90 percent solid. Scientists call the innermost part of the earth the **core**, and it is thought to be extremely hot. It is made up of a liquid outer core and a solid inner core. The theory of plate tectonics focuses on the top portion of the upper mantle. The plates are between 100 and 200 km thick, and the plates on land are thicker than the plates in the ocean. (See Figure 10.4.)

What happens during a volcano then? Where does the magma (molten rock) come from? Basically this happens in two different ways. At the trenches, rocks get pulled down into the mantle where they get heated up and melt. Sometimes these rocks have water mixed with them, which makes them easier to melt. At mid-ocean ridges, rocky material is moved upward and the heat that is generated causes the rocks to melt. This magma then rises to the surface as volcanoes erupt.

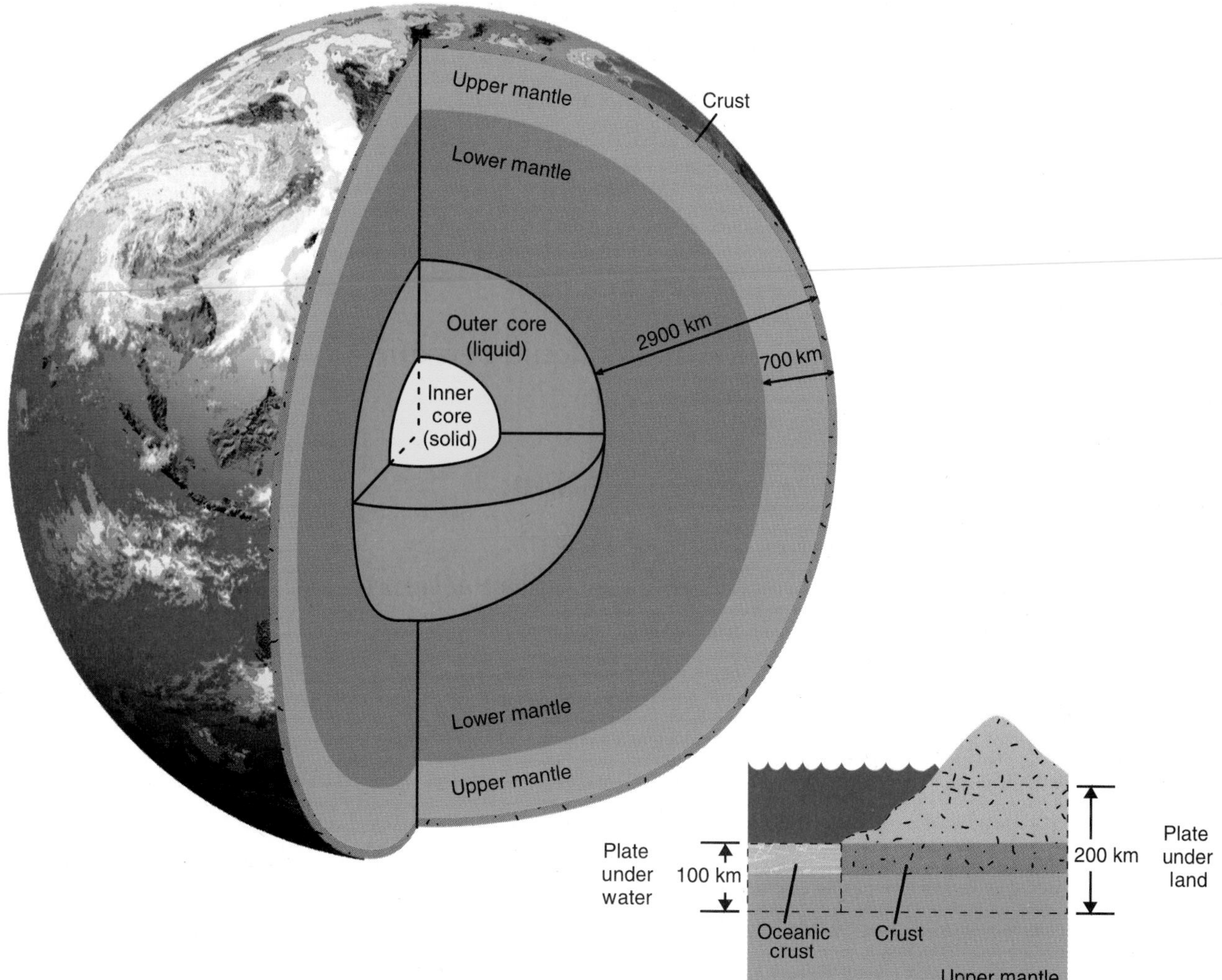

▲ **FIGURE 10.4**

The theory of plate tectonics focuses on the crust and upper mantle. Earth scientists have discovered that plates include slightly more than the crust because a small slice of the upper mantle moves with each plate. Plates are between 100 and 200 km thick. As you can see, the earth also includes a lower mantle and an inner and outer core.

You might wonder whether or not anyone has drilled a hole to see whether these ideas are accurate. Unfortunately no one has been able to—yet. From the upper mantle to the center of the earth is more than 6,400 kilometers, and we can dig down only 10 kilometers or so with our modern drilling equipment. Scientists have gathered their information about the earth's interior by observing how earthquake tremors travel through the earth and arrive at different places at different times.

Wrap Up

Participate in a class discussion of the following questions. Then write or illustrate your own answers.

1. What did the paper squares represent?
2. What did the hot water and the heat source represent?

3. When you added food coloring to the warm water, what pattern did you observe?
4. When you heat water, a pattern occurs. Use the pattern that you saw to explain why molten rock beneath the plates could cause the plates to move.
5. Explain how molten rock can become solid rock.
6 Why could rock on the ocean floor be recycled many times?
7. How might liquid beneath a solid rock plate help the plate move?

elaborate

Investigation: Near the Edges

Where does most of the action take place on the planet? If you answered that most action takes place near the edge of a plate, you are right. Even though it might seem that plates easily slide past each other, quite a lot of action takes place at the edges. Sometimes plates slide past each other, sometimes they move away from each other, and sometimes they move toward each other. These three types of motion—beside, away from, or toward—result in different types of boundaries. In this investigation, you will be working with teammates to describe what happens at different types of plate boundaries.

Working Cooperatively

Work cooperatively in teams of two until Step 5 and then join with two other teams of two. You will be in a jigsaw group—one that divides up a task among its members. As you work in teams of two, use the roles of Communicator and Manager. Throughout this activity, try practicing the new skill *Treat others politely*.

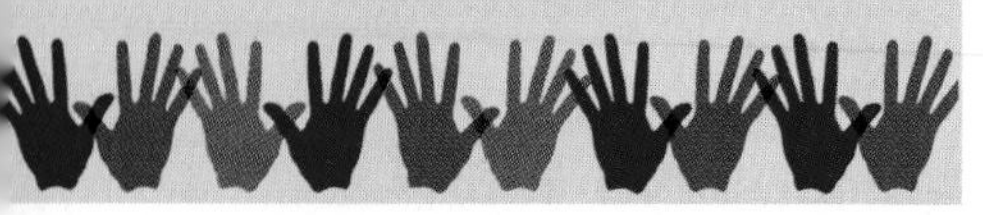

Materials for Each Team of Two:

- 1 stick of modeling clay
- 1 paper towel, cut in half

Process and Procedure

Part A—The Social Skill

1. With your teammate, think of two reasons why treating others politely is an important skill in cooperative learning and record your ideas in your notebook.
2. In your notebook, construct a T-chart for this skill.

Part B—Plate Boundaries

1. Get the materials.

2. Read the background information section assigned to your team.

   These readings are located after the procedure.
3. Divide the modeling clay into two pieces.

   The Communicator and the Manager each should have one piece of clay.
4. Decide how your team will use the modeling clay to demonstrate your type of plate boundary to two other teams.
5. Get into your jigsaw group.

   Share your T-charts for treating others politely.
6. Use the modeling clay to demonstrate your team's boundary to the other members of your jigsaw group.
7. Be sure that you understand each of the three types of boundaries so that you could demonstrate any of the three types to the rest of the class.

   If you do not understand something, ask your teammates for help.

Background Information

Ridges

The ocean floor makes up about 71 percent of the earth's surface. For centuries people thought that the ocean floor was almost entirely flat. They had no evidence to the contrary because no one could explore the deep ocean waters. Extreme darkness, icy cold, and great pressure near the ocean floor prevented exploration. During World War II, however, scientists developed technology to map the sea floor—special echo sounders and deep-sea cameras. The echo sounders allowed sailors to measure the depths of ocean waters and to determine where undersea mountains and canyons were. This work continued into the 1970s. Naval scientists then had enough information to make an accurate map of the ocean floor.

These maps show that parts of the ocean floor are flat. They also show that the ocean floor is made up of wide valleys, deep trenches, and towering mountain chains, called **ridges**, which are as high as 2,400 meters (7,880 ft.). Figure 10.5 shows ridges on the ocean floor.

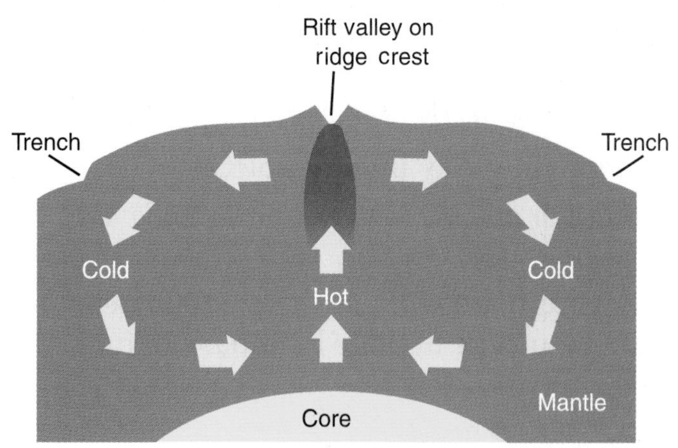

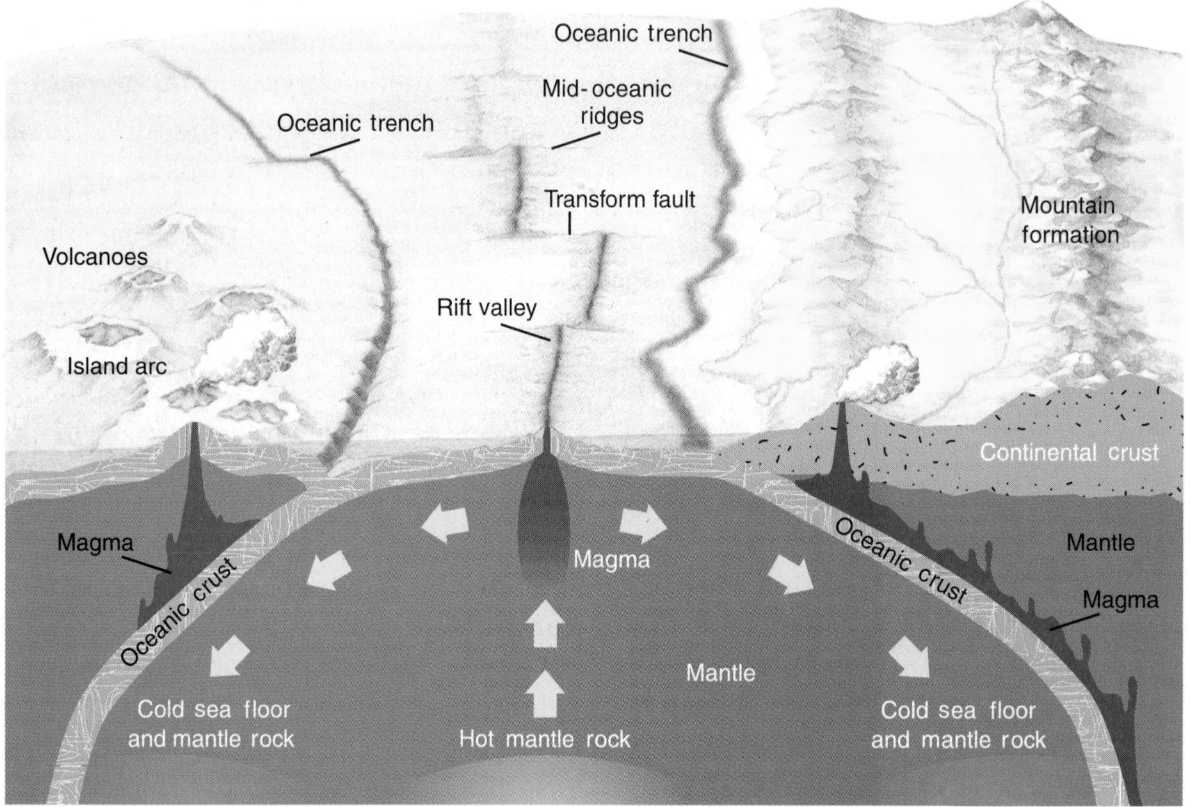

▲ **FIGURE 10.5**

Refer to this drawing as you read about ridges, trenches, and transform faults.

Underwater ridges, the longest mountain chains on earth, wrap around the earth like the seams on a baseball. In some places, the ridges are 4,800 kilometers (3,000 mi) wide—wider than the United States. Nearly all ridges are hidden under many kilometers of ocean water. Iceland and the Azores are actually the tops of ridges that rose out of the sea millions of years ago.

Most ridges are split down the middle by a valley. In the valley, the edges of the plates are spreading apart. This spreading opens cracks in the valley floor. Hot **magma** (molten rock) oozes out of the cracks. When it reaches the earth's surface, we call this magma **lava**. The lava hardens into new mountains of rock. As if they were on a huge conveyor belt, the mountains are moved away from where they formed. After the mountains are pushed away, they do not get any larger. The newest mountains, then, are nearest to the valley; the oldest are the farthest away.

Trenches

Trenches are the deepest parts of the ocean. At a trench, the edge of one plate bends and moves under another plate. This edge slowly moves down inside the earth where temperatures are hot enough to melt the rock. Sometimes the magma (molten rock beneath the earth's surface) may rise and break through the ocean floor to form volcanic islands. The islands of Japan were formed in this way. Figure 10.5 illustrates trenches and the formation of islands.

Scientists study rocks from the earth's crust to interpret earth's history, but rocks from the ocean floor that formed more than 200 million years ago have been pulled down into the trenches and have melted inside the earth. Thus to obtain rocks older than 200 million years, scientists must study continental rocks. Continents do not go down into trenches. This rock is lighter, and it essentially floats on top of the heavier rock below it.

Transform Faults

Transform faults occur when two plates, positioned side by side, slide past each other. When this movement occurs, it can produce earthquakes. The pressure between the plates builds until, suddenly, one plate moves past the other. This movement causes a rapid release of energy, which causes an earthquake. Figure 10.5 shows a transform fault. One example of a transform fault is the **San Andreas fault** in southern California. When the Pacific and the North American plates move past each other along this fault, earthquakes occur.

Some scientists think that transform faults may be the longest lasting type of plate boundary. After listening to the presentations of your jigsaw group, tell your group about transform faults.

Wrap Up

Work with your teammate to answer the following questions.

1. On the blank world map that your teacher provides, locate the ridges, trenches, and transform faults.
   a. Use the letters R (ridge), T (trench), and F (transform fault).
   b. Use Figure 10.5 as a resource. You may want to use other maps in Chapter 9 as well.
2. Using the concepts of ridges, trenches, and transform faults, describe the patterns that indicate the occurrence of
   a. volcanoes
   b. earthquakes
3. Discuss with your teammates ways to improve your practice of the social skill *Treat others politely*. Record these strategies in your notebook.

elaborate / evaluate

Investigation: Plate Tectonics Research

In this activity, you will further study one topic of your choice. The list includes many events that are related directly to plate tectonics. You will become an expert on the one topic so that you can make a presentation to the rest of your class. As you listen to the other presentations, you will see how the theory of plate tectonics has explained many features on the earth.

Working Cooperatively

You will work individually in this investigation. As you get help from others and as you listen to presentations, practice your unit skill and the skill *Treat others politely*.

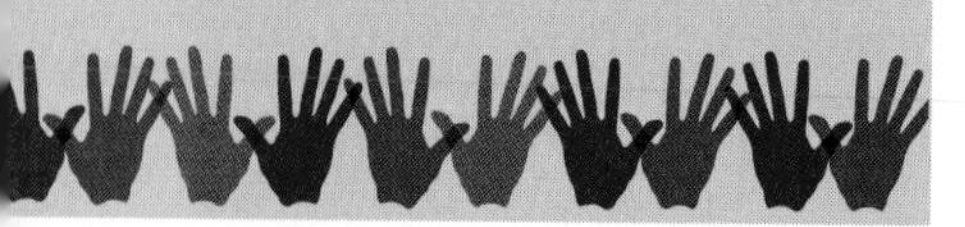

Materials for Each Student:

- 1 Presentation Review Sheet

Process and Procedure

1. Choose a topic that you would like to learn more about and record it in your notebook.

   You may choose a topic from the list at the end of this investigation, or you may choose a different one that your teacher approves.

2. Read any information in the Background Information that relates to the topic you chose.
3. Think about what else you would like to know about your topic and how you might find that information.

   You will need to visit the library in order to complete this investigation.
4. As you investigate your topic, do the following things:
   - Identify the question you are trying to answer.
   - Describe the answer you found.
   - Describe how the ideas connect with the theory of plate tectonics.
   - Use at least three references.
5. Research your topic.

   If you do not know how to do library research, see How To #6, How to Conduct a Research Project, for some help.
6. Design and organize a presentation for your classmates. Your presentation must include one of the following:
   - a 3-minute talk to the class,
   - a poster or demonstration large enough for the class to see, or
   - a two-page written description.
7. Show your teacher what you plan to do.
8. Make your presentation.
9. As you listen to other presentations, listen for the specific things listed in Step 4.

   Follow the example on the Presentation Review Sheet for each person you listen to, and write a review of each presentation in your notebook.

Questions and Topics for Presentations

1. How does the landscape change after a severe earthquake?
2. How do earthquakes affect buildings?
3. How could people's lives change after an earthquake?
4. How are rocks such as basalt and granite formed?

5. What is a tsunami (tsoo NAH mee), and how does it form?
6. Why are some rocks on land billions of years old but in the ocean the oldest rocks are only 200 million years old?
7. If most mountains are found on the edges of continents, how can you explain the location of the Ural Mountains?
8. Major earthquakes have occurred within the last 10 years in Mexico City, San Francisco, and the Philippines. Report on one of these earthquakes or another recent one.
9. Report on a relatively recent occurrence of volcanic activity, such as that in Japan, Hawaii, or the Philippines.
10. Choose one of the following mountain ranges: the Andes, Himalayas, Cascades, or Appalachians. Explain how that mountain range may have been formed according to the plate tectonic theory.
11. Use the theory of plate tectonics to explain why Mt. St. Helens erupted.
12. According to recent research, the continent of Africa is splitting apart. Describe and show where this is occurring and what the evidence is.
13. Describe what a hot spot is and how scientists can use a hot spot on the ocean floor to indicate the direction of a plate's movement.
14. Why do some volcanoes explode violently, like Mt. St. Helens and Pinatubo, and others erupt with much less force, like the volcanoes in Hawaii?

Background Information

This reference section contains information about some topics that are related to plate tectonics but have not yet been discussed in the readings.

Mountains

Mountains are formed in several different ways: by volcanic eruption, by folding when plates collide, and by movement along some types of faults. **Folding** means that the rock layers bend but do not break (see Figure 10.6).

▶ **FIGURE 10.6**

Folded mountains form when rocks have been squeezed from opposite sides and create folds.

Photograph provided by Dr. Carl Vondra, Iowa State University, Geology Field Station.

Faults form when the rock is pushed to the point of breaking. The broken block of rock may be pushed up, down, or sideways. Faults generally are evident in mountains when two different types of rock occur next to each other. Movement along the fault has pushed one type of rock next to another type of rock (see Figure 10.7). Many times mountain ranges form as a combination of folding and faulting.

Volcanic mountains form when volcanoes erupt (see Figure 10.8). The islands of Hawaii, Iceland, and Japan are examples of volcanic mountains. These mountains formed over hot spots, ridges, or near trenches.

Rocks

Rocks form in several ways. One type of rock forms when magma rises near the earth's surface and cools to form igneous (IG nee us) rocks. If the magma cools very slowly, large crystals have time to grow, and a rock such as granite forms. If the lava is thrown from a volcano and cools rapidly, a rock such as andesite (AN di zit) may form. A piece of andesite might weigh the same as a piece of granite, but the crystals in andesite would be tiny because the rock cooled so rapidly.

▶ **FIGURE 10.7**
Mountains that have formed by faulting often have different types of rock next to each other. When movement occurs along the fault, the crust breaks. As a result different types of rock appear next to each other.

Other rocks form because sediments (such as soil and pieces of animal shells) become cemented together. Just as a mixture of sand and clay can form a cement sidewalk, small particles of clay can dissolve in water and hold natural sediments together. We call these cemented rocks sedimentary rocks. Examples include limestone, shale, and sandstone.

If a sedimentary rock is in an area where mountains are forming, it may become deeply buried and subject to great heat and pressure. The heat and pressure at great depths can change the sedimentary rock. Limestone can change to marble, shale can change to slate, and sandstone can change to quartzite. We call rocks that change this way metamorphic rocks.

Volcanoes

When a volcano erupts, magma comes to the surface. Magma is molten rock that develops deep beneath the surface of the earth. When magma reaches the surface, it is called lava. Volcanoes are located over openings in the earth's crust and the material can come out through the

▲ **FIGURE 10.8**

Volcanic mountains form when molten rock erupts from inside the earth, and then the molten rock cools and hardens.

openings. This material is a combination of liquid rock and gases. If the gases are trapped or if a volcano is made of a particular rock type, then an explosion might occur. As the magma comes out, it separates into gas and lava. The lava cools rapidly and forms rocks such as basalt or pumice. Ash and cinders also come from the volcano and build up around the sides of the opening.

Hot Spots

Some places on the earth have had a lot of volcanic activity and yet are not near a plate boundary. These are called **hot spots**. Two examples of places affected by hot spots are the Hawaiian Islands (see Figure 10.9) and Yellowstone National Park (see Figure 10.10). Yellowstone National Park has a variety of volcanic rocks, hot springs, and geysers. A **geyser** (GUY zer) is like a small volcano. It erupts, but instead of hot lava, hot water and steam escape. The geysers are evidence that even if the rocks at the surface have cooled, there is still enough heat below to warm the water traveling through the ground.

▶ FIGURE 10.9

As a plate moves over a hot spot in the mantle, a small section of the plate melts, and magma rises up through the opening and forms volcanoes. But because the plate keeps moving slowly, one volcano after another is formed. This creates a chain of volcanoes, such as the volcanic Hawaiian Islands.

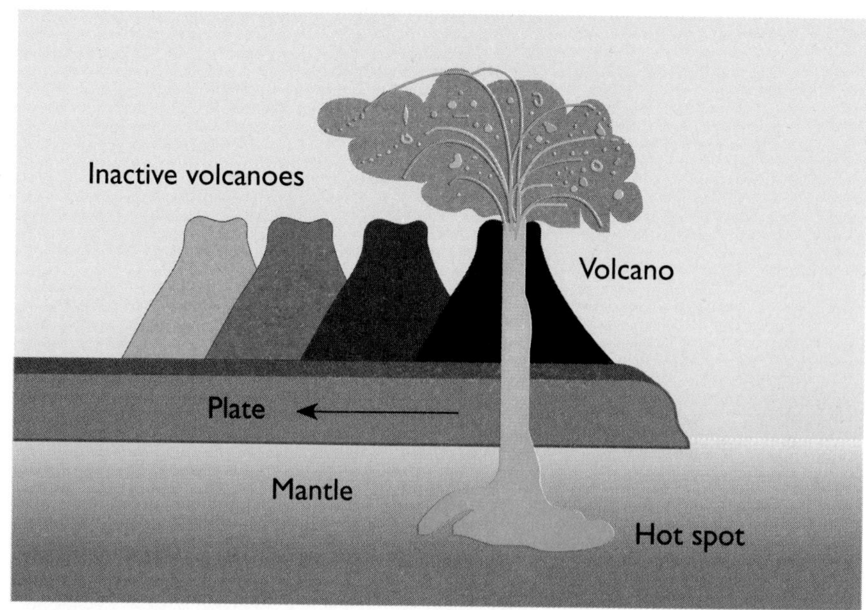

▶ FIGURE 10.10

Yellowstone National Park has hot springs and geysers like this one.

Connections:
Looking Back

evaluate

Look back at the terms and phrases you listed in your notebook during the Chapter 9 investigation, Patterns on the Earth. Which words and phrases are more familiar now? Which ones are still unfamiliar? Also review the questions your class posted during the Chapter 9 connections activity, Can You Explain the Observations? Which questions can you answer now? What new questions do you have?

In this chapter, we have introduced you to the theory of plate tectonics. Earth scientists currently use this theory to explain many features on the earth. But just because something is the currently accepted scientific theory does not mean it is correct. The evidence has been laid out for you, but you can still decide for yourself whether or not you agree with the conclusions presented in the chapter. Many scientists have disagreed with the current theories of their time. This is one way scientific advances take place.

Connections:
Listen to How They Say It

evaluate

At the beginning of Chapter 9, you looked at photographs and saw a film or video about earthquakes. In your class discussion, you probably discussed many ideas about what happens when volcanoes erupt and earthquakes occur.

Throughout this unit, you have been reading about and coming up with your own scientific explanations. In this activity, it is your turn to evaluate someone else's scientific explanation.

Before you watch the video or film that your teacher will show, review the readings in Unit 2. Think about the parts of a good scientific explanation. If you are hearing a complete scientific explanation, what things will the speaker tell you? What should you listen for? Write yourself a short list of the things you will listen for.

Watch and listen to the video or film. With your classmates, discuss how complete the scientific explanation was.

SIDELIGHT on History

Geologic Time

According to geologists, the earth was formed 4.6 billion years ago. That time span is difficult to understand. To better understand the earth's history, geologists have divided this long time span into shorter time periods. This sidelight depicts the important stages of the earth's history and correlates these events with the movement of the continents.

CAMBRIAN EARTH

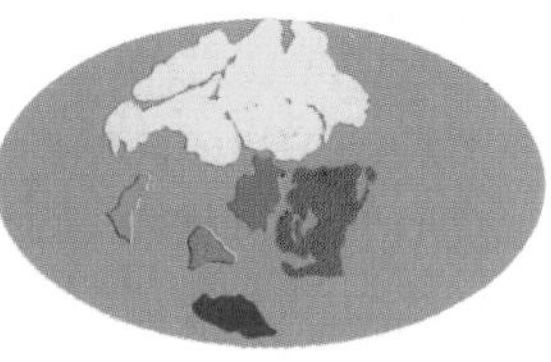

Four large (and two small) continents had been formed and were moving toward each other. Sea levels were high. Vermont mountains were formed.

DEVONIAN EARTH

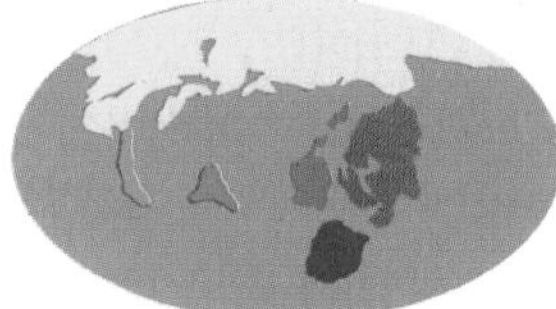

Laurentia and Baltica had collided to form one continent. Sea levels were low. In some regions there were periods of drought.

CARBONIFEROUS EARTH

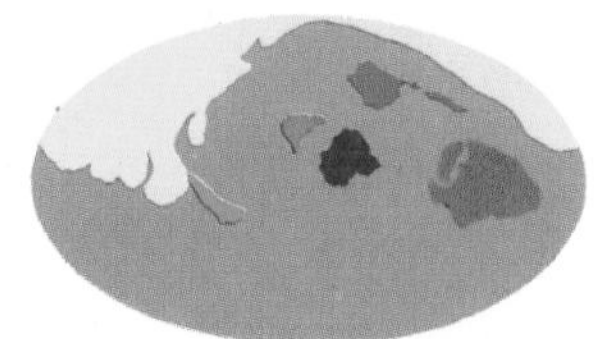

Because of high humidity, swamps and forests covered much of the land.

early sea life

marine plants

Vermont Mountains

clams and starfish

first fishes

first amphibians

insects

first air-breathing animals

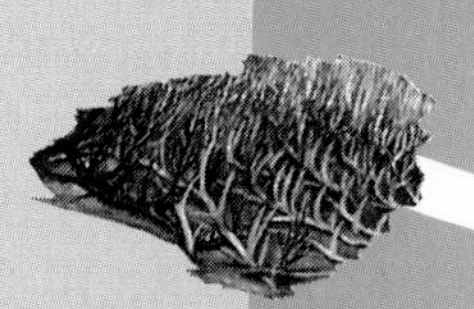

first land plants

Coal-age forests

PRE-CAMBRIAN	PALEOZOIC				
	Cambrian	Ordovician	Silurian	Devonian	Carboniferous

570 mya, 485, 435, 408, 360

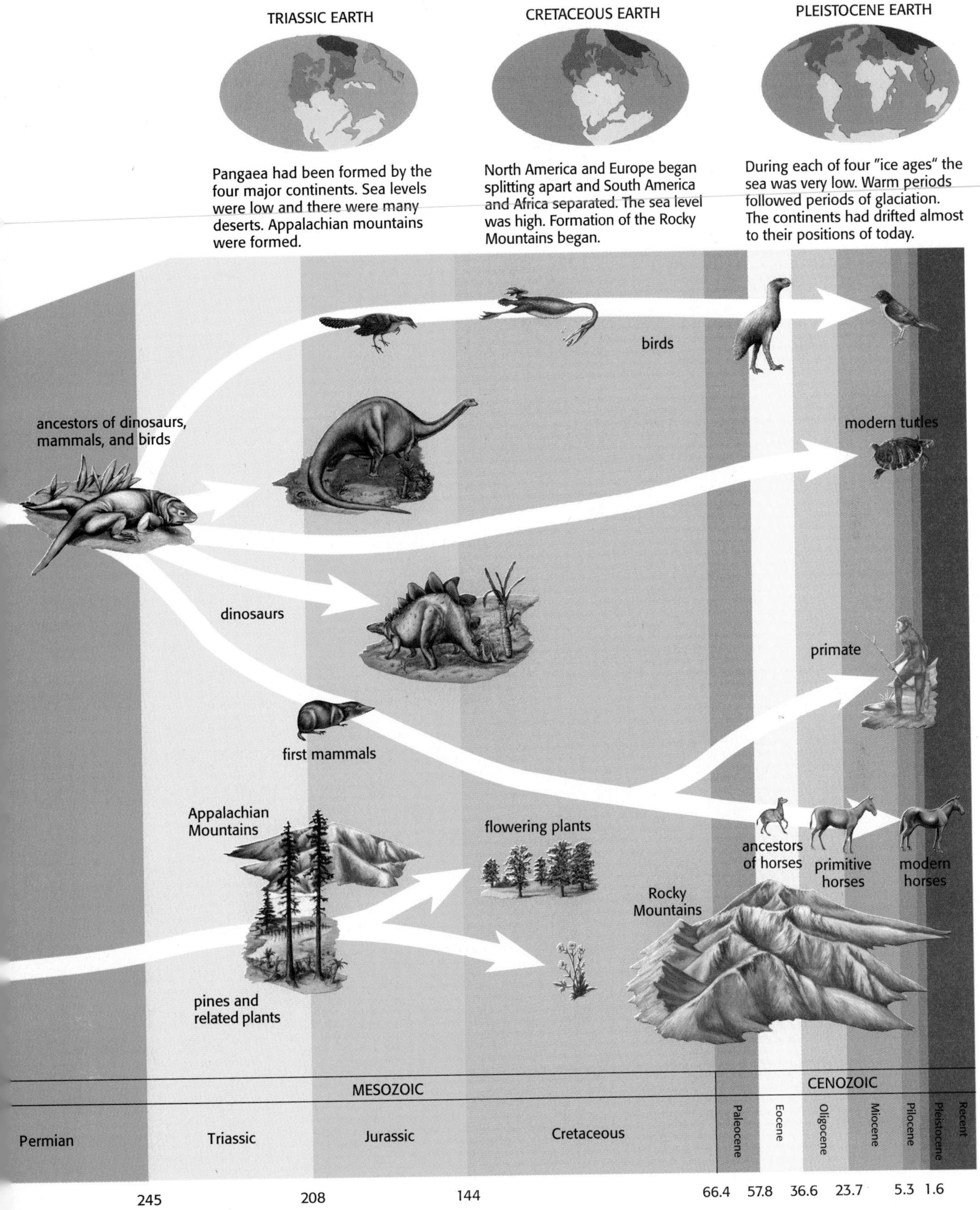

TRIASSIC EARTH

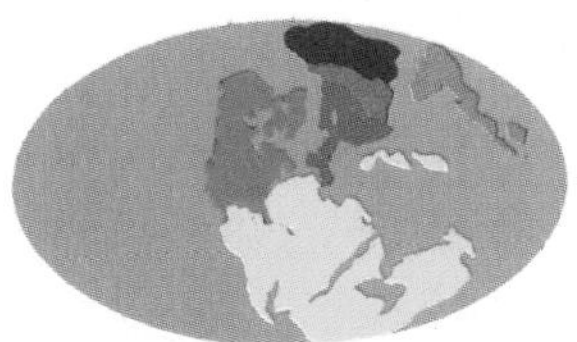

Pangaea had been formed by the four major continents. Sea levels were low and there were many deserts. Appalachian mountains were formed.

CRETACEOUS EARTH

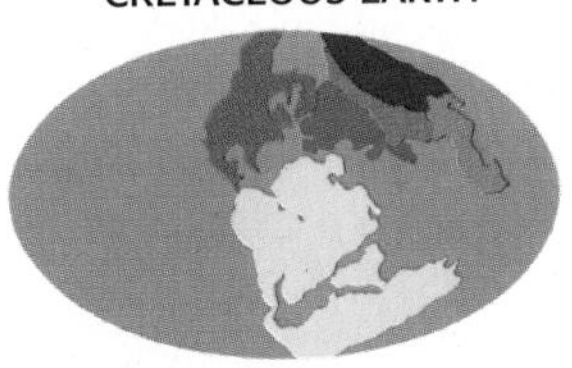

North America and Europe began splitting apart and South America and Africa separated. The sea level was high. Formation of the Rocky Mountains began.

PLEISTOCENE EARTH

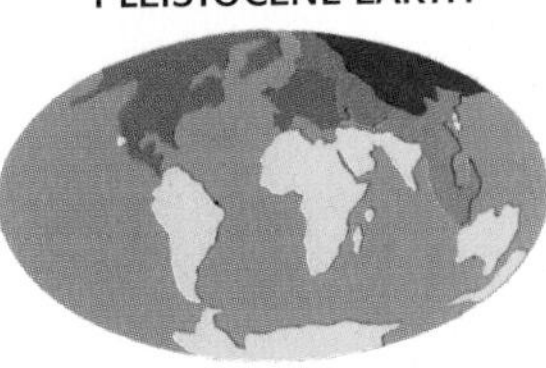

During each of four "ice ages" the sea was very low. Warm periods followed periods of glaciation. The continents had drifted almost to their positions of today.

birds

ancestors of dinosaurs, mammals, and birds

modern turtles

dinosaurs

primate

first mammals

Appalachian Mountains

flowering plants

ancestors of horses

primitive horses

modern horses

Rocky Mountains

pines and related plants

	MESOZOIC			CENOZOIC						
Permian	Triassic	Jurassic	Cretaceous	Paleocene	Eocene	Oligocene	Miocene	Pilocene	Pleistocene	Recent
245	208	144	66.4	57.8	36.6	23.7	5.3	1.6		

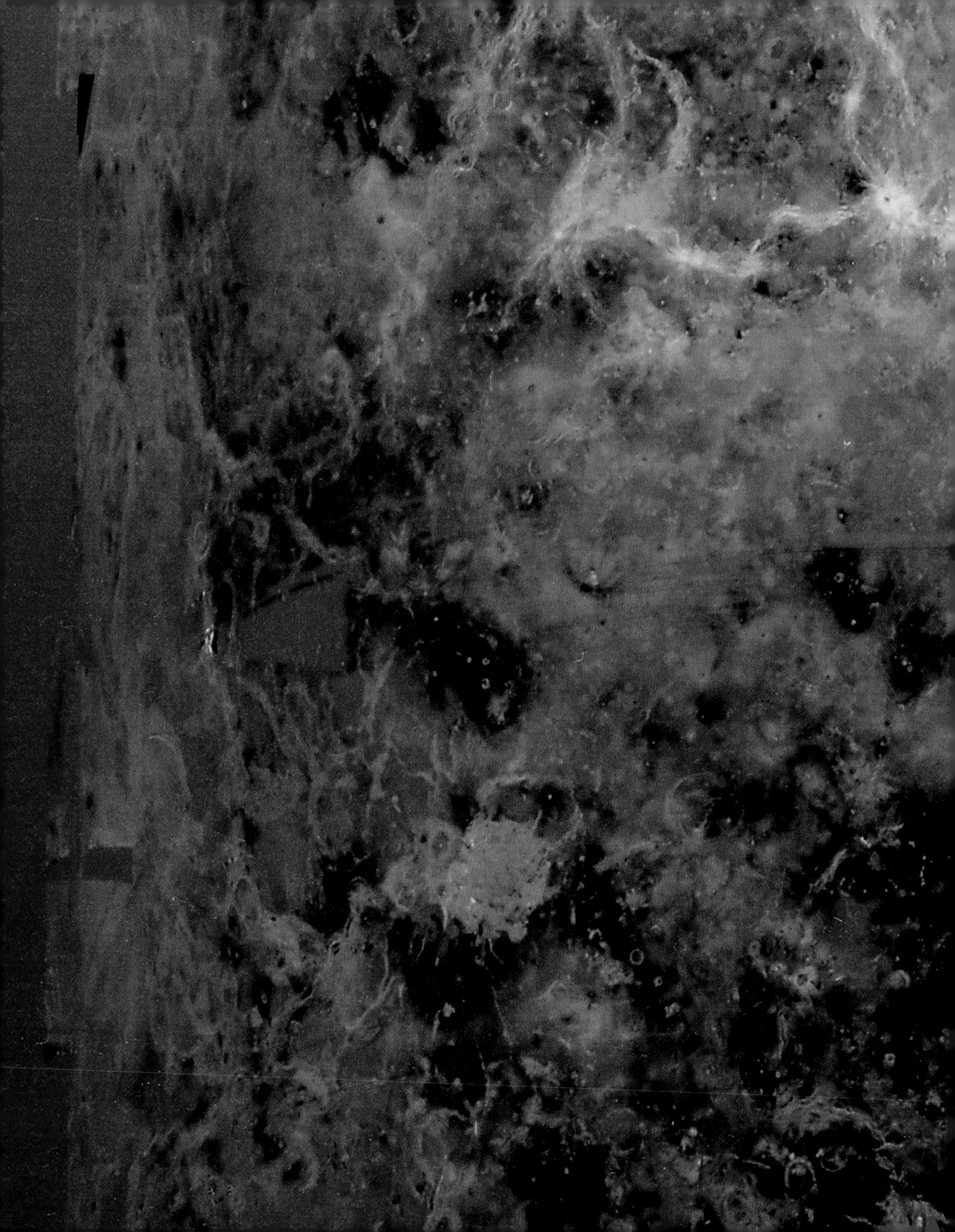

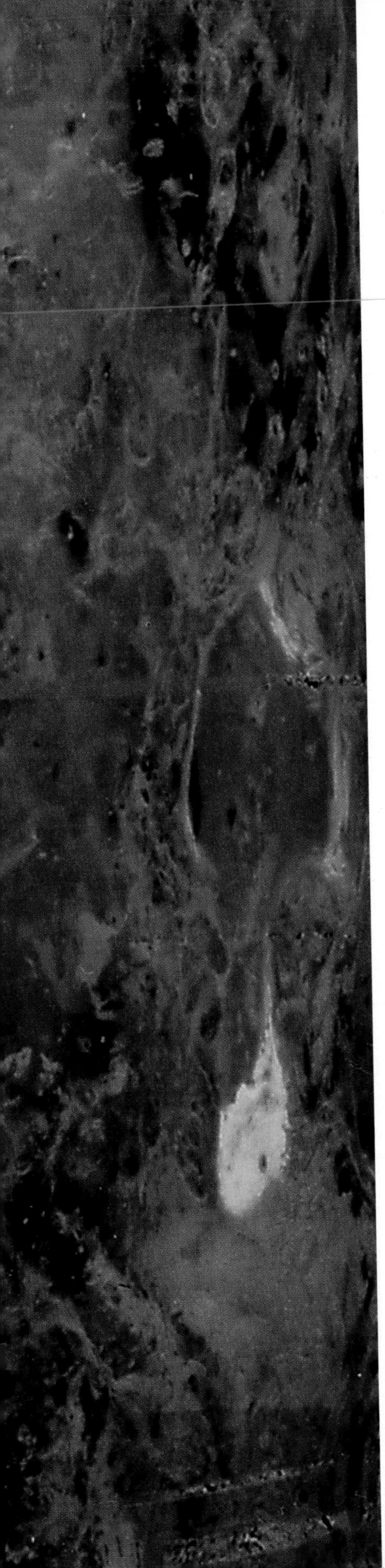

Using Scientific Explanations

This opening photograph is a color-enhanced composite image of the surface of Venus. These domelike hills may have formed due to the horizontal flow of lava. The image is assembled by a computer from data the *Magellan* spacecraft relayed back to the Earth. How would you describe the surface of Venus? Do you see any evidence that plate tectonics has occurred on Venus? What would you look for to find such evidence?

explore / explain

Reading: Scientific Explanations for Experts

explain

Reading: Explaining the Solar System

elaborate

Investigation: Plate Tectonics in Space

evaluate

Connections: What Would It Be Like If . . .

NASA

Reading:
Scientific Explanations for Experts

explore / explain

What have you learned about scientific explanations since Chapter 8? If someone were to ask you whether or not an explanation was really scientific, how would you decide? What would you look for?

Since the beginning of Chapter 8, you have gathered evidence to answer questions. At first the questions were very specific. You tried to discover the placement of the walls in a maze puzzle and to gather evidence for what was on the bottom of a cube. Next you used evidence to test your ideas about how an If–Then Box might work. As you tested ideas about the If–Then Box, you recorded your information and wrote if–then statements. Try to think of some if–then statements now. What examples can you give?

In Chapter 9, you looked at the patterns that people have observed in the occurrence of volcanoes and earthquakes. As you read the play, you learned that different people have observed patterns and proposed different explanations for volcanoes and earthquakes for thousands of years. Only recently have people tested their explanations by gathering evidence *after* they proposed their explanation.

People can gather more evidence about earthquakes and volcanoes today because they have better tools than they did in the past. As you saw in Chapter 9, maps are one tool that took a long time for people to develop. For hundreds of years, people could tell how far they were from the equator only by measuring how long daylight lasted on the longest day of the year. After many years of measurements, people finally could draw maps that showed the shapes of continents. Remember, in those times no one could observe the earth from space. When people were able to draw more accurate maps of the world, they could observe more patterns about the earth. When you looked at earthquake and volcano data plotted on a map of the world, you saw patterns to their occurrence.

The fact that volcanoes and earthquakes occur most often in a linear pattern at certain locations on the earth has intrigued many people. After many years of individuals asking questions and proposing explanations for this pattern, scientists combined their ideas into a theory. They called it the theory of plate tectonics.

Scientists proposed the theory of plate tectonics in the late 1960s. Since then many scientific explanations have changed. Currently **plate tectonics** is the most accepted theory that explains why earthquakes and volcanoes occur where they do: Giant plates of rock float on the earth's surface, and beneath them lies another layer of solid mantle. Within this mantle are pockets of hot molten rock. Where these plates meet, earthquakes occur. And along these plates where there are trenches, volcanoes occur.

▲ **FIGURE 11.1**
Advances in technology, such as this satellite in space, have helped mapmakers create more accurate maps.

You might now know more of the specific facts about plate tectonics, but what is the purpose behind all of these activities? If you had chosen to memorize the locations of all the plate boundaries, you would have some good information, but you wouldn't have the whole story. If you really have learned the material in this unit, you will know how to recognize and propose a scientific explanation. If you can recognize and propose scientific explanations, you have learned how to analyze information, and that is a very important skill.

explain

Reading:
Explaining the Solar System

The theory of plate tectonics is only one of many theories that scientists have proposed about the earth and our solar system. For over a thousand years, scientists have developed theories to explain many other aspects of our solar system including how it came to be.

Our **solar system** is part of a galaxy known as the Milky Way. By studying rocks from the earth and asteroids from space, scientists have been able to estimate that our solar system is about 4.6 billion years old. The evidence that scientists have collected about how matter and energy behave in different environments suggests that our solar system may have originated when a dying star exploded and formed a huge cloud of gas and dust. This cloud of material rotated faster and faster, and eventually most of the dust and gas collapsed into a spinning disk. The force of gravity may have pulled so much material toward the center that the pressure and heat caused a nuclear fire. As a result, this spinning disk—our sun—began to shine. Other material surrounding the sun began to form into other clumps of solids and gases, and these became the planets. Slowly the planets began to cool. In general the farther away the planets were from the sun, the faster they cooled; the small planets tended to cool faster than the large ones.

The sun, then, is the center of our solar system and its only star. The sun contains 99 percent of all the mass in our solar system. In addition to the sun, there are asteroids, meteoroids, comets, and nine planets that we know of.

The nine planets revolve around the sun as shown in Figure 11.2. Mercury, Venus, Earth, and Mars are closest to the sun and are often referred to as the inner planets. Each of these inner planets has a rocky exterior and scientists think each has a metal core. The outer planets are Jupiter, Saturn, Uranus, Neptune, and Pluto. All of these outer planets except Pluto are made of gas. These gaseous planets are encircled by rings of dust and ice. Scientists think that Pluto is made of ice.

All the planets orbit in the same direction around the sun, but the closer they are, the faster they revolve. Most of the planets move in almost the same plane except Pluto and Mercury. Each planet also rotates, or spins on its own axis. All of the planets except Mercury and Venus have one or more moons that revolve around it.

The outer planets are separated from the inner planets by a sea of asteroids. **Asteroids** are rock and metal

▲ **FIGURE 11.2**

Our solar system includes nine planets that orbit the sun. The inner and outer planets are separated by an asteroid belt.

NASA

► **FIGURE 11.3**

Saturn is one of the outer planets, and it is made of gas.

objects that are usually less than one kilometer in diameter. As they orbit, sometimes they collide with one another and small chunks—called meteoroids—break off. **Comets** also orbit the sun. They begin as a collection of frozen gas and dust. Scientists think that many comets originated at the time the solar system was forming. As a comet approaches the sun in its orbit, the heat from the sun vaporizes some of the ice and creates a cloud of gas and dust. This cloud of dust forms what we see as the tail, which streams away from the sun as the comet orbits. Some tails may be more than a million kilometers long.

Stop & Think

1. In what ways are the planets of our solar system the same and in what ways are they different?
2. If the solar system formed in the way scientists now explain it, how does that help us explain these similarities and differences?

▶ FIGURE 11.4
In 1997 the orbit of the comet Hale-Bopp came near enough for observers on Earth to watch it for several months.

elaborate

Investigation:
Plate Tectonics in Space

The managers of a new company called Tectonics Research have asked you to work for them. They have planned a trip to the earth's moon and several of the earth's neighboring planets and their moons. The head of this company is convinced that if the geologists knew more about plate tectonics on other planets, they could do a better job of predicting earthquakes on earth. They want you to join them on their journey. They are not certain whether plate tectonics occurs on other planets and moons. They want you to help them decide which planet or moon would be the best place or places to study more about plate tectonics.

Working Cooperatively

In this investigation, you will work alone.

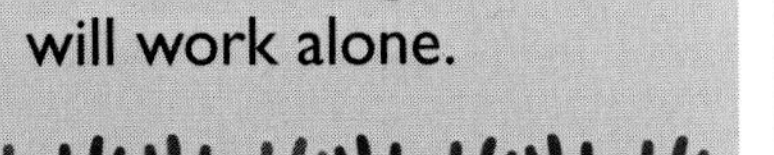

Materials for Each Student:

- ▶ 1 copy of the Evidence Chart

Process and Procedure

1. Participate in your class review of if–then statements.

   You will use if–then statements to test whether or not plate movements are occurring at the places you visit.

   "*If* plate tectonics is occurring, *then* I will expect to see mountain ranges in long linear patterns."

2. Think about the patterns you saw on maps of the world in Chapter 10. Then complete the following if–then statements for
   - earthquakes,
   - volcanoes, and
   - solid rock.

   For a and b in particular, think about the patterns you saw for earthquakes and volcanoes.

   a. If plate tectonics is occurring, then *fill in with a statement about earthquakes.*

   b. If plate tectonics is occurring, then *fill in with a statement about volcanoes.*

   c. If plate tectonics is occurring, then *fill in with a statement about solid rock.*

3. During your journey, test your if–then statements. Write down all the information you have on the evidence chart your teacher will hand out.
4. Read through the following example.

   The spaceship has landed on the earth's moon. You have your protective spacesuit on, and you step out. You find a cold environment. You are walking in a flat and dusty crater with a few mountains around the edge of the crater. The rocks are volcanic. Your captain tells you that no one knows of any earthquakes here during the past 25 years of exploration.
5. This is your evidence. What will you conclude? We have filled in one possible example for you (Figure 11.5).
6. Read the description of Stop 1.
7. Fill in your data table.

   There will be specific evidence for you to test, but any conclusion you can justify will be considered correct.

   Stop 1

   You land on a moon of Jupiter. This moon is called Io. When you climb out of the ship, you step onto a surface of bright yellow sulfur that appears to be from a volcano. You also can tell that this moon is extremely warm. Soon after you get out and begin to look around, you see a volcano in the distance beginning to erupt. As you run back to the spaceship, you feel the ground shaking beneath your feet. Once you are inside, the ship takes off immediately. You ask the captain to orbit this moon. From above, you see many volcanic mountains all over the moon, and many of them have very obvious pools of lava spilling out. You cannot see whether there is any pattern to where they occur, and although you see mountains, you see no linear patterns.
8. Read the descriptions of Stops 2 and 3.
9. Fill in your data table for Stop 2 and then Stop 3.

   Stop 2

   This time you decide to have the captain orbit the planet before you land. Below you is the planet Mars. You see tall cones of volcanic mountains, but you do not see any in lines. None of the volcanoes appear to be erupting. Even looking straight down into what appear to be volcanic cones, you do not see any lava. When you ask about quakes, the captain tells you that no quakes or volcanic eruptions have been recorded in recent history.

NAME: ____________________

EVIDENCE CHART

Stop	Results of first if-then (earthquakes)	Results of second if-then (volcanoes)	Results of third if-then (solid rock)
Example: Earth's moon	No known earthquakes	Saw volcanic mountains, but not in a line	Saw volcanic rocks
Stop 1 Io			
Stop 2 Mars			
Stop 3 Venus			

	Conclusions
Example: Earth's moon	We saw volcanic rocks, but most of the evidence does not indicate that plate tectonics is occurring today.
Stop 1 Io	
Stop 2 Mars	
Stop 3 Venus	

▲ **Figure 11.5**

This example shows how you might fill in the Evidence Chart after a visit to the earth's moon.

▲ **FIGURE 11.6** NASA

This NASA photograph shows the planet Jupiter, the planet in our solar system with the most mass. It has 16 moons; Io is one of them.

When the spaceship lands, you look out onto a red and dusty planet. It is extremely cold. You see that the mountains you observed from space are very tall, and some probably are bigger than any on Earth. The rock is volcanic, and you decide to look once more for lava flows from the volcanoes. Even after a long walk and several different stops on the planet, you don't find any molten lava.

Stop 3

As the spaceship approaches the planet Venus, it travels through thick layers of clouds. Even though you have planned to make observations from just above the planet, you cannot see very clearly. Then the spaceship emerges below the clouds, and you see many volcanoes in long rows, but all are quiet. After a careful approach, the spaceship finally lands. You can see mountainous rocks in the distance, and the surface appears fairly smooth but solid, as though it had been resurfaced. The captain notes a rise in temperature and recommends that the spaceship take off again.

▶ **FIGURE 11.7**

Like Earth, Venus is a planet that appears blue from space. Venus, however, has temperatures that are much hotter than those on Earth, and Venus has no moon.

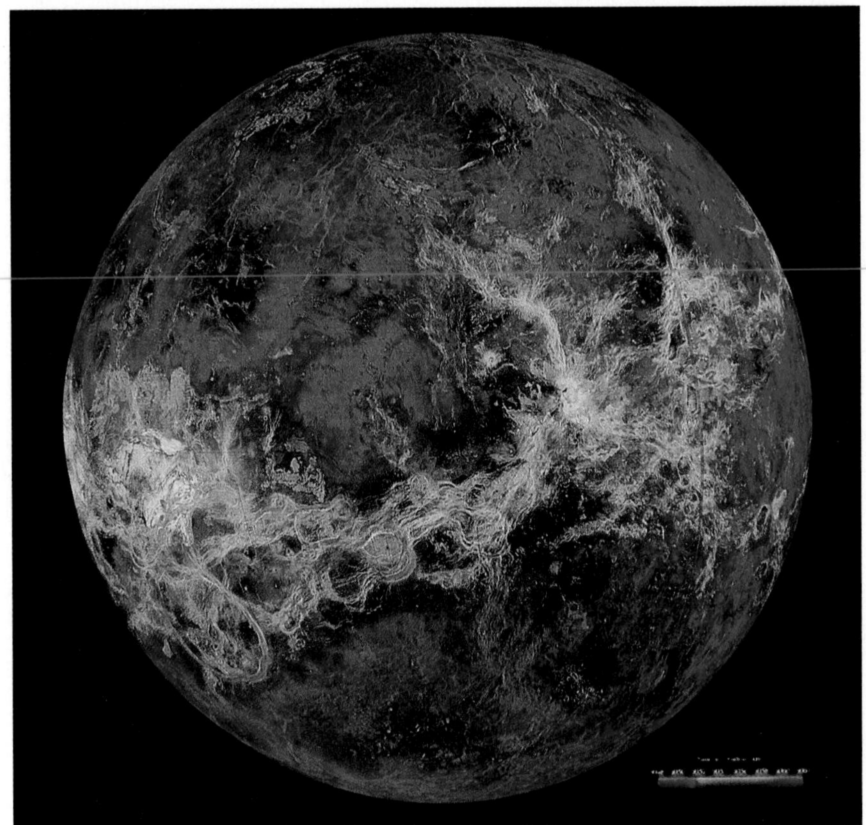

NASA

Wrap Up

1. Of the three locations you visited, which one or ones would be most suitable for studying plate tectonics?
2. For each place that you visited, explain why you think plate movement
   a. is or is not occurring now.
   b. has or has not occurred in the past.

evaluate

Connections:
What Would It Be Like If . . .

The theory of plate tectonics provides a strong scientific explanation for volcanoes, earthquakes, and mountains in part because it allows us to make predictions. If we know the pattern and can explain it scientifically, we can make more accurate predictions.

Use what you have learned about plate tectonics to describe and explain two possible, but distinctly

SIDELIGHT *on Nature*

A Martian Detective Story

Have you ever looked up into the night sky and wondered whether Earth is the only inhabited planet in the universe? For many decades, visitations from "Martians" or aliens from other galaxies have been the subjects of science fiction books, movies, and television shows. Interest in the possibility of extraterrestrial life, however, does not take place only in make believe worlds. The possibility that extraterrestrial life exists fascinates some scientists.

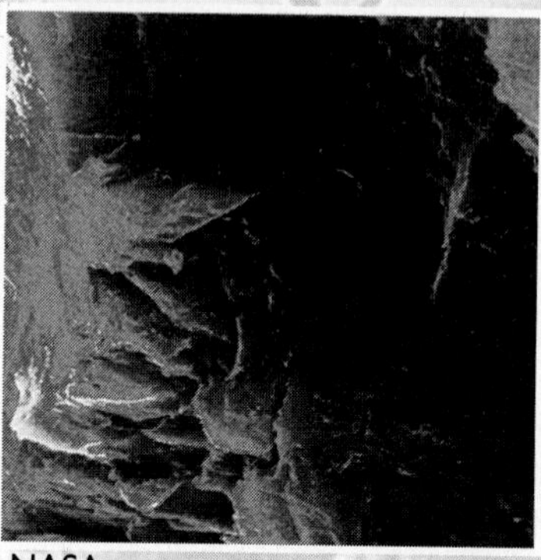
NASA

In August of 1996, a combined team of scientists from the National Aeronautics and Space Administration (NASA) and Stanford University, announced that they had found evidence to suggest that primitive life may have existed on Mars more than 3.6 billion years ago. Scientists have discovered much evidence to support their theory that bacterial life may have existed on Mars. The many steps on the road to their conclusion tell an intriguing Martian detective story.

During a National Science Foundation expedition in 1984, a researcher found a meteorite in Allan Hills ice field, Antarctica. The meteorite, now called ALH84001, is the oldest of only twelve meteorites identified. ALH84001 matches the Martian chemistry measured by the Viking spacecraft that landed on Mars in 1976. The meteorite is an igneous rock, which is a type of rock that forms when magma from a volcano has cooled. Scientists think that this rock crystallized from magma below the surface of Mars about 4.5 billion years ago. Scientists studying ALH84001 think that this meteorite provides evidence for the possibility of primitive life on Mars.

Why did it take scientists more than a decade after finding ALH84001 to announce the discovery of this evidence? The scientists from NASA and Stanford University have used very recent technological advances in high-resolution scanning electron microscopes and laser mass spectrometers to help with their findings. The photo in this sidelight was generated by an electron microscope scan. The photo shows a portion of

different, futures for the planet earth. Work alone to think about and write two descriptions and explanations of the earth as it might appear 500 million years from now.

1. Future One. In this scenario, imagine that plate tectonics continues on the earth for the next 500 million years.

the meteorite's surface. A few years ago, the technology to detect the minute features on the meteorite did not exist. With the use of this new technology, scientists can now see what they think are bacteria fossils on the surface of the meteorite. These fossils may be part of the history of life on Mars. The largest of the possible fossils are less than one-hundredth the diameter of a human hair! Imagine one thousand of these tiny fossils laid end to end would fill the space of the period at the end of this sentence.

Dr. David McKay, a planetary scientist who was a leader in the investigation said, "There is not any one finding that leads us to believe that this is evidence of past life on Mars. Rather it is a combination of many things that we have found." For example they found carbonate globules on the meteorite similar to those formed by bacteria on Earth. They also found that there are minerals with a shape and chemistry similar to bacterial products on the rock. An equally important piece of evidence is the presence of common organic molecules called PAHs. When microorganisms die, their organic molecules frequently break down into PAHs. The scientists used this evidence to explain and support their theory.

There are many flaws, however, in the scientists' theory. For instance, some of the evidence could have come from a nonliving origin. PAHs, for example, can be found in car exhaust. Also the fossils may be too small to be actual fossils. Although the scientists know that their theory is not airtight, they observed that all the evidence was clustered in the same area of the meteorite. This is a clue that a living organism may have left the evidence.

This team of scientists knows it has a long way to go before they have enough evidence for a strong theory. All of the evidence the scientists discovered is what we call indirect evidence. The scientists had to use evidence and inference as they developed their theory about life on Mars.

On 4 July 1997, the spacecraft Pathfinder landed on Mars. NASA scientists launched Pathfinder in December 1996. It took seven months to reach Mars. These scientists also built a rover, the size of a skateboard, to put inside the spacecraft. Upon landing on Mars, the rover, called Sojourner, exited Pathfinder. Sojourner moved slowly over the Martian landscape, surveyed its surroundings, and transmitted images back to scientists on Earth. Sojourner has helped scientists gather more direct evidence about Mars and its history.

2. Future Two. In this scenario, imagine that plate tectonics stops on the earth one million years from now.

Remember to use what you have learned about plate tectonics and about patterns to help you make these predictions and provide explanations for them.

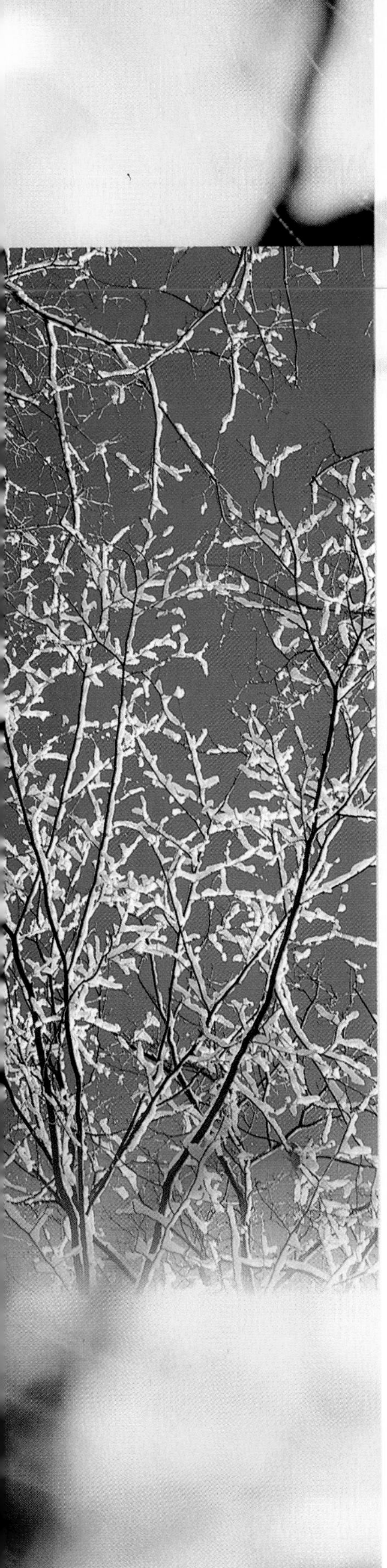

UNIT 3

Responding to Patterns of Change

By now you may feel that you have a fairly good understanding of what causes earthquakes and volcanoes, and of the patterns involved. Sometimes responding to changes in the weather is easy because of weather patterns that are familiar to us. At other times, responding to patterns of change in the weather is more difficult. There are other natural events that have patterns that people must respond to. What can people do when they know that certain events may occur? In other words, how can knowing about patterns help better prepare us to respond?

Cooperative Learning Overview

The better you are at working in a team, the better able you are to use challenging skills. Think about it. You started by trying to express your ideas and listen politely. In the next unit, you practiced respect for the ideas that others were expressing. Now that you can express your ideas aloud and can respect the ideas of others, you can learn to encourage others to share their ideas. This will allow you to hear many different opinions. You also can encourage people who do not want to help to be part of the team. You really are becoming a team player!

Now that you have come this far in cooperative learning, you probably have definite opinions about it. Some of you might have found that working cooperatively is not limited to your science classroom. You might not work in teams in other classes, but think of group situations in which you cooperate. The characters have introduced you to your Unit 3 skill of encouraging others to participate. Before you begin Chapter 12, be sure that you have created a T-chart for this skill. Also share your feelings about cooperative learning with your new teammates. Be sure to express both the positive and negative aspects of cooperative learning that you have discovered.

You again will have social skills for each activity. Remember to use your unit skill in each cooperative activity as well as the activity skill. Also try to remember and keep using the social skills you worked on in past units. Finally review the role descriptions with your new teammates so that together you can answer any questions you might have about the duties of each role.

Hmm... encourage others to participate... how do you do that without saying, "Why don't you participate?" This seems like a hard skill.
Well, we already know how to show respect for other's ideas. All we have to do is add something extra, like "You usually have good ideas–what do you think about this?"
We're so used to working in pairs. Now that we're working in threes, someone might feel like a third wheel. We could say things like, "While I'm doing this, will you do that and you do that?" so that no one feels left out.

What Causes Weather Patterns?

Weather can be as calming as the soft sound of rain on the roof or as frightening as the rising flood waters from a hurricane. As you know, weather events can be as dramatic as earthquakes and volcanoes. People attempt to predict the weather because severe weather can cause hazardous situations. Weather forecasters warn people about these potential hazards so that they can take action to protect themselves and their belongings. For example, before a hurricane people will listen to a forecast, along with the warnings and recommendations, and then may evacuate the area.

People can make weather predictions because they have learned some of the factors that affect weather patterns. Can you explain how rain forms or how wind blows? By the end of this chapter, you should be able to do just that and to describe the patterns related to the occurrence of weather.

engage

Investigation: Water on the Move

explore

Investigation: Cooking Water
Investigation: Wind in a Box

explain

Connections: Thinking about Density in the Atmosphere
Reading: Changing Weather Patterns

explain / elaborate

Investigation: Winds above a Rotating Earth

elaborate

Connections: Picture This

evaluate

Connections: Science in Your Bathroom

engage

Investigation: Water on the Move

If you have ever been soaked in a rainstorm or even surprised by a thundershower in the desert, you know that water is a big part of the weather. Rain, snow, hail, and fog are all examples of water on the move. Even when you cannot see it or feel it, water is moving around you. What evidence can you find in this investigation that water is on the move?

Working Cooperatively

Work cooperatively in your new teams of three. Move your desks together or sit at a table. Use the roles of Manager, Tracker, and Communicator. Practice the social skill *Use your teammates' names.*

Materials for Each Team of Three:

- 1 empty can, soup size
- water, room temperature (½ to ⅔ of a can)
- 3 ice cubes
- 1 stirring stick
- 1 paper towel

Process and Procedure

Part A—The Social Skill

1. Write your teammates' first and last names in your notebook.
2. Design a logo that uses all of the team members' first names.

   Notebook entry: All team members should have a copy of the logo in their notebook.

Part B—A Chilling Experience

1. Obtain the materials for Part B.
2. Fill the can about half-full of room-temperature water.
3. Observe how the can looks and feels on the outside.

   Notebook entry: Record your observations.
4. Add three ice cubes to the can.

   The Communicator should do this.
5. Stir the water and ice slowly.

   The Manager should do this. Do not hold the outside of the can while stirring.
6. Keep stirring for 3 minutes.

   The Tracker should keep track of time.

7. Look at the can and touch the outside.
   Notebook entry: Record these observations.
8. Empty the can and dry it off. Then return your materials.
   Check to be sure that the outside of the can is dry.
9. If you haven't looked closely at it yet, observe the glass containers that your teacher has set up.
   Notebook entry: Record your observations. Make sure that your observations account for the differences between the setups.

Wrap Up

Discuss the following questions with your teammates. Record your own answers in your notebook. Each of you should be prepared to explain your answers if the teacher calls on you during a class discussion.

1. Explain what you think happened to the outside of your can.
2. How might you test the explanation you provided in Question 1?
3. What similarities did you see between what happened with your can of icy water and what happened in the demonstration?
4. Write a two-line rhyme that describes how well you used each other's names as you worked. Record this two-line rhyme in your notebook alongside the logo that you created in Part A.

explore

Investigation: Cooking Water

From your everyday experiences, you are familiar with the different states that water can be in—a solid, a liquid, and a gas—also known as ice, water, and vapor. What are the distinctions between these states? What type of energy is involved as water changes from one state to another? With water, what does this mean for the weather conditions? In this investigation, you will begin to discover some of the answers.

Working Cooperatively

Work cooperatively in your teams of three. You will need a Manager, a Tracker, and a Communicator. Monitor your success with the unit skill *Encourage others to participate.*

Materials for Each Team of Three:

- a set of 3 balloons
- 4 ice cubes
- heat source (small hot plate or Bunsen burner)
- small wooden spoon
- large metal spoon
- small pan or heat-resistant beaker
- clock or stopwatch
- 3 pairs of goggles

Process and Procedure

Part A—Exploring States of Water

1. Collect the materials that your team will need for this investigation.
2. Copy the data table in Figure 12.1 in your notebook so that you can record your team's data.
3. Examine the three balloons carefully. Each balloon contains water in a different state. Record the state of water in each balloon along with your observations.

   How are the balloons similar and how are they different? Use the ruler to gently manipulate the balloons as you explore the similarities and differences. Look especially at shape, feel, and ease of movement.

Part B—Exploring Changes in States of Water

The heat source and the water will be very hot and could cause burns. Remember to wear your goggles.

	Data Table for Cooking Water	
PART A		
	State of Water Inside Balloon	Observations
Balloon 1		
Balloon 2		
Balloon 3		
PART B		
Phase	Total Time in Seconds	Number of Seconds For each phase (relative amount of energy)
Ice cubes melt completely		
Water begins to boil		
Water evaporates completley		
Observations of large, metal spoon (Step 5)		

▲ **FIGURE 12.1**

Copy this data table into your notebook so that you can record your observations and results.

Water spills may cause slippery floors.

1. Turn on the heat source as your teacher indicates and place the small pan on it.

   The Manager should make certain that the heat source remains at the same setting throughout the experiment.

2. After about one minute, place four ice cubes in a small heat-resistant container.

3. Use the clock or stopwatch to begin timing how long it takes for the ice to completely melt.

   The Manager should stir the ice cubes and be in charge of the heat source. The Tracker should keep track of the time. The Communicator should record the time in his or her data table.

4. Continue timing until the water begins to boil.

   The Manager should continue stirring. The Tracker should not start timing over again, but should continue timing. The Communicator should record the time in his or her data table.

5. Continue timing until the water has evaporated completely. During this time, take the large, metal spoon and hold it over the edge of the pan. Observe what happens.

   The Team Members should continue their roles. Record your observations.

6. Turn off the heat source and let the materials cool before putting them away as your teacher instructs.
7. Study the times that you have recorded in your data table and determine the number of seconds that it took for each of the following:
   - for the ice to melt completely,
   - for the water to begin to boil, and
   - for the water to evaporate completely.

   Record these numbers in your data table. All team members should copy all the data into their own data tables.

Wrap Up

Because you tried to keep the temperature of the heat source constant, you can assume that the amount of heat energy from the heat source remained constant and that the heat energy that was transferred to the pan and then to the water can be stated in terms of the time interval. That is, the heat energy required for each step of the process is equal to the energy per second times the number of seconds each process took. So the number of seconds also tells us about the amount of energy. (Because you are making a comparison, you don't need to know the specific units of energy.)

1. Did it take more energy to melt the ice or for the water to begin to boil?
2. Which step took the most energy? Did this step take a little more energy, or a lot more energy compared with the other steps?
3. Think about the process of evaporation that you just observed in terms of the movement of water on the earth. Also think about what you know about the conservation of energy. Now where is the energy that was used to melt the ice and evaporate the water?

4. Think about the observations that you made in Step 5 (refer to your notebook if you need to). After the water evaporated and then condensed on the spoon, what happened to that energy?
5. How can you use your responses to Questions 2–4 to more accurately describe certain weather patterns?
6. How does this investigation help you understand the energy that is stored and released during storms, for example?

explore

Investigation: Wind in a Box

After one particularly long, hot day at school, Marie arrived home feeling exhausted and thirsty. She went to the refrigerator to find something cool to drink. When she opened the refrigerator door, she noticed a particular phenomenon. What do you think happened? In this investigation, you will have the opportunity to investigate this and other similar patterns.

Working Cooperatively

Work cooperatively in your teams of three. Use the roles of Manager and Communicator. As you work, concentrate on the skill *Treat others politely.*

Materials for the Entire Class:

- 1 box of safety matches
- 1 large bucket of water
- 1 fire extinguisher

Materials for Each Team of Three:

- 1 convection box with candle
- 6 wooden splints
- 3 pairs of goggles

Process and Procedure

Part A—The Social Skill

1. Discuss what it means to be polite when doing team work.
2. Discuss the strategies your previous teams used when practicing this skill.

   Share your ideas about what seemed to work and what didn't work.

3. Record three ways you and your teammates can be polite to each other.

Part B—The Box

1. Prepare your work space for the safe use of the convection boxes.

Safety procedures include moving all papers and extra notebooks to the side of the classroom, tying back long hair, wearing goggles, and moving slowly while the boxes are in use. NEVER LEAVE THE BOX UNATTENDED.

2. Stand the box on its side, with the tubes up in the air. Take off the lid of the box.

   This is the Tracker's job.

3. Carefully light the candle and place it directly under one of the tubes (see Figure 12.2).

   This is the Manager's job. Be careful not to place the candle too near the back or sides of the box.

4. Put the lid on the box.

5. Carefully light a wooden splint and then blow it out. Lower the smoking splint 1 or 2 cm into the tube above the candle.

   This is the Communicator's job.

A smoking splint can cause burns and fires because it is very hot. Be careful not to touch yourself, a teammate, or the box with the smoking part of the splint.

6. Observe what happens to the smoke.

7. Lower the smoking splint 1 or 2 cm into the other tube and observe what happens.

   Take turns doing this. Notebook entry: Record your observations.

8. Extinguish the candle.

   This is the Tracker's job.

9. Return the materials.

▼ **FIGURE 12.2**

Before you light the candle that goes in the convection box, be certain that you've taken all the precautions you can to avoid fire hazards.

Wrap Up

On the basis of your experience with a convection box, discuss the following questions as a team. Record your own answers in your notebook. Be sure each of you can justify your answers in a class discussion.

1. How did the smoke help you observe what the air was doing?
2. If you were outside, what would you call the moving air?
3. If you could stand inside the convection box, where would you be standing if you felt air sinking down on you?
4. Where would you have to stand inside the box if you wanted to feel air rising upward?
5. Would you find rising air above a warm area of the earth's surface or above a cool area?
6. Rate your team on politeness: good, fair, or poor. If you rated yourself *fair* or *poor,* agree on one way you could improve your rating.

explain

Connections:

Thinking about Density in the Atmosphere

As you know, our atmosphere is made up of gases. These gases include mostly nitrogen, along with oxygen, carbon dioxide, water vapor, and a few others. The water vapor in the atmosphere gives us some interesting weather. Believe it or not, the gas in our atmosphere has weight. Each square inch column of air in our atmosphere weighs about 15 pounds. When you take this weight and divide it by the area of the column, you get a **pressure**—that is, 15 pounds per square inch.

Remember from the investigation Cooking Water that the solid, liquid, and gas in the balloons each behaved somewhat differently. Gases can be compressed, but solids and liquids cannot. If we exert a pressure on a gas, its particles are forced closer together. Their mass has not changed, but now they occupy less volume. When this happens, the density of the gas increases.

Now for a thought experiment. (You might want to do this at home later, or your teacher may have you do this in class.) Think about some large compressible objects (Let's use pillows. They have foam or feathers and a lot of air in them). Now imagine making a very high stack of them. The pillows at the bottom carry the weight of all of those on top. We can say that the pressure is greater at the bottom, and so the pillows get compressed. The density of pillows at the bottom, then, is also greater than at the top. The same thing happens in our atmosphere. The density of the air at the earth's surface (at the bottom of a column of air) is about three times greater than it is five miles up.

Another interesting thing about gas is that when you compress it, its temperature will increase. If that is the case, do you think the temperature of the air is warmer at sea level or 5000 feet up? Have you ever experienced this change in temperature? Share your experiences with your classmates.

explain

Reading:
Changing Weather Patterns

If you have ever lived in a place where the temperatures can plummet from comfortably warm to freezing cold in just a few hours, you know how drastic weather changes can be. If you ever have been soaked in a rainstorm, trapped in a snowstorm, or sunburned by overexposure to the sun, you have experienced the results of weather patterns. To understand why certain weather patterns exist, think about some of the things you have experienced in this chapter.

Stop & Think

1. In your experiences during this chapter, where have you seen water?
2. Explain how the water got to those places.

The air around you has water in it, water that you cannot see under normal circumstances. Water in the air is present in microscopic particles. If you live where it is very humid during the summer, you probably have experienced the feeling of water in the air. If you live in a dry area, you may have never detected the water that is in the air and all around you. When the tiny water particles in the air come in contact with something cool, they clump together to form drops of water. This process is called **condensation.**

Stop & Think

3. What happens to the water in a glass when you leave the glass out for a week or more?

When tiny water particles move into the air, the process is called **evaporation.** People often think that when water evaporates, it disappears, but, in fact, the small particles of water are now in the air.

The process of water evaporating and then condensing is happening all the time in nature. This is because heat from the sun is constantly warming the earth's surface. When the sun warms the water in lakes, rivers, oceans, and even puddles, the water gradually evaporates. As the moist air rises away from the warm surface of the earth, the air cools. When the air becomes cool enough, water in it condenses into tiny water droplets and forms clouds (see Figure 12.3).

When a lot of water condenses, the droplets in the clouds become larger and heavier so that they eventually fall as rain.

Stop & Think

4. Think back to the fish bowl demonstration. How could you keep the cycle going? See Figure 12.4 if you need a reminder.

The pattern of water movement on earth is called the **water cycle.** Water is constantly on the move. In some places it is going into the air, or evaporating, and in other places it is coming out of the air, or condensing.

▶ FIGURE 12.3
Because water is always losing heat energy (and condensing) or gaining heat energy (and evaporating), water particles are constantly moving.

▶ FIGURE 12.4
When your teacher originally set up the fish bowl with the water in it, the sides of the fish bowl were dry. Where did the water droplets come from?

The movement of water is responsible for much of the weather. Remember that when rain or snow is falling, water is moving out of the air. In another place, where perhaps it is a sunny day, water is evaporating and moving into the air.

Stop & Think

5. Think about your explanations for why you saw water on the can and in the fish bowl. How might you revise those explanations now?
6. Look at the diagram in Figure 12.5. The teakettle is plugged in, and the glass plate is cold. Describe what will happen as the water in the teakettle continues to heat. You may draw and label a diagram in your notebook or write several sentences to explain what will happen.

But why does water move? The short answer is because of heat energy. The sun's energy warms the earth's surface—including the water on the surface. If the water is heated enough, it changes from a liquid (the way we usually think of it) to a vapor, or a gas. When water is a gas, its particles are farther apart. When it's a liquid, its particles are closer together. When water continues to lose heat energy, it changes from a liquid to a solid. In other words, it becomes ice.

The heat energy that warms the water on the surface of the earth also warms the air. This causes the air to move. This moving air is the wind you feel outside. Wind is one of the factors that contributes to weather patterns.

But how does heat energy cause wind? As the sun's energy reaches the earth's surface, the heat is absorbed unequally. This happens in part because the earth's surface is covered with land as well as water, and solid materials absorb heat differently from the way water

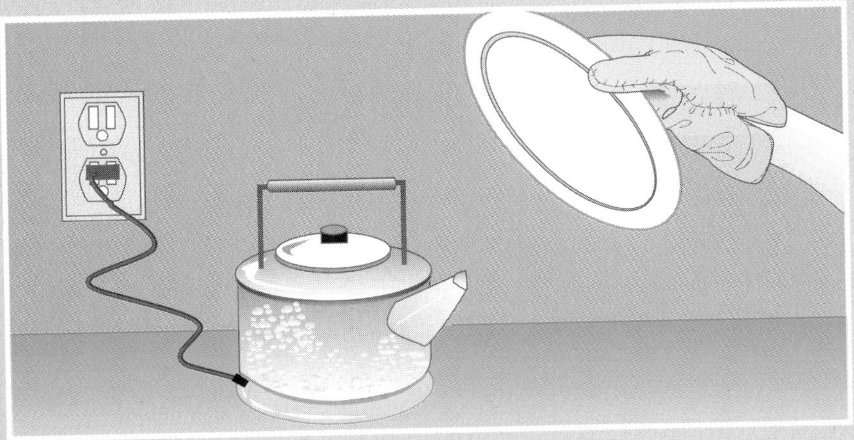

▶ **FIGURE 12.5**
The water in this teakettle is being heated. What will happen to the water?

does. The sun's rays also strike the earth more directly at the equator than they do at the poles. As a result, the air in some places is warmer than in others.

Stop & Think

7. Look at Figure 12.6. What parts of the convection box represent the following:
   - a warm place like the land at the equator?
   - a cool place that does not receive direct rays from the sun?
   - the wind?
8. Describe the patterns you see in Figure 12.6.

The type of circulation or movement shown in Figure 12.6 is a convection cell. When air moves in a convection cell, you can feel it. For example, when cold winds in the Northern Hemisphere rush from the north to the south, those winds are part of a convection cell. In fact one definition of wind is: air moving horizontally in a convection cell.

Stop & Think

9. If you have seen a hot air balloon like the one in Figure 12.7, you have seen an object floating in the air. How can this happen?

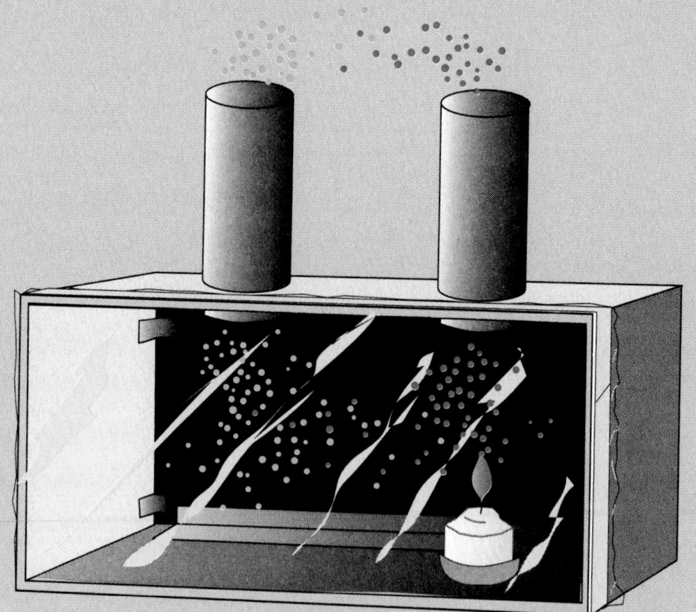

FIGURE 12.6
This diagram shows air particles in a convection box.

Stop & Think

10. Why do certain objects sink and other objects float?

▲ **FIGURE 12.7**
Why do you think hot air balloons are able to float?

Remember that density was the critical factor in the investigation, Will It Sink or Float, in Chapter 5. The molecules in warm air are farther apart because the extra heat energy makes them bounce around faster. The density of warm air is less than the density of cool air.

When we replace the cool air with warm air, which is less dense, we get an upward **buoyant force.** If this force is large enough to balance the weight of the balloon and all that it is carrying, the balloon will float. If the weight is larger than the buoyant force, then we have a problem. (Do you think you could get the air hot enough to escape into space?)

You have explored many factors that cause the weather patterns that we see on the earth. The principal source of the energy for these weather patterns is the sun, of course. Near the equator, the sun's rays strike the earth's surface at right angles. Near the poles, the sun's rays are more parallel to the earth's surface. Because of this difference, more heat develops over a square meter at the equator than over a square meter at the poles.

In the early 1700s, George Hadley, a British scientist, thought about this situation and reasoned that these conditions should generate a very large convection cell, with warm air rising at the equator and cold air at the surface of the earth moving from the poles toward the equator (see Figure 12.8). This simple global model seemed to account for the heat at the equator. The circulation

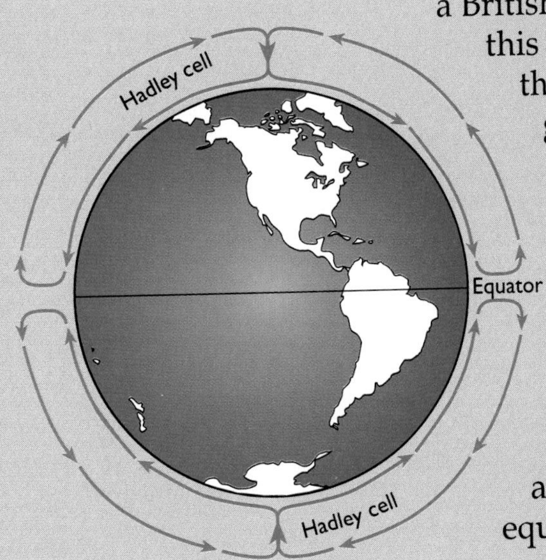

► **FIGURE 12.8**
Hadley was the scientist who proposed this model. He envisioned two convection cells that covered the earth like bowls.

pattern, then, would distribute this energy to the higher latitudes. However this model left many other questions unanswered.

The winds near the surface of the earth behave in complicated ways. For example there is friction with the earth's surface and the lifting of air over mountain ranges. The heating of the earth's surface differs over land and water. Also evaporation and condensation occur in many places at different times all over the earth. Because of these complexities, we expect temporary differences in atmospheric pressure to occur.

Finally there is an additional complexity in describing the motion of the atmosphere because it moves above a rotating earth. In the next investigation, you will come to understand that what you observe depends on your point of view.

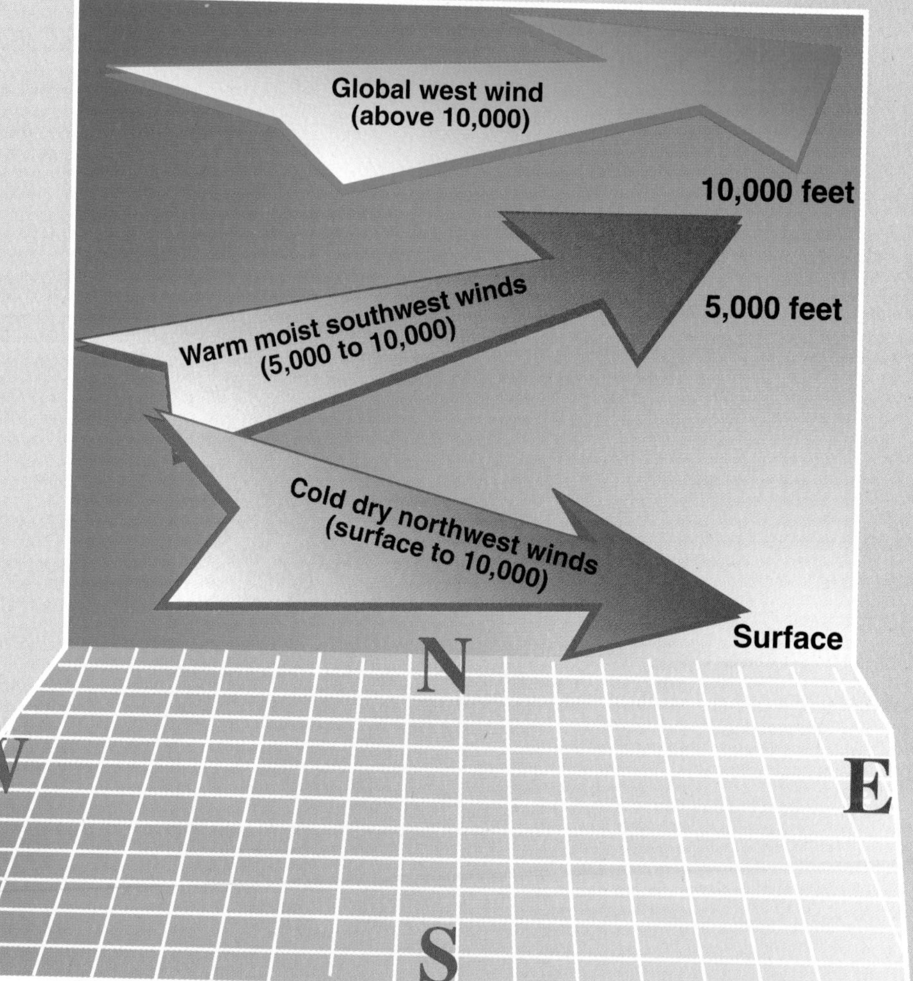

FIGURE 12.9

This diagram shows a low-level, or surface, wind blowing from the northwest, a mid-level wind blowing from the southwest, and a high-level (global) wind blowing from the west.

SIDELIGHT on Technology

Sailing in the Doldrums

Sailing ships once followed the prevailing winds across the globe to carry their cargo from one continent to another. But some places on the globe do not have prevailing winds.

Have you ever heard anyone say that he or she is "in the doldrums"? What did that person mean? Above the hot tropical regions of the world, the air warms and rises, but on the surface of the land and sea, only light breezes blow. These near-surface breezes often change direction and never blow strongly in any one direction. This area along the equator was dangerous for the great sailing ships of the past and was known as the "doldrums." There was so little wind that sailing ships often became stuck in one area for weeks.

Farther north and south of the equator lie two other regions that also were hazardous to sailing ships. In these subtropical areas, the air that has risen from the equator cools enough so that it sinks. This cool, dry air creates an area of fair weather. Most of the world's deserts are in these regions. Sailors called these belts of calm, high-pressure air the "horse latitudes." Some people say that this is because horses sometimes died of thirst while on these ships stuck in calm waters.

Because of the work of the early explorers, modern-day sailors have learned to avoid both the horse latitudes and the doldrums.

explain/elaborate

Investigation:
Winds above a Rotating Earth

You now have observed several patterns caused by moving air and water. In this investigation, you will see whether you can apply your understanding to a new pattern. You will try to answer the question, How does the earth's rotation affect the movement of the wind?

Materials for Each Team of Three:

- 1 square of corrugated cardboard, at least 25-by-25 cm
- 1 pen or pencil
- 1 sheet of paper, 8½-by-11 in.
- masking tape, 5 cm

▶ **FIGURE 12.10**
This is an aerial photograph of clouds over the earth. This photograph was taken from space.

NASA

Working Cooperatively

Work cooperatively in your teams of three. You will need a space beside your desks or table where each of you can stand and move freely. Use the roles of Manager, Communicator, and Tracker. As you work, use the strategies and ideas you developed for the social skill *Treat others politely.*

- 1 felt-tip pen
- 1 ruler, 30 cm (12 in.), or 1 piece of string, at least 30 cm long
- 1 pair of scissors

Process and Procedure

1. Obtain the materials.
2. Trim the paper to fit your piece of cardboard.
3. If there is no hole, poke a pencil through the center of the cardboard as shown.
   The cardboard should spin freely on the pencil. See Figure 12.11.
4. Tape the sheet of paper onto the cardboard.
   The pencil should stick through the paper so that the paper and cardboard can spin together as shown in Figure 12.11.
5. Spin the cardboard on the pencil.
   The Communicator should do this.

▶ **FIGURE 12.11**

This diagram shows the cardboard ready to spin on the pencil. The paper is on top of the cardboard, and the ruler is held horizontally above the cardboard.

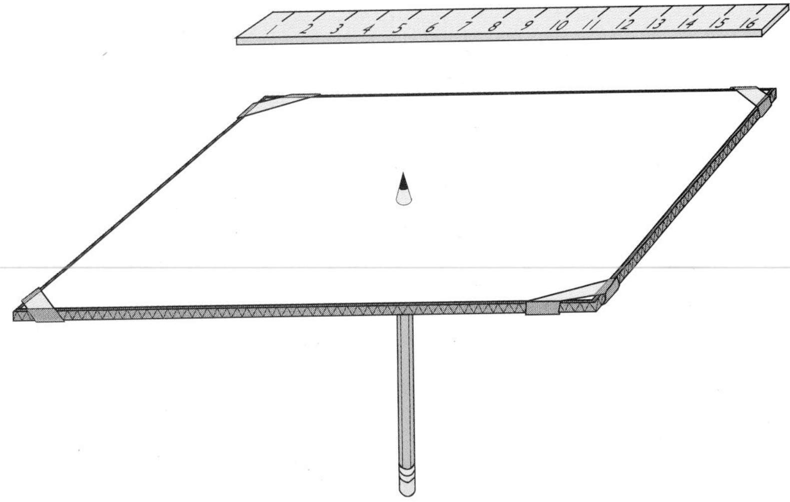

6. Hold a ruler 5 cm above the middle of the cardboard.

   The Manager should do this as in Figure 12.11 (do not move the ruler).
7. On the spinning cardboard, draw a line on the paper with a felt-tip pen while keeping the pen against the ruler.

   The Tracker should do this as shown in Figure 12.12.
8. Take turns switching jobs so that each teammate has a chance to draw a line across the paper.
9. Read the Sidelight on the Foucault pendulum and then the Background Information about the Coriolis Effect.

▶ **FIGURE 12.12**

As the cardboard is spinning, move the pen along the ruler.

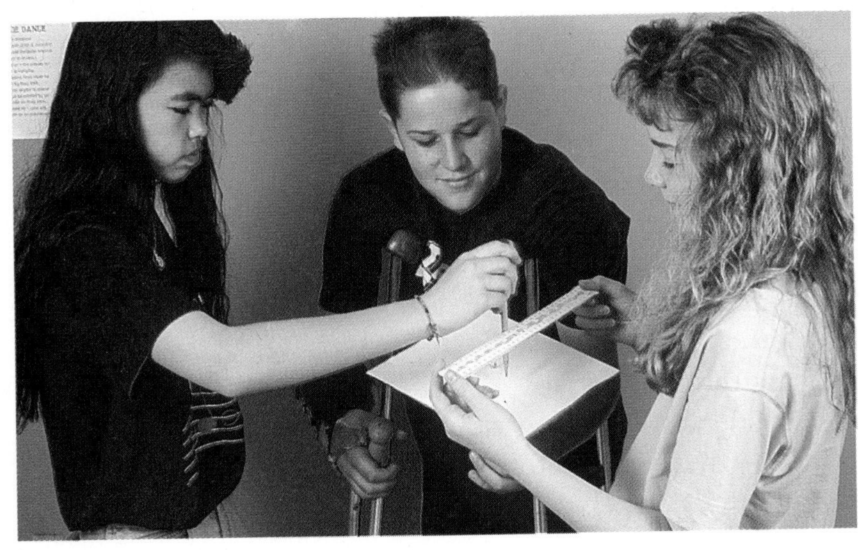

Background Information

The Coriolis Effect

After completing this investigation, you can now appreciate the difference in describing the motion of the atmosphere as you view it from a rotating earth than if the earth were not rotating. This difference is known as the **Coriolis Effect.** When we describe the winds from the perspective of our rotating surface, we must take into account the earth's rotation along with convection cells, friction, and differences in pressure.

The model shown in Figure 12.13 provides a global picture of the atmosphere's circulation. Calculations that scientists make with the model must take into account the large portion of energy that is transported by the water vapor, which has been produced by evaporation in the tropics. Scientists also would have to make modifications for specific, local situations. The temporary differences in pressure that arise and the evaporation-condensation cycle produce local weather systems that are well defined. In the midlatitudes, these local weather systems move along with the prevailing westerlies (winds from the west). In fact, scientists believe that the local weather systems we see every few days play an additional important role in redistributing the sun's energy.

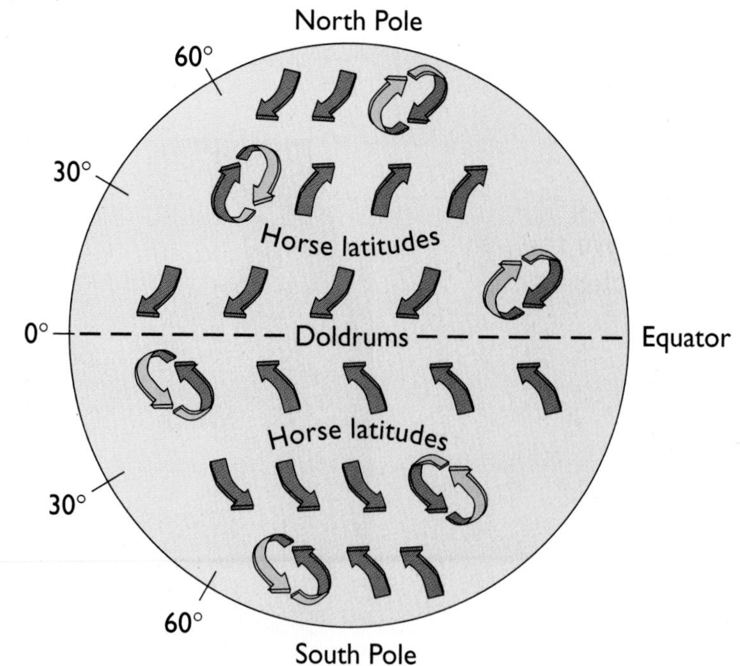

▶ FIGURE 12.13

This general circulation model improves upon the simple Hadley convection cell. This model has three convection cells and takes into account the earth's rotation. This model accounts for the trade winds at the low latitudes and the prevailing westerlies at the midlatitudes. The darker portion of the arrows indicate the near-surface winds, and the lighter portion of the arrows indicate the high-level winds.

As the ground is heated by the sun, scattered cumulus clouds grow and become heavy with water droplets. Soon scattered showers occur. Late in the afternoon, anvil cirrus clouds are visible high in the sky. They are called anvil cirrus because they are shaped like an anvil. This pattern, with the cirrus clouds on top and the cumulonimbus clouds on the bottom, is shaped like an anvil. Through convection, heavy cumulus clouds have formed and this

These scattered cumulus clouds form quickly in a moist air mass when the ground is heated by the sun.

A blunt wedge of cold air is rapidly approaching from the west. This cold, dry air is a cold front. The very high, thin, overcast cloud is an ice crystal cloud. The overall result is an anvil-shaped cloud.

pattern has been increased by a fast-moving wedge of cold air from the northwest. You can hear a distant rumble of thunder, and occasionally you can see lightning make brief connections between the leaning tower of dark clouds and the earth. Suddenly you are pelted with hailstones, and gusts of cold wind blow from beneath the fast-approaching, low roll of clouds. Soon there is a scattering of large, cold raindrops followed by a downpour. Puddles and small rivers of rainwater form. This storm continues for an hour or so with a grand display of nature's violence—lightning, thunder, gusty winds, and heavy rains.

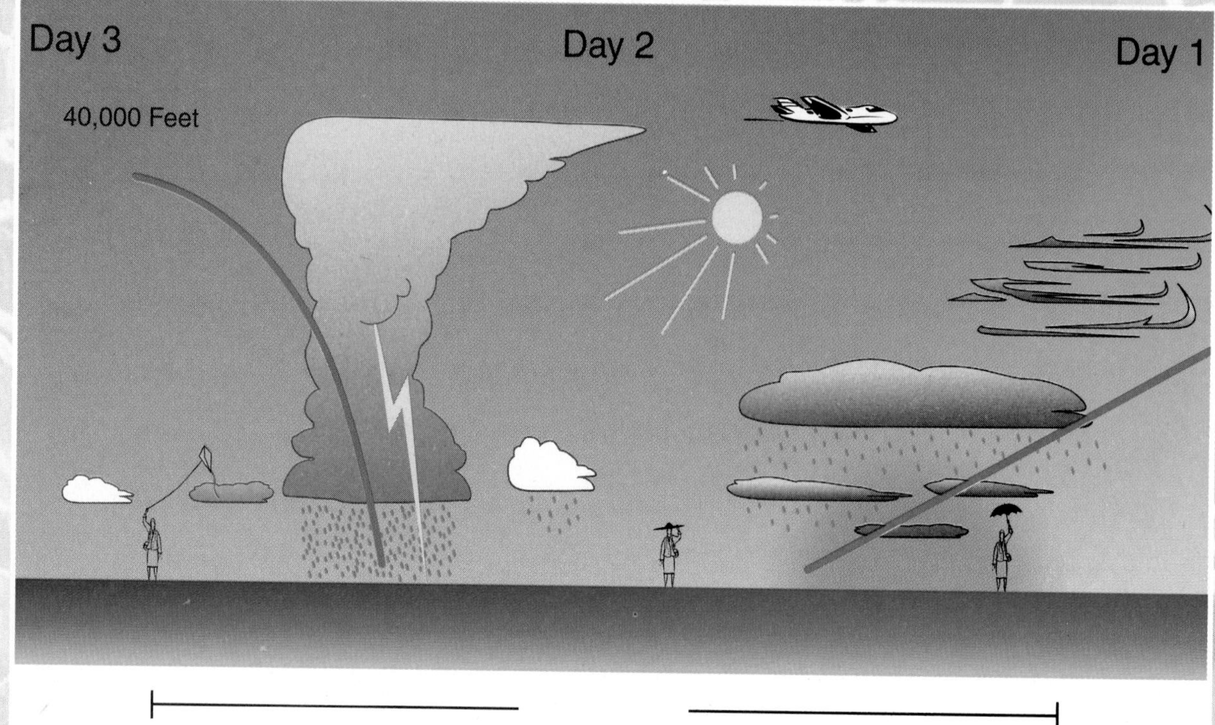

Day Three

By early the third morning, a brisk but dry wind from the northwest with stratocumulus clouds replaces the violent storm. The clouds chase the storm, which has moved off to the east. By the afternoon, a clear blue sky has reappeared. A lavender twilight tells you that the air is clear of dust and pollutants.

Day Four

The following dawn is clear. There is a gentle west wind. A few fair-weather cumulus clouds appear by the middle of the day. The bottoms of these clouds show a typical convective formation, but the tops are flat. This pattern indicates that the air mass is stable again. In a day or so, another weather system will arrive from the west.

evaluate

Connections:
Science in Your Bathroom

You have just studied some of the earth's weather patterns and explored some ways that air and water move in cycles. Can you apply your understanding to everyday phenomena? Try to explain what happens in the following two situations you might encounter in your bathroom.

Situation A
You take a shower and the mirror fogs up.

1. Where does this water come from?
2. How does it get to the mirror?

Situation B
You take a hot shower, and the curtain billows in and brushes against your legs.

1. What causes the curtain to move like this?
2. What would happen if the water were cold?

When Natural Events Become Disasters

At times weather patterns do more than cause a light snow or a gentle rain. Some weather-related events are extremely powerful and can cause significant problems as in this opening photograph. As you begin the activities in this chapter, see whether you can decide what the problems are and how you might deal with them.

engage

Connections: Extraordinary Events

explore

Investigation: Miniature Events

explain

Connections: Piecing Together the Weather
Investigation: Presenting Events

elaborate

Connections: Legends
Investigation: Twisters

elaborate / evaluate

Investigation: Wind and Water

▶ **FIGURE 13.1**

This photograph shows clouds of ash erupting from a volcano in Alaska on 27 March 1986. It has erupted explosively six times since 1812. It is similar to Mt. St. Helens, which is a volcano in the state of Washington. A major eruption of Mt. St. Helens occurred on 18 May 1980.

Connections:
Extraordinary Events

engage

Life can be frustrating at times. Perhaps the bus is late or your locker will not open. Sometimes, however, it is much more serious— flood waters wash away someone's house or destroy entire neighborhoods. To better understand the impact of some natural events, look at the photographs that follow. As you look at them, think about your own experiences with natural events that are out of the ordinary.

Look at each of the pictures in Figure 13.1 to 13.8 and read their descriptions. Then read the questions at the end of this activity. Think about how you would answer each question and discuss your answers with your teammates. Finally write answers in your notebook and be prepared for a class discussion of all the questions.

▶ **FIGURE 13.2**

These cars were trapped in a lava flow from Mt. Kilauea on the island of Hawaii. Lava flows from Mt. Kilauea stopped in 1960 and began again in 1983. Many different flows have occurred; the one that covered these cars occurred in 1987.

▶ **FIGURE 13.3**

These buildings collapsed during the Los Angeles earthquake in 1994.

▶ **FIGURE 13.4**

These buildings on the South Carolina coast were hit in 1989 by Hurricane Hugo's storm surge. As you can see, the building on stilts suffered less damage than the other one.

▶ **FIGURE 13.5**

Heavy rains that hit the midwest in 1993 caused immense flooding.

▶ Figure 13.6

This is Armour Station, Missouri on 16 October 1953. The lakes at Armour Station dried up due to a severe drought. The baked soil has cracks 25 to 35 centimeters (10 to 14 inches) deep.

The Corbis-Bettmann Archive

▶ Figure 13.7

The Yellowstone fires of 1988 created so much smoke that the sky appeared to be yellow.

▶ **FIGURE 13.8**

Denver, Colorado, 15 June 1988. A tornado moves above the airport. Several tornadoes were sighted; two of them caused damage and minor injuries.

1. What evidence of natural events did you see in the photographs? Without looking at the pages, list all you can remember. Then look at the photographs again to see whether you missed any.
2. Rank the events you listed from most severe to least severe and justify your ranking.
3. What natural events have you heard about that have occurred in your community?
4. Often during natural events, people are more cooperative and helpful than they are at other times. Why do you think this could be true?

explore

Investigation:
Miniature Events

Often you must experience something firsthand before you truly can understand it. But if a hurricane or a tornado strikes, you might not want to experience too much in person. Not, that is, if you want to be safe. As you move through the stations in this investigation, try to imagine how these miniature events are like the actual events.

Working Cooperatively

Work cooperatively in your teams of three. Use the roles of Communicator and Tracker. As you move from station to station, review your use of the skill *Stay with your group.*

Materials for Each Station:

Station 1 (Fires)

- 1 drinking glass or jar
- 1 votive candle
- 1 box of safety matches

Station 2 (Droughts)

- 1 lamp
- 2 thermometers
- 2 pots or cups of soil
- 1 cardboard shade

Station 3 (Floods)

- 1 floodplain setup
- water supply and container
- water disposal container

Station 4 (Hurricanes)

- 1 psychrometer set up
- 1 calibration chart

Station 5 (Tornadoes)

- 1 tornado bottle setup

Process and Procedure

1. Gather at your first assigned station.
2. Follow the instruction card for that station.
3. Observe what happens.

   Notebook entry: Record your observations and answer any questions that appear on the instruction card.

4. Move to other stations when your teacher says it is time.

   You should have notebook entries for all five stations when you have finished.

Wrap Up

In your notebook, write an explanation for what you saw at each station and why it occurred. In each of your five explanations, include the following:

- station number,
- what the results you saw had to do with a particular type of event (fire, drought, flood, or so on), and
- what natural processes caused whatever you saw.

explain

Connections: Piecing Together the Weather

In some of the previous investigations, you have explored situations that play a major role in the weather. You have seen the role of density in determining buoyancy. You discovered that large amounts of energy are required for water to evaporate. The idea of conservation of energy explains that this energy will be released when the water vapor condenses. You also learned that air is cooled when it goes from high to low pressure and that air is compressible. This means that the atmospheric pressure and the density decrease as we go up and that the temperature of the air usually decreases as we go higher. How do these ideas piece together in real storms?

Energy that is added by the sun's radiation gradually will add water vapor to the air through the process of evaporation, especially evaporation from the ocean. You know that warm air is less dense than cold air. You also know that when the sun heats the earth's surface and warms the air, the force of buoyancy will cause convection currents. The air cools as it moves up to an altitude of lower pressure. Its water vapor may condense in droplets and form cumulus clouds. Because of the heat energy that is released during condensation, this air is frequently warmer and less dense than the surrounding air. In this case, the buoyant force will be greater than the weight of this air. If there is enough moisture from below, the cloud will continue to grow upwards. The droplets in the clouds will increase in size until they fall as rain. If these upward currents of air are strong enough, thunderstorms are likely to develop. These storms are very helpful in returning water to the land and in cleansing the atmosphere. The circulation of the atmosphere may transport the moist air many miles from the ocean.

How might the climate and weather patterns affect the lives of plants, people, and other animals?.

explain

Investigation: Presenting Events

You have survived a set of miniature events, and you might be wondering what they had to do with the actual, potentially dangerous events. In this investigation, your team's task will be to become experts on one type of event and to teach your classmates how the miniature events are like the real ones.

Working Cooperatively

Work cooperatively in your same teams of three. You will need a work space large enough for a piece of newsprint paper. One of you will be the Manager. Continue to practice the social skill *Treat others politely.*

Materials for Each Team of Three:

- 1 sheet of flip chart paper, newsprint, or 1 overhead transparency
- 1 colored marker or transparency marking pen
- any other materials you need for your presentation

Process and Procedure

1. Read the information on your assigned topic.

   Your teacher will assign your team to read about fires, droughts, floods, tornadoes, or hurricanes. At the end of this investigation, your team will present this information to the class.

2. Discuss the reading with your teammates and make sure that you can answer these questions:
   a. What causes this type of event?
   b. How does it affect humans?
   c. How does it affect the environment?
   d. What do humans do about this type of event?
   e. What are some examples?
   f. How is the actual event like the miniature event you observed?

3. Meet with the other team that has your same reading.
4. Decide how you will divide up the tasks for the presentation.

   One team of three should present answers to questions 2a, b, and c. The other team should present answers to questions 2d, e, and f.
5. Prepare and practice your presentation.

   For your presentation, you may prepare a poster, a collage, a concept map, or summarize your discoveries with words.
6. Give your presentation to the class.

   As you give your presentation and as you listen to others, show the rest of the class how politely your team can treat others.

Background Information

Jigsaw Reading 1: Fires

For a fire to start and continue burning, three elements are necessary: fuel, oxygen, and heat. Fuel is anything that burns. In a forest fire, the fuel could be trees, bushes, grass, or debris on the ground. In a house fire, furniture,

insulation, carpeting, clothing, and other household items serve as fuel for the fire. The hotter a fire gets, the more things will burn.

Oxygen is needed for something to burn. Because the air contains oxygen, oxygen is usually available. The process of something igniting, or bursting into flames, is called **combustion.** During combustion oxygen combines with the fuel to make a fire. As the fire burns, it makes heat. This heat causes higher temperatures that help more things burn. For example, a wet log will not burn in a low-temperature fire. If the temperature rises, however, the water will boil out of the log and then the log will burn.

Together these three things—fuel, oxygen, and heat—represent the fire triangle. Just as a three-legged stool will not stand up if one of its legs is missing, a fire will not keep burning if one of these elements is missing. To put out a fire, fire fighters try to eliminate one or more of these elements. When fighting a forest fire, they often will

attempt to remove the fuel from the path of the fire. They do this by creating fire lines—long ditches where they remove all the vegetation (plants and trees) by hand or by bulldozer. When the fire reaches the fire line, there is nothing left to burn. Fire fighters also spray water on a fire to reduce the temperature or cover it with dirt to cut off the oxygen supply. When one or more of the three elements are eliminated or reduced significantly, the fire goes out.

A fire burning in a building or forest creates convection currents that make the fire even harder to extinguish.

Stop & Think

Take a minute to review the convection box activity from Wind in a Box. As you review, think about these questions:

1. How did the smoke move in the box?
2. In a burning building or forest, what is the hotter air likely to do?
3. How will this pattern help the fire spread?

Weather conditions also play an important role in whether a fire keeps burning. On the one hand, dry, windy conditions increase the chances that a fire will start. On the other hand, rain and snow help keep fuels cool, so they do not ignite. Rain or snow also can smother the flames by keeping oxygen out. These wet conditions, however, only stop fires of low temperatures.

The temperature and moisture of the air can influence how easily a fire will start or how well it continues to burn. Temperatures below -18° Celsius (0° Fahrenheit) make it very difficult for a fire to start. High humidity (lots of moisture in the air) also decreases the possibility of fire because the fuel is moist. Moisture keeps the temperature of fuel lower and reduces the chance of combustion.

Fires can be helpful in some places. For example, when fires burn in some forests, it becomes easier for new trees to grow. After a fire, seedlings receive more sunlight because there are no older trees to block the light. Some species of trees (lodge pole pines and jack pines) need the high temperatures that fire provides. High heat allows their cones to open and release their seeds.

Fires also can benefit wildlife and other animals that eat grass. When fires burn down trees or shrubs, sometimes grasses will spring up. People have begun to use this phenomenon in the plains region of western and central North America. By starting small, controlled fires, people have found that grasses will grow back into areas taken over by shrubs. Grasses continue to grow as long as periodic burns occur.

In wilderness areas, we can see patterns of fire because trees and grass act as fuel. Lightning strikes can easily ignite woodlands and grasslands when it is dry enough and there is enough fuel. When scientists examined the giant sequoias in California, for example, they found that fires occurred in the sequoia forests every eight years. These fires did not damage the trees because of their thick bark. Instead the fires cleared the ground so that new trees could sprout. This pattern ended after humans began putting out fires in parks where the sequoias grow.

People have affected the patterns of fire occurrence in other forests as well. Another example is Yellowstone National Park. The summer of 1988 was hot and dry across much of the United States. The combination of heat, dry weather, strong winds, and several fires that had been started by lightning resulted in a forest fire that burned one million acres. It also started an ongoing controversy.

In 1988 the National Park Service had a policy called "let burn." Under this policy, certain types of fires (primarily those started by lightning in isolated areas) were to be allowed to burn and follow their natural course. This would allow forests to go through the

▶ FIGURE 13.9

Many national camping and nature areas post fire danger signs. Depending on the weather conditions, some days present a higher risk of fires than others.

natural cycles of burning out debris and encouraging new growth. The policy, however, had been in effect only since 1970, while from the 1930s to the 1970s, park officials had put out every fire. As a result, many areas of Yellowstone had at least forty years' worth of accumulated debris on the ground. This debris was available as fuel for the lightning fires of 1988.

The controversy about the 1988 fire centers on whether or not national parks, which people use for recreation, should be artificially maintained or left more to natural processes. On the one hand, advocates of human control say that people's needs, wants, and safety should come first, so we should strictly control and put out fires. On the other hand, advocates of natural processes say that natural burns help maintain balance in the forest. Without these fires, wild areas cannot regenerate, and wildlife will lose valuable food sources.

Stop & Think

Should fire fighters control fires in our national parks, or should we let natural processes control the fires?

Much more information is available on the Yellowstone fires. You may want to investigate further before you answer this question.

Melbourne, Australia— February 1983

During 1982 and 1983, Australia had very little rainfall. One careless spark could ignite the grasslands into a horrible blaze. In February 1983, a eucalyptus forest caught fire. Eucalyptus trees contain a lot of oil that burns easily and explodes when the trees are hot. Wind carried sparks from these explosions into the small town of Maceddon, which was burned to the ground. By the time this fire was put out, seventy-five people were dead, 8,000 were homeless, and 815,000 acres of forest and farmland were burned.

Chicago, Illinois—October 1871

On 9 October 1871, the city of Chicago experienced a tragic fire. Chicago sits on the western shore of Lake Michigan. During much of the year, the difference in temperatures between the land and the water results in a constant breeze or wind blowing through the city. The year 1871 was very dry, and Chicago was a town with mostly wooden buildings and no fire department. Legend has it that Mrs. O'Leary's cow kicked over a lantern in the barn, and a raging fire resulted. The fire burned only for one day but left 100,000 people homeless and caused millions of dollars in damage.

When the citizens of Chicago rebuilt their town, they used stone for downtown buildings, laid the streets out on a logical grid, and established a fire department. These changes prepared the city to fight future fires.

Jigsaw Reading 2: Droughts

A drought (DROWT) happens when there is no rain for a long period of time. Droughts are slow-acting events, but they have affected more people than you may realize.

Some places on earth tend to have dry seasons, but enough rain or snow falls during the wet season to fill water-storage reservoirs. During the dry seasons, people can use the stored water to farm the land and to grow food. When the wet season occurs again, as expected, enough snow or rain falls to make up for long periods of dryness.

Review the diagram of the water cycle from Chapter 12. Also think about weather patterns.

During the summer of 1988, the pattern of winds did not carry moist air over Minnesota and Iowa as was usual, but instead blew the moist air farther north, over Canada. That summer was wetter than usual in Canada and much drier than usual in Minnesota and Iowa. So while there are drought years in some places, there may be wet years in other places.

A drought is a slow natural disaster. Many people may die in a severe drought that lasts several years because there is not enough water to grow food, and people simply starve. People also become more susceptible to disease, and they may die from sickness. Droughts have killed many people throughout history. In China one drought lasted from 1876 to 1879. It is estimated that between nine and thirteen million people died. People in other parts of China tried to send food, but some people were too weak even to come to the road to get the food. It was hard for the wagons to get to the center of the drought-stricken area because of poor road conditions.

Similar disasters have happened in other places. Near the end of the 1800s, more than five million people died in a drought in India. In 1921 and 1922, roughly five million people died during a drought in Russia.

More recent droughts in Africa have claimed hundreds of thousands of lives. From 1968 to 1975, a devastating drought affected the Sahel region of Africa. It ended the way of life for many nomadic people. The

▶ FIGURE 13.10

Drought conditions can be so severe that river tributaries, such as this one, dry out.

nomadic people who did reach the cities were exposed to a range of diseases caused by overcrowding. Many of the children who survived suffered from deformed bodies and mental retardation, simply because they had not had enough to eat when they were very young. The African country of Ethiopia is another example; it has been drought stricken from 1981 into the 1990s.

When a drought strikes, plants and animals are affected as well as people. During the summer of 1988, people in the United States noticed that some of the water wildlife was dying. When the ponds received less rainwater than usual, bacteria known as clostridia became more concentrated in the remaining water. Many of the ducks that drank the water died of botulism, a disease caused by certain types of clostridia.

Droughts also may make an area more susceptible to fire. Plants dry out so much that they can burn easily. So if a drought happens, fires are more likely, and there is less water to put out the fires.

Historically people have had very few defenses against drought. When a severe drought struck the central United States during the 1930s, many people had no other solution but to leave the area. Many of them moved all the way from Oklahoma to California. During those years, such states as Oklahoma and Nebraska were part of what was called the Dust Bowl.

Once the drought of the 1930s was over, people in the United States began to look for better ways to protect themselves from drought. People planted trees as windbreaks to slow down soil erosion. This action would help keep the farmland fertile. People also built reservoirs to store water and began to store food for the years when droughts might strike again.

Jigsaw Reading 3: Floods

Beneficial rain or snow can become too much of a good thing and turn into a disaster. The result may be a flood. Floods can occur suddenly or gradually and can last for hours or days.

Floods happen because of a combination of events. Usually for a flood to occur, three things must happen: There must be heavy rain, the soil must be so completely soaked that it cannot hold any more water, and stream channels or rivers must be filled with more water than they can carry.

As you might have thought already, heavy rain or melting snow is the primary cause of flooding. But what causes rain? Rain is water falling from the air.

Stop & Think

How did water (rain) get into the air? If you don't recall the answer to this, review the Chapter 12 reading on weather patterns.

Even if a heavy rain does fall, flooding will not necessarily happen. If the soil and vegetation absorb a lot of the water, streams may not overflow. If a stream had a very low water level before the storm, the stream channel may not overflow. If it does overflow, this is the beginning of a flood.

Floods happen in a variety of places—everywhere from near the oceans to inland deserts. Sometimes heavy rains occur near the coast because the air is near a large body of water. Here it is easy for the air to gain and then suddenly lose large amounts of water as the clouds move inland. In these coastal areas, floods can occur during or after heavy thunderstorms or during the heavy rains that accompany hurricanes. When hurricanes move onto land, a surge of ocean water pushed by winds also can cause flooding.

For places farther inland, floods occur mostly along rivers. Most rivers have channels in which the water usually flows, but they also have flat areas alongside them. The flat area alongside a river is called a **floodplain.** This is the land where water from a flooded river will go first.

Floods also can occur in areas that are not close to oceans, lakes, or rivers. Sometimes a thunderstorm will occur over a desert area. There are few plants, and the soil cannot absorb all the water. The water comes rushing down the hillsides and into the valleys below. Places

▶ **FIGURE 13.11**
In the spring of 1993, the midwest received an immense amount of rainfall, which caused damaging floods. In Decorah, Iowa, local residents sandbagged the Upper Iowa River to try to prevent the water from flooding their town.

with dry stream beds suddenly fill with gushing water that can throw aside anything in its path. Because these floods occur so suddenly, they are known as flash floods.

Flash floods often take people by surprise. People have come out of buildings in such places as Las Vegas, Nevada, to find that a sudden storm had washed away their car. People who are caught in flash floods often try to drive to safety. They rarely succeed. If you are in a car, the best idea is to get out of the car and immediately walk, run, or climb to the highest ground in sight.

Floods have caused millions of deaths. In the United States, flooding is responsible for more deaths than fires, droughts, hurricanes, or tornadoes. Some deaths occur because people do not want to leave their homes or cars.

Two severe floods in the United States happened when thunderstorms occurred near mountain canyons. After one such thunderstorm in 1972 in Rapid City, South Dakota, 232 people died in a flood. In Colorado, the Big Thompson River flood of 1976 killed 139 people. These were tragedies, but they were mild, compared with some of the deadliest floods in history. For example, in 1887 the Hwang-ho River of China overflowed its banks and caused the deaths of 800,000 people.

One way that people try to eliminate the danger from floods is by building reservoirs. When a heavy storm occurs, the reservoir can hold the extra water. This works, however, only if the rain falls over the reservoir or over the river upstream from the reservoir. If the storm is downstream from a dam that holds back the reservoir water, there still will be a danger of flooding. Expecting a dam to protect people from flooding is not always a good idea.

It is important to avoid constructing buildings and homes on floodplains. Floodplains are usually flat and sometimes scenic, so people often want to build there. For safety's sake, however, city planners are wise to forbid such building.

What do floods do besides hurt people and cause property damage? For one thing, they can enrich the soil. Some rivers have mild floods every year. Rivers carry nutrients and fine dirt, and when a flood recedes, or withdraws, it leaves these nutrients behind. During

► **FIGURE 13.12**

This is a photo of the Nile River from space.

NASA

floods the rivers also wash excess salts out of the soils. Annual flooding makes the soils very fertile. Some of the good farmland along the Nile River and the Mississippi River was a result of flooding. But people have built dams along many rivers such as the Nile, and so the annual flooding in some of these locations has stopped. As a result, the soils have been drained of their nutrients and do not produce the same quality of crops.

Jigsaw Reading 4: Hurricanes

Hurricanes form when warm, moist air rises, condensation occurs, clouds form, and thunderstorms develop. But the storms that can produce hurricanes occur only over warm oceans. Hurricanes develop fairly near but not exactly at the equator. This is because the Coriolis effect is not experienced at the equator. So hurricanes begin slightly north or south of the equator in warm, moist regions.

Hurricanes, which are called typhoons in the Pacific Ocean, require two basic conditions to develop. First the atmosphere must contain large amounts of moisture. This is most frequently found over the warm oceans where cumulus clouds form easily. If the atmospheric temperatures are favorable, the clouds can grow to fill the sky because a large amount of moist air is available. This

▶ FIGURE 13.13

This photograph shows how hurricanes appear from above. In the center of the hurricane is the eye.

pattern has the potential to develop into a large region of clouds and rain showers. Second a storm circulation pattern must be established. The atmospheric pressure in this warm, sea-level region is likely to be low. If this happens at the equator, nearby air will move in quickly. Pressure differences do not last long here. Not far from the equator, however, we will see a small Coriolis force acting to the right of the wind and, in the northern hemisphere, the circulation will begin counterclockwise around the area of low pressure. The energy that the sun has stored in the moist atmosphere will continue to be released in the form of condensation, and the winds and rain will increase. When the winds reach speeds of 40 miles per hour, it is called a tropical storm. When winds are 74 miles per hour or greater, it is called a hurricane. Strong downdrafts in the center of the storm actually warm the air. Here the clouds disappear and the winds die. This section is called the eye of the hurricane.

The storm drifts slowly to the west because of the easterly winds at high altitudes, and the storm may gradually curve northward. These steering currents are weak, however. The forces within the storm and the energy available in its moisture may affect the storm's path. These circumstances sometimes make predictions difficult.

The hurricane will weaken when there is less energy available to add to the storm. This often happens when the storm leaves the warm ocean reservoir of energy and moves over land. It is on land, however, where most of the damage occurs because of the strong winds, heavy rains, and high ocean surges ahead of the storm. The Weather Service tracks the storm with information from satellites and from radar reflections from stations on the earth. A hurricane watch is issued to alert people living in communities along the coast. When the storm is close, a hurricane warning is issued. At this stage, officials may recommend that people evacuate certain vulnerable areas.

Stop & Think

Review what you know about convection cells from Chapter 12. Then see whether you can find the convection cells in Figure 13.14.

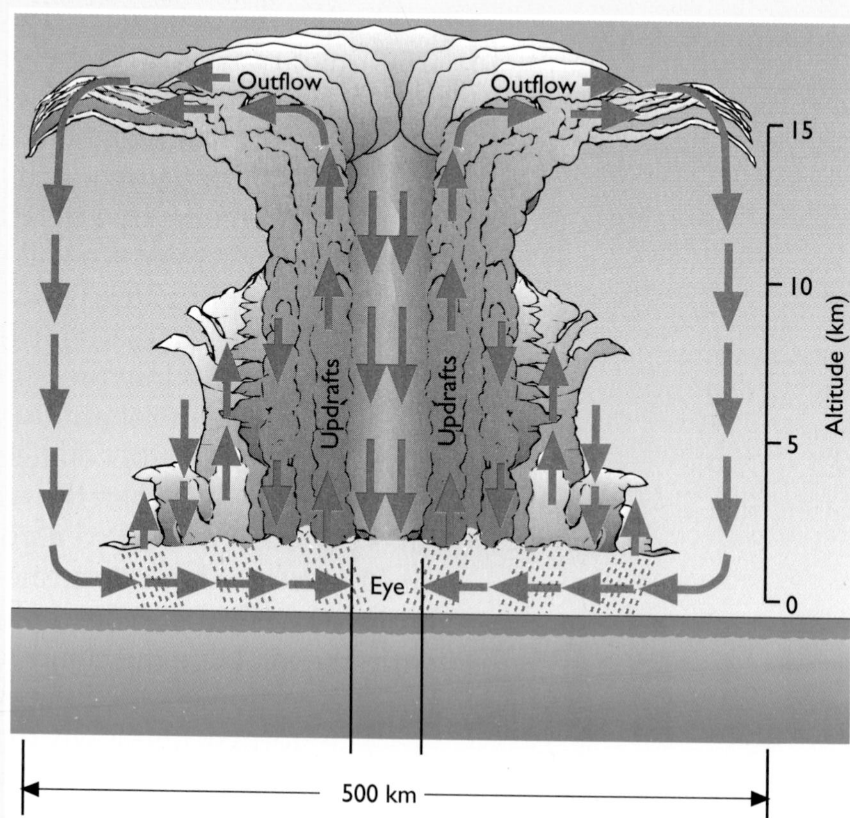

FIGURE 13.14
This diagram shows the side view of a hurricane. Bands of thunderstorms are around a calm area in the middle.

One hurricane that is well-remembered occurred in Galveston, Texas, in 1900. Galveston is built on a large island off the coast of Texas. People in Galveston knew that hurricanes had struck the island before, but they thought their homes were hurricane-proof. Tragically they were wrong. When the 1900 hurricane struck the island, more than 7,000 people were killed. The bridges to the island were destroyed, and people could not escape even when they finally realized that their homes were not safe. Many people drowned. One young woman was extremely fortunate. She clung to a floating tree branch and when the flood waters finally went down, she found herself 29 kilometers (18 miles) from home. Fortunately the only injuries she suffered were scrapes and bruises.

Sometimes people forget the lessons of earlier times. When Hurricane Camille struck the coast of Mississippi in 1969, no one was prepared for its strength. Camille was a category five hurricane, the strongest known. Homes and buildings along the coast were flooded and smashed. Even the leaves were stripped off the trees. People learned that the best way to be safe in a hurricane is to follow advice from the weather service. When you are advised to evacuate—do so!

Jigsaw Reading 5: Tornadoes

Tornadoes are swirling masses of air with wind speeds from 112 to 480 kilometers (70 to 300 miles) per hour. Their swirling winds can rip a building to shreds in a matter of seconds. Tornadoes strike suddenly and may accompany hurricanes. One hundred fifteen tornadoes occurred with Hurricane Beulah in 1967. Tornadoes are even more common in certain inland areas—they have ripped apart towns from Xenia, Ohio to Limon, Colorado.

The tornado believed to be the largest ever recorded occurred in 1925. It was a huge funnel cloud that bore down on Missouri, then moved to Illinois, and then to Indiana. It lasted far longer than tornadoes typically do, striking 23 towns as it moved across the three states. Along its path, the tornado killed more than 600 people and injured hundreds of others.

Of course there are also amazing stories of survival. In 1981 a man in Sumner, Texas, huddled in a bathtub during a sudden tornado. The tornado picked up the man and the bathtub and dropped them 0.4 kilometers (a quarter of a mile) from the demolished house.

But what causes tornadoes?

Stop & Think

To understand what causes tornadoes, review what you learned about winds in Chapter 12. Remember that air is constantly moving across the earth's surface. Near the equator, warm air is rising. Near the poles, cool air is sinking. But these **air masses** (sections of air with similar temperatures and humidity) do not sit still. They move, and sometimes they meet.

Although tornadoes are exceptionally violent, the funnel cloud is usually quite small, with a diameter of less than a mile. Buildings in the direct path of the tornado can be completely demolished while a few miles away, only brief showers may occur. It is nearly impossible to predict the amount of destruction for a particular location.

The Weather Service will issue a tornado watch when the general conditions are favorable for a tornado to develop. This tells people to listen for further developments and to pay attention to the sky. The Weather Service, then, will issue a tornado warning when someone has observed an actual tornado. At this point, changes can occur rapidly and it is important to watch for funnel clouds and to seek safe and sturdy shelter.

The conditions for tornadoes to develop are particularly favorable in the Midwest of the United States in the spring. Warm, moist air frequently moves in along with south winds from the Gulf of Mexico. During the day, the ground will be heated by the sun, and this will begin convection currents. Cumulus clouds will form as the air is cooled when it is lifted. Condensation will release some heat energy so that this air may end up with a lower density than the air around it. The buoyant force continues to lift the air and form very large thunderstorms (see Figure 13.15). A dangerous situation

▶ **FIGURE 13.15**

In this diagram, a cold, dry mass of air that has moved south beside the Rocky Mountains meets a warm, moist air mass from the Gulf of Mexico. In this example, a warm, dry air mass from the southwest also enters the storm area.

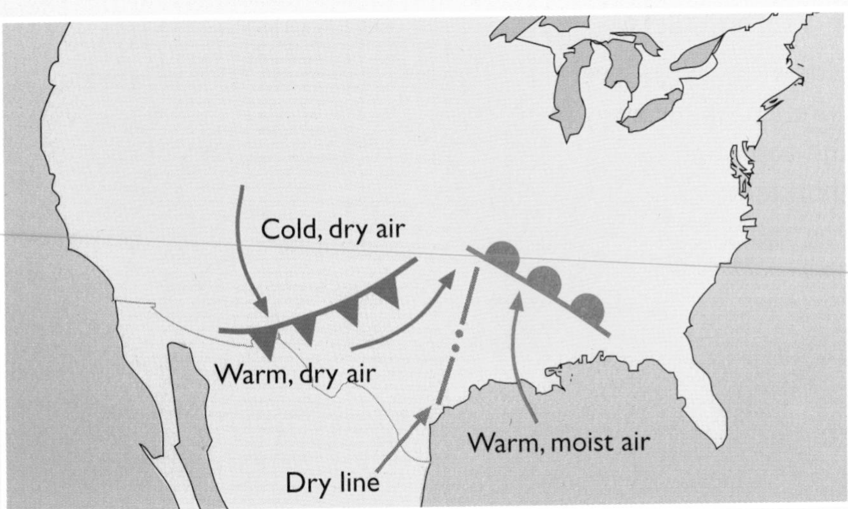

occurs when a cold, dry air mass from the west moves rapidly over the warm, moist air mass. This warm, moist air may be much less dense than the cold dry air and very violent updrafts will occur (see Figures 13.16 and 13.17). The condensation during these thunderstorms releases a large amount of stored energy and a tornado is likely to develop. A tornado releases forces much greater than ordinary storms do. Wind speeds are very high on the edge of the funnel, and the atmospheric pressure inside the funnel is very low. Buildings are likely to explode when they are engulfed by the funnel. A tornado is usually very short-lived—perhaps lasting only a few minutes, but a lot can happen in those few minutes.

On warm, muggy spring days, you often expect to see cumulus clouds develop and rain showers begin. The development of tornadoes, however, requires an additional unstable condition high up in the atmosphere. The Weather Service uses weather balloons to obtain some information and satellite cameras to spot violent thunderstorms that are very high. The Weather Service also uses modern ground-based radar systems to detect the characteristic rotation patterns of tornadoes. Because of these warnings, people can be alert for further developments and can take actions to protect themselves. This warning system saves many lives.

▶ FIGURE 13.16

Side view: High-level winds push air away from the top of a thunderstorm and warmer air is lifted.

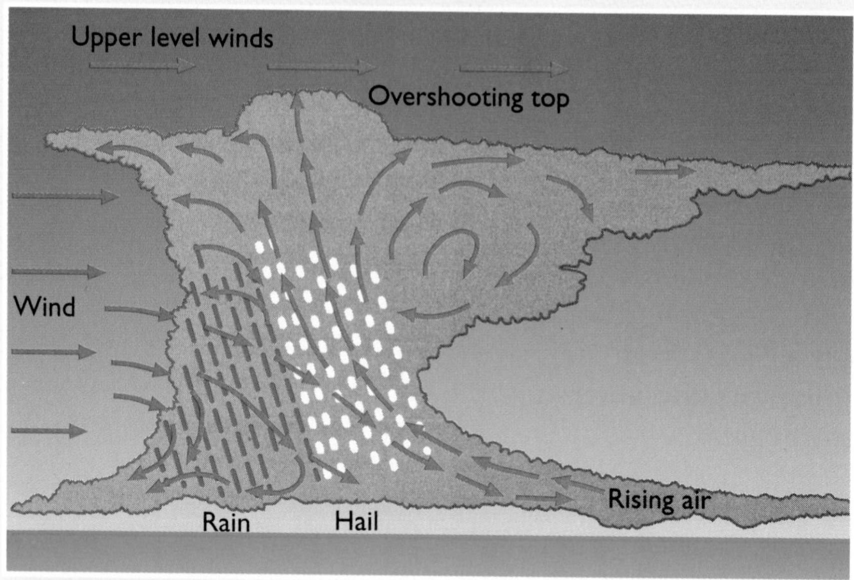

▶ FIGURE 13.17

In this diagram, air that is lifted will begin to rotate counterclockwise as it reaches 10,000 feet.

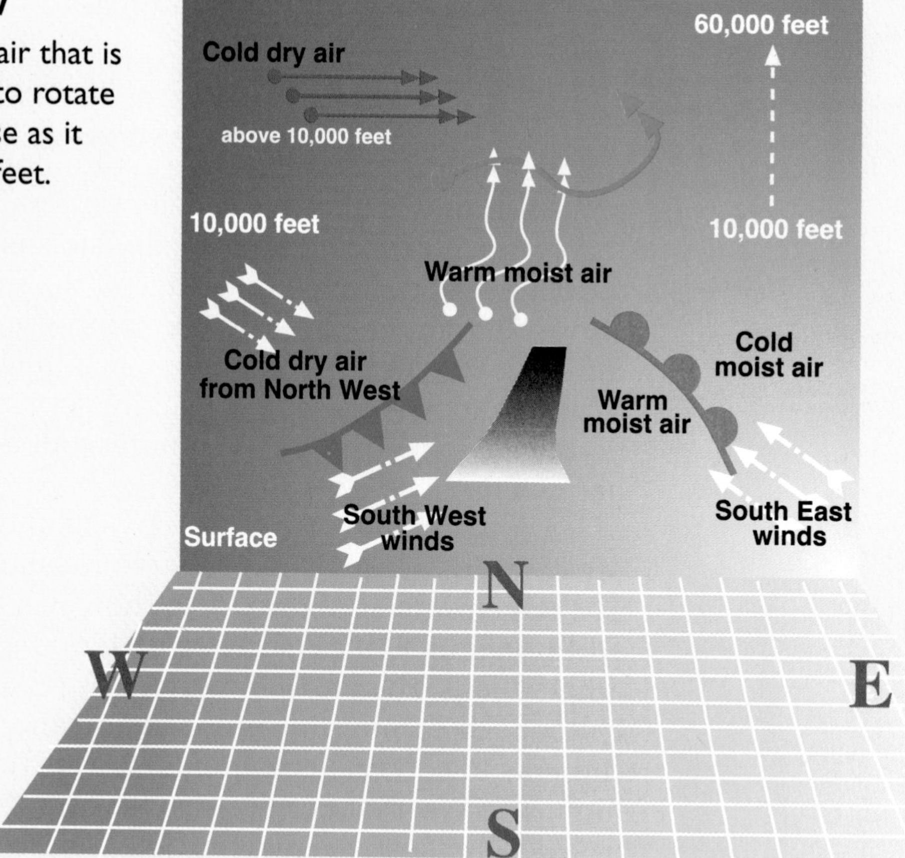

Wrap Up

After you have heard all of the presentations, consider the following questions. Write your answers in your notebook and prepare to discuss them with the rest of the class.

1. Revisit your wrap-up questions from the Investigation: Miniature Events. Revise your answers based on the information you now have.
2. Which natural events tend to occur together? Why is this so?
3. Explain how each of the following sets of words are related.
   a. convection cells: fires, floods, hurricanes, tornadoes
   b. water cycle: droughts, floods, hurricanes
   c. winds: droughts, fires
4. How did you benefit from working with a larger group on your presentation?

elaborate

Connections: Legends

Read the following paragraph and record your answer to the question in your notebook.

People do not always use scientific explanations to explain natural events. Some legends propose that an angry evil spirit causes storms. For example, the Seneca Indians of the Iroquois Confederacy told stories about Jijogweh (jih JOH gway), an evil monster bird that caused horrible storms and killed humans. In a Blackfoot Indian legend, the reckless horse Red Wind lived in the sky and caused tornadoes. When Red Wind decided to cause trouble, he came to earth, and his dancing caused the tornadoes.

Why do you think legends such as these portray angry spirits as the cause of many natural events?

SIDELIGHT *on History*

Fire in London

In the seventeenth century, London was a town with very narrow streets and many houses and other buildings built close together. The houses had thatched roofs (woven straw). Back then houses did not have running water and the town had no fire department. The summer of 1666 was very hot and dry. In early September, a baker's wood pile caught on fire. When the baker noticed the fire, he tried to put it out, but he couldn't because everything was so dry and there was a strong wind. Finally he gave up and escaped through the roof.

The wind carried the sparks to other thatched roofs, and the fire spread quickly. By six o'clock the next morning, all of the houses and shops on Pudding Lane, where the bakery stood, were on fire. Most of the buildings on the next street over, Fish Street, and the houses on the London Bridge were burning too. The fire was out of control. People did not stay to fight the fire. Instead they collected their belongings and left for the countryside.

The wind blew nonstop for three days, and the fire kept spreading. Finally four days after the fire had started, the wind died down and so did the large flames. The fire burned itself out completely, but not before it had destroyed 80 percent of the buildings in London. Few people died, but 13,900 homes were burned, leaving three-fourths of the town's population homeless. The fire had burned more than 400 acres and ruined eighty-seven churches and cathedrals.

Investigation:

Twisters

elaborate

Have you ever experienced a tornado? Probably most people in your classroom have not, but some may have. Some people live where they are likely to see a tornado. It might seem that tornadoes just "appear" out of a cloudy sky, but there are patterns to when and where tornadoes occur. Because scientists have learned more about the weather patterns that are closely associated with tornadoes, fewer people are injured or die during tornadoes now than previously. In this investigation, you will look at information about tornado occurrences. See what patterns you can find.

Working Cooperatively

Work cooperatively in your teams of three. As you work, *Encourage each other to participate*. Use the roles of Manager and Communicator. Sit together and remember that you are all Team Members.

Materials for Each Team of Three:

- 1 copy of a Tornado Data Sheet for at least one state
- 1 sheet of graph paper
- 1 calculator

Materials for the Entire Class:

- 1 overhead projector
- 1 overhead transparency, United States Map with Boxes
- 4 transparency marking pens of different colors
- 1 United States map, wall-size

Process and Procedure

1. Pick up the graph paper and a Tornado Data Sheet with your team's number on it.

   Teams will count off to get a number.

2. Find your assigned state's location on a United States map.

   Your Tornado Data Sheet is based on information from a particular state. Be ready to locate this state on a map.

   STOP: Is everyone participating? If not, how can you encourage more participation?

3. Study your team's Tornado Data Sheet.

4. As a team, find as many patterns in the data as you can.

   Averaging some of the numbers will help. If you do not know how to average numbers, do How To #9, How to Average Numbers.

5. Describe any patterns you find.

   Notebook entry: Record your descriptions of patterns.

Wrap Up

Use the patterns that you have found to respond to the following scenario. Discuss your ideas as a team and write your policies in your notebook. Encourage each other to participate by making sure that everyone has equal input in writing your policies.

1. You are an insurance agent working for a company that writes policies all over the country. People buy policies to pay for damage that might happen to their homes. If disasters occur, your company pays. Predict where most disasters would occur. With your teammates, choose three states. Each of you should write a policy for one state. Explain what you would charge for home insurance in three different states you have heard about and why. For the three policies you write, you must answer the following questions:

   a. How are tornado patterns different or similar in the three states?

SIDELIGHT on Nature

Dust in the Wind

Have you ever traveled in a desert? Even if you haven't, you probably know that a desert has a lot of dry ground and few trees. When the wind moves across the desert, it picks up sand and dust and carries it along, up to a meter above the ground.

Maybe you have seen pictures of winds blowing dust and sand over the land. Sometimes tiny "twisters" form in those dust storms; these are called dust devils. If you have ever encountered one of these, you probably remember it. A dust devil is a storm that develops from very warm air, particularly over bare ground. The warm air carrying sand and dirt is pushed up into the cooler air above it, and the air currents begin to swirl. The larger the area of bare ground, the larger the area of very warm air, and the longer the storm can last. This is why dust devils are common in deserts.

Although dust devils may look like tornadoes, they are not. A dust devil starts at the ground surface and moves upward quickly. A tornado begins in the clouds and moves downward quickly and violently.

People often think of dust devils as part of the American West. But they occur in other deserts too. In the Sahara Desert of Africa, dust devils have been strong enough to blow people out of tents.

b. Of all tornadoes that occur, where do most of them take place?

c. When do most tornadoes occur?

elaborate / evaluate

Investigation: Wind and Water

As you know by now, hurricanes can be extremely powerful storms. But again some patterns will allow you to make predictions. Imagine that you want to make predictions about hurricanes. If you look at some information that has been gathered already, you may be able to recognize certain patterns. As you look at this information, what patterns do you think you will find?

Materials for Each Student:

- 1 sheet of graph paper
- 4 strips of transparent tape, 5 cm each

Working Cooperatively

You will be working individually.

Materials for the Entire Class:

- 1 world map, wall-size

Process and Procedure

1. Obtain the materials.
2. Read Background Information, Part 1.
   This information follows the procedure.
3. Study the hurricane data chart. (See Figure 13.18.)
4. Decide how you can graph what the data chart is showing.
   If you need help, you might consult How To #3, How to Plot Data on a Graph.
5. Make a graph of the data and tape it into your notebook.
6. Read about the hurricanes assigned to you.
   These are in Background Information, Part 2.
7. Look at the description of
   - the hurricane's size,
   - how long it lasted,
   - where it went,
   - whether or not it hurt anyone, and
   - how fast its winds blew.

   Do this for each hurricane reading you were assigned.
8. Share your hurricane information with the class and discuss with your classmates the groups of hurricanes that seem to best reflect the information that you read.
   Try two or three groups and see which hurricanes fit into each.

Background Information

Hurricanes begin as storms near the equator. These storms are sometimes called tropical storms. If the tropical storms' wind speeds become strong enough, they are then classified as hurricanes.

In the hurricane data chart that you will use in this investigation, some storms are listed as "T" (for tropical storm), while others were strong enough to be listed as "H" (for hurricane).

► FIGURE 13.18

This hurricane data chart lists the tropical storms and hurricanes from three different years.

Hurricane Data Chart

1994	Type	Name	Date
	T	Alberto	June 30 - July 7
	T	Beryl	August 14-19
	H	Chris	August 16-23
	T	Debby	September 9-11
	T	Ernesto	September 21-26
	H	Florence	November 2-8
	H	Gordon	November 8-21

1995	Type	Name	Date
	H	Allison	June 3-11
	T	Barry	July 5-10
	T	Chantal	July 12-22
	T	Dean	July 28 - August 2
	H	Erin	July 31- August 6
	H	Felix	August 8-25
	T	Gabrielle	August 9-12
	H	Humberto	August 22 - September 1
	H	Iris	August 22 - September 7
	T	Jerry	August 22-28
	T	Karen	August 26 - September 3
	H	Luis	August 27 - September 12
	H	Marilyn	September 12-27
	H	Noel	September 26 - October 7
	H	Opal	September 27 - October 6
	T	Pablo	October 4-8
	H	Roxanne	October 7-21
	T	Sebastien	October 20-25
	H	Tanya	October 27 - November 3

1996	Type	Name	Date
	T	Authur	June 17-23
	H	Bertha	July 5-17
	H	Ceasar	July 24-28
	H	Dolly	August 19-25
	H	Edouard	August 19 - September 6
	H	Fran	August 23 - September 10
	T	Gustov	August 26 - September 2
	H	Hortense	September 3-16
	H	Isidore	September 24 - October 2
	T	Josephine	October 4-16
	T	Kyle	October 11-12
	H	Lili	October 14-29
	H	Marco	November 13-26

Source: National Oceanic and Atmospheric Administration (NOAA).

Descriptions of Hurricanes

Hurricane Andrew, 1992

Andrew began as a tropical wave that crossed from the west coast of Africa to the tropical North Atlantic Ocean on 14 August. The wave continued westward at 22–25 miles per hour and on 15 August passed to the south of the Cape Verde Islands. The storm became a tropical depression on 16 August as narrow bands of spiral-shaped clouds formed around the center of the storm. This depression continued to grow stronger and by 17 August, it became the first tropical storm of the Atlantic season. Andrew continued to head west, moving rapidly and then west-northwest in the direction of the Lesser Antilles Islands. During the next few days, Andrew was affected by other low pressure systems in the Atlantic and began a more northwestward course (see Figure 13.20). The area near the storm changed significantly by 21 August and after sunrise on 22 August, Andrew had reached hurricane strength. An eye formed that morning, the storm strengthened, and Andrew continued due west. Late on 23 August, Andrew ripped through the Bahamas with winds up to 150 miles per hour.

Andrew continued moving west toward Florida and on 24 August, smashed into Dade County, Florida, with winds of 160 miles per hour and gusts up to at least 180 miles per hour. It demolished homes and businesses and toppled palm trees and telephone poles alike. Andrew left thousands of residents homeless. Homestead, Florida, was the hardest hit; the entire farming and retirement community was nearly wiped out and Homestead Air Force Base was completely demolished. The storm moved quickly west across Florida and weakened somewhat. Then it continued out into the Gulf of Mexico and began a west-northwest course. The storm came ashore again in a sparsely populated area of the Louisiana coast on 26 August. Andrew again weakened quickly as it moved across land. It became a tropical storm in about 10 hours and a tropical depression 12 hours later, but it continued to produce heavy rains.

Although it was not the most intense storm to ever hit Florida, it caused more than $25 billion in damages.

FIGURE 13.19
Extensive damage such as this, made Hurricane Andrew the most expensive natural disaster to date in the United States.

This makes Andrew the most expensive natural disaster in the United States. At least twenty-six people were killed: three in the Bahamas, fifteen in Dade County, and eight in Louisiana. Several areas that did not experience Andrew directly, experienced tornadoes that were spin-offs from Andrew. Dozens of tornadoes popped roofs off houses and scattered possessions.

Hurricane Gabrielle, 1989

Gabrielle moved off the coast of Africa on 1 August. It was first classified as Tropical Storm Gabrielle. As it moved across the ocean, it was reclassified as a hurricane (see Figure 13.20). Gabrielle turned north on 4 September. It missed the Caribbean islands by about 480 kilometers and slowly stopped about 280 kilometers southeast of Cape Cod, Massachusetts. By 12 September, it had lost most of its strength.

Gabrielle was a large hurricane. The eye was never less than 37 kilometers across, and sometimes it was as large as 93 kilometers (58 miles). Gabrielle's winds also were extremely strong, up to 112 kilometers (69 miles) per hour, even 232 kilometers (144 miles) from the center of the storm. Gabrielle's winds generated ocean swells as high as 9 meters (30 feet). These swells hit shorelines from Bermuda all the way to Canada. The ocean swells caused eight deaths in the mid-Atlantic and New England regions. In some cases, boats capsized while trying to enter or exit coastal inlets, and in other cases people were washed from jetties while watching the large swells.

Hurricane Hugo, 1989

Hugo was first identified as a group of thunderstorms off the coast of Africa on 9 September. This group of storms moved gradually westward and continued to gather strength. When wind speeds were measured on 15 September, the best estimate for surface speeds was 260 kilometers (161 miles) per hour in the fastest moving parts of the storm. Hugo moved over the island of Puerto Rico and then struck South Carolina. Storm tides ranged from 2.4 to 6 meters (20 feet), and the storm surge was as high as 1.2 meters above normal, even several hundred kilometers up the coast. Heavy rains fell as far away as eastern Ohio. By 22 September, Hugo had weakened to a tropical storm. It continued to move northward. On 23 September, it was no longer classified as a tropical storm. It moved across eastern Canada and into the far northern Atlantic Ocean. Along the way, Hugo caused $10 billion worth of damage and claimed forty-nine lives (see Figure 13.20).

Hurricane Gilbert, 1988

Gilbert began as a storm off the coast of Africa. It moved away from the African coast on 3 September and reached hurricane intensity on 9 September. Gilbert moved south of Puerto Rico and crossed directly over Jamaica. Then Gilbert landed on the Yucatan Peninsula of Mexico. It continued to move northwest, crossed over the Gulf of Mexico, and made its final landfall in northern Mexico on 16 September (see Figure 13.21). At this landfall, Gilbert's winds were 296 kilometers (183 miles) per hour—the strongest that had been recorded during any hurricane since 1969. Gilbert then moved north across Texas and into Oklahoma. Storm tides caused by Gilbert were as high as 4.5 meters. An estimated 318 people died as a result of

▶ FIGURE 13.20

This map shows the tracks for hurricanes Andrew, Gabrielle, and Hugo.

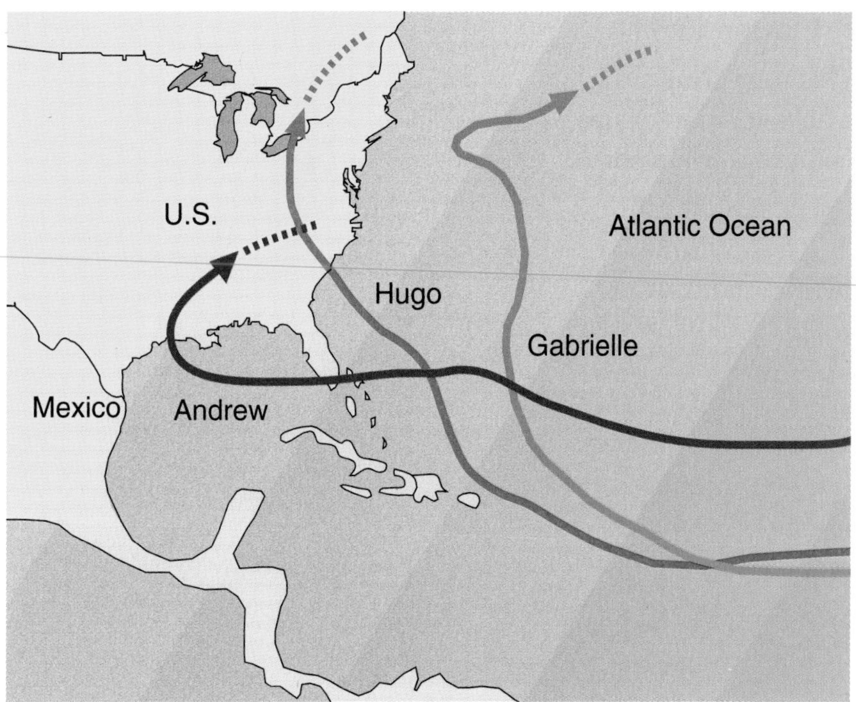

Source: National Oceanic and Atmospheric Administration (NOAA).

Hurricane Gilbert, and $5 billion worth of damage was done.

Hurricane Helene, 1988

As Hurricane Gilbert was moving into the Gulf of Mexico, another storm was moving off the coast of Africa on 15 September. By 21 September, Helene was a hurricane moving through the midtropical Atlantic. On 23 September, Helene moved northward. Helene's wind speeds were up to 232 kilometers (144 miles) per hour. Helene was a hurricane for nine days, the longest-lasting storm of the season (see Figure 13.21).

Hurricane Joan, 1988

Joan was a hurricane with a very unusual path. On 11 October, Joan was classified as a tropical storm. It moved farther south than Atlantic hurricanes usually do and affected the north coasts of Venezuela and Colombia. Joan then moved back over the waters of the Gulf of Mexico. As the storm moved across the water, it strengthened to become a hurricane. By the time Joan came ashore on the coast of Nicaragua, it was an extremely strong hurricane with wind speeds of 232

▶ **FIGURE 13.21**
This map shows the tracks for hurricanes Gilbert and Helene.

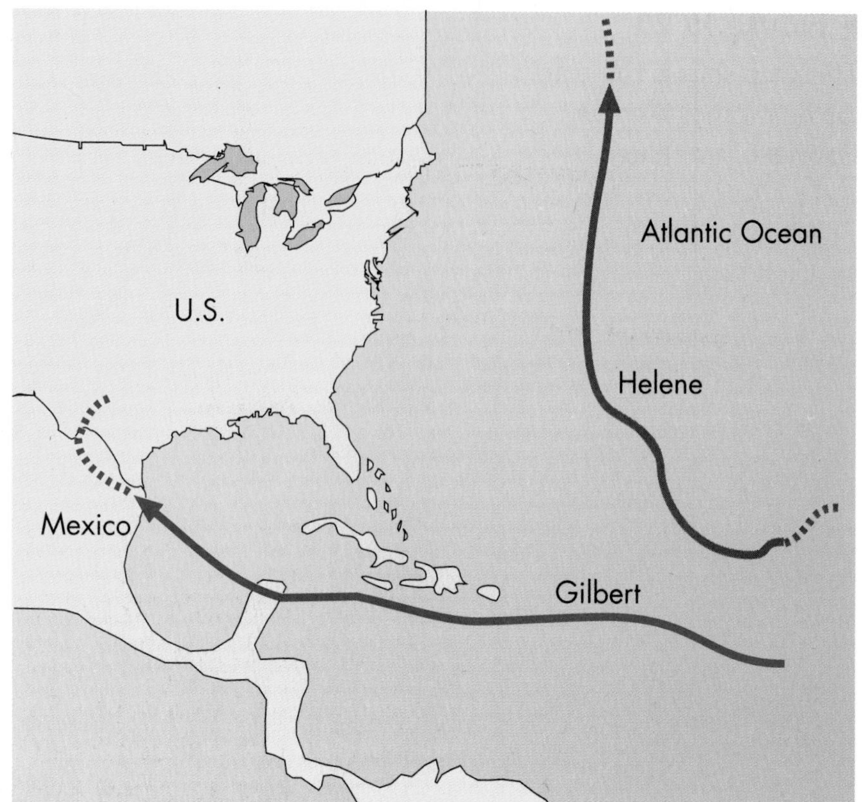

kilometers per hour (see Figure 13.22). Along its path, Joan was responsible for approximately 216 deaths, many in Nicaragua. Joan also caused more than $2 billion worth of damage. Once Joan crossed Central America, it continued as a storm into the Pacific.

Hurricane Emily, 1987
Emily began as a storm off the coast of Africa and was classified as a hurricane on 20 September. Emily was a small storm during this relatively mild hurricane season. Emily moved across the Atlantic Ocean. By the time the storm crossed over Bermuda, wind speeds had gusts up to 187 kilometers (116 miles) per hour. Emily was strong enough to pull out part of a dock, sending a cruise ship to float out into the stormy harbor. Luckily the captain and crew were able to keep the ship stable in the harbor as the hurricane passed over the rest of the island. Hurricane Emily caused approximately $35 million worth of damage to Bermuda, but fortunately no lives were lost (see Figure 13.22).

▶ **FIGURE 13.22**

This map shows the tracks for hurricanes Joan and Emily.

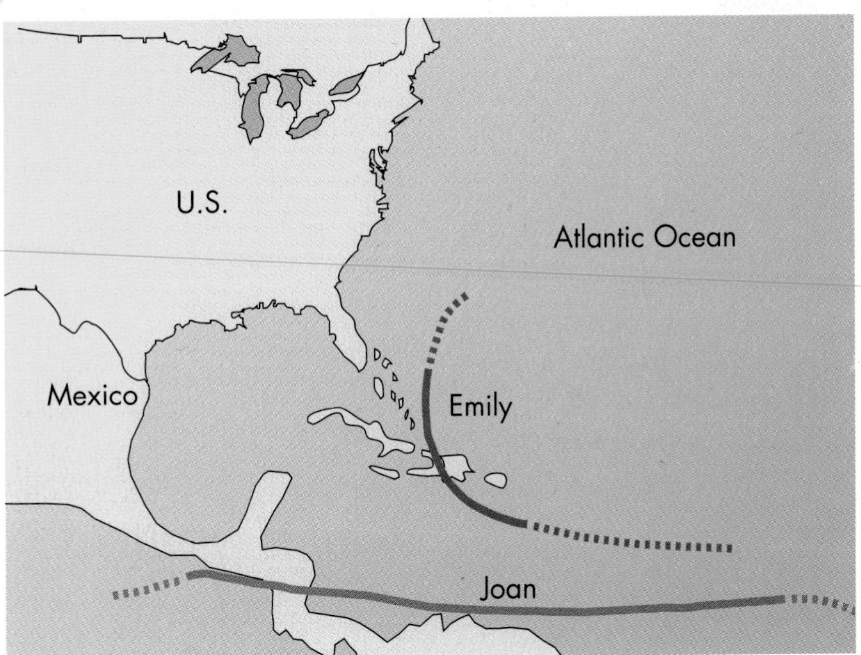

Wrap Up

Write answers to these questions in your notebook.

1. Of the hurricanes you read about,
   a. Where did most of them begin?
   b. Which direction did each travel?
   c. What patterns are associated with hurricanes?
2. How might people use hurricane patterns to prevent loss of life and property?
   Refer to the graph you made from the hurricane data chart.

Making Decisions to Solve Problems

People try to protect themselves from the dangers of natural events. For example, people stay in basements or storm cellars while a tornado passes by or evacuate an area when there are flood or hurricane warnings.

For protection against some natural events, people can even alter the designs of buildings. For example, this photograph shows one way that people protect their homes from high water: they have built houses on stilts. Now flood waters that accompany a hurricane can pass beneath. The people still may have to evacuate before the storm, but if the hurricane is not too severe, their houses on stilts may not be damaged by the storm. When people choose to live in any area, they usually have to adapt to the natural events that are likely to happen there.

In this chapter, you will use your understanding of natural events to make decisions. To learn about one situation in which people's decisions were very important, watch the video or film your teacher will show. See whether you can decide what problem people were trying to solve. What do you think of their solution?

engage/explore

Investigation: Standing against the Wind

explore

Investigation: The House on the Windy Plain

explain

Reading: A Process for Solving Problems
Connections: The Popcorn Cube
Reading: Decisions Are Part of the Process

elaborate/evaluate

Investigation: Designer's Dilemma
Connections: A Balancing Act

▶ Figure 14.1

Many buildings today are wind resistant because of decisions that architects and builders made.

engage/explore

Investigation:
Standing against the Wind

Wind can have destructive effects on the things that people build. In some parts of the world, people have to design buildings that can withstand extremely strong winds—winds blowing across a desert or perhaps out of a mountain canyon. Today people have found ways to strengthen buildings against the wind. Because of the materials builders use and because of the way architects design buildings, winds do not damage many buildings in the western world today. In this investigation, see whether you can use materials and shapes to make a structure that will stand against the wind.

Working Cooperatively

Work cooperatively in your teams of three and use the roles of Manager and Communicator. You will need a work space that allows each of you equal access to a building project. As you *Encourage others to participate*, be sure to *Treat others politely*.

Materials for the Entire Class:

- 1 model house
- 1 large box fan or blow dryer
- 1 wind scale, mounted on a box

Materials for Each Team of Three:

- 1 pair of scissors
- 1 metric ruler
- 4 index cards, 3-by-5 in.
- 4 sheets of construction paper, 9-by-12 in. (1 for Part A, 3 for Part B)
- 1 sheet of white, unlined paper, 8½-by-11 in.
- 3 strips of transparent tape, 5-cm lengths (Part A)
- 3 strips of transparent tape, 5-cm lengths (Part B)

Process and Procedure

Part A—Testing Materials

1. Watch the demonstration your teacher will do.
2. Think about how to build a stronger house than the one you just saw.
3. Read the Background Information that follows the procedure.
4. Pick up the materials for Part A.
5. Cut out four rectangles of construction paper and four rectangles of white paper. Make them the same size as the index cards.

   Use one sheet of construction paper and one sheet of white paper to do this.
6. Tape four index cards together as shown in Figure 14.2 These are the walls of your index-card house.
7. Tape the pieces of construction paper together in exactly the same way that you taped the index-card house together.

   This house should look just like the index-card house but be made of construction paper.
8. Make a house out of plain paper that looks exactly like the other two houses.

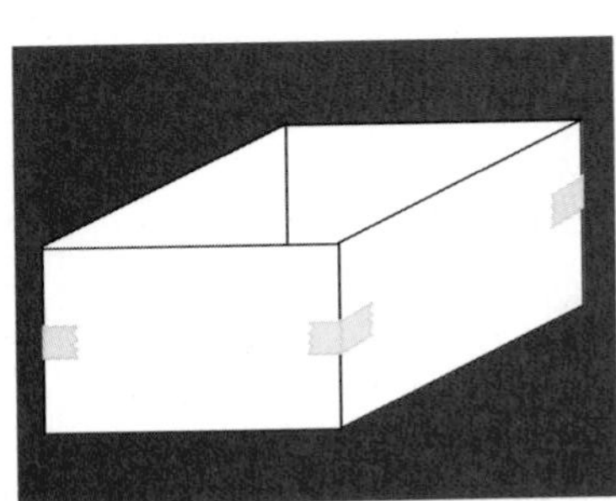

▲ **FIGURE 14.2**
Tape your index cards together as shown to form a square.

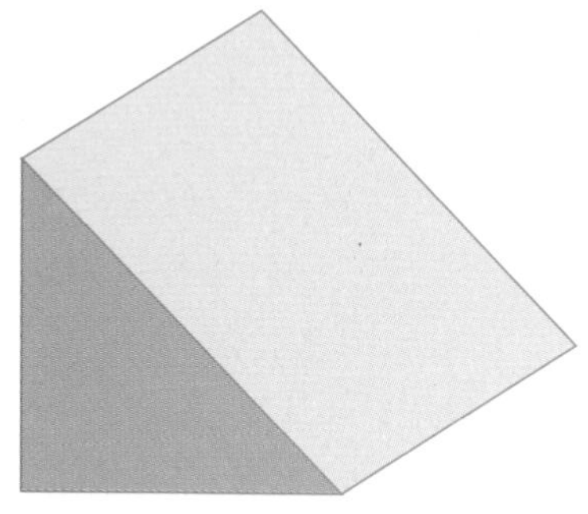

▲ **FIGURE 14.3**

This diagram shows a triangular shape, which also is known as a wedge.

▲ **FIGURE 14.4**

This diagram shows a tube shape, which also is known as a cylinder.

9. Take turns with other teams and test your team's three houses in front of the wind source.

   Your teacher will show you the wind source.

10. With your teammates, summarize the results for Part A.

    Notebook entry: Record your summary and describe which material stood up the best against the wind.

Part B—Testing Shapes

1. As a team, decide how to conduct a fair test to determine what *shape* of house will best withstand a strong wind.

   You should test at least the following shapes

   - a rectangular or cube shape,
   - a triangular shape, and
   - a cylindrical shape.

   Use the following guidelines.

   - Each shape should be made of construction paper.
   - Each shape should use no more than one piece of construction paper.
   - Each shape should be closed on the top and sides, as shown in Figures 14.3 and 14.4.
   - Each shape should be at least 6 cm high and 6 cm wide.

2. After your teacher approves your plan, build the shapes.
3. Conduct your test of each structure's ability to withstand the wind.
4. Clean up the materials.

Background Information

A Fair Test

During this investigation, you will be given instructions on how to set up a fair test. If you are not familiar with the idea of a fair test, think about a controlled experiment. Controlled experiments are basically the same as fair tests. During Chapter 4 of Unit 1, you conducted a controlled experiment when you planted seeds and made sure that the conditions were the same for all the bean seeds, except for one factor, such as the amount of water the plant

▲ **FIGURE 14.5**

A lighthouse has to be resistant to both wind and water. How effective do you think this shape is?

received. A fair test or controlled experiment means that everything is the same, except for one thing that you are comparing or testing. If this is not clear to you yet, read this description again before you do the wrap-up questions.

Wrap Up

Write answers to the following in your notebook. Do this task individually.

1. Why did the three houses that you built in Part A need to look exactly alike? Why did they have to be placed the same distance from the fan?
2. Which material worked best for building a wind-resistant house, and why?
3. Why was the entire class required to use construction paper for Part B?
4. Would the results of your test be different if you used materials other than construction paper? Why or why not?
5. If you were going to build a house that needed to withstand strong winds, in what shape would you build it? Why?
6. Describe how much your team has improved in treating others politely since the beginning of this unit.

Investigation:
The House on the Windy Plain

explore

You now know a little about what types of houses might best withstand strong winds. You could go on testing factors such as materials and shapes for a long time, but maybe it's time to try to build the ideal, wind-resistant house.

Working Cooperatively

Work cooperatively in your teams of three. Use the roles of Manager and Communicator. Practice your Unit 3 skill. You will need a large work space for a building project and a common testing area. During the testing, *Treat others politely.*

Materials for the Entire Class:

- 1 box fan or blow dryer
- 1 wind scale, mounted on a box
- construction materials (that your teacher will sell in the class supply store)

Materials for Each Team of Three:

- 1 empty cereal box
- 1 metric ruler
- 1 pair of scissors
- 30 plastic tokens

Process and Procedure

1. Read the Background Information that follows the procedure.
2. Read the following guidelines for planning your house:
   a. It must have a floor, walls, and a roof.
   b. It must be large enough for a 6-cm person to be able to stand up and lie down inside.
   c. The house must stand on the cereal box, which represents the ground.

   You may decide to poke holes into this ground, but you may not make the holes bigger than a pencil.
3. Discuss the optional materials with your teammates. Decide what you will buy.

   You must build the house by using the materials you buy at the class supply store. See Figure 14.6 for a list of the materials and their prices.
4. Decide how to build a house that will stand best against the strong wind.

   Use what you know about materials, size, and shape.

FOUNDATION CONNECTING MATERIALS
Clay: 40¢ per sphere (pea size)
Toothpicks: 10¢ each

WALL AND ROOF MATERIALS
Index cards: 50¢ per card
Construction paper: $1.00 per half-sheet
Plain paper: 60¢ per sheet

FASTENER MATERIALS
Glue: 60¢ per bottle
Tape: 10¢ per cm
Weights: 20¢ each

▲ **FIGURE 14.6**
You may purchase construction materials from the class supply store. Your plastic tokens are worth 10 cents each for these supplies.

5. Draw your house plan on paper.
   Make sure that you have allowed for a roof, walls, and a floor, and that your house will be large enough for a 6-cm tall person.
6. Show your house plan to your teacher.
   This is the Communicator's job.
7. Build your house according to your team's plan.
   You may buy additional materials if you have tokens left over.
8. When your house is completed, use a pen or pencil to outline where your house is sitting. This line will mark the foundation of your house.

Scale for Rating Houses
You might want to use the following point system
POINTS:
4 It withstands the wind (needs no repair); or
3 The roof comes off the house (needs slight repairs); or
2 The house moves off its foundation (repairable); or
1 The house completely falls apart (destroyed).

▶ **FIGURE 14.7**
You may want to use a point system for rating your house and those of other teams.

▶ FIGURE 14.8

This igloo made of snow and ice serves as a shelter for people who live in areas like Alaska. How do you think a dwelling made of something so cold can keep people warm? Think about the function of other structures that you see pictured in this chapter.

9. Participate in the class test of the houses and use the scale shown in Figure 14.7 to rate your house (and other houses).
10. As a team, discuss the characteristics of the house that stood up best against the wind.
11. With your teammates, redesign your house using what you learned from the class test.
12. Test your house again.

Background Information

People build houses to provide shelter for themselves or others. In some parts of the world, a house provides shelter against the heat and glaring sun. In other places, a house protects against snow, rain, and cold. In some places, houses must be able to withstand at least a mild hurricane. People have developed different types of houses to adapt to different situations.

A house typically has several basic parts: a foundation, a frame, floors, walls, and a roof. Many modern houses are called frame houses because the builders construct a frame of wood and then attach the walls and roof to this frame (see Figure 14.9). Other

houses, such as some log cabins, do not have a frame; the logs are the only materials used to construct the walls.

If you were building a house in certain parts of the world, you would want a house that could stand against strong winds. You would want a strong roof and walls, and you would want to attach them securely to the foundation. As you work through this investigation, look for the choices that will make your house best able to withstand the wind.

Wrap Up

Discuss with your teammates all of the characteristics of your team's final house design. If your teacher calls on you in a class discussion, each of you should be prepared

▶ **FIGURE 14.9**
This photograph shows the roof, frame, and foundation of a house.

to explain your team's design and how you encouraged each other to participate. Then complete the following activity as a team.

1. In your notebook, draw a sketch of your team's final house and describe what you did to make it wind resistant.
2. Imagine that you are trying to sell this house; design an advertisement that highlights its wind-resistant characteristics.

Reading:
A Process for Solving Problems

Everyday people all over the world are recognizing and solving problems. If people need food, they will look for ways to get or to grow food; if people need shelter, they generally can find it or make it. People are inventive; they look for solutions to their problems. For example, if the house that you built falls over in a strong wind, you will recognize that there is a problem and then try to do something about it as you rebuild it.

The knowledge that people use to design and construct things to solve problems is called **technology.** People often think that technology means computers, light bulbs, or space shuttles. Those objects were developed through a process of problem solving that involved technology, but technology is much more than fancy machines and computers. Even something like a paper clip or a piece of tape is the result of the process of technological problem solving. The paper clip solves the problem of loose papers, and tape can repair torn papers.

Stop & Think

Did you think that you were using technology as you built your tiny house? Why or why not?

People have been using the process of technology for thousands of years. But recently, people have used technology to develop new inventions. Sometimes new inventions build on other inventions; that is, the invention of one object sometimes contributes to the

▶ FIGURE 14.10

Native Americans in Nevada use charcoal ovens like these.

invention of other objects. For example, people invented wheels for carts, glass windows for houses, and large engines for boats and trains. Then about 100 years ago, people built new, smaller engines and combined them with wheels, glass, and metal to make the first automobiles.

Often as one problem is solved, another arises. After people had cars to get from one place to another more quickly, they wanted cars that were also safe. So designers investigated ways to build better brakes, safety belts, and child safety seats. This is one example of people using technological problem solving to find solutions.

explain

Connections: The Popcorn Cube

Do you remember the cubes that you looked at in Chapter 8? During the investigation, Numbers, Names, and Cubes, you saw a cube that had a number on each side, but you could not see the bottom. Think about that cube and review your notes from that activity.

Now here is the problem. Imagine that you want to use one of those cubes for a new purpose: holding buttered popcorn. In addition, you want to be able to eat the popcorn while you watch a movie, and you want the

▶ Figure 14.11

Popcorn poppers such as this one were invented to meet a special need in movie theaters. What problems did it solve?

popcorn to stay warm for half an hour. How would you change the cube? Spend some time thinking about this question before you continue. Be sure to record your solution in your notebook.

As you thought about the popcorn cube, you were engaged in the process of technological problem solving. You were not trying to explain what was on the bottom of the cube, as you did in Unit 2. This time you have been thinking about changes that you would make in the cube in order to solve a problem. People engaged in science seek answers to questions about the natural world. People engaged in technology try to solve problems that are associated with humans and their environment.

explain

Reading:
Decisions Are Part of the Process

As you thought about the perfect cube for holding popcorn, did the cube suddenly appear before your eyes? Probably not. Did the walls of your wind-resistant house put themselves together into the strongest shape? No. You did the thinking and the building, and along the way you made some decisions. As you look back on it, you probably will see that you and your teammates had several decisions to make.

Stop & Think

1. List some of the decisions that you made as you built your wind-resistant house.

When people use the process of technological problem solving, the situations almost always require decisions. So you might be wondering how people make good decisions.

One way to make a decision is to consider all of the **benefits** and **costs.** The benefits are all the positive things that could result from a decision. The costs are all the

The Smithsonian Institution

▶ **FIGURE 14.12**

As the Wright Brothers tried to design a plane that would fly, they made countless decisions along the way. Decades later as others designed commercial planes, such as the one in the next photograph, these designers made many other decisions.

negative things that could result from a decision. Some people call the potential costs of making a decision its risks. Suppose for example, that you decided to spend four of your tokens to buy toothpicks for your model house. The benefit of this decision would be that you could use the toothpicks to support the walls of your house. The cost would be that now you could not use your tokens to buy extra tape or a weight.

So here's a strategy for making decisions: First consider a certain choice. Then make a list of the positive things that will or could happen (benefits) and a separate list of the negative things that will or could happen (costs) if you make that choice. If you can predict that more negative than positive things will happen, usually the choice is not a good idea.

Stop & Think

2. Provide an example of something you've done that has had both benefits and costs.

One cost may outweigh many benefits, or sometimes one benefit may outweigh many costs. Someone might dare you to do something dangerous and even offer you money. The costs of refusing to do this might be that people will laugh at you and that you will not get the money. But you might decide that being safe is wiser. So perhaps you decide not to take the dare just because the one benefit (safety) is more important than all the costs.

Here is another example of a type of decision you already may have made. You are working on a model house for a contest. You were supposed to finish it last night, but did not. The contest is this morning at school. To make matters worse, your bottle of glue has dried out. In a kitchen drawer, you find a tube of glue that your brother used on his model airplane. It is really strong glue, and you know it worked great on the plastic airplanes. You don't know, however, if it will work on wood and the directions have rubbed off. Also your brother is not home so you cannot ask him if you can use it. But you really want to finish your house, and you think this glue should work really well.

Stop & Think

3. What are the benefits and costs to using the strong glue?
4. What will you do, and why?

By now you probably have decided what you would have done. The decision you had to make was whether or not to use that particular tube of glue. As you thought about it, though, you might have realized that you had several additional options. For example, you could try it on a small piece of wood to see if it would hold before you used it on the entire model house. You could ask your parents for permission since your brother is not at home, or you could see whether a friend had some other glue that you could borrow.

When you are making a decision, you usually have several options. Therefore when you are making decisions, get as much information as you can. Imagine what the results of your decision would be and then list the benefits and costs. Finally make the best decision you can.

elaborate/evaluate

Investigation: Designer's Dilemma

In this investigation, you and your team will examine an everyday object. To get some practice, look at the objects pictured below and think about what decisions the designers made when they were creating them.

Materials for Each Team of Three:

- 1 object assigned by the teacher

Process and Procedure

1. Collect the object assigned to your team.
2. Pass your object around to each person in the group, then place it in the center of the table.
3. Read each of the questions below and have each member of the team offer an answer.

   Notebook entry: Write an answer to each question after your team has discussed it. Answer all the questions.

Working Cooperatively

Work cooperatively in your teams of three. Sit in a triangular configuration. Use the roles of Manager, Tracker, and Communicator, as well as Team Member. Practice reviewing the skill that your teacher has assigned.

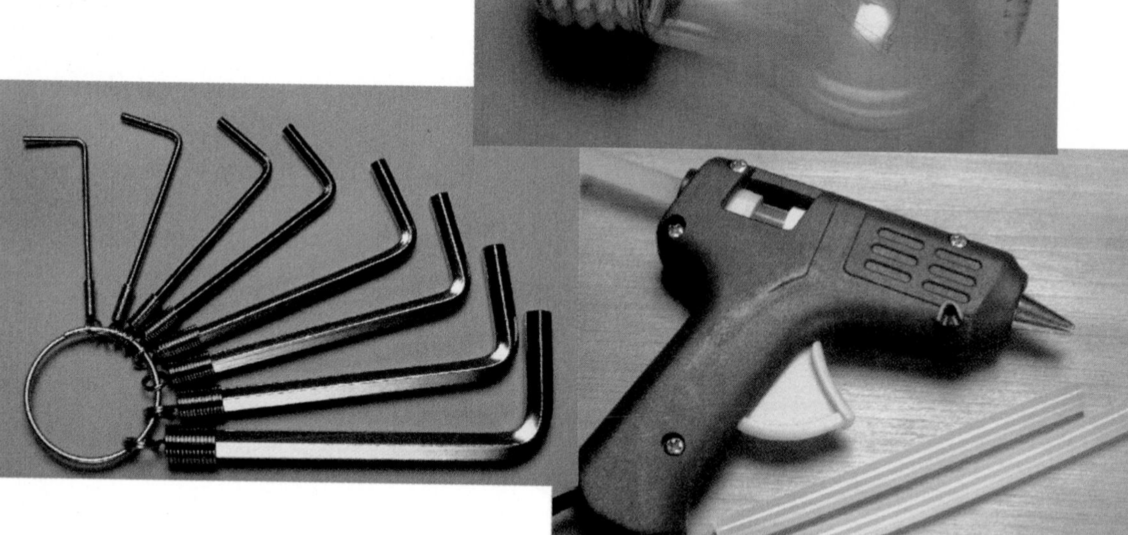

▶ FIGURE 14.13

This photograph shows an astronaut writing with a special pen designed for use in space. What problem did this object solve?

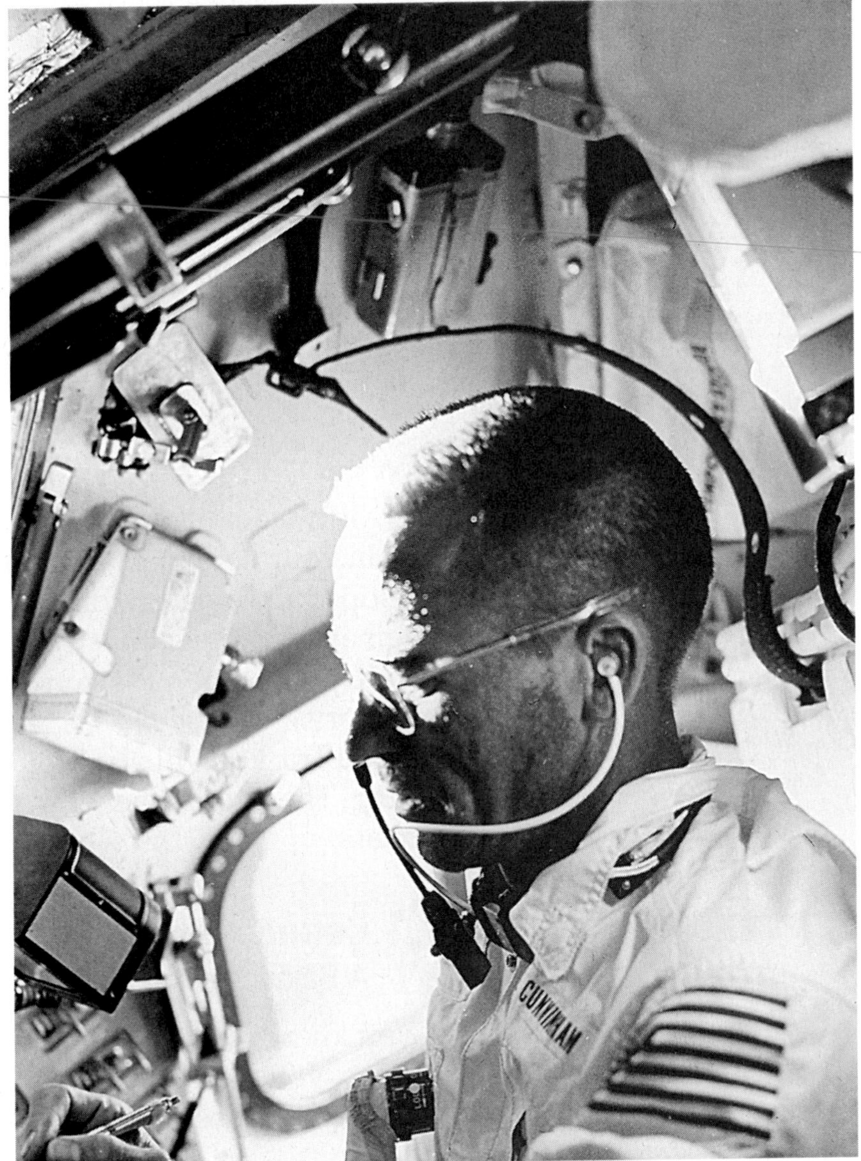

NASA

a. What is the purpose of this object?

b. Does the object solve any problems? If so, which ones?

c. Why do you think the designer chose this material?

d. How do you think the designer decided on the size of the object? Is size important in how the object works?

e. How much could you change the shape of the object and still have it do the same job?

f. Would the object serve the same function if it were another color?

g. How would you change the structure of your object so that a small child could use it?

h. Suppose NASA decided to use your object on the next shuttle mission. The object would need to work in space where the force of gravity is minimal. How would you change the design of the object so that people could use it in space?

Wrap Up

After your team has answered the questions, write a story in your notebook about how the designer developed the object. Work by yourself. Use your imagination and creativity in your story. Be sure to include your team's answers to questions *a* through *h* in your story.

The Tracker will give you 30 minutes to finish writing. Then your teacher may ask you to share it with the class.

Connections: A Balancing Act

elaborate/evaluate

As you know by now, when you want to make a wise decision, you often must consider the costs and benefits. In this activity, see whether you can make some balanced decisions.

Follow these steps for the first situation:

- read about the situation;
- draw two blank cost and benefit charts, one for choice *a* and one for choice *b;*
- fill in your cost and benefit charts;
- answer any questions in your notebook; and
- explain what your decision would be.

Repeat the steps above for the second situation.

Situation #1

You have been selected to serve on a town committee. The town has raised money to build a new apartment

▲ **FIGURE 14.14**

When builders construct new buildings or remodel old buildings, there are many safety factors to take into account. What are some of them?

complex for senior citizens. The town has selected a builder, and a company representative tells you about the two options for completing the project. You are asked to choose between these two options:

a. You could build a one-story complex of apartments at a convenient and scenic area in town. People would have easy access to stores and clinics. But because this is a scenic area, you are limited to one-story buildings; anything higher would block the view. The design of the one-story complex would allow some people to have small porches and yards, but there would be room for only ten apartments. Currently the town has a waiting list of more than 30 people who want to move into the complex.

b. You could build a taller building on a different lot. This building could have two or three floors of apartments and room for many more people than the first site. There would be no porches or balconies. The three-story building would allow twenty-five of the people on the waiting list to move in. The building itself would not be in the scenic area of town, and it is more than seventeen miles from the more convenient site.

1. Which choice has the most benefits and the fewest costs?
2. Which benefits are most important, and why?

The Corbis-Bettmann Archive

▶ **FIGURE 14.15**
Historic buildings, such as this one, contribute to the character of our cities. Sometimes there are modern safety concerns that require remodeling.

Situation #2

In another building situation, your committee has to make a decision about safety. An old office building is being restored. It is a beautiful building in the downtown area, with woodwork and designs from the early 1900s. But here are the safety concerns.

a. Currently the building has a stairwell but no elevator. People want to make the building accessible to the handicapped, but there are problems. In order to put in an elevator, part of the building must be torn out to make room for the elevator shaft. But for fire safety, the owners must have a stairwell. This stairwell must be of a certain size to allow many people to leave the building at the same time. Here's the problem: If the elevator is put in, the current stairwell will be too small for fire safety regulations. So the builders have proposed building a second, iron staircase outside the building. With the inside and the outside stairs, the building would meet the fire code and the elevator would allow handicapped people access to all the floors. Some people have argued, however, that the outside staircase is not a good idea because the building could then be vandalized more easily.

b. The second choice would be to make a larger inside stairwell, in addition to the elevator. This plan calls for no outside stairway. This plan would allow handicapped people access to all floors, as well as provide a fire escape and ensure a safe building. There are opponents to this plan too, however. Constructing the larger inside stairwell will cost much more money. If the owners raise the rents in the building to cover these costs, small businesses may not be able to afford the rent.

3. For situation #2, which solution would you choose, and why?

Big and Little Decisions

By the time you have reached this point in the unit, you have looked at photographs of many natural events. You have learned how you can make some predictions about these events through the use of patterns. You also have seen examples of how people can use technology to solve problems. In this chapter, you will learn more about how people can make decisions about hard-to-predict events.

As people decide how to make their homes and communities as safe as possible, they have to decide which types of natural events are most likely to occur and what problems they might cause. In the Florida Keys, designers need to design long bridges to connect one Key to the next. These bridges need to withstand wind and water during hurricanes. If you lived near the Gulf of Mexico where floods and hurricanes were a problem, you would build a house on stilts to protect your belongings and you would not be as concerned with making your house earthquake-proof. But if you lived in California, your decision probably would be different because of the frequency and severity of earthquakes there.

engage

Connections: Those Difficult Decisions

explore

Investigation: It's in the Bag

explain

Reading: Probable Outcomes

elaborate

Investigation: What Are the Chances?
Investigation: What Will Happen Here?

evaluate

Connections: Patterns, Problem-Solving, and Probability
Connections: You, the Decision Maker

engage

Connections:
Those Difficult Decisions

People base their decisions on what they think is most likely to happen. People often watch weather forecasts to help them make decisions. If you have planned to attend an outdoor baseball game, but then learn that heavy rains are predicted for that afternoon, you might decide not to go. Sometimes numbers are included in the forecast. You might hear a weather forecaster say on the news, "Tonight's forecast calls for a 20 percent chance of rain." Is this forecaster predicting that it is or is not going to rain? Listen for more examples of forecasts as you watch the video your teacher will show.

explore

Investigation:
It's in the Bag

How do people decide what risks they will take? As you have read before, people look for patterns and make predictions. Often they identify costs and benefits. Sometimes they even use numbers to show how certain they are about their predictions. As you and your teammates go through the investigation, see whether you can discover how people use numbers in predictions.

Working Cooperatively

Work cooperatively in your teams of three. Use the roles of Tracker, Communicator, and Manager. Agree on a social skill from this year that your team needs to practice the most. Report the skill you chose to your teacher.

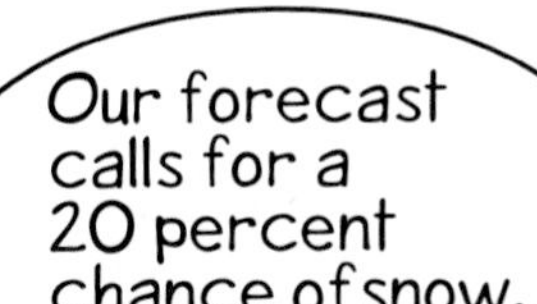

Materials for Each Team of Three:

- 20 plastic pieces, 10 red and 10 white
- 1 paper bag for holding the pieces

Materials for the Entire Class:

- an additional 200 plastic pieces, 100 red and 100 white
- 2 paper bags
- 1 large map of the United States

Process and Procedure

Part A—The Demonstration and More

1. Participate in a demonstration with your teacher.
   See whether you can predict what the chances are that snow will fall in Bozeman.
2. Read How To #10, How to Make Sense of Percentages.
   You will use percentages in this investigation.

Part B—Bozeman, Montana

1. Set up a data table in your notebook.
   See Figure 15.1. You will use a data table like this in which to record your results for Parts B, C, and D.
2. Obtain the materials.
3. The Tracker should put two white pieces and eight red pieces into the paper bag and gently shake the bag to mix the pieces.
4. Read about the following situation in Bozeman, Montana.

Situation A

As Isaac has pointed out, there is a 20 percent chance of snow for Bozeman, Montana, today. Looking at the long-range forecast, the situation should remain much the same for the next ten days. So for each day during the next ten days, there is a 20 percent chance of snow.

▶ **FIGURE 15.1**

Copy this data table into your notebook.

Did snow fall in Bozeman?

Day	Yes	No
1		
2		
3		
4		
5		
6		
7		
8		
9		
10		

5. To play out the weather day-by-day in Bozeman, do the following:
   a. The Tracker should hold the bag while the Communicator draws out one plastic piece without looking into the bag.
   b. Observe whether or not it snowed.

      If the Communicator draws out a white piece, then it snowed in Bozeman that day.

      If the Communicator draws out a red piece, then it did not snow in Bozeman that day.
   c. The Manager should record in his or her table whether or not it snowed on Day 1.
   d. Return the colored piece to the bag so that there are again ten pieces in it and shake it to mix the pieces.
6. Repeat all parts of Step 5 nine more times, one time for each day.

   The Manager should record whether or not it snowed on Days 2 through 10.

Part C—Baton Rouge, Louisiana

1. Remove the pieces from your bag and replace them with five red pieces and five white pieces.

   The Communicator should do this. There should be ten pieces altogether in your team's bag.

2. Read the forecast for Baton Rouge, Louisiana.

   Situation B

   As Marie has said, we might get a little rain. The forecasters say there is a 50 percent chance of rain in Baton Rouge for both today and tonight. Tomorrow and the next day each have a 50 percent chance of rain and thunderstorms.

3. Make a data table in which to record whether or not it rained on Baton Rouge for each of these days.

4. To play out the weather day-by-day in Baton Rouge, do the following:

   a. The Manager should hold the bag while the Tracker draws out one plastic piece without looking.

   b. The Communicator should record in his or her table whether or not it rained in Baton Rouge on Day 1.

   c. Return the plastic piece to the bag.

5. Repeat all parts of Step 4 two more times, once for Day 2 and once for Day 3.

   The Communicator should record the results for Days 2 and 3.

6. Fill in your own data table for Parts B and C.

   Be sure that you have your team's results recorded for Bozeman and Baton Rouge.

7. Participate in the class discussion.

   Notebook entry. Listen to find out how your team's results differed from or were similar to other teams' results.

Part D—Clean Energy Town

1. Read about Clean Energy Town.

   The utility company in Clean Energy Town, U.S.A. has built a nuclear power plant. It wanted to make sure the plant would be safe. Clean Energy Town has the slight possibility of an earthquake. The chances are three out of 100 that a major earthquake will occur in any year. If a major earthquake hits Clean Energy Town, there is a chance that the nuclear plant would be damaged or would release dangerous pollutants.

2. Make a data table for recording earthquake occurrences in Clean Energy Town.

   Notebook entry: Use a full page and make two columns, one labeled "yes" and the other labeled "no." Allow space in your table for fifty years.

3. Discuss with your classmates how you will represent the probability of an earthquake.

4. Participate in the class drawing and record the results in your data table.

   Each drawing will represent what happened in a particular year. Remember that after each drawing, you must place the plastic pieces back into the bag.

5. Put away the materials.

Wrap Up

Discuss the following questions with your teammates and write the answers in your notebook. Each of you should be able to explain your answers during a class discussion.

1. With a 20 percent chance of snow in Bozeman, how many days did it snow for your team and the two teams nearest you?
2. Suppose the forecast for Baton Rouge, Louisiana, includes a 60 percent chance of rain for each of the next three days.
   a. Is it possible that the next three days in Baton Rouge will have no rain?
   b. Is it possible that it could rain each of the next three days? Explain your answers.

▲ **FIGURE 15.2**

When designers and engineers work together to design a dam like this one, they need to take into account the natural events that are likely to happen that might damage the dam.

3. You read about a place with a 3 percent risk of a major earthquake occurring that could trigger a catastrophe in a nuclear power plant.
   a. Is an earthquake likely to occur?
   b. Is the site safe enough for a nuclear power plant? Why or why not?
4. Use your own rating system to evaluate how well you used the skill you chose.

explain

Reading: Probable Outcomes

Statements of Probability

You might wish that the weather forecaster could just tell you whether or not it is going to rain or snow. Why do forecasters say that there is a 25 percent chance of rain? They say this because they do not know for certain. We

▶ FIGURE 15.3
Look at this picture of falling number cubes. How is predicting rainy weather like rolling number cubes? How can you use your observation skills to make accurate predictions about weather patterns?

can use some types of patterns to make very accurate predictions. But other patterns, such as weather patterns, are not always as predictable. We do not always have enough information, and sometimes things do not follow definite patterns. So sometimes we use the information we have, to say what probably will happen.

Here is an example. Suppose one of your friends plays basketball three days a week but not always on the same days. In some weeks, he plays on Monday, Thursday, and Friday. Other weeks he plays on Tuesday, Saturday, and Sunday, and so on. Now suppose someone asked you whether your friend will be playing basketball on a Thursday three months from now. Could you give a definite answer? No because you do not have enough information to make the prediction—your friend has not established an exact pattern. But there is a general pattern. You know that your friend plays three days out of every seven. That is a little less than 50 percent of the days. So although you could not state for sure whether or not your friend would be playing on that Thursday, you *could* say something like, "There is a little less than a 50 percent chance that he will be playing basketball on that Thursday."

We call statements like this, **statements of probability.** They are statements that indicate what could happen or what is likely to happen, but they do not say for sure what *will* happen. Think back to when you selected plastic pieces to determine whether it snowed in Bozeman, Montana. Each team used the same probability—a 20 percent chance of snow each day. But each team probably did not get the same results. Maybe it did not snow at all for some teams, and for other teams it may have snowed four days or more. Of course for most teams, there probably were more days without snow. That is because a probability of 20 percent, or 20 out of 100, is a fairly small probability. If the probability of snow were 70 percent, you could expect that most teams would end up with more days of snow than they did with a probability of 20 percent.

Stop & Think

1. For Bozeman and Baton Rouge, why did you have to replace the plastic piece each time and always draw from a bag that had ten pieces in it?
2. If the weather forecasters in Bozeman are predicting a 20 percent chance of snow, would you still plan a drive through fifty miles of the Montana countryside? Explain your answer.

Making Decisions Based on Probabilities

In Chapter 12, you learned that one way to make a decision is to weigh the costs and benefits that would result from the possible decision. But sometimes you don't know what the costs and benefits will be. For example, if you were planning to go to an outdoor flea market on Saturday and you knew that it was going to rain, you could decide whether enjoying the market (a benefit) is worth walking around in the rain (a cost). But people do not always know for sure whether or not it is going to rain. What if there is a 70 percent chance of rain? This makes your decision more difficult because you only know what is likely to happen.

Stop & Think

3. During the investigation It's in the Bag, it might have seemed to you that a 20 percent chance was a low risk for snow but that a 3 percent chance was a high risk for a major earthquake that could damage a nuclear power plant. Why might people think differently about the probability for these two events?
4. Describe another pair of events in which one could be an inconvenience and the other could be a disaster.
5. Describe how the type of event (an inconvenience or a disaster) changes the percentage of chance that you are willing to accept.

Investigation: What Are the Chances?

elaborate

The sun always rises in the east. The winds probably will increase later today. A snowstorm in July is unlikely in Florida. There is a small chance that I will pass my history test without studying. These statements all have something in common. Each one describes the chances or probability of an event occurring. In this investigation, you will have an opportunity to rate such statements according to how likely you think they are to occur.

Working Cooperatively
You will work by yourself.

Materials for Each Student:

- 1 copy of Words by Chance
- 1 pair of scissors
- glue or tape

▶ FIGURE 15.4
Can you tell from your front door which direction is east? The sun has its own pattern. It rises in the east and sets in the west.

Process and Procedure

1. Draw a line like the one shown in Figure 15.5 near the top of a page in your notebook.
2. Write "Low Chance" on the left edge of the page and "High Chance" on the right edge.

   This will be your scale.
3. Cut out the words from Words by Chance.
4. Lay the pieces of cutout paper on your open notebook, below the line you have drawn.
5. Group the words so that ones describing approximately the same chance of something happening are together.
6. Then arrange these groups on the paper in order from low chance to high chance.
7. When you are satisfied with your arrangement of the cutout words, attach or copy the words into your notebook.

Low chance — High chance

▶ FIGURE 15.5
Draw a line like this in your notebook.

Wrap Up

1. Use the words from Words by Chance to describe the probabilities that the following events will occur.
   a. The sun will rise tomorrow.
   b. A coin will land head up.
   c. You will be absent from school at least one day this year.
   d. A blizzard will occur in Hawaii in August.
   e. The next baby born in your town's hospital will be a girl.
   f. An earthquake will occur in California during the next century.
2. Look at the probability scale in Figure 15.6 and draw one just like it in your notebook. Leave at least 10 centimeters of vertical space between this scale and the scale you drew in Step 1.

▶ **FIGURE 15.6**

Note that the marks on this scale divide it into 10 parts.

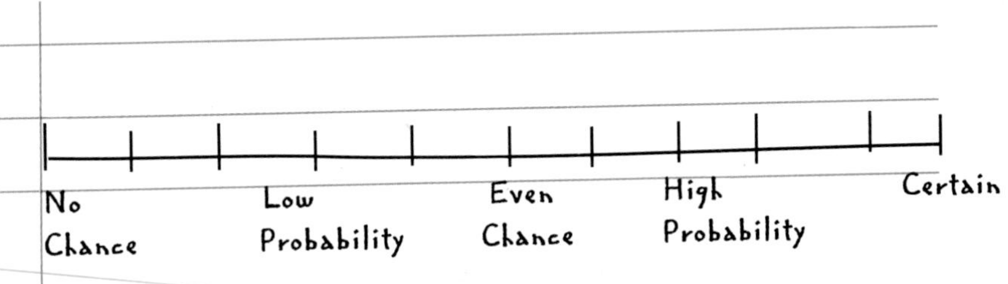

Answer the following questions by using percentages and enter the numbers above the line of the scale.

a. On the probability scale you have drawn, what number should you assign to a certainty?

b. What number should you assign to an even chance?

c. What number should you assign to no chance?

Answer these questions by using percentages.

3. What is the chance that the sun will rise tomorrow?

4. What is the chance that the next baby born in your town's hospital will be a girl?

▶ **FIGURE 15.7**

What is the chance that the next baby born in your town's hospital will be a girl?

5. Suppose that the last fifteen babies born in the hospital were boys. What is the chance that the next baby born in your town's hospital will be a boy?
6. What is your chance of winning a drawing if you bought five of the 100 tickets sold?
7. What is your chance of winning if you bought twenty-five of the 100 tickets sold?

elaborate

Investigation:
What Will Happen Here?

By now you realize that you can use probability to make predictions about all kinds of things, from whether or not you should wear a rain jacket to school one day to whether or not someone in your class has the same birthday as you. In this investigation, you will use probability to decide which types of events are most likely to occur at a given location.

Working Cooperatively

Work cooperatively in your team of three. You need to sit in a configuration that allows all Team Members equal access to the map and the list that your team will have. Practice your Unit 3 skill *Encourage others to participate.*

Materials for the Entire Class:

- 1 wall map of the United States

Materials for Each Team of Three:

- 1 copy of the Natural Events List
- 1 copy of the U.S. Map with Location Dots

Process and Procedure

1. Obtain the materials.
2. Read the Background Information.
3. Look at the map you have.

   Notice where the letters and dots indicate six locations.
4. Read the Natural Events List.
5. Decide which numbered set of events should go with which location.

   Mark a number beside each letter to indicate which set of events is likely to happen at each location.

   STOP: Remember to encourage others to participate.
6. Discuss your opinions with your teammates.

You do not need to agree with your teammates, but be ready to justify your answer.

7. Participate in the class discussion.

   Listen as other teams explain why they think a particular set of events would occur at a certain location.

▼ **FIGURE 15.8**

This is a computer graphic drawing of the state of California. Why do you think certain natural events are more likely to occur in California than in other parts of the United States?

Background Information

During this investigation, you will read about the probability of certain natural events occurring. As you try to decide which events would occur at each location, you might find that the following information is useful.

Hurricanes mostly affect the land only along coastlines. In the United States, hurricanes usually occur in the eastern and southeastern parts of the country.

Tornadoes may occur almost anywhere in the United States. Check your notebook and Chapter 12 to remember where most tornadoes occur.

Fires may occur in any location where there is fuel to burn.

Droughts may occur in any part of the country, although they usually are associated with the western, midwestern, and southwestern parts of the United States.

Snowstorms may occur almost anywhere in the United States, but they occur much more often in the northern and mountainous parts of the country.

▲ **FIGURE 15.9**

What do you think it takes to keep farmland like this in a healthy state?

Wrap Up

For the activities in this section, work individually and write answers in your notebook.

1. Choose one of the following questions to answer:

   What is the best method you have found to encourage others to participate?

   What is one example you saw during class of someone effectively encouraging someone else to participate?

2. Choose one of the six locations in the investigation. Write down which set of events your team decided would be most likely to happen there. Then write about what has happened at that location during the last year, the last 100 years, or what will happen in the future. This work might be a short story, an essay, or a play for example.

Connections:

Patterns, Problem-Solving, and Probability

evaluate

As you can see, Isaac, Marie, and Al are satisfied that they have solved a problem with a model bridge they have built. If you think over what you know about houses and bridges, perhaps you can decide what problems the bridge solved.

1. What are some of the natural events that architects and engineers must consider when constructing buildings and bridges? If you do not remember, look back at the readings in Chapters 12 and 13.

   Natural events have the power to destroy people and the structures they live in. When such destruction occurs, we consider the event a disaster and make an effort to change the way we live and the way we construct buildings. People begin to adapt when they make observations about natural events and recognize the patterns associated with these events. Think back to Chapter 14 and review the answers you wrote in your notebook.

2. What are some of the patterns associated with hurricanes and tornadoes?

▲ **FIGURE 15.10**

Look at these two photos. What difference do you see in the time of day they were taken? What pattern are you observing here?

People have used patterns not only to predict events but also to predict how to solve problems. When you designed houses and tested them in the wind, you might have noticed that some shapes and materials always stood up well in the wind. As you made the observations, you found the key to solving a problem, and you learned more about creating a house that would withstand a strong wind. Your new knowledge helped you to solve a technological problem.

3. Explain how the process of solving a technological problem is different from developing a scientific explanation.

   An important part of technological problem solving is making decisions. Every technological decision involves costs and benefits. Sometimes the best answer or solution is not easy to find because one cost or one benefit may outweigh many of the other benefits or costs.

4. What is one example of a situation in which one benefit can outweigh many costs?

When we make decisions, we want to know what is most likely to happen. In some cases, we use probability statements. People use probability statements when their decisions involve hard-to-predict events.

5. An example of a probability statement is, "There is a 40 percent chance of rain tonight." What does this statement mean?

So how do people use patterns to adapt to natural events? People look for patterns to discover what has happened, to predict what will happen, and to figure out how to solve problems that might result from the events. As you proceed through the next activity, see whether you can apply what you know about natural events, technology, decisions, and probability.

Connections:
You, the Decision Maker

evaluate

A citizens' group has selected you to serve on a committee that is studying a scenic area in a semi-arid location, which has been struck by a terrible drought. This is the third year of the drought. The committee must make some decisions that involve technology.

Solution A

One possible solution for easing the drought would be to pipe water to the area. A place not too far away has a water reservoir, and this place is likely to have a rainy season this year. To make sure that there is enough water for both places, however, some of the people in charge of the reservoir have said that they would have to raise the height of the dam to allow the town to store more water.

Opponents of this idea say that if too much water is added to the reservoir, the weight of the added water will put too much pressure on the faults below and could trigger an earthquake. They believe that increasing the height of the dam is a dangerous idea. Several engineers have come to the area and studied the

▲ **FIGURE 15.11**

There are many areas in the world that do not have enough water to sustain communities. By diverting water from distant rivers, certain areas are now able to support large communities. What other problems does this solution raise? What are the costs and benefits of this solution?

problem. They have listed the probabilities of natural disasters as follows:

drought: 98 percent per year
earthquake: 20 percent per year

Solution B

Other people have suggested that a solution might come from even farther away. Some areas along the coast have heavy rains and plenty of water. Large trucks could haul drinking water from there to the areas that really need it. Also the cost of hauling the water by truck would be much less expensive than raising the dam. Only if trucks hauled water for six years would the expenses equal the cost of raising the dam.

But some people have argued that these large trucks will cause extra air pollution and create a traffic hazard along narrow and scenic roads. Much of this coastal area is a forest wilderness that people are trying to preserve. They also believe that the trucks would create noise pollution and that the sight of so many trucks along the roads would be a type of visual pollution. This is a tourist area, and the increase in pollution may decrease the number of tourists and hurt the economy. Scientists have reported on the probabilities as follows:

drought: 98 percent per year
increase in air pollution: 20 percent per year

1. Draw a chart that shows the costs and benefits for Solution A and another chart that shows the costs and benefits for Solution B.
2. Explain what you think should be done and why.
3. Describe at least one other possible solution to the problem. What are the costs and benefits of this solution?

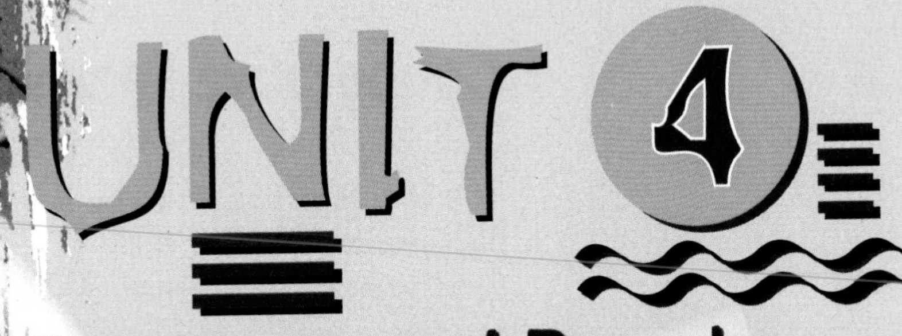

UNIT 4

Patterns and People

So far this year, you have investigated patterns that people have discovered. People saw patterns in the changes of the moon and used those patterns to devise calendars. People noticed patterns in events on earth and found ways to explain such things as hurricanes, earthquakes, and volcanoes. People have used the patterns associated with certain natural events to build structures that can withstand these natural events. Some patterns though, are created by people such as these vapor trails, fireworks, ancient ruins, and windmills. What are some other patterns that people create? As you continue through this unit, see what patterns you can find.

Cooperative Learning Overview

The characters seem to be feeling pretty good about their cooperative learning skills, and they certainly have a right. Unit skills, activity skills, roles, evaluating your cooperative learning progress during wrap-up sections—these all represent a good deal of hard work.

Stop and think for a moment about how you have progressed from being new to cooperative learning to where you are now. What was the hardest part of cooperative learning? What was the best part?

- Do you have all the skills you need to be able to work cooperatively with others at any time?
- How do you think that the characters might answer the preceding question?
- Using a maximum of three speech balloons, write a conversation among the characters that you think would follow Al's comment. Write this conversation in your notebook.

Before you begin the next chapter, add your ideas to a class T-chart for the new Unit 4 skill of including everyone in discussions. Remember that discussions occur in small groups (like your individual teams), as well as large groups (like your class). Also be sure to discuss with your team not only the unit skill but also what you have learned in previous teams about cooperative learning.

The last unit skill of the year! I remember when we didn't know anything about cooperative learning and we were trying to make a T-chart for the first unit skill.
Now think of all the skills we've used, like expressing your thoughts and ideas aloud, and listening politely to others. It makes so much sense now!
How about showing respect for others and their ideas or encouraging others to participate. They seemed hard at first, but they did help us work well together. Gee, what could be left? Isaac? Marie? Do you know what the new unit skill is? Oh well, let's take a look in the book.
Hey! What about me? No one asked me what the new skill is, and I just happen to know. Get this you guys...INCLUDE EVERYONE IN DISCUSSIONS!

It's Everywhere

As you look at these pictures of covered and uncovered landfills, you might wonder what types of patterns you possibly could find. Garbage dumps, after all, contain a lot of junk jumbled together and stacked in heaps. Eventually some landfills are reclaimed as this one has been. As you might know already, garbage disposal is a major problem in many places. Around the world, especially in developed countries, people generate too much garbage. In this chapter, you will learn about people's patterns of garbage disposal and about some patterns that people are beginning to change.

engage / explore

Connections: Look at the Evidence

explore

Investigation: All in a Day's Garbage

explain

Reading: The Garbage Crisis
Connections: Garbage through the Years

explain / elaborate

Investigation: Recycling Choices

elaborate

Investigation: Everything in Its Place

evaluate

Connections: Down by the River and Out in the Desert

Connections:
Look at the Evidence

engage / explore

Maybe when you think about garbage, it is something you just want to throw away. But what if you could not get rid of it? The garbage would keep piling up in the hallway or at the curb, and of course the mound would keep growing because you would keep using things and throwing them away.

Imagine a time when the garbage company could not pick up the garbage because of bad weather or a garbage strike. You then might have an idea of what too much garbage is like. Today getting rid of garbage really is a problem. People in many countries are running out of places to dispose of garbage. Dumps that city planners expected to last for 100 years have filled up within 15 years. By the time you read these words, there will be even less space because of the amount of garbage that people throw away daily. In the United States, every day each person throws away an average of four pounds of trash. That may not seem like very much trash, but it adds up to over 207 million tons every year. But why should you care about garbage? It all gets thrown away somewhere, doesn't it?

Study Figures 16.1 and 16.2. In your notebook, record your ideas about how the garbage in each picture got to where it is.

In your notebook, record answers to the following questions.

1. What things do you usually throw away every day?
2. How much garbage in pounds or kilograms do you think you throw away each day? Explain your answer.
3. What are some things you think you and your family or school could do to throw away less?

By the end of this chapter, you may have some more ideas.

▲ **FIGURE 16.1**

Certain kinds of plastic products floating in the water can kill animals. Sometimes animals swim into the plastic and drown; sometimes they eat it and die. Some of the more vulnerable animals are birds and sea lions. Sea lions often swim into plastic fishing nets that fishing crews have thrown away. Roughly 50,000 sea lions become entangled and die in the nets each year. We have no estimates on how many birds die from eating plastic or swimming into it.

Investigation:
All in a Day's Garbage

explore

During the 1980s and through the 1990s, we could see a trend in garbage disposal. Many people have thrown away more and more garbage every year. As you read in the beginning of the chapter, some areas are running out

▶ FIGURE 16.2
Sometimes when litter washes up on beaches, it causes health hazards. Sometimes things like hypodermic needles and sewage are floating in the water.

of room for garbage. In the United States and some other countries, this is happening because our current pattern of garbage disposal is to throw away large quantities of garbage every day. As you and your classmates conduct the following investigation, see whether you can determine how garbage patterns have changed through the years.

Working Cooperatively

You will work as a class and then individually. As you participate, practice the new unit skill *Include everyone in discussions.*

Materials for the Entire Class:

- props

Process and Procedure

1. Discuss as a class how detailed you want the production of the following play to be. You might
   - act out the play without props,
   - act out the play with props, or
   - have each team discuss one scene and then present the information you learned.

   If you want to use props, think about ideas and materials that you can contribute.
2. Participate in the investigation according to the procedures that you agreed on during the class discussion.

TRAVELS WITH TRASH

Scene 1: The Year 2000

Narrator: Al, Marie, Isaac, and Rosalind are spending the afternoon at Isaac's house.

A nearly full garbage bag is sitting in the kitchen corner near a garbage can.

Al: Hey Isaac, looks like you didn't take out the trash this week.

Isaac (*offended*)**:** Yes, I did take out the trash this week. That's just today's garbage. I can see you're not in charge of the garbage at your house, Al. You obviously have no idea how fast this stuff builds up!

Ros (*opening the tied-up garbage bag and stuffing a sack into the already full garbage bag*)**:** Thanks for the snacks, Marie. They were really good. Hey Isaac, looks like you guys had frozen food this week too—oops.

The bag splits open, spilling plastic milk bottles, cereal boxes, frozen food boxes, and paper towel rolls.

Sorry Isaac, I'll help clean it up.

Isaac: That's okay; I broke a trash bag last week too.

He gets out a fresh bag.

At least you didn't see any aluminum cans, did you? I recycle those at school.

Marie: My grandfather says that he used to take out the trash just once a week when he was growing up.

Al: Maybe he forgot to take it out on the other days.

Marie: No I don't think so. I think he meant there really wasn't much to take out.

Ros (*beginning to get excited*)**:** I know how we could find out. We could go back to that time travel place and see whether we could get another free ticket for time travel. Then we could visit your granddad!

Isaac: Well I guess we could, but you know, Ros, the probability isn't very high of us getting free tickets twice.

Marie: Maybe not but I'd like to try. I'm sure my grandfather wouldn't have made that up.

Al (*heading for the door*)**:** Well, let's go.

Scene 2: At the Travel Agency

Narrator: On the street corner where Time Travel is located, the characters find a surprise.
The agency has a sign out front that states "Closed for the day. Please take a free card." Al reaches the door first.

Al: Hey look a free card.

Al picks one.

Isaac: No way!

Ros (*looking over Al's shoulder and reading aloud*)**:** Why don't you take one too? This ticket is good for four stops. Just stand on the painted square, hold the card, and state the place you want to go . . .

Ros stops and checks where she is standing.

Well we're right in the middle of the square.

Isaac: Now wait, I'm not sure I want to . . .

Marie (*moving into the painted square with the other characters*)**:** My grandfather's house, when he was my age!

Narrator: And with a "poof" all four characters disappear.

Scene 3: The 1930s

Narrator: The characters find themselves watching a family eating breakfast.

Al: Hey Marie, is this your grandfather's home?

Marie: I'm not sure. I don't recognize anybody. But if this is when my grandfather was a boy, it has to be before World War II.

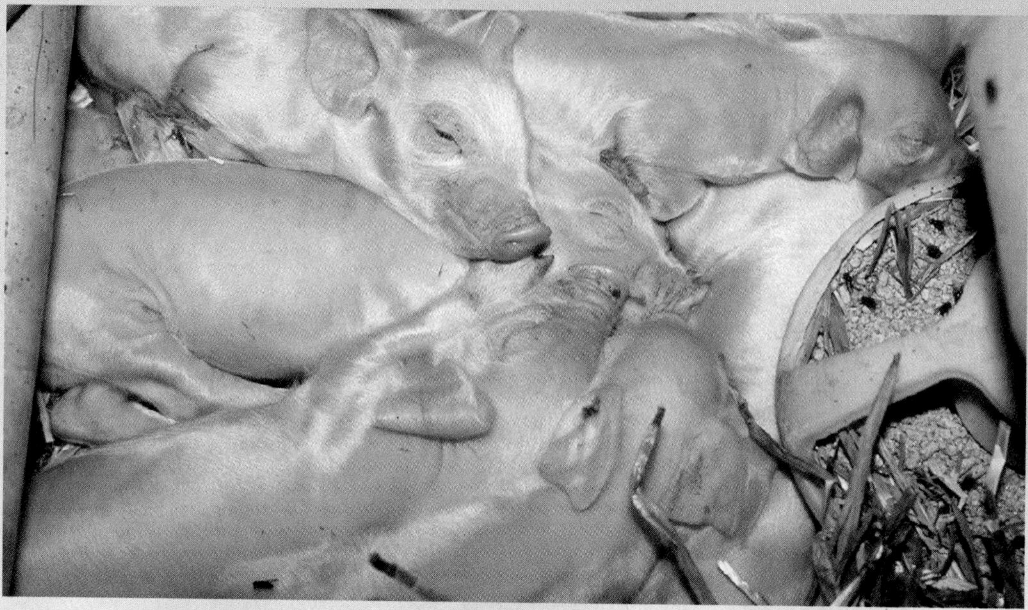

Isaac: Hey they've got a huge wood stove. And I see chickens outside that window. We must be on a farm.

Ros: Look at all those kids!

Six children are seated around the table.

Mother (*standing up as they finish eating*)**:** Miguel, will you take these eggshells out to the compost heap and bring me back the bowl? Ana, will you take this bucket of scraps out to the pigs?

Ana: Oh do I have to?

Father: Ana, remember, those pigs give us food, so we should give them food.

Ana: I know, waste not want not.

Ana turns to one of the boys.

Juan, it's your turn tomorrow!

Marie: Hey, Juan was my grandfather's name.

Ana goes out with the bucket. Miguel goes out with the bowl.

Ros (*doubtfully*)**:** Uh oh. Maybe that's why he took the garbage out just once a week. They all took turns.

Isaac: Yeah, but that was a small bucket, and it was just food scraps. Besides, I don't see any plastic bags, foam packaging, junk mail, or anything else like the stuff we have in our garbage today.

Isaac and Marie walk over to Juan. Marie taps him on the shoulder.

Marie: You know you look a little bit like my grandfather.

Isaac: Yeah, Juan, I know your granddaughter.

Juan (*jumping up*)**:** Huh? Hey, who are you kidding? Who are you?

Isaac: Well I do know your granddaughter—but let's skip that part. What I really want to talk about is your garbage. How come you don't have more garbage—I mean, with six kids in your family and all that? Don't you have to put out big sacks for the garbage collector to come and pick up?

Juan: My garbage? Four strangers here to talk to me about garbage? Oh well, okay. I'll tell you about it. It seems to me like we have a lot of garbage. Every week there are food scraps for the pigs or stuff for the compost heap. Nobody hauls garbage away for us. If we want to get rid of something, we haul it to the dump ourselves.

Al and Ros walk over to them and join the conversation.

Al: Really? But what about all the little stuff? You know, paper cups, plastic bags, foam containers.

Juan: Plastic bags? Foam containers? I don't think we have those. But sometimes we take a brown bag lunch to school. After we use a bag several times, we just burn it with the rest of the burnable trash.

Marie: Aha! So you get rid of trash by burning it. What do you burn?

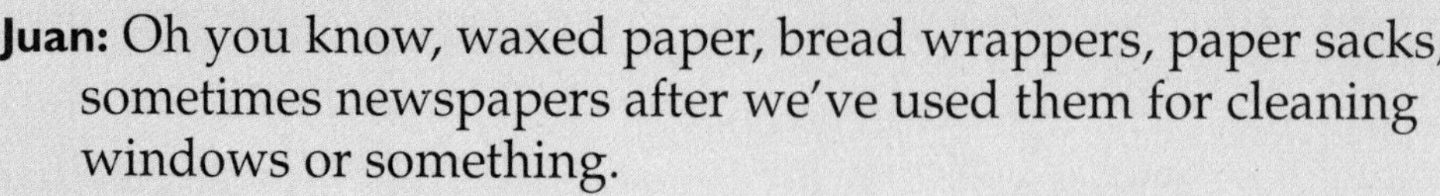

Juan: Oh you know, waxed paper, bread wrappers, paper sacks, sometimes newspapers after we've used them for cleaning windows or something.

Al: Yeah, I saw that stack of newspapers and it looks pretty skinny to me. (*He walks over to it and picks up a few pages.*) Where are all the ads?

Ros: So what is at the dump if there's no food and no paper?

Juan: Oh I don't know—old tin cans I guess, if we haven't used them for holding nails or something, old cars, washing machines—just big stuff, mostly. Hey, you guys wait here, and I'll take you to meet my grandfather. He knows a lot about what people used in the old days.

Juan walks over to the characters.

It's okay if I go for only a few minutes. I'll take him some eggs.

He picks up the basket of eggs.

Scene 4: Hearing about the 1890s

Juan's grandfather: Hi, Juanito! What have you got there?

Juan: Hi Abuelo. Oh nothing too much. I just brought you some eggs. Would you like to meet my new friends? Now what are your names?

Marie: I'm Marie, and this is Isaac, Al, and Rosalind.

Grandfather (*chuckling*)**:** Well, Juan, you have some nice invisible friends.

Juan: Oh I guess you can't see them. Mom couldn't either. Well anyway, Abuelo, I wanted to ask you about the old days. When you were little, what kind of things did you throw away in the garbage?

Grandfather: What got you to thinking about that? For one thing, I'll tell you that there certainly wasn't so much waste. I mean, newspapers were smaller and most of them came out just once a week. And we weren't wasting all this metal, letting cars rust away because there weren't any cars when I was a boy.

Grandmother (*coming onto the porch and joining in the conversation*): Hello Juan! I couldn't help overhearing your conversation. And when we were children, back in the 1800s, there were no electric light bulbs, or aluminum foil, or radios—none of this modern stuff. And there wasn't a wagon you couldn't fix.

Ros: So they weren't even throwing out much metal. Hmm.

Isaac: Sounds like taking out the trash would've been easy back then, at least most of the time.

Al: Yeah but maybe they had to do other things that we don't.

Juan: Well I've got to get back home. See you later, Abuelo! Bye!

Marie: I guess we'd better go, too. Bye, Juan. See you later.

Juan: You will? Okay, bye.

He walks away.

Marie: Look here's another square to stand on.

The characters all move onto the square.

Ros: Where should we go next?

Al: Let's go look at somebody in my family history!

Isaac: Okay when?

Al: Let's just say, "Way back then!"

Narrator: The characters are caught up in a dark cloud, traveling far back in time.

Scene 5: The Year 1500

Narrator: The characters find themselves standing on a narrow street paved with stones. They are in Europe in the Middle Ages in about the year 1500.

Marie looks up. She sees that someone is about to pour something out of an upstairs window.

Marie: Look out everybody! Move!

Just as the characters step inside the doorway, dirty dishwater comes pouring down beside them.

Narrator: The characters then look inside the house. They see a group of people inside, apparently a mother, father, and several children.

Ros: Hey, Al, one of those kids looks a lot like you! But what funny clothes everyone is wearing!

Marie: I wonder what year it is?

Isaac: Hey I think I can hear what they're saying. It's some sort of celebration of the year 1500. Listen . . .

Walter: So he let you bring home a piece of paper for us?

Father: Yes but he wants me to bring it back tomorrow. It's just for you to look at. It will be one of the pages used in a book for the King!

Mother: So this is paper. Well, I never thought I'd see the day when we'd actually have a piece of it in this house. Isabella, be careful with it! Remember, your father said it took several hours to make that sheet!

Isabella (*smiling*): Well if only the King and a few other rich people can use it, I guess we won't see much of this, will we?

Walter (*laughing*): No, I guess not.

Al: Hey he sounds like me, doesn't he?

Marie: Yeah, Al, he kind of does. You know, it sounds as if they didn't even have newspapers to throw away!

Isaac: This throwing out the garbage job is looking easier all the time, but I don't like the water getting thrown out of the window.

Ros: No, sinks are pretty handy. So they didn't even have any paper that they would throw away. Imagine no paper towels even!

Isaac: Well time to go! I guess I'll hold the card and get us home. I think I need another snack.

Ros: No Isaac—we have one more stop!

Scene 6: A Time in Prehistory

Narrator: Instead of ending up at home, the characters find themselves in a dim light. They are gathered near a small fire and several people are sitting around the fire eating.

Isaac (*seeming upset*)**:** Oh, no. Where are we now?

Young man #1: Hey I wasn't done with that bird yet. Where did you throw the bone?

Young man #2: Well it's on the garbage heap with the other bones that have been there all year.

Ros (*noticing that she is standing near the heap of bones*)**:** Oooh, yuck.

She moves.

Young man #1 (*retrieving the bone*)**:** So much for this bone. It looks like there are ants crawling on it.

Woman #1 is walking around with an animal hide.

Woman #2: Be sure you don't put that animal hide on the garbage heap. We need it for the children's clothes.

Woman #1: No I wouldn't throw it away. You know it's time to dig a hole for this heap and bury it. I'll make a digging stick from this bone.

She picks up a bone from the stack.

Isaac: That's their garbage heap for months and months? Bones?

Marie: It looks like there are also a few arrowheads. And they even must have used quite a few of the bones, because there aren't very many in the heap.

Al: Okay so they didn't have very much garbage. Now let's go home!

Scene 7: Back to the Present

Narrator: The characters find themselves standing in Isaac's kitchen. Beside them is another mess because the garbage bag has broken again.

All four characters: Oooh, yuck.

In the closing scene, the characters bend over and begin quickly picking up the "garbage" again.

Wrap Up

Write answers to the following in your notebook. Be prepared to share your ideas if the teacher calls on you during a class discussion.

1. Describe how people disposed of garbage differently in each time period: (a) 1930s, (b) 1800s, (c) 1500s, and (d) prehistoric times.
2. Archaeologists can learn a lot about groups of people who have lived in the past by studying what they left behind. Some archaeologists learn a lot about groups of people living today by studying what they throw away. What do you think archaeologists might learn about you by studying what you throw away during one month? What might they learn about your school by doing the same thing?

Reading:

The Garbage Crisis

Today, we know that everyone should recycle whatever they can, but do you have a good understanding about why recycling is important?

Stop & Think

1. If people have been throwing things away for so long, why is there a problem now? Why do certain problems exist today that did not exist in the past?

People have more to throw away today than they did ten years ago. For example, if plastic bottles didn't exist, you couldn't throw them away. It might not seem very important when you throw away a plastic bottle. Every hour of the day, people in the United States make that decision. Americans throw away more than 2.5 million plastic bottles every hour. And every year, the United States produces ten pounds of plastic for every person in the world.

What do we do with our garbage? Typically we put it into a plastic bag and expect that the garbage collectors will take care of it. In the United States, people throw away more than 209 million tons of garbage each year. In other words, about four pounds per person, every day of the year. What might four pounds of your garbage consist of? If you are like many Americans, more than half of your garbage is paper and plastic. The rest of your garbage is probably food scraps, glass, metal, and lawn trash. Even if you don't have a lawn or garden, your average portion of garbage includes the lawn trash from public parks.

Landfills

Garbage collectors usually haul the garbage to a **landfill** and dump it. A landfill is most often a large hole in the ground, unless it becomes so large that it is a mound. Layers of garbage are covered with dirt each day to keep the garbage from blowing away and to keep away rodents and other pests. In the United States, 73 percent of our garbage is hauled to landfills (see Figures 16.4 and 16.5).

The problem with landfills is that they are filling up. This is particularly true in some coastal areas with large populations and in the northeastern United States. People in these locations often have chosen what seemed to be the simplest solution: They have hired truckers or large garbage barges to haul their garbage to far-away landfills. But there are problems with using distant landfills as well.

▶ **FIGURE 16.3**

Today more companies all over the world are discovering ways to use recycled materials to develop new products. These products are made from recycled trash in Thailand.

▶ FIGURE 16.4

This pie graph shows the composition of garbage in the United States.

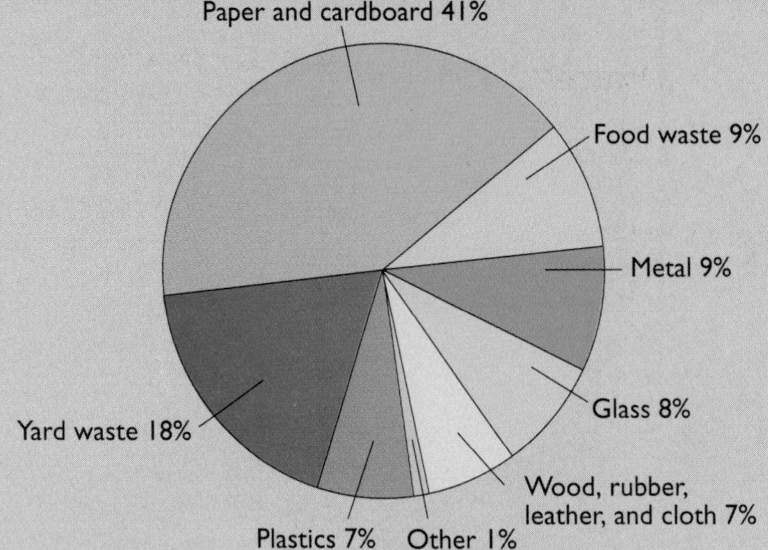

▶ FIGURE 16.5

This pie graph shows how we dispose of our garbage in the United States. Today, 73 percent of our garbage is hauled to landfills.

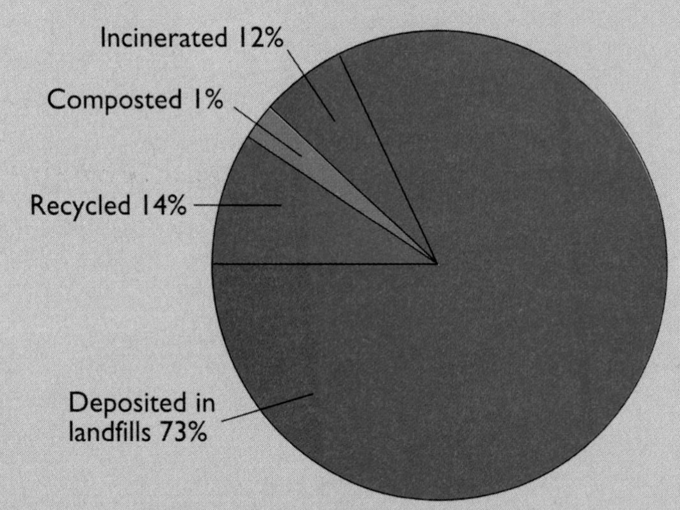

Source: Environmental Protection Agency

Transporting garbage for long distances is expensive, and sometimes the managers of the receiving landfill will not accept the garbage shipment. If the garbage is not accepted, the likelihood increases that the garbage haulers then will dump the garbage illegally, either in the ocean or on land—because hauling the garbage back home would be expensive. And people simply cannot find a place for the garbage back home. For example, in New York State in

1985, there were 294 open landfills. By 2006 there probably will be only thirteen landfills remaining open. Clearly people in this state are running out of room for their garbage. As their garbage is hauled to other parts of the country, landfills in other places will begin (and have begun) to fill up as well.

It might seem that people just should continue to dig more and deeper landfills wherever it is possible. There are problems with this approach, however. First, many people protest if officials are considering a landfill near them. In some places where there might be room, people have put up strong protests. They don't want landfills in their backyards. This is a big change from the 1960s and early 1970s, when people didn't think of landfills as dangerous places (see Figure 16.6). Second, people cannot dig landfills much deeper than they are already. Soil is only so thick, and below it is solid rock (or underground water).

To make the problem worse, landfills are leaking. When people first began digging landfills, they were not concerned about leaks. But through the years, rain has soaked into the landfills. Because water doesn't stay in one place unless it is held by something watertight, eventually the water in old landfills moves down farther into the ground and into lakes and streams. Water that moves through the soil and underground is called **groundwater.**

▶ **FIGURE 16.6**

People once thought that garbage dumps were full of safe junk. Now people know that landfills are not always sanitary.

Groundwater that moves through landfills often becomes polluted by the material that it passes through, such as paint thinner. The danger is that this polluted water may turn out to be someone's drinking water.

Among the first people to learn about hazards from industrial landfills were the residents of the Love Canal area of New York in the 1970s. (An industrial landfill is one where manufacturing wastes are dumped.) The people living near that landfill had unusually high rates of cancer and higher than usual rates of birth defects among their children. Many people felt sick for no apparent reason. Then they discovered that they were living on top of a landfill in which harmful chemicals had been dumped and then covered over, an action that took place in the 1950s. People recognized the strong correlation between the number of sicknesses and the old landfill. City officials finally called in medical experts who determined that some materials in the landfill were causing many of the illnesses. In some homes, polluted water was even bubbling up into the basements. Officials evacuated the school and many of the homes around the landfill. The residents of the Love Canal area filed a lawsuit against the company originally responsible, hoping to force it to pay for some of the damages. Even decades after filing the lawsuit, many of the issues of this court case remain unresolved.

Trash that is potentially harmful to people is called **toxic waste** or **hazardous waste.** Toxic means "poisonous." You would not want your drinking water to contain toxins. We define hazardous wastes as "things that might cause fires, corrode metals, or make people sick in different ways." If people throw away such things as motor oil, paint thinner, or car batteries, they can expect that small amounts of oil, paint thinner, or the lead from batteries might end up in somebody's drinking water. These wastes can cause sickness. When too much lead is in our drinking water, for example, lead poisoning can occur. Lead poisoning can cause mental retardation or even death. People never used to worry about dissolved lead or other hazardous wastes in their water. But now that we understand more about the patterns of water flow, people are concerned.

FIGURE 16.7

How do you or your parents dispose of these household products?

People have taken steps to prevent toxic chemicals from leaking into the groundwater below landfills. Modern landfills (those built since the 1980s) have plastic liners or 2-foot layers of clay at the bottom to trap any water that might fall through. Collection tanks hold the trapped water. Landfill workers then treat the trapped water to remove pollutants and sometimes circulate the water back through the landfill. When the water is recirculated, the decomposition of materials in the landfill speeds up, because moist materials decay faster. Some water probably still does get through to the ground after many years, but it is a tiny quantity compared to the leaks from old landfills.

Stop & Think

During this chapter you might have noticed some patterns associated with garbage disposal.

2. Use what you know from this reading so far to describe trends and correlations associated with garbage disposal. What predictions can you make about how these patterns will be different or the same in the next decade?

Incineration

Some city officials are looking for other solutions because they know that people will not allow new landfills near them and that the garbage problem will not go away.

One solution is to return to burning garbage. Garbage is burned in furnaces called **incinerators.** People stopped using incinerators during the 1960s because the burning garbage produced smoke and people wanted the air pollution to stop.

In the late 1980s, new incinerators became available that could get rid of half of the problem: They burn things at very high temperatures, and their chimneys filter out ash, so there is no smoke to see. However they still do cause air pollution but the particles that spew from the new incinerator chimneys are simply too small for people to see. In addition to causing some air pollution, other problems are associated with the new incinerators. They are expensive to build and operate. It has cost some cities hundreds of thousands of dollars to hire experts who know how to run the incinerators properly. And even with the advice of experts, sometimes the incinerators break down and so leave the city without a method of garbage disposal.

When incinerators do work and city officials use them to burn all kinds of trash, another problem arises: Toxic waste becomes concentrated in the ash. Modern incinerators trap the ash that flies up the chimney and the ash that settles at the bottom of the furnace. The ash is all that remains of huge amounts of garbage. The incinerators do help reduce the amount of garbage, but some toxic waste doesn't burn. Liquids evaporate and papers are burned, but some metals are left behind. This concentration of metal can be toxic and must be disposed of in a landfill designed especially for hazardous waste.

Using incinerators does have benefits, however. First, when cities use incinerators, the landfill crisis is lessened. Second, engineers who design the new incinerators claim that they can build incinerators that release almost no poisons. In addition the heat from a certain type of incinerator can be used to generate electricity. Some countries, such as Japan and Sweden, and a few cities in the United States have waste-to-energy systems that generate electricity from burning garbage. Maybe you can find out more about these systems.

Stop & Think

3. Why do you think that some big cities have chosen incinerators as part of the solution to their garbage problem?

Recycling

Another solution to overcrowded landfills is **recycling.** Recycling means that materials repeat a cycle or, in other words, that people use them more than once. Currently people in the United States recycle only about 14 percent of their garbage. Experts estimate that we could recycle 40 to 60 percent of our garbage. But recycling requires more effort than just bagging up the trash. People must sort the trash and then possibly take it to a special location for collection. In the 1990s, however, many waste disposal companies began to pick up recyclables as an important service in addition to their regular garbage pick up service. The most commonly recycled materials include aluminum, glass, paper, certain plastics, and motor oil.

Recycling has many benefits. First, it reduces the amount of garbage going to landfills and saves energy. For example when aluminum is recycled, it produces 95 percent less air pollution, 97 percent less water pollution, and requires 95 percent less energy than mining and processing the same amount of aluminum ore from a mine. Second, because people are not simply tossing the materials away, recycling plants generate three to six times more jobs in a local area than either landfills or incineration plants. And third, many communities that require people to recycle have greatly reduced their landfill costs.

Recycling does not end with the collection of materials—it also involves careful purchasing, or **precycling.** To make recycling a choice that works, people must buy products that can be recycled, and products that have been recycled. For example, if people do not insist on purchasing recycled paper, the market for it decreases. It is also important to buy products that have the least amount of packaging. In 1996 Americans spent more on the packaging of food than American farmers received in net income. Packaging waste accounts for almost one-third of all of the garbage we send to the landfills.

Recycling does have limits. Some materials require too much energy to recycle effectively, and others are of too poor a quality to use again. But we can recycle paper up to twelve times before the wood fibers in it are too short to recycle again. We cannot recycle paper that has glues or adhesives on it. If paper and plastic materials or different types of plastic are laminated together, they cannot be recycled either. So even though recycling is a partial answer, it does not solve the entire garbage crisis.

Reducing and Reusing

Reduction simply means that people avoid unnecessary disposable products and demand less packaging. An example of reduction would be carrying a thermos of juice to school instead of a drink packaged in a disposable drink box. Because you could reuse the thermos many times, you would have reduced the amount of garbage required to provide you with servings of juice.

Stop & Think

4. Some environmentalists have a slogan: reduce, reuse, recycle. Explain how this phrase could (or could not) help solve the garbage crisis.

Composting

Compost is a mixture of garbage that breaks down into nutrient-rich material. After this process occurs, garbage becomes a useful resource because it can add nutrients to soil. It might seem that all garbage in landfills would rot anyway because the heaps of garbage are just sitting there. The garbage in most landfills, however, does not break down or does so very slowly because it is buried so deeply that air cannot get to it. Even items such as leftover food and newspaper can last for more than thirty years.

Materials in a compost heap decay within a few weeks or months. Composting requires the presence of several factors: air, water, warmth, and soil microbes. (Soil microbes are plants or animals that live in the soil and are so small that you cannot see them without a microscope.) To have all these factors work, compost must be kept near the surface.

Composting provides several advantages. First, composting costs very little, even on a large scale. The only costs are shredding the garbage and occasionally turning the compost so that it breaks down more quickly. Second, garbage that is composted becomes nutrient-rich material. This material is useful as fertilizer or as a covering for landfills. Third, if cities use this material as a covering for landfills, they will save money because they won't need to buy soil covering from rural areas or developers. Finally and perhaps most importantly, composting reduces the amount of garbage sitting in landfills. In the United States, we could compost about 20 percent of our garbage each year.

Stop & Think

5. List the costs and benefits of each of the methods of garbage disposal described in the previous reading.
6. What new questions do you have about garbage disposal? Ask your teacher about ways to find out the answers.

explain

Connections: Garbage through the Years

Study Figure 16.8. What does this graph show you? What trends, correlations, or cause-and-effect relationships can you determine from this graph? Which is increasing faster in the United States, the number of people or the amount of garbage that we throw away each year?

▶ **FIGURE 16.8**

This graph shows the population in the United States from 1960 to 1995, along with the number of tons of garbage generated.

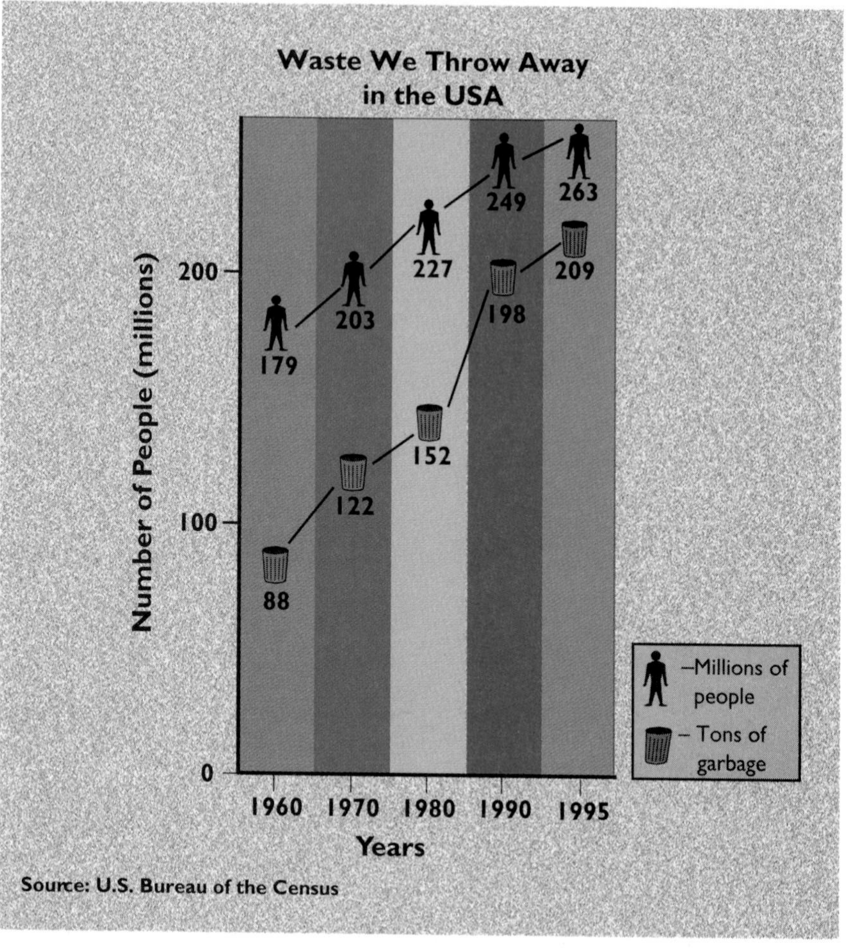

explain/elaborate

Investigation:
Recycling Choices

You make decisions about garbage every day. Some decisions make it easier to get rid of garbage, and some make it more difficult. In this investigation, you will play a game about these decisions. The goal of this game is to get rid of your garbage. You and your classmates will decide on the consequences of twenty-four different actions before you play the game.

Materials for Each Team of Three:

- ▶ 1 Recycling Choices game board
- ▶ 1 bowl for discarding plastic pieces
- ▶ 1 spinner
- ▶ 3 tokens

Working Cooperatively

Work cooperatively in your teams of three. Practice the skill *Treat others politely.* Use the role of Manager. Push your desks together or work together at a table.

Material for Each Student:

- 20 plastic pieces or pinto beans (to represent trash bags)

Process and Procedure

Part A—The Game Board

1. Obtain the materials and set aside all except the game board.
2. Read the actions described on the squares that are assigned to your team.

   Each square describes an action that someone could take. You and your classmates will decide the consequences of each action.
3. Decide whether each action will make the garbage crisis worse or improve conditions.

   Each square describes one action, such as recycling paper. Your task is to decide whether this action could help lessen the garbage crisis a little, quite a bit, or very much. If you decide that this action will make the garbage crisis worse, you are to decide whether it will make the crisis a little worse, quite a bit worse, or very much worse. Assume that 1,000 people are doing the action in each square.
4. Agree on the number of plastic pieces that people are to pick up or discard if they land on that square. Decide between one, two, or three pieces.

   Each plastic piece represents a bag of garbage, and the goal of the game is to get rid of the garbage.
5. Participate in the class discussion of the game board.

   Be ready to share your team's ideas about what should be in the squares.

Part B—Playing the Game

1. Choose the token that you will use.

   If your teacher did not supply individual tokens, you may use items that you have, such as a pen cap, a ring, or a coin.
2. Count out 20 plastic pieces for yourself.

   All Team Members should take these from the bowl that the Manager picked up. Put the extra pieces back into the bowl.

Rules for Recycling Choices

- To take your turn, use the spinner. The number that the spinner stops on shows how many places you should move your token.
- Move your token.
- When you land on a square, read it and do what it tells you to do. Discard or take the number of pieces that your class agreed on for that square.
- It is all right for more than one person to be on the same square at the same time.

▲ **FIGURE 16.9**

The rules in this box describe how to play the game.

3. Decide who will go first by using the spinner.

   The high number goes first, the middle number goes second, and so on.
4. Read the rules for the game (see Figure 16.9).
5. Play the game.

Wrap Up

Discuss the following questions with your teammates, then record your own answers in your notebook. Be prepared to explain your answers if you are called on in a class discussion.

1. Look over the squares on the game board. Do you strongly agree or disagree with what is stated on any of the squares? Choose at least two squares; write down what is stated in each square; and write down why you agree, disagree, or are neutral about the information on those two squares.
2. What one thing could you do differently about your own contribution to the garbage crisis in the United States? What one thing could your community do differently?
3. If you could change one thing about your use of the skill of treating others politely, what would you change?

SIDELIGHT *on Numbers*

How Big is 209 Million?

How big is 209 million tons of trash? How much space does all that trash really take up? The short answer is—a lot. One year's trash in the United States takes up 20,700,000 truckloads, based on the average 10-ton load of 20 cubic yards that the average garbage truck carries. This is enough garbage to completely fill 1,000 professional football stadiums every year. What a lot of trash.

You already know that paper and cardboard products account for over 40 percent of the total weight of our trash. And in terms of volume, paper and cardboard make up over 50 percent of our trash. So in one year, more than 500 of the 1,000 football stadiums would be filled with nothing but paper and cardboard.

You also know that people recycle only about 14 percent of the paper they discard. That represents only 60 of the 500 football stadiums that would be filled with paper. We could be recycling 400–500 football stadium's worth of paper each year, not just 60. And that is just the paper. The other 500 football stadiums would contain plenty of trash that could be recycled—probably 50 percent of it. That would represent another 250 football stadium's worth of trash that we could recycle.

If everyone in the United States recycled as much as they could, we might have as few as 300–500 football stadium's worth of trash each year instead of 1,000.

▶ **FIGURE 16.10**

The choices we make about things such as landfills have consequences for the health of rivers such as this one.

elaborate

Investigation:
Everything in Its Place

As you read in *The Garbage Crisis*, landfills can leak; that is, rain or snow can wash down into them, seep through the garbage, and pick up pollutants. The polluted water then may move into rivers and lakes. So water that once was clean can become polluted and can move elsewhere. People who have studied relatively safe landfills have found that some soil types allow less movement of polluted water than other soil types. As you do this investigation, try to discover the answer to the following question: What type of soil would you want underneath a landfill, and why?

Working Cooperatively

Work cooperatively in your teams of three. Use the roles of Manager, Communicator, and Tracker. In class discussions concentrate on using the unit skill. In your team of three, use the skill *Treat others politely.*

Materials for Each Team of Three:

- 1 clear-sided plastic box with a 2.5 cm layer of soft clay or coarse sand
- 1 wood block, approximately 2.5 cm high
- 1 sprinkler container or spray bottle
- 1 soda straw
- powdered soft-drink mix without sugar (1 Tbsp or 1 packet)
- 1 bowl
- 1 graduated beaker or 1 ruler

Materials for the Entire Class:

- ▶ water source
- ▶ clock

Process and Procedure

1. Watch your teacher's demonstration of the procedure. In this investigation, different teams will be testing soils at different sites.
2. Review with your classmates what a controlled experiment is.
3. Discuss with your classmates what each team will need to do to conduct a controlled experiment.

   Listen to the suggestions that people make for how the experiment might be set up to test your landfill sites. Your goal is to decide which soil type would be the best for a landfill.
4. Obtain the spray bottle, water, and a bowl.
5. Pump the spray bottle ten times, allowing the water to spray into the bowl.
6. Measure the amount of water in the bowl.

   Use a ruler or a graduated beaker. This will allow you to be sure that all teams use the same amount of water. What other things must all teams do in the same way to control the experiment?
7. Obtain the rest of the materials.
8. If the soil is not already in the box, put a 2.5-cm layer into your team's plastic box.
9. Use a straw to dig a small hole 1 cm deep.
10. Open the packet of powdered drink mix and pour all of it into the hole.

    The Communicator should do this.
11. Cover the powdered drink mix with soil.

    The Tracker should do this.
12. Tilt your box as shown in Figure 16.11.

    This is your landfill site.
13. Divide the work as follows:
    - the Manager holds the box and observes it;
    - the Tracker keeps track of time and says when to add water.

▶ **FIGURE 16.11**

How to set up the landfill site before adding water.

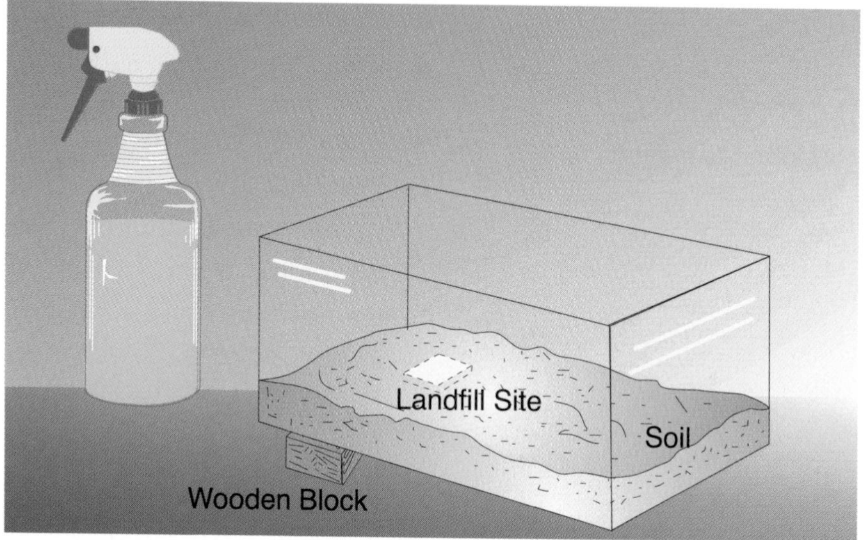

14. When the Tracker says "Go," the Communicator should add the water at the rate that the class agreed on.

If you have a controlled experiment, all teams will be adding the same amount of water at the same rate.

15. Continue adding water and observing your landfill site for the amount of time that your class decided on.

Notebook entry: Write down any notes that you want to remember for the class discussion, such as the results that you saw.

16. Clean up your materials as instructed.

From: Movement of Groundwater and Contaminants, which appears in Groundwater Quality Protection in Oakland County: A Sourcebook for Teachers, pp. 22–26 Copyright © 1984 by East Michigan Environmental Action Council, Bloomfield Township, Michigan. Adapted by permission.

Wrap Up

Write your own responses to the following questions in your science notebook.

1. In your controlled experiment, what was the one factor that varied from team to team?
2. What conditions did your class agree on so that all teams were doing a controlled experiment?
3. When you want to compare data from two or more landfill sites, why is a controlled experiment important? Give an example of when a controlled experiment could be important.

4. What type of soil did your team test? Describe what happened when you added water to your landfill.
5. What soil type do you think should be beneath a landfill, and why?

evaluate

Connections: Down by the River and Out in the Desert

How might you use patterns to solve a mystery? Recall from Unit 1 that scientists often must work like detectives when they are trying to solve problems. As you proceed through this connections activity, you will look for patterns to solve two mysteries. To do this, take the following steps:

- individually, read Part A—Down by the River;
- write out your answers for the class discussion; and
- then go on to Part B—Out in the Desert.

Part A—Down by the River

Pleasant Isle is a small town along the Atlantic coast. The region is a pleasant place to live, except that it has a history of flooding. Pleasant Isle was built mostly during some unusually dry years in the 1940s, and many people didn't know about the flood patterns before they built their homes and shops. Since 1950 floods of some sort have happened almost every year. During early spring, heavy rains fall and the streams become full. Sometimes the streams overflow only slightly; sometimes the floods cover the entire floodplain. Even during the years with floods, the waters are rarely more than 30 centimeters deep. During these floods, many people have wet yards and some water in their basements. A few people have built their homes higher on the hills, but most residents have stayed near the downtown area on the floodplain in their original homes. When new people move into the area, their neighbors usually tell them not to store anything but junk in their basements because the basements usually get flooded. Most people in Pleasant Isle think of the floods as a minor annoyance but nothing more.

People in this region have had very few health problems. But lately there is an unusually high number of people with kidney problems. For several years it seemed that many more people than usual had flu-like symptoms and just didn't feel well during the spring floods. Then after a few years, about one out of every ten people developed kidney problems. People began talking to each other about their problems, and soon they realized that many people in Pleasant Isle were sick.

Townspeople contacted the state health department and asked for help. They learned from the officials that a number of toxic materials could cause their symptoms. Sources of toxic waste could be such things as old car batteries, paint thinner, and chemical cleaning compounds.

Health officials began to survey the area. No dumps were nearby that they could find. The community had no major industries. On the main street of the town there were several clothing stores, a grocery store, a dry cleaning store, and a hardware store. Because of hard economic times, a clothing store and the dry cleaners closed. During the following spring, health officials returned to the area and collected samples of the floodwater. Again people were sick. When the officials plotted the locations of sick people's homes on a map, they found the pattern shown in Figure 16.12. Then the officials began checking basements of all the buildings in town. Which do you think was the first basement they checked. Why?

1. This reading has described several patterns. What are they?
2. Once the officials completed their survey, they knew immediately what to look for. What other information do you need to solve the puzzle?

Part B—Out in the Desert

After reading Part A, you might think that a desert would be a much safer place to live than the floodplain of a river. After all you wouldn't be near much polluted water, right? Right. But potential risks are in the desert as well.

Imagine that you work for a company that advises people on how to handle hazardous waste. A member of Congress has asked your company to make some decisions about a hazardous waste dump in the desert. Currently the wastes are stored in an isolated area of

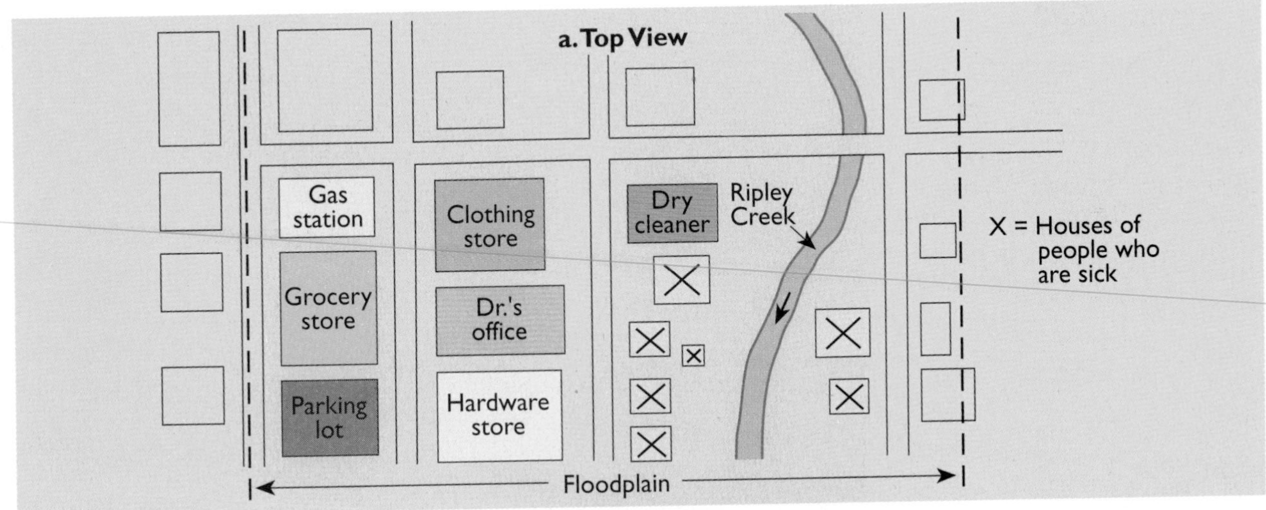

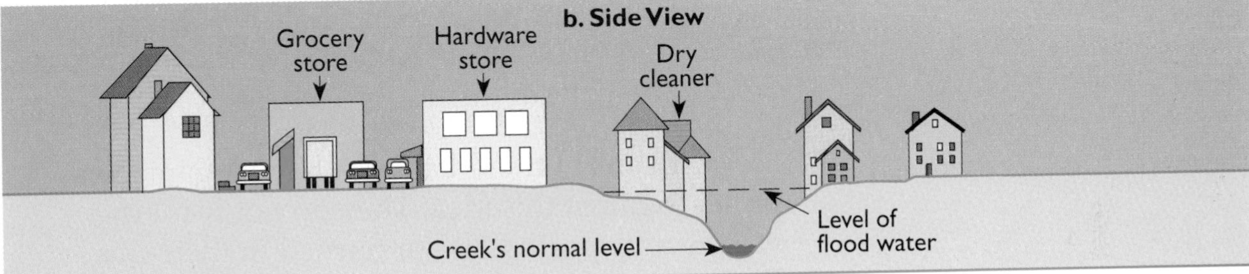

▲ **FIGURE 16.12**

This diagram shows the patterns that the health officials found. The two views are a view from (a) above and (b) a view from the side.

Nevada. Very few people live nearby. Recent studies by geologists, however, have shown that the area has a high potential for earthquakes. The wastes are liquid and are stored in steel barrels. These are your choices:

a. Leave the wastes where they are. The probability of an earthquake affecting the barrels is 9 percent each year for each of the next thirty years. After thirty years, the barrels will be slightly more rusted and more easily damaged if an earthquake occurs. Then the probability that an earthquake will affect the barrels goes up to 15 percent. If a leak occurs, there will be no way to stop it.

b. Transport the wastes to an urban waste incinerator to be burned. The probability of a traffic accident while the trucks are moving the barrels is 8 percent. In the urban area, the company could burn the wastes in a modern incinerator. When the liquid waste is boiled away, the waste would be reduced to ash. Then the company could cement the ash into concrete blocks.

▶ Figure 16.13
Landfills have serious consequences even for isolated areas like this desert in Nevada. What are some of them?

Citizens in the urban area have organized a protest against this idea. They do not want the wastes transported into or burned in their city. Furthermore they do not even want the concrete blocks of burned waste to be stored nearby. To transport the blocks away from the city would mean two-way costs for transportation. This would raise the price of this disposal method to $60 million. If the incinerator has a scrubber added to it to catch ash and reduce air pollution, the cost of the project would be $70 million. If this method is adopted and completed without accident, there would be no future fears of chemical leaks from this waste.

c. Build an incinerator near the current dump. Burn the waste that is now in the barrels and cement the ash into blocks. Because the company would need to transport many workers to this isolated area, along with the materials they would need to build the incinerator, the cost for this project would be $70 million. The probability of increased air pollution is 16 percent. The ash could reach a small city 200 miles away. Again the option of a scrubber is available, but this would raise the cost to $80 million. If this project is completed, there will be no future leaks to worry about.

d. Move the wastes to another isolated area with a lower risk of earthquakes. Again the probability of traffic accidents is 8 percent. The cost for this would be $2 million. This probably would prevent damage to the barrels from an earthquake, but the old barrels would rust eventually, and there would be no way to stop leaks when this occurs.

e. Place the barrels on the ocean floor because there are no earthquakes there. This would cost $6 million. The company would have to transport the barrels through a large urban area, and the probability of a traffic accident in this case is 12 percent. There still would be a potential for leaks when the barrels rusted.

Write your own answers to the following questions in your notebook.

1. One of the choices above contains false information. Discuss with your teammates which one you think it is.
2. Develop a costs-and-benefits table for each of the four options that do not contain false information.
3. Why do you think the hazardous wastes originally were stored in the desert?
4. Which choice do you think is the best solution for the wastes stored in the desert? Justify your answer.

Solving Problems

The neatly stacked tires in this photograph show one way that people are solving a particular garbage disposal problem—getting rid of tires. Used tires are a problem in many landfills. The tread on the tires has become too worn to keep using them on vehicles, and the tires won't stay buried because they are lighter than the dirt around them. In addition the tires can be a fire hazard because the oil that they contain is highly flammable. But some people have worked out a solution to this problem. They use worn tires as building material. In this example, the tires are stacked and filled with concrete (or another weight). The tires then absorb heat and insulate these mostly underground houses against cold winters. In this case, used tires have become a useful resource instead of a garbage problem.

Most garbage experts agree that the choices we make can affect the garbage crisis. Also reusing materials rather than buying new materials conserves our supply of many natural resources. Although solving the garbage crisis is a complex problem, it is one that individuals can work on. In this chapter, you will discover ways that you and others can make a difference.

explore

Connections: On Almost Every Corner

explore / explain

Investigation: The Choice Is Yours—Projects, Part I

elaborate / evaluate

Investigation: Presentations—Projects, Part II

evaluate

Connections: St. Louis and San Diego: Opposite Decisions?

explore

Connections:
On Almost Every Corner

In Chapter 16, you read or heard about how people's patterns of garbage disposal have changed through the years. One reason that those patterns changed is because the type and amount of materials changed. The more materials people have, the more materials they throw away.

Because people have caused the problem of too much garbage, maybe people also can solve the problem. As you know by now, solving a problem usually is easier after you have recognized a pattern.

Take litter for example. Maybe you have noticed that you often see litter in cities on streets and in many parks. What are the patterns that have to do with litter? Participate in the litter hike that your teacher will organize. As you walk, record the following information in your notebook:

- all the places you find litter,
- where you find the most litter,
- what's nearby (such as a store, school, houses, or other buildings),
- the variety of litter, and
- what types of litter you see most often.

When you are finished with your survey, record any trends that you find and any ideas that you have about how to solve the litter problem.

explore / explain

Investigation:
The Choice Is Yours—Projects, Part I

It might seem that your daily four pounds of garbage does not really amount to very much, but it does. Four pounds per day means that you throw away 1,460 pounds per year. And if you multiply your amount of garbage by 263 million (the population of the United States), then the amount of garbage is huge. But there are ways that you can make a difference. You probably know some ways already. If you don't already have ideas, this investigation will help you find some.

Working Cooperatively

In this investigation, you will work individually.

Materials for Each Student:

- individual project materials

Process and Procedure

1. Think of something that you would like to change about the garbage pattern in the United States.

   Notebook entry: Write this down as a goal.

2. Read through the project ideas.

These are in the Background Information that follows this procedure. As you read, think about whether you would like to do one of the projects listed or another one of your own.

3. Decide on a project that interests you and that is related to the garbage crisis.

   Your choice does not have to be one from the project list.

4. Decide what procedure you will need to follow to complete your project.

   For example, you might decide to write letters or to look up information in the library. If you do, write down those steps. Refer to the resource list in the Background Information for other sources of information. You also might want to review How To #8, How to Conduct a Research Project, to help you remember some of the steps involved in gathering information. After you have completed your list, have your teacher check it (see Figure 17.1).

5. Prepare to discuss your proposed project with the class.

   As others discuss their projects, listen for additional steps that you might need in your project. Also be prepared to make suggestions about other projects.

6. After the discussion, revise the steps of your project if necessary.

7. Record in your notebook what project you have chosen and begin your project.

   Keep this in mind: You will use the information from this project to make a presentation after your project is complete.

8. Take notes as you find information and follow the guidelines in Figure 17.2.

Ros and Marie's Brainstorming List
Project Steps – Recycling Metal

- Write a letter to State Recycling Agency.
- Look in library for information about aluminum or steel.
- Contact local scrap metal dealers.
- Let people know where they can recycle metal.
- Find an example of recycled metal for presentation.

▶ **FIGURE 17.1**

This is one example of what your procedure list might look like.

▶ FIGURE 17.2

Use these guidelines to help you decide whether you have the quantity and quality of information that you need.

Project Guidelines

- Use either four library resources or some combination of library resources and outside information (e.g., two library resources and surveys from two stores). Using a combination of sources might give you much better information for your project.
- Describe both the costs and benefits of any action that you advise.
- As you work on your project, you might decide that you need additional or different steps to complete your project successfully. Be prepared to change your project if you need to.

Background Information

Part A—Project Ideas

1. Make recycling work! Conduct a survey in several local stores to find out what recycled products they sell. Then write letters to the school board or the city council and give them information about where to buy such materials as recycled paper and plastic lumber for your school or your community. Let the city council or school board know that plastic

lumber is ideal for picnic tables and outdoor playground equipment. Find and bring some examples of recycled products for your presentation. Use the library to find examples of designs that could be built with plastic lumber as well as designs or uses that will not work with plastic lumber.

2. Help stop the pollution caused by used motor oil! Find out who recycles motor oil in your local area. Organize a public awareness campaign to let people know how they can and why they should recycle motor oil. Let them know at least one store where they can buy recycled motor oil and one place to turn in used motor oil for recycling.
3. Which towns and cities have successful recycling programs? What makes these recycling programs work? If there are places where recycling experts think recycling will not work well, what are their reasons? Study four locations (cities, states, or countries). Find two where a successful recycling program is operating and choose two where you think it probably would not work well at this time or where it does not yet occur but could begin quite easily. In your presentation, include your ideas of what makes recycling projects successful. If no one has started a recycling program in your school, use your ideas about successful programs to start one. If a recycling program already exists, expand it.
4. What are the benefits of recycling? Study at least three types of materials. You might choose from aluminum, glass, paper, motor oil, and plastic. What are some of the effects when people do not recycle these materials? Are there materials that people should not recycle? Include examples of how people or wildlife can be affected if recycling does not occur.
5. Many communities now have curbside pickup for recycling. In other communities, people must carry their recyclables to a store or other central location. What recycling facilities are available in your community? What do they recycle? How many

people use the facilities? What can you do to increase both numbers?

6. Identify ten products that you use regularly. Do research to define and find out whether or not the products are "environmentally friendly." Find at least two or three that are available in an "environmentally friendly" form and switch to them for several days at least. In your project, be sure to include how you defined an environmentally friendly product. Also describe what factors you think about when you decide whether you are willing to switch to a product.
7. Are there hazardous wastes in your home? Pick two or three specific items that you think might be hazardous, such as several kinds of batteries or different types of cleansers or solvents. If these products are toxic, find out what makes them toxic. Do a survey at your home and the homes of several classmates or an entire neighborhood. Find out how many households have these products and how people dispose of them. Look for information about safer products that people could use. Write a commercial that tells people about safer products that they can use instead of toxic ones or how they can dispose of some hazardous materials safely.
8. What are some effects that landfills have on animal and plant populations? If possible study the wildlife in an area such as a canyon used for a landfill. Also make use of library resources to learn more about wildlife in landfill areas. If you discover that a landfill is having a negative effect on local wildlife, develop an advertising campaign. Convince people to recycle or to produce less garbage in order to preserve the wildlife habitat. If you discover that the landfill is beneficial for some animals or plants, you might decide to describe that effect too.
9. Start a compost project at home or school. What arrangements would you need to make to get your project started? What patterns do you need to change? Are people throwing away food scraps that they could put into compost? Once the compost is ready, how would you use it? Would it be practical for your school

to compost food wastes? Build a container for small-scale composting. Bring it to class and describe how you would use it.

10. Some scientists state that we are putting garbage into the atmosphere. One example is the propellants that we put into the atmosphere when we use aerosol sprays. How can you find out what aerosol propellants people commonly use? What are some of the effects of using aerosol sprays? What are some alternatives to using aerosols?

11. How might incineration play a part in solving our garbage crisis; that is, what are the methods of incineration, which methods are best, and why should we use them? Why do some people want incinerators to be shut down? Prepare a poster that describes how modern incinerators work. Choose one type of incinerator that you would consider to be the best designed; that is, describe the incinerator that offers the best technology in your opinion. After your research, describe the part that incineration should or should not play in garbage disposal. If appropriate, consider sending a summary of your findings to the city council.

Part B—Resource List

The following organizations and resources might have information that you are looking for. Your teacher also has a list that includes names and addresses for some national sources. If you have access to the Internet, you will find some useful information on the Web. Your teacher will have some current web addresses for you to check.

The Recycler's Handbook. This book lists recycling ideas and includes names and addresses of state recycling agencies, as well as many national organizations involved in recycling.

Iowa Department of Natural Resources. This organization provides information about household hazardous wastes.

Partnership for Plastics Progress. This organization publishes information about recycled plastics as waste and about recycling plastics.

Bureau of Mines. This branch of the federal government is interested in recycling metals and in retrieving lead from batteries, among other projects.

Recycled products catalogs. Your teacher has addresses for sources of such materials as carpet made from plastic, rechargeable batteries, nontoxic cleaners, plastic lumber, and recycled paper.

Local landfill operators or scrap metal dealers. Consult these people for information about the efforts of your local merchants to promote recycling, as well as the difficulties they have encountered.

Wrap Up

Write a one-page summary of your project in your notebook. Be as thorough as you can. Describe what you did and what you learned from your project. Also describe any decisions that you made about actions to take and the costs and benefits of these actions. (An example of a personal action would be to buy an environmentally friendly product rather than one that is not. Your action should match the type of project you did.) At the end of your summary, list the sources you used.

Investigation:
Presentations—Projects, Part II

elaborate/evaluate

The way you present an idea can have a big impact on how people receive it. Before you can convince people of the value of your idea, you must understand clearly what you want to say and what you want to show to your audience. In this investigation, you will find ways to present your ideas and to let people know that solutions to the garbage crisis really matter. The purpose of this investigation is to prepare and present what you discovered during your project.

Materials for Each Student:

- materials for presentations

Process and Procedure

1. Think about your project and what ideas you would most want people to remember.

Working Cooperatively

You will work individually and as a class. You will make a presentation and listen to the presentations of other students in your class. As you discuss presentations, be sure to *Include everyone in the discussion.*

2. Decide what information you will present to your class.

   Look over the summary that you wrote about your project and review your findings as well as how you gathered information.

3. Prepare your project presentation.

   Think of your audience and remember that they do not know all the details of your project the way you do. No matter what format you use, your presentation must include the following information:

   - *a description of what you chose to study,*
   - *how you gathered your information (e.g., what resources you used—the World Wide Web, books, magazines, or people you interviewed), and*
   - *the argument that you are making (what you want to let people know).*

4. Practice your presentation.

   Make it as appealing as possible.

5. Make your presentation and listen to your classmates' presentations.

6. As you listen to other presentations, write a summary of each one. Use two or three sentences to answer the following:

   - What project did your classmate choose?
   - What information did your classmate gather?
   - What were the results?

Wrap Up

After you and all of your classmates have given presentations, answer the following in your notebook.

1. Describe in a few sentences which project you liked the best and why.
2. How would you change or improve your project if you did it again?
3. Write down which project ideas you think you could carry out and which ones you think you couldn't. Explain what would make some ideas possible and some more difficult.

evaluate

Connections:
St. Louis and San Diego: Opposite Decisions?

As you might have noticed during this unit, if people are concerned about garbage, they must make careful choices about the products that they buy and use. Many people want to use products that cause the least pollution or that have the least negative impact on the environment. Many grocery store owners are faced with a dilemma of what to supply to their customers: paper or plastic bags.

Sometimes two people might be trying to solve the same problem and yet they might make two different decisions. Can the different decisions both be helpful to the environment?

Read the following excerpts and see what you think. Two grocery store owners are telling about their decisions. Schnucks is a chain of grocery stores in St. Louis, and Big Bear Markets is a chain in San Diego.

Why Recyclable Plastic Bags Make Sense

by Terry Schnuck

Several years ago, we introduced polyethylene plastic grocery sacks in our stores. We did so for three basic reasons. First, the bags we chose are photo degradable (they break down in the presence of air and sunlight). Second, the manufacturer uses water-based inks. Using this type of ink means the bags cannot cause harmful leaching when placed in landfills. Third, we felt the bags represented a quality product at a reasonable cost.

Since introducing the plastic bags we have found they offer many other benefits. Schnucks' environmental philosophy, which we communicated to the public on Earth Day 1990, is comprised of three critical points—reduce, reuse, and recycle. Plastic bags can address all three:

- They require less energy to produce than paper bags.
- They are reusable in the home.
- They are completely recyclable.

Later, we placed recycling containers at all of our 59 supermarkets. When the containers are full, the bags are transported from our stores to a central warehouse where they are baled for shipment to our bag supplier, Sonoco Products.

The bags are then used to make a variety of new products such as irrigation pipes, protective edge molding, plastic trash cans, sign posts and non-food packaging materials.

Even if the bags are not recycled, but instead end up in landfills, they take up only one-seventh the space of paper bags. They also burn cleanly when incinerated.

Some scientists have come to regard plastic bags as less damaging to the environment than paper bags. Papermaking contributes to water pollution, acid rain, releases dioxin and depletes our forests.

Our customers have come to prefer plastic bags (three to one over paper) for a variety of reasons. Elderly customers and customers who have to walk up stairs prefer plastic because the handles make them easier to carry. Other customers have told us the bags are great for all types of reuses because they are waterproof. But their single most redeeming feature is that they can be recycled.

Customer response to this recycling effort has been extremely positive. People want to help, and welcome an opportunity to address the solid waste problem in even a small way.

Yet the very nature of our business makes us incompatible with recycling on any major scale. Bringing products for recycling to a food store presents a potential sanitation problem.

For this reason, we have placed the bins for milk and soda containers a considerable distance from our stores on our parking lots; there is somewhat less of a hazard with the plastic bags. Nevertheless, we are pleased to be part of both these recycling programs.

There are programs companies can institute in-house as well. At Schnucks, we have reduced the number of polystyrene foam cups our office personnel use by at least 2,000 per week. We asked them to bring their own coffee mugs and drinking cups in exchange for a lower price for a cup of coffee. We also have a receptacle in our cafeteria for aluminum cans, which volunteers then take to recycling centers.

Finally, as a visible and involved member of the communities in which we do business, Schnucks strives to present a balanced view on environmental issues. For example, when talking with customers, we make it clear that our plastic bags are not biodegradable, but only photo degradable.

That is to say, we try to explain that the bags will degrade if exposed to sunlight and air—which addresses the litter problem—but they will not degrade in a landfill. However, it is equally important to point out that the bags are non-toxic and take up significantly less space in landfills than paper bags, and that they can be recycled.

From "Why Recyclable Plastic Bags Make Sense," by Terry Schnuck, The Progressive Grocer Special Report: The Environment, © 1990 by The Progressive Grocer. Excerpted with permission.

Why We Switched Back to Paper Bags

by Tom Dahlen

At Big Bear Markets, we feel it is our responsibility to be the environmental conscience of our customers. We must provide them with the information to make environmentally sound shopping decisions that can have a positive impact on our community and quality of life.

The issue with Big Bear is not so much paper vs. plastic, but the specific challenges that must be faced to protect

San Diego's environment. There is a serious landfill shortage and the health of wildlife and marine life to consider.

While both paper and plastic bags have some trade-offs, experts from the Audubon Society have pointed out that paper bags are preferable in coastal areas because plastic bags can entangle and trap marine life. Paper bags—which quickly degrade if they find their way to the sea—do not pose this danger. Some would argue that plastic bags can degrade as well, but as we have all seen, the issue of degradable plastics has become extremely controversial.

By educating our employees and our customers about the paper bags, we have attained greater productivity at the checkstand and savings in supply costs. Our customer research indicated that we had been wasting 10 percent of each bag—which were rarely filled to capacity. So besides having our bags made out of recycled paper, we had our supplier make them 3 inches shorter than traditional sacks.

This has resulted in better loading, easier carrying and less likelihood of toppling over in the car or when being unloaded at home. We also are paying consumers two cents for every large paper bag returned to our stores to pack subsequent orders.

We let the customers vote, and don't make them feel guilty about their choice. While we don't mind working with plastic, we do ask customers, "Is paper okay today?" About 95 percent of the time the answer is "yes."

We are also selling recycled paper bags with handles, and donating proceeds to *I Love a Clean San Diego*. The bag supplier has committed to planting three seedlings for every tree they cut down.

The initial switch to paper did have its costs. For example, we spent $7,000 retraining our employees to pack paper bags properly. And we spent another $20,000 in advertising to educate our customers about the change—and the reasons behind it. There was also some expense involved in removing the plastic bag racks and printing promotional material.

But six months after the switch, we have toted up some significant benefits. Supply costs are down $35,000. Big Bear is using fewer bags per unit of retail sale since paper bags hold more product. This accomplishes our goal of using up fewer natural resources.

In addition, productivity studies indicate a significant improvement in checkstand speed—over 15 percent on average. Finally, paper bags are easier to use and in the long run require far less bagger training. Since we are faced with increased labor costs, this is a significant cost advantage.

Our paper bags represent recycling in action. Our old corrugated boxes return as carryout bags. All in all the response to our switch to paper bags has been overwhelmingly positive—the amount of media coverage and support phenomenal.

From Tom Dahlen, "Why We Switched Back to Paper Bags," The Progressive Grocer Special Report: The Environment, © 1990 by The Progressive Grocer. Excerpted with permission.

SIDELIGHT *on Technology*

Closing the Loop

You might have seen the recycling arrows on many products. These recycling arrows stand for the three phases of recycling: collecting, remanufacturing, and remarketing.

When people collect, remanufacture, and resell products such as aluminum cans, manufacturers say that closed-loop recycling has occurred; that is, the product made it all the way around the loop. People sometimes forget the third part of the loop: buying recycled products. People who recycle paper have a saying: "If you're not buying recycled products, you're not recycling!"

Why do you suppose recyclers say this? It is because of supply and demand. If there is no demand for products that have been recycled, the supply will dry up. Recyclers will go out of business because they cannot sell their products. If no companies recycle products, then there will be nowhere to take used aluminum, glass, cans, or paper. These products will end up in the garbage along with the other types of wastes.

Wrap Up

Read through the following and write your answers in your notebook. Prepare to share your ideas with the class.

1. Describe how Big Bear Markets changed a pattern in its customers' use of grocery sacks.
2. Describe the customers' patterns of using grocery sacks at Schnucks' Markets.
3. What do the owners of Schnucks' Markets consider the costs and benefits of their decision to be?
4. What do the owners of Big Bear Markets consider the costs and benefits of their decision to be?
5. Some people think that paper or plastic is not a choice they need to consider because they use cloth bags. What do you think the costs and benefits of this decision would be?
6. Write a paragraph expressing your opinion of the decision the Schnucks' Markets made, the decision the Big Bear Markets made, and the paper versus plastic controversy.
7. What would you decide to do if you owned a large chain of grocery stores? Explain your answer.

HOW TO Round Off Numbers #1

When you measure the length of someone's foot with a ruler, the measurement you get will not always be a whole number. In fact the measurement is more likely to be *between* two whole numbers on the ruler. So which whole number should you write down as the measurement of the person's foot?

How did Isaac, Ros, and Al decide to round off the measurements they made? They made use of **millimeters (mm),** the small spaces between the **centimeter (cm)** marks, on their rulers. (The centimeter marks are the whole numbers.) See Figure H1.1.

Each centimeter contains 10 millimeters. In other words, each millimeter equals one-tenth of a centimeter. That relationship (10 millimeters = 1 centimeter) makes it easy to show measurements that fall between two centimeters. All you have to do is write the number of millimeters as a decimal following the whole number of centimeters. After you work through some examples, you will understand how to show measurements using centimeters and millimeters.

Let's say you measured the length of a toddler's foot and the measurement was between 11 and 12 centimeters—the exact measurement was 11 centimeters plus 3 millimeters. Because each millimeter equals one-tenth of a centimeter, you can represent 11 centimeters and 3 millimeters as 11.3 centimeters. (This is the same as saying the toddler's foot is 11 and three-tenths centimeters long.) Another toddler's foot might be 11 centimeters plus 8 millimeters in length, which is the same as 11.8 centimeters, or 11 and eight-tenths centimeters long (see Figure H1.2).

Now you know how to write measurements to the nearest millimeter. Your assignment in the investigation *Getting Off on the Right Foot*, however,

▼ **Figure H1.1**

How many millimeters are between the centimeter marks on a metric ruler?

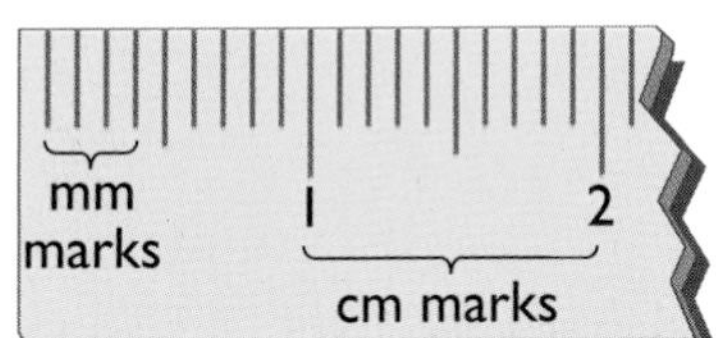

▶ **FIGURE H1.2**
What are the exact measurements of two toddlers' feet that are between 11 and 12 centimeters long?

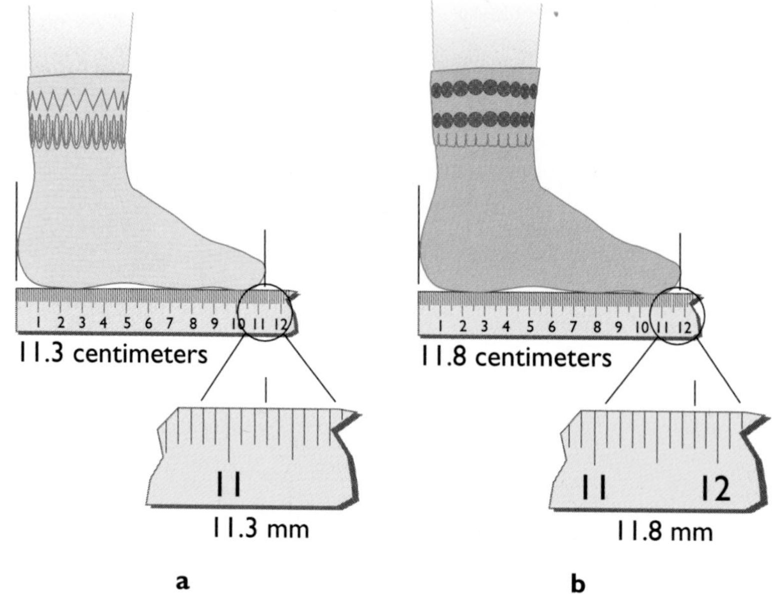

was to determine the length of your foot to the nearest centimeter. To do this, you must round off your measurement to the nearest whole number. For example, if your foot were 20.2 centimeters long, that measurement is closer to 20 centimeters than to 21 centimeters, so you would round off your measurement to 20 centimeters. If your foot measured 20.7 centimeters, that measurement is closer to 21 centimeters than to 20 centimeters, so you would round off your measurement to 21 centimeters. Look back at the picture of Isaac, Ros, and Al and review their decisions about rounding off their measurements.

In summary to round off a measurement to the nearest whole number, first look at the ruler. If the measurement is closer to 20, write 20. If it is closer to 21, write 21. If the measurement is exactly halfway, for example 20.5 centimeters, then round the measurement to the next higher number, in this case to 21 centimeters.

HOW TO Identify the Parts of a Graph #2

Graphs are useful tools because they help us see a lot of information at one time. We organize graphs in a certain way so that we can *read* easily the information the graphs contain. Graphs also help us find patterns in the data we have collected.

A graph has two lines, one that runs crosswise (horizontally) and one that runs up and down (vertically). These lines have special names. We call the line that runs crosswise the **horizontal axis** and the line that runs up and down the **vertical axis.** The point where these two

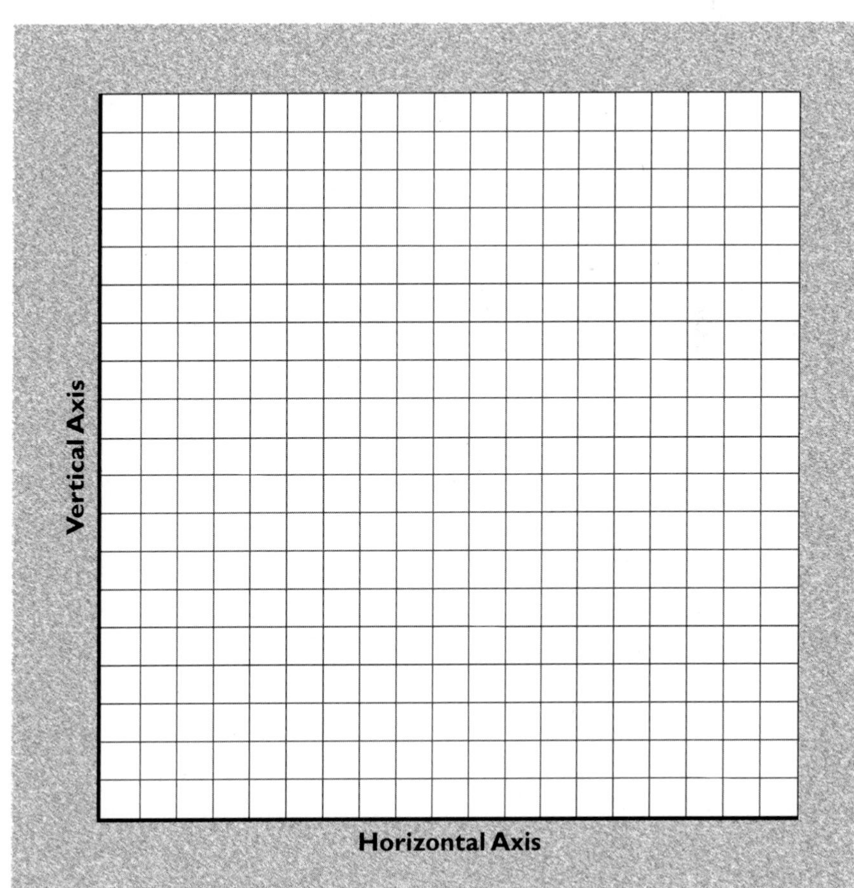

FIGURE H2.1

The names of the axes on a graph are the horizontal axis and the vertical axis.

▶ FIGURE H2.2

These are possible labels for the sample graph in *Getting Off on the Right Foot.*

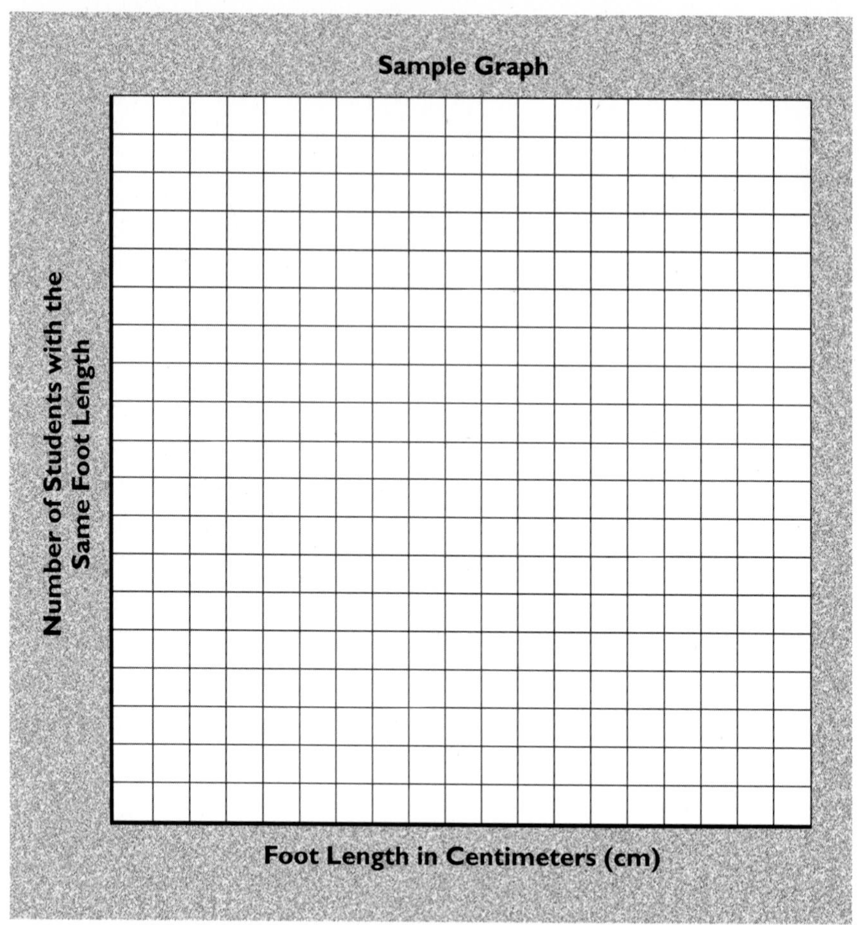

lines, or axes, meet is the place where the graph begins. (The term **axes** is the plural for the term **axis.**)

Before you began the investigation *Getting Off on the Right Foot,* your teacher probably set up a horizontal axis and a vertical axis for your class graph.

To find out what kind of information a graph displays, you need to look at the labels next to each axis. Your teacher probably used the following labels for the graph in the investigation *Getting Off on the Right Foot.*

Both axes of a graph often have a sequence of numbers called a **number scale.** You read the numbers on the horizontal axis from left to right and those on the vertical axis from bottom to top. For example, in your class graph for *Getting Off on the Right Foot,* the number scales probably looked like those in Figure H2.3.

The numbers on the horizontal axis represent possible foot measurements; the numbers on the vertical axis show how many students had the same foot measurement. The difference between numbers next to each other on the horizontal axis is one; the difference between numbers next to each other on the vertical axis is also one.

The number scale on one axis does not have to be exactly the same as the number scale on the other axis (see Figure H2.3). The difference between the numbers next to each other on an axis must be the same, though. Look at the graphs in Figure H2.4. One graph has a number scale that will work, and the other has a number scale that will not work. Which graph's number scale will not work? Be prepared to explain why you chose the one you did.

Often you will draw your graphs on a special kind of paper called graph paper. Graph paper is special because it has evenly spaced lines: The distance between the lines is the same from side to side and from bottom to top. This even spacing helps you show that the difference

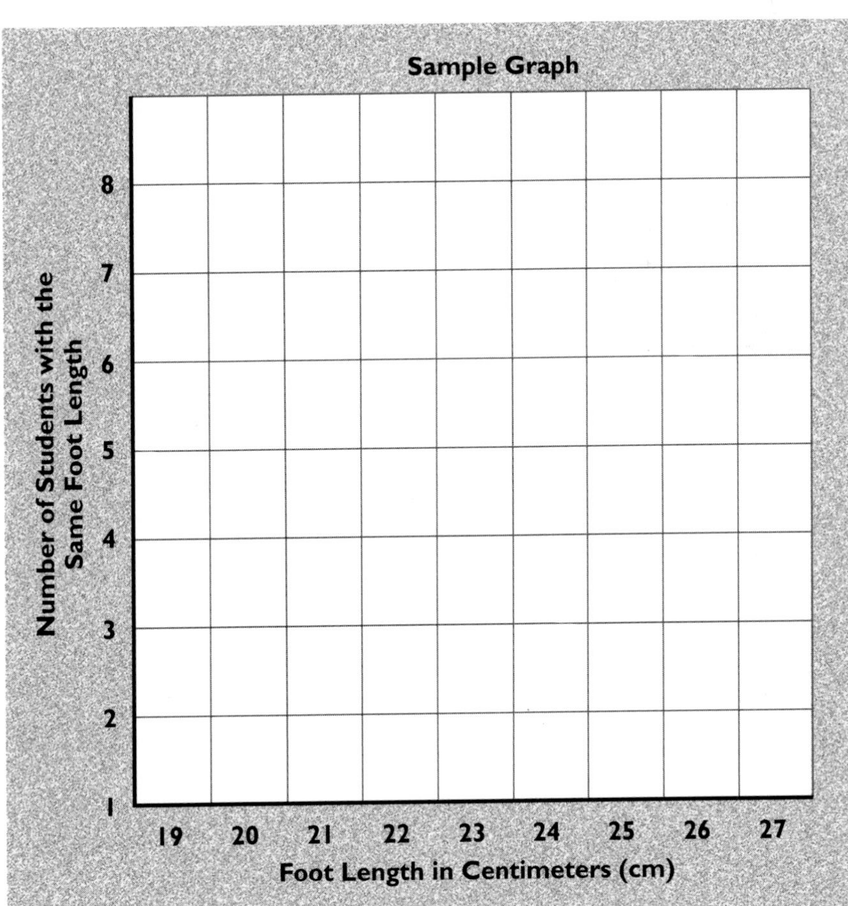

▶ **FIGURE H2.3**
In addition to the labels, this diagram shows the number scales for the sample graph in *Getting Off on the Right Foot.*

▶ FIGURE H2.4

Which graph's number scales will not work for graphing data?

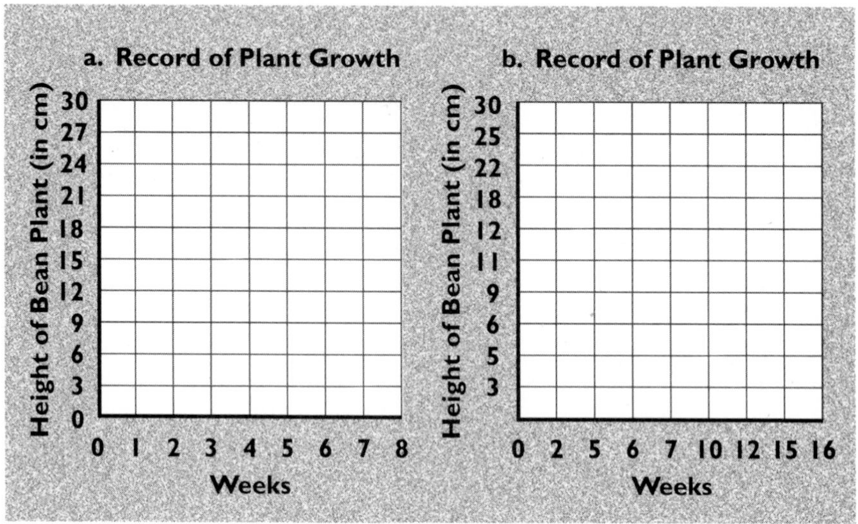

between numbers on your graph's number scale is the same from one number to the next (see Figure H2.5).

One last important feature of a graph is its title. We gave the graphs in this How To the titles of "Sample Graph" and "Record of Plant Growth." Your class graph for the investigation *Getting Off on the Right Foot* might have been titled "Class Graph of Foot Lengths." The title should tell the reader something about the purpose of the graph.

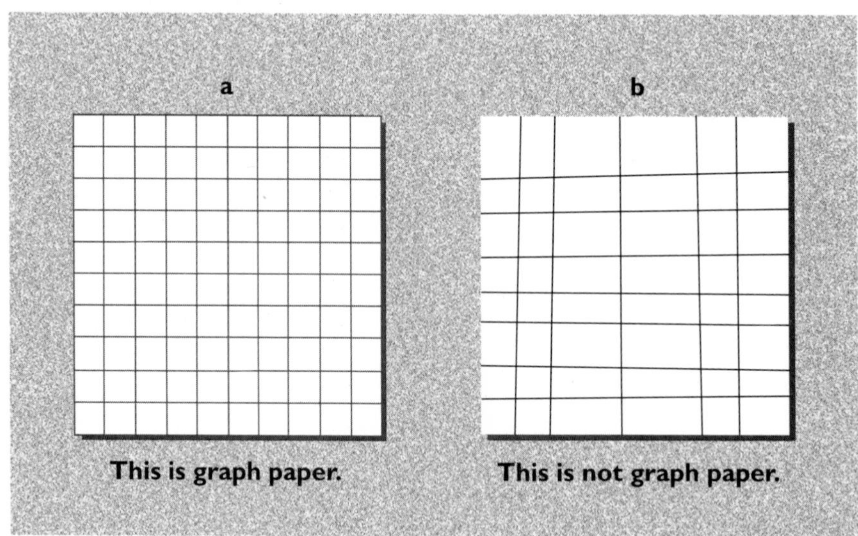

▶ FIGURE H2.5

Can you explain why the example shown in B is not graph paper?

HOW TO

Plot Data on a Graph

#3

If you have read How To #2, you know that graphs have the following parts: a horizontal axis, a vertical axis, labels on each axis, a number scale on each axis, and a title. (If you have not read How To #2 or if you do not remember the parts of a graph, review How To #2 before you continue with this How To.) You also know how to organize those parts so that the graph makes sense. But no graph can really make sense until you plot some information, or data, on it.

How do you get the information, or data, onto the graph in the right places? The answer to that question is what this How To is all about: learning how to plot data on a graph. On graph paper, draw a graph and plot the data from each of the sample data tables. The following steps will help you, and some hints and checkpoints appear along the way.

Part A—The Steps

1. Review the data you have recorded.

   For this example, you will use the data we recorded in Figure H3.1.

2. Draw the horizontal axis and the vertical axis for the graph.

   It helps if you draw your graph on graph paper because graph paper provides evenly spaced lines and squares. The spaces on graph paper keep the distance exactly the same between the consecutive numbers on each axis, that is, the numbers next to each other on an axis.

3. Label each axis by using the headings in the data table (see Figure H3.2).

4. Set up the number scales on each axis.

   Be sure to provide space on the horizontal axis and on the vertical axis for all the numbers that are included in the

► **FIGURE H3.1**

This data table shows daily high temperatures in degrees Fahrenheit (°F) over a two-week period in Phoenix, Arizona.

Daily High Temperatures in degrees Fahrenheit °F, Phoenix, Arizona	
Day, Week 1	**Temperature (in °F)**
1	103
2	104
3	105
4	104
5	105
6	102
7	102
Week 2	**Temperature (in °F)**
8	103
9	105
10	101
11	102
12	104
13	100
14	99

► **FIGURE H3.2**

These are possible labels for a graph of daily high temperatures.

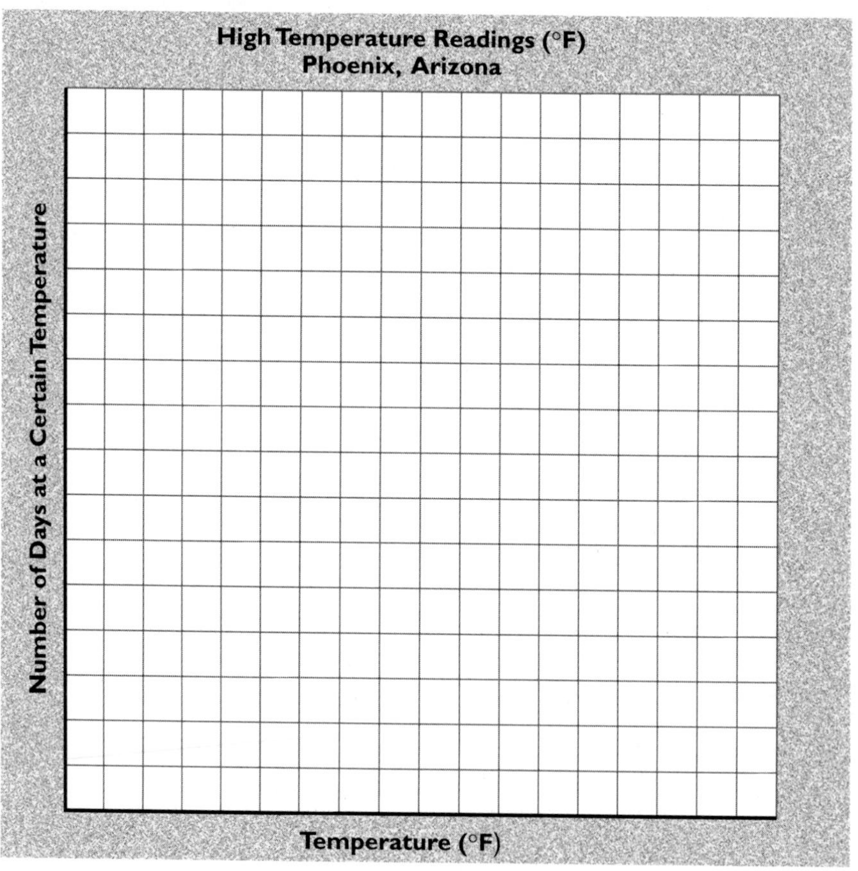

data table. Remember, a number scale does not always have to start with the number 1 (see Figure H3.3).

5. Give your graph a title.

   You might title this graph "Daily High Temperatures (in °F) over a two-week period in Phoenix, Arizona."

6. Plot the data on your graph by doing the following:
   - read one piece of data from the data table,
   - find the square on your graph where that piece of data fits, and
   - place an X in that square.

Repeat these steps for all the pieces of data in the data table.

First locate the first piece of data in the data table. It tells you that the high temperature on Day 1 in Phoenix, Arizona was 103°F. Next find 103 on the horizontal axis of your graph. Then place an X in the first square above 103.

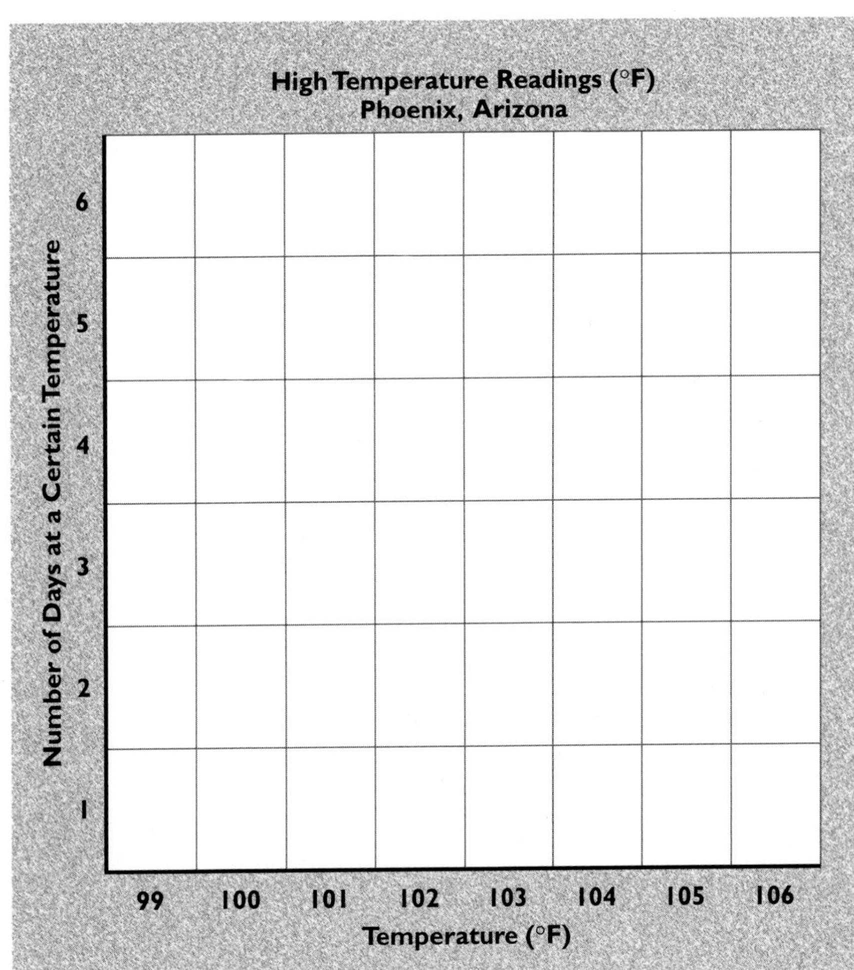

▶ **FIGURE H3.3**

This outline shows the labels and number scales for a graph of daily high temperatures.

This data point indicates to anyone reading the graph that the high temperature on one day during the two-week period in Phoenix, Arizona, was 103°F. (Note that on this type of graph you will not be able to show that the temperature on Day 1 was 103°F. What you will show when you complete the graph is the *number* of days that had a high temperature of 103°F.)

Go to the second day. The data indicate that the high temperature on Day 2 was 104°F. Find the first square above 104°F on the horizontal axis and place an X in it.

Plot the data for the first four days. Your graph should look now like the graph in Figure H3.4. Note that when you have two data points that are the same—104°F, for example—that the graph shows two Xs in that column.

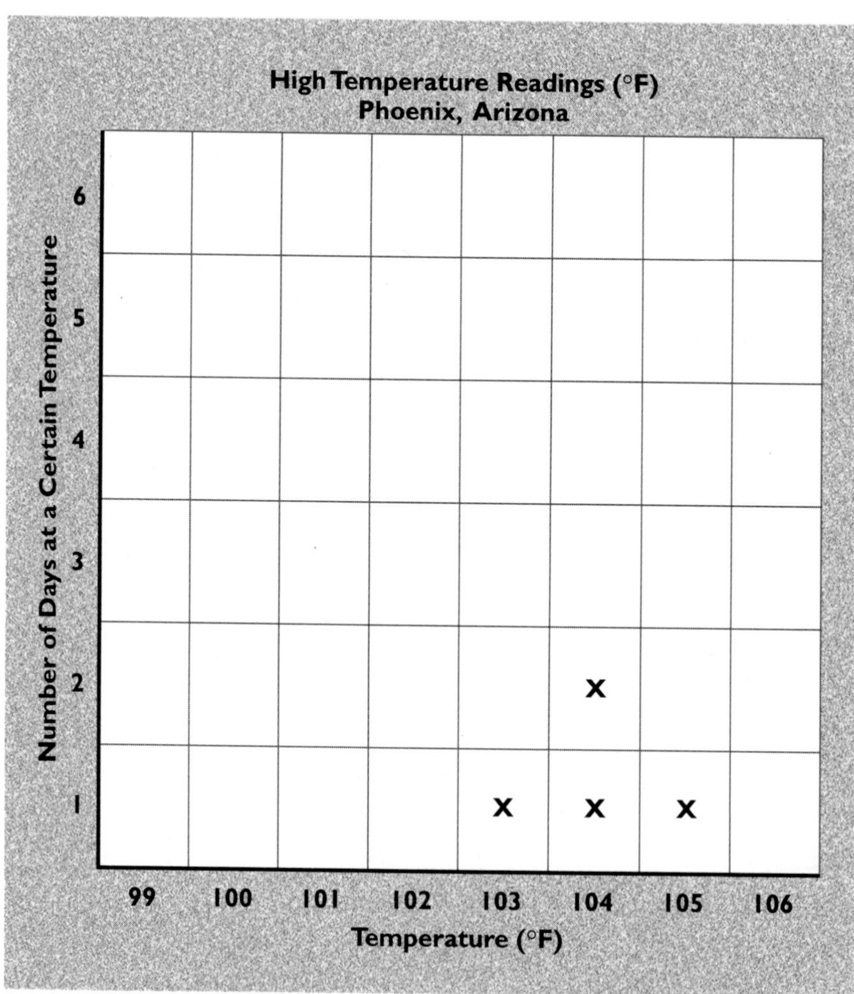

▶ **FIGURE H3.4**

Does your graph look like this one?

FIGURE H3.5

This data table shows daily high temperatures for a third week in Phoenix, Arizona.

Daily High Temperatures in degrees Fahrenheit (°F)	
Day, Week 3	Temperature (in °F)
1	100
2	99
3	103
4	101
5	101
6	99
7	102

Part B—Additional Practice

Suppose that someone recorded the daily high temperatures in degrees Fahrenheit (°F) in Phoenix, Arizona, for a third week. Figure H3.5 shows the high temperatures during the third week.

Plot the additional data on your graph and then answer these questions.

1. What was the most common temperature over the three-week period?
2. On how many days was the high temperature 104°F?
3. During the three-week period, did the temperature reach a high of 102°F more often than it reached a high of 99°F?

Part C—More Practice with Bar Graphs

So far in this How To you have learned how to plot data on a graph by placing Xs in the appropriate squares on the graph. In doing this, you have made a type of graph called a **bar graph.** You might see why this type of graph is called a bar graph if you shade each square that contains an X. The shaded squares line up on top of one another to make bars.

Sometimes in creating bar graphs, though, you will not always have data that you can plot by marking one X at a time in a square on your graph. Sometimes you will make a bar graph by shading the entire bar at one time. If you work through the following example, you will find out how to make a bar graph by shading each bar all at once.

Look at the data table in Figure H3.6. In this data table, you will find the names and approximate heights of some mountain peaks from around the world. (The column label reads "*Approximate* Height" because the numbers are not exact. We rounded off the numbers to make them easier for you to plot.) By plotting these data on a bar graph, you can compare the heights of these mountains. Can you use an atlas to find the location of each mountain?

Remember the six steps you used in the first example? You will follow the same steps in this example, but step 6 introduces a few changes. The steps are:

1. Review the data.

   Use the data recorded in Figure H3.6.

2. Draw the axes.
3. Label each axis.

   Because vertical bars usually are easier to read than horizontal ones, you should label the vertical axis "Approximate Height (in meters)" and the horizontal axis "Mountains." This way, the bars will run up and down and not across the graph. Can you see what would happen to the bars if you exchanged the labels on the axes?

4. Set up the number scale on each axis.

   In this graph, only the vertical axis has a number scale. The horizontal axis uses names instead of numbers. With some graphs, names instead of numbers will be more appropriate as labels. Also place the numbers on the vertical axis next to the lines, not between the lines (see Figure H3.7).

Approximate Heights (in meters [m]) of Mountains around the World	
Name of Mountain	**Approximate Height (m)**
Kilimanjaro	5,900
Mount Cook	3,800
Mount Elbrus	5,600
Mount Everest	8,800
Mount Fuji	3,800
Mount McKinley	6,200
Mount Whitney	4,400
Orizaba	5,700

▶ **FIGURE H3.6**
Which bar will be the tallest on your graph?

▶ **FIGURE H3.7**

Find the location on your bar graph for the first piece of data.

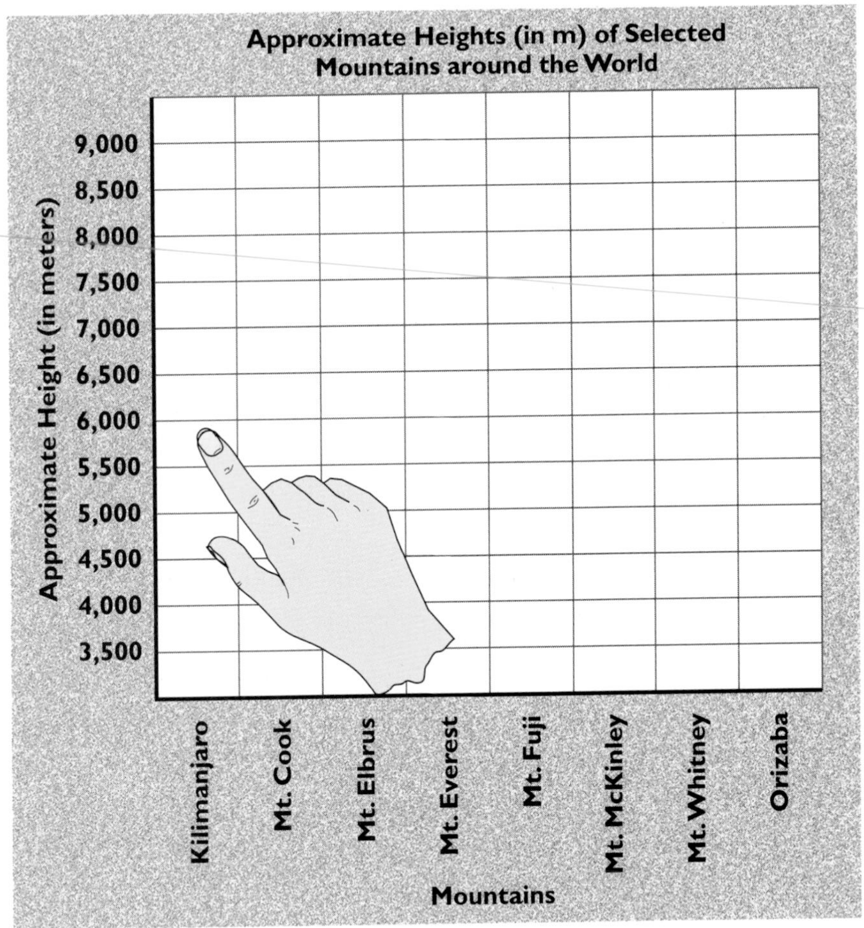

5. Give your graph a title.

You might title this graph "Approximate Heights of Mountains around the World."

6. Plot the data.

The parts of step 6 that you followed before do not fit the graph for approximate heights of mountains because you cannot plot each piece of data in the data table as one X on your graph. To make this graph, you must draw the entire bar to show the approximate height of each mountain. The following steps will tell you what to do differently.

- Read one piece of data from the data table.

The first piece of data tells you that a mountain named Kilimanjaro is approximately 5,900 meters high.

- Find the label for that piece of data on the horizontal axis.

The label on the horizontal axis for this piece of data is "Kilimanjaro."

- Trace your finger up the column above the label to the place on the vertical axis that shows where that piece of data fits.

The height of Kilimanjaro is approximately 5,900 meters. That height is between 5,500 meters and 6,000 meters on the vertical number scale. You can see in Figure H3.7 that the top of the bar for Kilimanjaro is between those two marks, but much closer to 6,000 meters than to 5,500 meters.

- Draw a horizontal line at the correct height to make the top of the bar.
- Color in the bar from that line down to the horizontal axis (see Figure H3.8).
- Repeat the parts of step 6 for all the pieces of data in the data table.

Now you know two different ways to plot data so that you can make a bar graph. In How To #6, you will learn how to plot data to make a line graph, another type of graph that displays data by using lines instead of bars.

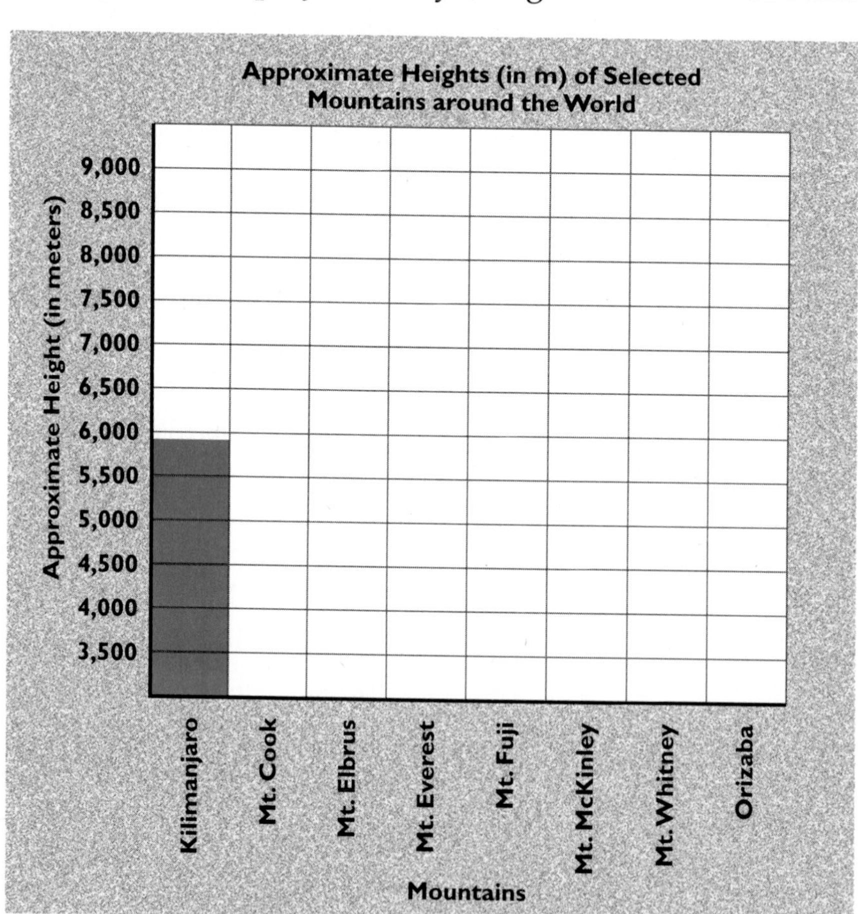

▶ **FIGURE H3.8**

This bar graph shows the first colored bar. You can do the rest.

HOW TO Construct a Data Table #4

Whenever you work on an activity in this program, you collect information. For example in the first unit you collected information about things such as the length of classmates' feet; the lengths of your ears, forearms, and little fingers; plant growth; and floating and sinking objects. We refer to such information as **data.** Data can be things such as measurements, numbers, observations, dates, or times. (We say "data are," not "data is," because the word *data* is plural. The singular form is *datum,* a word that means "one piece of information.")

Usually data do not make sense until they are organized in some way. In Chapters 3 through 7, the directions in your book helped you organize your data. But beginning in Chapter 8, you will not get as much help from your book. For example, when you worked with maze puzzles in the first investigation in Chapter 8, your book did not tell you how to keep track of your observations about the maze puzzles. The instructions suggested that you and your partner test your ideas and record your results, but the instructions did not tell you *how* to record what you observed. You might have run several tests before you and your partner realized that you needed to keep track of the observations as you made them. How did you keep track of the data from your tests? Were your data organized like Al's?

Al definitely needs a better system for organizing his data. What might you suggest to Al so that he is better organized next time? You might suggest that he organize his data in a **data table.**

A data table is a chart that helps people keep track of observations, or data, so that they can use the data later to make decisions, predictions, or graphs. You probably are familiar with data tables because you used them throughout Unit 1, but you might not have tried to construct a data table on your own. It's not too hard if you have some steps to follow.

Let's suppose that one of your tasks in the investigation *How Do You Know* was to construct a data table. How might you have done it? The following steps will show you one possible way. The steps also can help you construct data tables for other investigations, such as *The If–Then Box.*

1. Read the entire investigation so that you know its purpose.

   As you read the investigation, ask yourself, "What am I supposed to find out in this investigation? What question am I trying to answer?"

   In the investigation How Do You Know, you were supposed to decide what the inside of your and another team's maze puzzles looked like, without actually looking inside the puzzles.

2. Make a list of the types of information that you have or that you will need to collect during the investigation.

   In the case of How Do You Know, especially if you and your partner did not agree about what was inside the maze puzzle, you needed information about the following:

   - which test you were doing: Test #1, Test #2, and so on
   - what you did in each test: Which way did you move the maze puzzle—up and down, from side to side, from left to right?
   - what happened when you conducted each test: Did the marble stop in a particular place? Did the marble roll freely along the edge?
   - your conclusion about what happened: Do your results mean that a straight wall is probably inside the puzzle? Do your results show that the marble probably goes in a circle?

3. Review your list from Step 2 and the purpose from Step 1 and decide whether you are collecting enough information.

   This probably is the hardest step. You might ask yourself, "If I collect only what is on my list, will I collect enough information to find the answer to the main question?"

Remember that it is better to have too much information in a data table than too little. If you do not record all the information you will need, then you might have to repeat parts or all of the investigation to get the information you left out or forgot. This step will become easier as you construct more data tables.

4. Construct the outline of your data table by drawing one column for each item on your list.

   For the investigation How Do You Know, you would have had four things on your list: (1) which test, (2) what you did, (3) what happened, and (4) your conclusions. Therefore you would have needed four columns in your data table.

5. Label the columns in your data table.

   For the maze puzzles you would have used the items in your list from Step 2 as the column labels (see Figure H4.1).

6. Give your data table a title.

   The title should be simple but one that makes this data table different from any other data table you might use. A title also gives you a handy way to refer to this particular data table. You might have used "Maze

▼ **Figure H4.1**

This is a possible outline of a data table for the investigation *How Do You Know.*

Test number	What we did	What happened	Conclusion

Puzzles Data Table" as the title of your data table for the investigation How Do You Know.

7. Fill in your data table as you do the investigation.

   Figure H4.2 shows an example of what your data table might have looked like after you conducted two tests of one maze puzzle. (Your results might or might not agree with this example. The sample data table does not contain actual data, only examples of what the data might have been.)

   Be sure to complete one row of the data table after each test. If you write your observations and results right after you complete each test, then you do not have to worry about remembering what you did and what happened. But if you wait to record your observations until you have completed three tests, you might not remember exactly what you did in each test and what happened.

If you had made a data table in the investigation *How Do You Know,* would you have followed steps similar to these? If not, what would you have done differently? Would your method have worked just as well? Take a few minutes to share your strategies with your classmates. You might find that the steps you would have followed

▼ **FIGURE H4.2**

This sample data table shows possible results after testing one maze puzzle.

Test number	What we did	What happened	Conclusion
1	We held the puzzle up so that the marble was at the bottom. Then we slowly turned the puzzle in a clockwise direction.	The marble rolled along the bottom about 1 inch and then stopped.	There is a wall or part of a wall on the right side of the maze.
2	We tipped the puzzle so that the marble was resting at the top of the maze puzzle. This time we turned the puzzle counterclockwise.	The marble rolled about an inch again and stopped.	There is a wall that stops the marble on the right side.
3	We tipped the puzzle so that the marble was at the bottom and as far as it would go to the right. Then we tipped the puzzle down.	The marble rolled straight to the top.	Now we're sure there's a wall on the right side.

are slightly different from these. That is all right, as long as you would have ended up with a data table in which your data were organized and easy for you and others to read. The true test is whether you can use the information in your data table easily to help you answer the main question of the investigation. If your data table does not help you, then either you did not organize your data well or you forgot to collect and record some important data.

Do not worry if the first data tables you construct are not perfect. You will have other chances to practice constructing data tables in the investigation *The If–Then Box*. Follow the steps and use the sample data tables from the maze puzzles to help you construct your data table for this investigation. You will become better at constructing data tables with each try.

HOW TO Have a Brainstorming Session #5

Having a brainstorming session can be a lot of fun. During a brainstorming session, you can voice any idea that comes to your brain, no matter how crazy it might seem. You can say *any* idea that you think might provide a solution. Sometimes the ideas that seem far-fetched at first can lead to other ideas that really work. The main purpose of a brainstorming session is to create a storm in your brain so that you become very creative.

During a brainstorming session, you have permission to be as different in your thinking from others as you like. Your goal is to come up with as many different ideas as possible. After you finish your brainstorming session, you can come back to your task and use your ideas to solve a problem or to answer a question.

The process of brainstorming has a few guidelines:

1. State any idea about the topic that comes to your mind.
2. Record everyone's ideas. Do not judge whether the ideas are good or bad. Write them all down.
3. Keep thinking of ideas for at least five minutes. Continue for as long as you can or until your teacher tells you that your time is up.
4. If you cannot think of a new idea, look at something that is already on the list. Try to add something to that idea or change the idea slightly.
5. If you are working in a group, take turns. Be sure that each person has a chance to suggest ideas. Remember that some people might need a little more time to think before suggesting something.

After you finish your brainstorming session, look at your list and decide which ideas might be better than others for solving the problem or answering the question. You should have a great list from which to choose!

HOW TO Draw a Line Graph #6

In Unit 1 you learned about graphing. You learned about the parts of a graph in How To #2. In How To #3, you learned how to plot data to make bar graphs. In this How To, you will use what you learned in How To #2 and How To #3. Instead of showing the data with bars, though, you will use a line to connect the data points. When you connect the data points in this way, you make a **line graph.** A line graph helps you understand events that happen over time.

You and your classmates have just described what you saw on the maps in the investigation *Patterns on the Earth.* Probably a lot of what you described were the *patterns* that you observed on the maps. You could describe those patterns easily because you could see the data plotted on the actual maps, and you could point out the patterns to one another. But what if you had to explain the patterns to someone who was not in class and who did not see the actual maps? There is another way to show some of the patterns you observed. You can use a graph.

In this How To, you will use the data from the Ages of Rocks map to show a pattern on a graph. Before you can make a graph, though, you must organize your data into a data table. (If you do not remember how to construct a data table, review How To #4.) To show the pattern from the Ages of Rocks map, you will need to display the ages of the rocks and their distance from the coast of South America. Your data table might look like the one in Figure H6.1.

To set up your graph, follow the same basic steps as you did in How To #3. Steps 1 through 5 will be the same. Plotting the data on your graph (Step 6) will be different, however, because you will draw a line instead of bars. Let's go through the process one more time.

1. Review the data you have recorded.
   You will use data from the data table in Figure H6.1.

2. Draw the horizontal axis and the vertical axis for the graph.
3. Label each axis, using the headings in the data table.

   Because you want your line graph to help you see a pattern of something that happened over time, you should put the heading about time on the horizontal axis. In this case the heading for time is "Millions of Years." The other heading relates to distance, not time, so distance will be the label for the vertical axis.
4. Set up the number scales on each axis.

   Use the data table to help you with this step. Notice that the numbers on the horizontal axis are from less than 1 million years to 190 million years and that each line represents 5 million years. The numbers on the vertical axis are from 0 kilometers to 2,200 kilometers, and each line represents 100 kilometers.
5. Give your graph a title.
6. Plot the data on your graph by doing the following:
   - Read one row of data from the data table.

   The first row of data tells you that the rocks that are 0 kilometers from the coast of South America (those rocks that are actually on or near the coast of South America) are 190 million years old.
   - Find the number on the horizontal axis where that piece of data fits.

   In this case, the number you want on the horizontal axis is 190. Move your finger to that number.

▼ **FIGURE H6.1**

This data table presents the data from the Ages of Rocks map.

Distance from the coast of South America in kilometers	Ages of rocks (in millions of years)
0	190
1000	65
1500	37
1900	22
2100	5
2200	<1

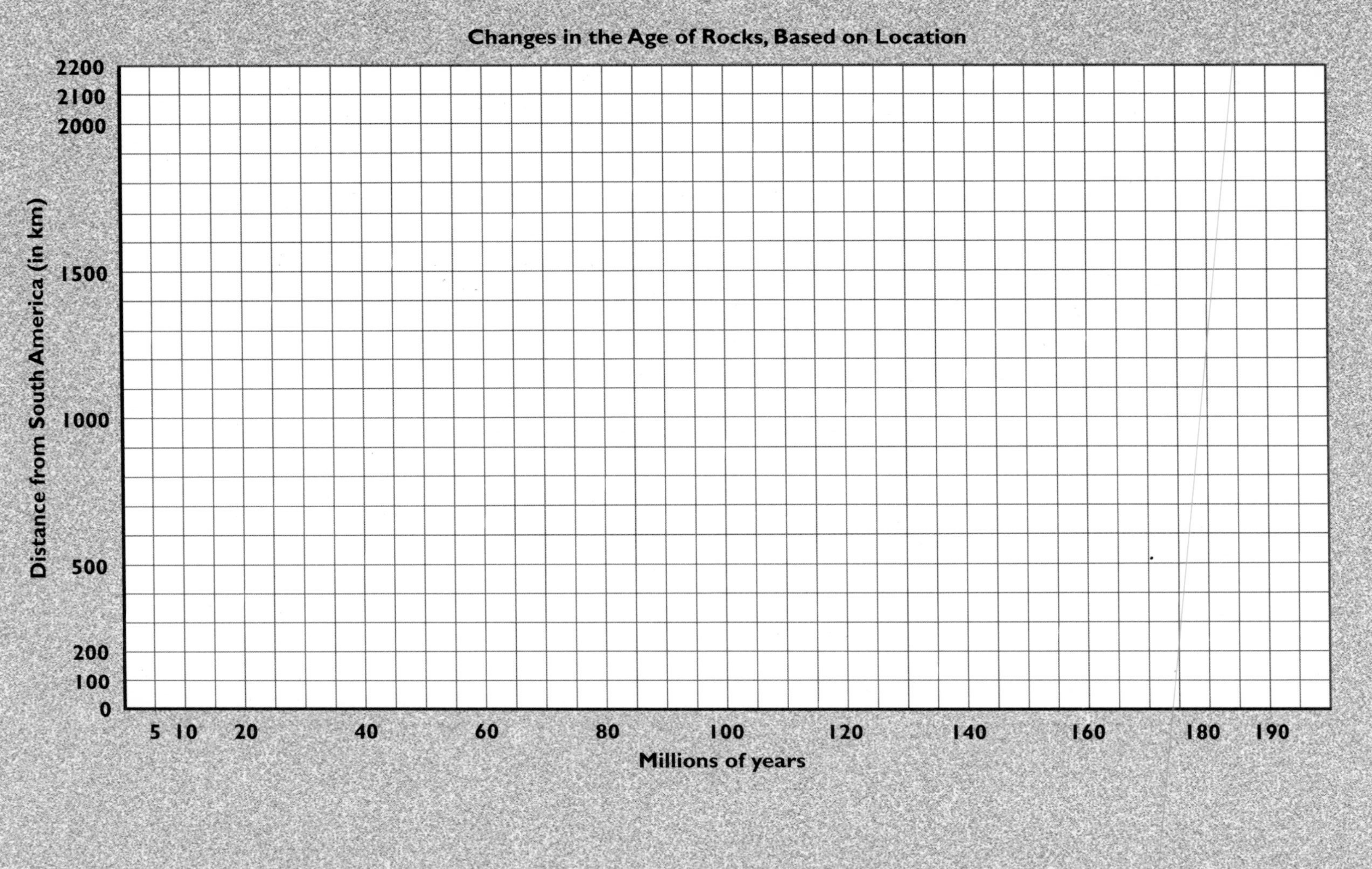

▲ **FIGURE H6.2**
Now you are ready to plot data on your graph.

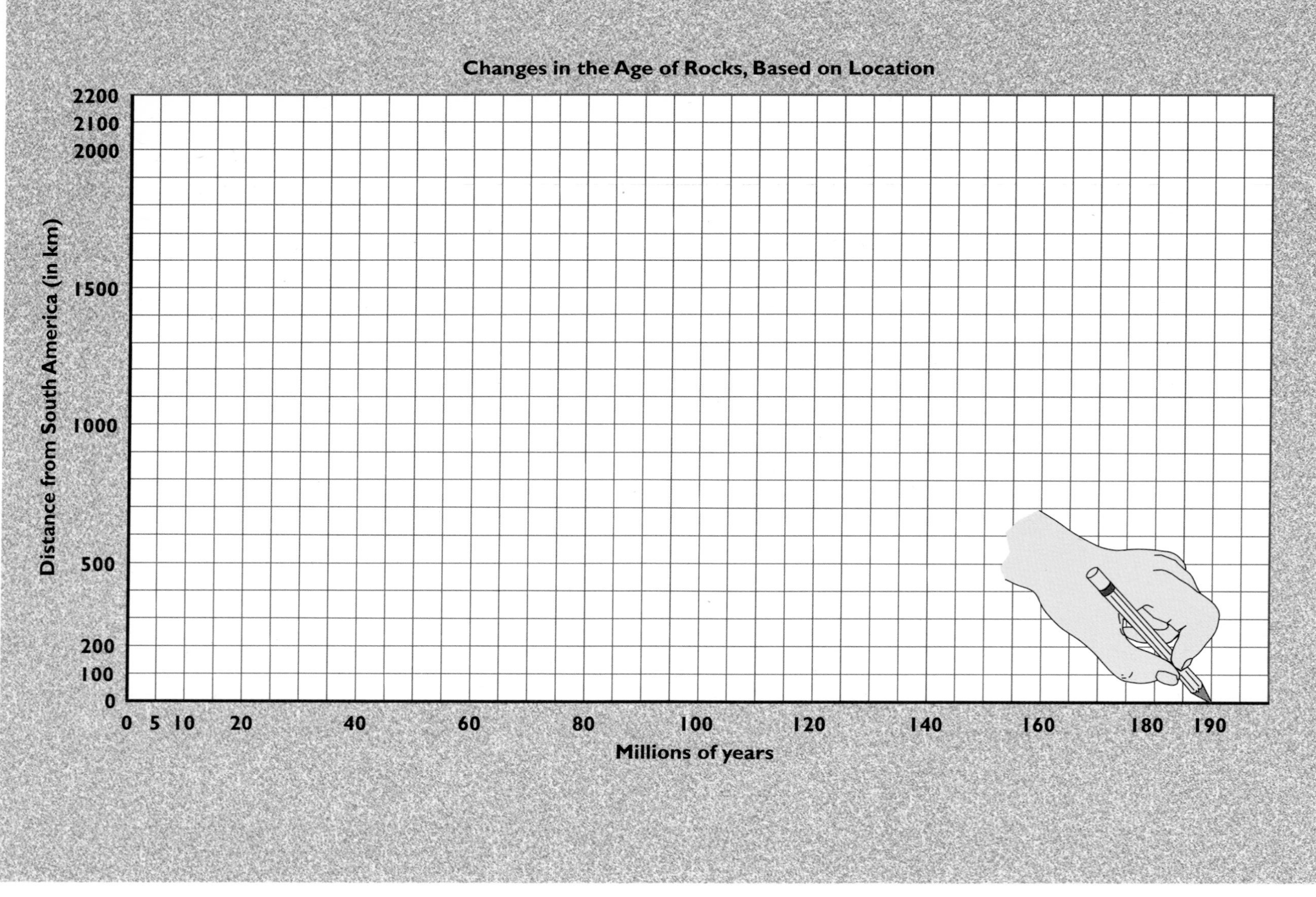

▲ **FIGURE H6.3**
This graph shows the first data point.

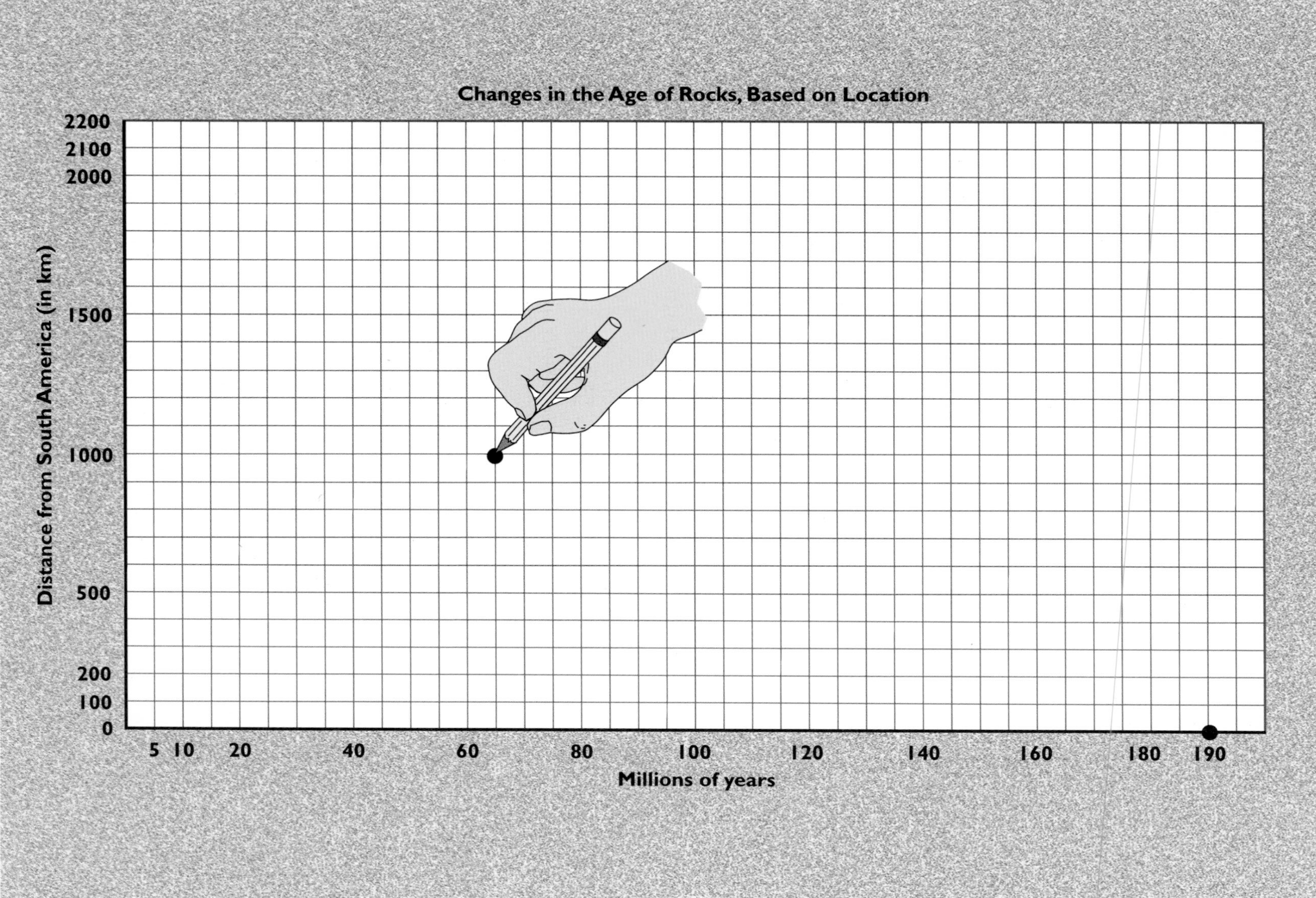

▲ **FIGURE H6.4**
Can you begin to see a pattern?

- Move up from the number on the horizontal axis to the place on the vertical axis where that piece of data fits.

In this case you do not need to move your finger at all because the distance at 190 million years is 0 kilometers, which is on the horizontal axis (see Figure H6.3).

- Draw a dot, called a **data point,** at that place.
- Repeat the four parts of step 6 for every row of data in the data table.

For example, to plot the second data point, move your finger across the horizontal axis to the 65 million year mark and then up that line to 1,000 kilometers on the vertical axis (see Figure H6.4). Make a dot for the second data point. Do the same for the rest of the data in the data table.

7. Draw a smooth line from left to right that connects all the data points.

You have completed a line graph that displays the data in the data table. Look at the pattern shown on the graph. Describe that pattern in terms of the age of the rocks and their distance from the coast of South America.

Questions:

1. As the rocks get older (in millions of years), do you move farther away from or closer to the coast of South America?
2. Where would you find the youngest rocks—near the coast of South America or toward the middle of the Atlantic Ocean?
3. What kind of pattern does this graph show?

HOW TO Use a Bunsen Burner #7

A Bunsen burner is a type of heat source that burns fuel gas. This burner was designed in 1855 by a German scientist named Robert Bunsen. The Bunsen burner was a much more convenient and efficient heat source for a laboratory than either stoves or candles, which were the only other heat sources available then. The design of the Bunsen burner has changed little since Bunsen invented it, almost 150 years ago.

▼ FIGURE H7.1

A Bunsen burner has few moving parts and is easy to use. A Bunsen burner burns with an open flame, though, so you must always be careful when you use one.

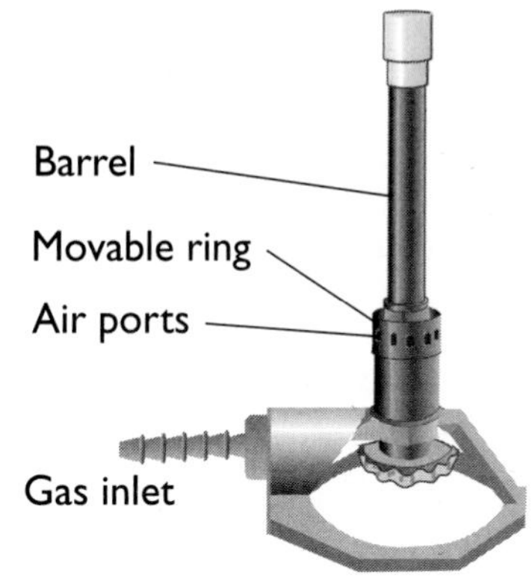

Part A—The Parts of a Bunsen Burner

The Bunsen burner has very few parts (see Figure H7.1). It has a fuel gas inlet, which is connected to the gas jet with rubber tubing. The burner has a movable ring near the base, which has openings called air ports. (The air ports look like small holes around the base of the Bunsen burner.) The air ports allow air to enter the barrel of the burner and mix with the fuel gas. Once ignited, the air and gas mix in the barrel to produce a flame at the top of the barrel.

You can change the size of the air port openings by rotating the ring. By changing the size of the air ports, you can control how much air enters the barrel of the burner. The amount of air entering the Bunsen burner is important because fuel gas cannot burn without air. If not enough air is mixing with the gas, then the gas will not burn completely, and the flame will not get very hot.

Part B—Safety Cautions When Using a Bunsen Burner

Always be careful when lighting and using a Bunsen burner. Wear eye protection at all times. Be sure you do not put your face near the top of the barrel at any time. Tie back long hair and remove scarves, ties, or jewelry that might hang down into the flame. Remember that the flame of a Bunsen burner burns very hot; do not play around during an investigation that requires the use of a Bunsen burner or any other heat source.

Strike the match *before* you turn on the gas jet. Place the match to the side of the barrel, just below the top. As soon as you hear the gas, light the burner. The gas should not be on longer than a few seconds before you light it. If you have trouble lighting the burner, turn off the gas and try again. *Do not keep the gas flowing while you wait to light a new match.* If you fail to light the burner after a few attempts, ask your teacher for help.

After you have finished with the burner, be sure you turn off the gas jet completely so that no gas escapes into the room.

Part C—How to Light and Adjust a Bunsen Burner

Follow these steps in lighting and adjusting a Bunsen burner.

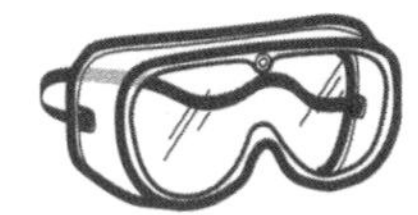

1. Put on your safety goggles.
2. Turn the ring near the base of the burner so that the air port openings are open just slightly so that a little air flows through them.
3. Strike a match. (Use a long wooden one.)
4. Turn on the gas jet.
5. Hold the match just to the side of the barrel of the burner.

   The burner should light and probably will burn with an orange flame. The orange flame is a sign that the gas in the burner is not burning completely.
6. Adjust the flow of air and the flow of gas until you see a blue flame.

   When the burner is burning properly, you will see a blue flame that has two distinct parts (see Figure H7.2). To get the blue flame, slowly open the air ports. This will add more air to the fuel. You might need to adjust the flow of gas from the gas jet as well. Keep adjusting the air port openings and the gas flow until you get a steady, blue flame.

   The gas should burn quietly. If you hear a roaring sound, then too much gas probably is coming into the barrel. You should reduce the flow of gas and possibly close the air port openings a little, too.
7. After you have finished with the Bunsen burner, turn off the gas jet completely and close the air ports.

   The flame should go out quickly.

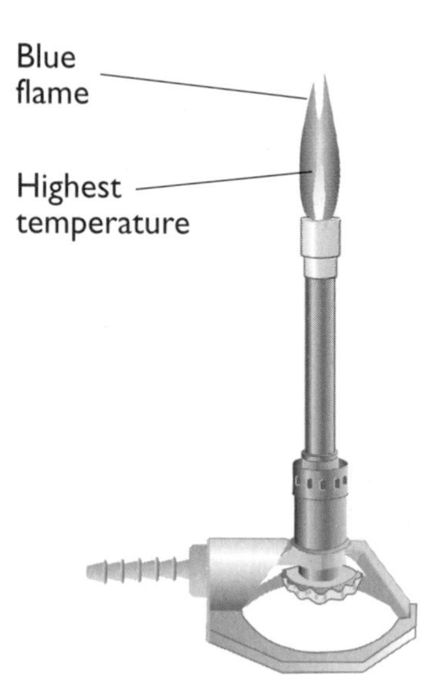

▲ **FIGURE H7.2**

When you have adjusted your Bunsen burner properly, you should see a flame that looks like this.

HOW TO Conduct a Research Project #8

So you are going to do a research project. It might seem like a pretty big deal, but it is not if you take it one step at a time. Actually conducting a research project *will* take more time than a simple homework assignment, but it also should be more interesting. There are two keys to conducting good research for a report or a presentation: (1) Choose a topic that interests you, and (2) get organized. If you go about your research in an organized manner from the beginning, then it will be a snap to put your presentation or report together. This How To has some tips that will help you get organized.

You might be wondering what research is. How is conducting research different from completing other assignments? According to the *American Heritage Dictionary,* to research a topic means to study the topic thoroughly. Therefore conducting research is different from just reading one article in a newspaper, a magazine, an encyclopedia, or a textbook. When you conduct a research project, you gather as much information as you can about the topic you are researching. Then you put the information together in an organized way that will make sense to someone who listens to your presentation or reads your report.

Tips for Conducting a Research Project

Part A—Choosing Your Topic

Tip #1: List several topics that interest you.

Usually you cannot just think up your own topics. Your teacher or your textbook probably will limit your choices to a general area of research. In this case, your assignment is to research a topic that is related in some way to plate tectonics.

To get started, list at least five possible topics that are related to the general subject of your research—plate tectonics. Then rank the topics and circle your first and second choices. (You always should have two choices, because you might not be able to find enough information about your first choice.)

Stop now and make your list of five or more possible choices. You may write your list on BLM HT8.1.

Part B—Getting Organized

Tip #2: Think about your topic before you read anything. You might ask yourself these questions about the topic you have chosen:

- What do I already know about the topic?
- What books or magazines have I seen that might have some information about the topic?
- What would I like to know about the topic?
- What about the topic would I like to share with my classmates?

If you organize your thoughts first, then it will be easier to organize the information you find.

Let's say you chose the topic of geysers (GUY zerz) for your research project. After thinking about the topic of geysers, you decide you want to answer the following questions:

- How are geysers formed?
- What do geysers look like?
- What makes geysers shoot up into the air?
- What are the names of some famous geysers around the world?

You might organize your research by writing each of those questions at the top of one sheet of paper. Then as you find information that answers one of those questions, you can write the information on that sheet of paper. That way you may organize your notes before you even start. (For your notes, you may use note cards instead of sheets of paper. If you do use note cards, you probably will need more than one card for each main idea or question.)

As you read, stay open to new ideas. You might think of new questions about your topic that you would like to answer. Start a new sheet of paper or a new set of note cards for each main idea that you find interesting.

Stop now and write some things you already know about the topic and some of the questions you would like to answer. You may write your ideas and questions on BLM HT8.1.

Part C—Finding Information

Tip #3: Look at more than one source for information. Several different resources are designed especially to help you locate information:

- The World Wide Web
- *Reader's Guide to Periodical Literature*
- on-line catalogs or databases
- the card catalog

But how can you find the right sources that will have information about your topic? First you need to know enough about your topic to identify a few **key words.** Key words are important words related to the topic you want to study. Sometimes you also can come up with key words by brainstorming a list either by yourself or with a partner. Ask yourself:

- What do I already know about my topic?
- What words do I associate with my topic?

For example, let's use the topic of geysers again. To get started, you might look up the word "geyser" in an encyclopedia or in a dictionary. There you might find words, such as "hot springs," "geothermal energy," and "hot spots." Then you remember reading about a geyser named "Old Faithful." The words inside the quotation marks are all possible key words because they tell you something about geysers.

You will need to have some key words in mind before you can use effectively the card catalog, an on-line data base, or the *Reader's Guide to Periodical Literature.* If you have not used those resources before, ask your media specialist, librarian, teacher, or a friend for help.

Stop now and list the resources you will use to get started. Then list a few key words that will help you find out more about your topic. You may add to your list of key words as you do your research. Write your lists in the appropriate spaces on BLM HT8.1.

After you have learned to use the *Reader's Guide to Periodical Literature,* the on-line data bases, or the card catalog, these resources will lead you to specific articles in newspapers or magazines or to books about your topic.

In addition to these sources of information, the following sources of information might be helpful:

- The World Wide Web
- audiovisual materials such as films, filmstrips, videotapes, videodiscs, CD-ROMs, slides, audiotapes, and television specials or documentaries
- people who are experts on the topic or have experience related to the topic
- encyclopedias
- science dictionaries
- pamphlets

Part D—Taking Notes

Tip #4: Take notes in your own words.
Sometimes you might think it is easier just to read something in an encyclopedia and copy whatever it says. That type of library research has two problems. First, copying what someone else has written and using it as your own work is called plagiarism (PLAY-jer-ism), and plagiarism is illegal. Second, your report or presentation will be much more interesting if you put the information together in your own words. You might add something humorous that you found out, or you might weave your information into an exciting adventure story about a geologist who discovered a new geyser. Copying from encyclopedias probably will make your report uninteresting to your classmates, too.

Sometimes, though, you might want to write down the exact words someone wrote or said. That is okay, as long as you use those words as a quote. Quotes can make your presentation or report more interesting, because a quote can add humor or authority to your report. When you use a quote in your presentation or report, you must use the exact words and tell or write down who said the words and where you found the quote. Using a quote is not plagiarism because you are giving credit to the person who said or wrote those words. You are not trying to say that those are your words. Be sure each quote you use is not more than about 50 words long. You should use quotes to "spice up" your report, not to be your report.

You might want to keep track of the direct quotes you find by writing them on BLM HT8.2.

Part E—Making a Reference List

Tip #5: Write complete information about all of the reference materials you use.

Before you put away a book, magazine, or pamphlet from which you took notes, write down the following information:

- the title of the book or magazine
- the title of any specific article you read from a book, magazine, or pamphlet
- the author or authors (if any)
- the publisher
- the city where the book or magazine was published
- the copyright date of a book
- the volume if it is an encyclopedia, and the date if it is a magazine or newspaper
- the page numbers you read

Your teacher probably has a certain way she or he would like you to list your references. Be sure you know how you should list your references before you put those references away. It is time consuming to go back and find all your sources again if you need more complete information.

As you use reference materials for your research project, write down the necessary information about each reference on BLM HT8.2. That way, you will have your reference list almost ready when you finish taking notes.

Part F—Organizing Your Notes

Tip #6: Separate your notes into different main ideas.

After you have gathered all the information you need, look through your notes. Decide what information you want to include in your presentation or report and what information might be unnecessary. You do not have to use all of the information that you gathered, just because you have it. It is always better to have more information than you need.

Then if you have not already done so with separate papers or note cards, divide your notes into different main ideas. Go back to Part B—Getting Organized, and review the main ideas you wrote on BLM HT8.2. Use those main ideas and others that you chose as you gathered information.

Finally organize your main ideas into a logical order. What do you want to talk or write about first, second, and third? Write down your main ideas in order on BLM HT8.3. Then decide what information would make the best introduction and what information would make the best ending. Write your ideas for an introduction and for an ending in the appropriate boxes on BLM HT8.3. If you know how, you might put your notes into an outline form.

Before you go to Part G, decide what information would be best to show on a poster or with a model or diagram. Separate that information from the rest of your notes and write down your ideas on BLM HT8.3.

Part G—Writing Your Report or Planning Your Presentation

Tip #7: Do not worry about every detail in your first draft. When you conduct a research project, you will write more than one draft of your report. Do not try to get all your ideas down exactly the way you want them on your first draft. The most important thing to decide is the order of your main ideas. (Review what you wrote on BLM HT8.3.) Then you can decide which details best support those main ideas. After you complete the first draft of your report or presentation, you can go back and add details, check the flow of your ideas, and be sure you have not left out anything important. You now are ready to write a revision of your paper or presentation.

Begin with a strong introduction to catch the interest of your classmates. Be sure to state the most important idea in your introduction.

Organize your information into complete sentences that flow in a logical order. Move smoothly from one main idea to the next, supporting all your information with examples and quotations from your research. Be sure to support your opinions with information, quotes, and examples from your research. Also think about what information would be best to present on a poster, in a diagram, or as a demonstration.

Decide how you will end your presentation or report. Your conclusion should tie all your information together and summarize your main ideas.

Use the information you have organized on BLMs HT8.2 and HT8.3 to help you through this process.

Part H—Congratulating Yourself on a Job Well Done

Conducting a research project might not be the easiest thing you have ever done, but it can be rewarding. Often you will find interesting information that you never knew before. You probably will remember it longer, too, because you really had to think about how all the information fit together. When you have finished your report, congratulate yourself on a job well done.

HOW TO Average Numbers #9

Averaging numbers can be a useful skill when you want to find out what *usually* happens or what is likely to happen in a particular situation. For example, let's say that your family plans to take a vacation in August and that you want to travel to a state where tornadoes are unlikely to occur. Before you could decide where to go, you would need to know how many tornadoes usually occur in different states in August. Look at the data in Figure H9.1.

Part A—Finding an Average

When you look at these data, you will see that the number of tornadoes that occurred each year in each state was not always the same. In some years, quite a few tornadoes occurred in August, and in other years few or no tornadoes occurred. How could you predict how many tornadoes might occur this year in August in each state? The best way to make your prediction would be to find the **average** of the numbers of tornadoes that occurred each year in August in each of the states.

You need to follow only two steps to find an average.

1. Find the **sum** (the total) by adding all the numbers together.

   The total number, or sum, of tornadoes in August in Nebraska from 1985 through 1989: 6 + 3 + 4 + 3 + 4 = 20.

2. Divide the sum by the number of data points you have.

   In this case, you would divide the sum by 5 because you have data for 5 years, each year from 1985 through 1989.

   In Nebraska the total number of tornadoes in August from 1985 through 1989 was 20. You have 5 years' worth of data, or 5 data points, so divide 20 by 5:

   20 tornadoes in August ÷ 5 years = 4 tornadoes per year in August

Year	Number of Tornadoes in August in Nebraska
1985	6
1986	3
1987	4
1988	3
1989	4
Year	**Number of Tornadoes in August in Florida**
1985	9
1986	9
1987	6
1988	2
1989	4
Year	**Number of Tornadoes in August in Wisconsin**
1985	5
1986	0
1987	5
1988	6
1989	0

▲ **FIGURE H9.1**

Which state is likely to have the highest number of tornadoes in August?

Now you know that the average number of tornadoes that occurred in Nebraska in August from 1985 through 1989 was four. This means that you might expect four tornadoes to occur in Nebraska each year in August. As you can see from the actual data, the number of tornadoes was above the average some years and below the average other years. The average simply tells you the number of tornadoes that *usually* occur in August in Nebraska.

Part B—More Practice Finding Averages

Look at the data for the other two states. Answer these questions before you find the average number of tornadoes for those states.

Questions:

1. How will the average number of tornadoes in August in Florida compare with the average number of tornadoes in August in Nebraska? (Will the average in Florida be higher or lower?) Explain your answer.
2. How will the average number of tornadoes in August in Wisconsin compare with the average number of tornadoes in August in either Nebraska or Florida? (Will the average in Wisconsin be higher or lower?) Explain your answer.

When you look at the data for Wisconsin, you will notice that *no* tornadoes were reported in August in 1986 or in 1989. How will you find the average when some of the data points are zero? You still follow the same steps.

1. Find the **sum** by adding all the numbers together.

   $5 + 0 + 5 + 6 + 0 = 16$

2. Divide the sum by the number of data points you have.

   Even though some of the numbers are zero, you still have one data point for each year for 5 years. Some of those data points just happen to be zero. You still divide the sum by 5 because you added 5 numbers (5 data points) together to get the sum.

   16 tornadoes ÷ 5 years = 3.2 tornadoes per year

   (You also can write 3.2 tornadoes per year as 3 tornadoes per year with a remainder of $\frac{2}{10}$ or $\frac{1}{5}$.)

As this example shows, sometimes the numbers do not divide evenly, and you end up with a whole-number average with some amount left over. In those cases, you will use a skill you already have: the skill of rounding off numbers. (See How To #1 if you do not remember how to round off numbers.) It is not possible for there to be $\frac{2}{10}$ths of a tornado; there either is a tornado or there is not one. So in the state of Wisconsin, you would say that the average number of tornadoes in August is three.

Before going on to Part C, follow the steps and find the average number of tornadoes that occurred in August in Florida.

Part C—Using Averages to Make Predictions

Does the average tell you *exactly* how many tornadoes will occur in August in each of these states this year? No, averages do not give you exact numbers. They simply tell you what is likely to happen based on the data you have.

Averages can be very useful numbers, especially if you want to make predictions based on what usually happens. For example, if you are a baseball pitcher, you might like to know which batters are more likely to hit the ball when they are up to bat. How would you find out? You would use each batter's batting average, which is based on the total number of hits the batter got, divided by the number of times that batter was at bat. Those players who have a high batting average are more likely to get a hit when they come up to bat than those players who have low batting averages.

Weather forecasters also use averages when they discuss the weather. Sometimes temperatures in the summer might be unusually high, and the weather forecaster might say, "The temperatures continue to be above average for this time of year." This statement means that the temperatures are above those that usually occur at that time of year.

Scientists called climatologists also make use of average temperatures. They are studying average temperatures over time to decide whether the earth is experiencing something called "global warming." Those scientists are trying to find out whether temperatures around the world are increasing over time or whether they are staying basically the same. To make their predictions, scientists use recorded average temperatures from many places around the world over many years.

Listen carefully to news reports and weather forecasts on television. How many times do you hear the newscasters or weather forecasters talk about averages? The next time you hear someone use the term "average," you will know exactly what he or she means.

HOW TO Make Sense of Percentages #10

What does 20% mean? Are Marie's chances of winning good or poor? The symbol % stands for **"percent."** The word "percent" means "out of 100." So 20% reads "20 percent," or "20 out of 100."

To make percentages easier to understand, let's use a diagram. Suppose 100 total chances were available in Marie's sweepstakes. We will use a grid of 100 squares to represent the 100 chances. Thus on this grid each square represents one chance (see Figure H10.1).

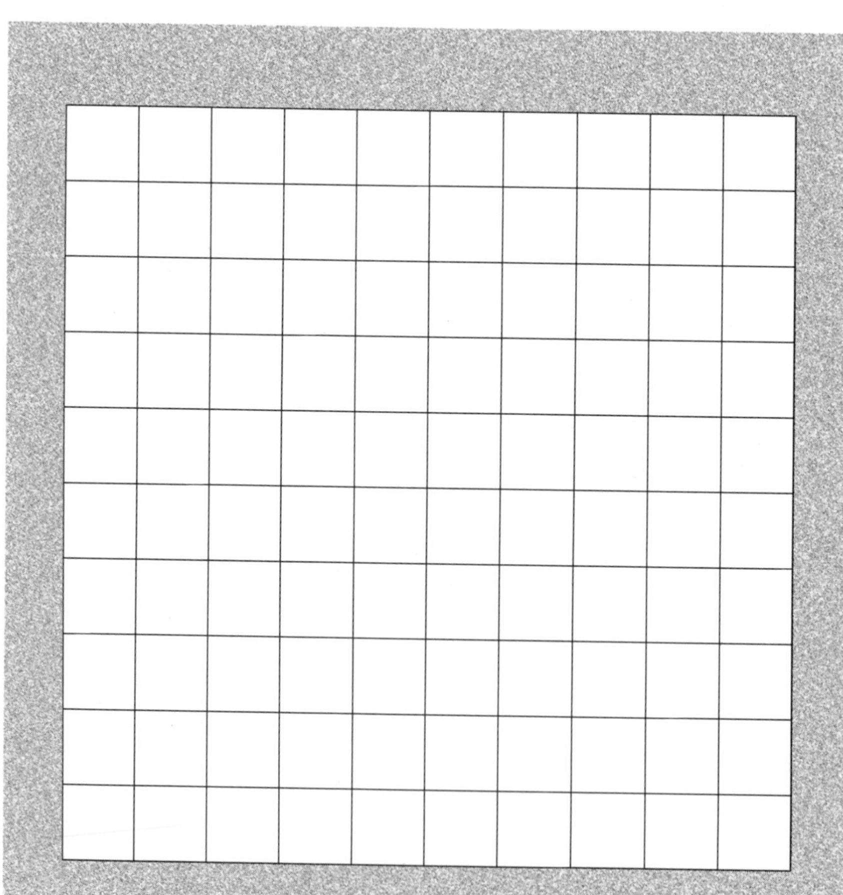

▶ **FIGURE H10.1**
This grid shows all the possible chances in Marie's sweepstakes. Each square represents one chance.

▶ FIGURE H10.2

This grid shows the 20 chances of winning as 20 red squares.

The certificate suggests that Marie has a 20 percent chance of winning. If we say that each red square represents one chance of Marie winning, how many squares of the grid would be red? (See Figure H10.2.)

That's right. If 20 percent means 20 out of 100, then 20 of the 100 squares would be colored red.

Look at the grid in Figure H10.2 again. What do the 80 white squares stand for? If the 20 red squares stand for the number of chances Marie has of *winning*, then the 80 white squares stand for the number of chances Marie has of *not winning* (100 total chances – 20 chances of winning = 80 chances of *not* winning.) So are Marie's chances of winning good or poor? Use the data shown on the grid to answer the question. Be prepared to support your answer.

Often people use percentages to represent **probability.** (Remember that probability can tell you how *likely* something is to happen, but it cannot tell you that

▶ FIGURE H10.3

Twenty percent, or 20 out of 100, of these pieces are red.

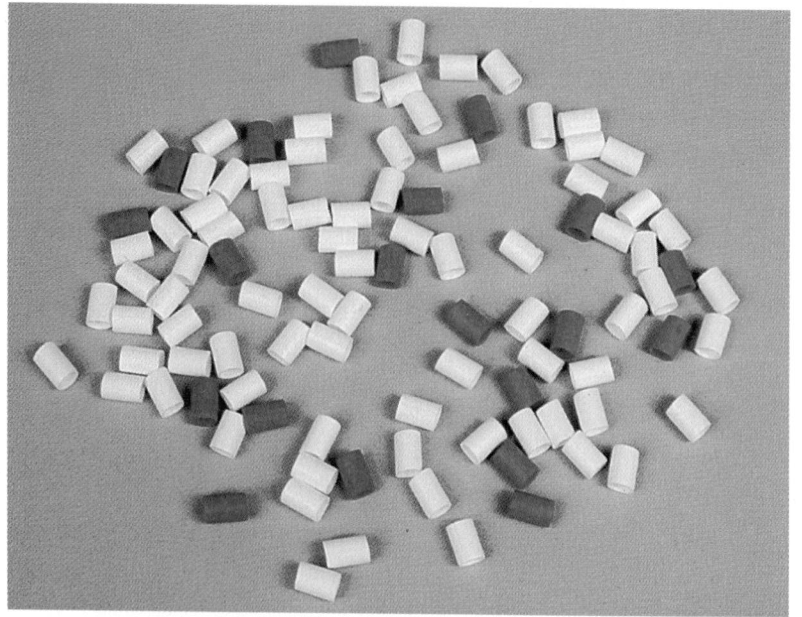

something *will* happen for sure.) Let's go back to Marie's sweepstakes. This time, we will use 100 plastic pieces to represent the total chances of winning. We will show Marie's 20 percent chance of winning by including 20 red pieces in the 100 total pieces. The other 80 pieces will be white. The white pieces show the chances Marie has of *not* winning.

Imagine that you put these 100 plastic pieces into a bag and that, without looking into the bag, you drew out one plastic piece. Do you think the piece is likely to be white or red? Because the majority of the pieces are white, it is more likely that you would draw out a white piece. But you *could* draw out a red piece, couldn't you? It is just not as likely that you would draw a red piece because there are so few of them. So once again this shows that Marie's chances of winning the sweepstakes are not very good.

Suppose that Marie's sweepstakes certificate had said that she had a 60 percent chance of winning. Look at the change in the plastic pieces when 60 percent of them are red. If the red pieces represent the chances of winning, decide whether you think Figure H10.4 accurately shows a 60 percent chance of winning.

Percentages usually are not difficult to understand when you have exactly 100 of something. But suppose you have 50 plastic pieces and that 20 percent of them are red. How many of the 50 pieces would be red? Look back at the photograph of the 100 pieces when 20 percent

▶ **FIGURE H10.4**

Would Marie be more likely to win if she had a 60 percent chance of winning?

were red. Then imagine that someone divided the 100 pieces into two *equal* piles. To be exactly equal, each pile would have exactly the same number of white pieces and the same number of red pieces (see Figure H10.5).

Now you have 50 plastic pieces in each pile. Count the number of red pieces in each pile. You should count 10 red pieces in each pile. This means that 10 red pieces out of 50 total pieces is the same as 20 red pieces out of 100 total pieces. The portion of pieces that are red, compared to the total number of pieces is the same. You can look at this in terms of fractions, too:

$$\frac{\textbf{20 red pieces}}{\textbf{100 total pieces}} = \frac{\textbf{10 red pieces}}{\textbf{50 total pieces}}$$

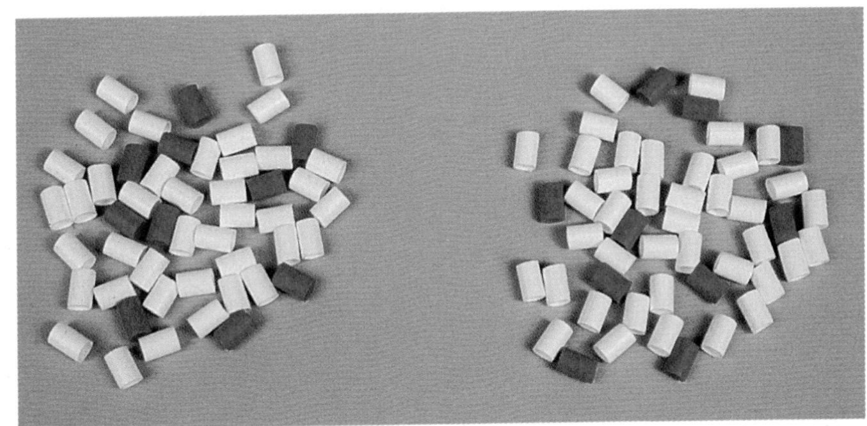

▶ **FIGURE H10.5**

This photograph shows the 100 plastic pieces divided into two equal piles.

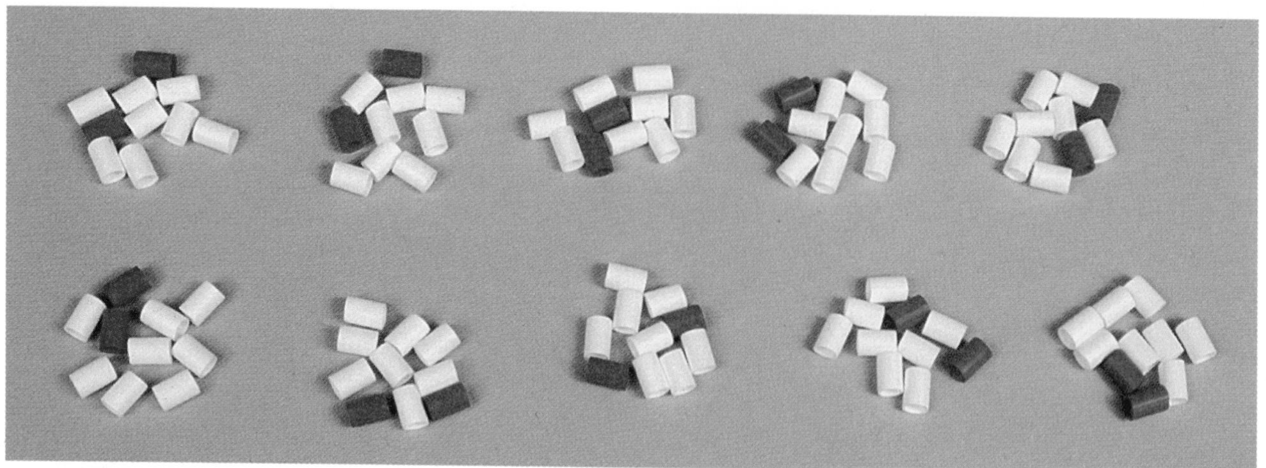

▲ **FIGURE H10.6**

How many red pieces are in each pile if 20 percent of the pieces are red?

Suppose you have a total of only 10 plastic pieces and that 20 percent of those are red. How many of the plastic pieces in each pile of 10 would be red? To find out, divide the original pile of 100 pieces into 10 equal piles. (To make the piles equal, each pile of 10 must have the same number of white pieces and the same number of red pieces.) If you make the piles equal, you should count 8 white pieces and 2 red pieces in each pile of 10.

Look back at the photographs. Do you see that 2 red pieces out of 10 is the same distribution as 10 red pieces out of 50 and 20 red pieces out of 100? You can look at the relationship between the numbers in terms of fractions:

$$\frac{\textbf{20 red pieces}}{\textbf{100 total pieces}} = \frac{\textbf{10 red pieces}}{\textbf{50 total pieces}} = \frac{\textbf{2 red pieces}}{\textbf{10 total pieces}}$$

Now try to solve these problems:

1. You have 10 plastic pieces and 40 percent of them are red. How many pieces are red and how many are white?
2. You have 10 plastic pieces and 60 percent of them are red. How many pieces are red and how many are white?

Glossary

air mass: An air mass is a large region of air characterized by a particular temperature and humidity.

area: The area of a surface is the product of the length times the width. The area has units squared (cm^2, for example).

average: To calculate an average, find the sum by adding all the numbers together. Then divide by the number of data points or items that you have. For example, a store owner might sell 10 bags of carrots in 2 days. The bags of carrots are the data, and the owner collected data for 2 days. The owner sold an average of 10 divided by 2, or 5 bags of carrots per day.

axis: An axis is the horizontal or vertical line in a graph on which we write numbers or labels. Most graphs have both a horizontal and a vertical axis. The place where these two lines meet is where the graph begins. (The plural of axis is axes.)

bar graph: A bar graph uses bars to illustrate the results of a survey or an experiment.

benefits: Benefits are the positive effects of a decision.

buoyant force: Buoyant force is the upward force on an object when it displaces a fluid, like water. An object will float if its weight is balanced by the buoyant force, and it will sink if its weight is greater than the buoyant force.

cause and effect: Cause and effect is a pattern in which one or more factors make something happen.

centimeter (cm): A centimeter is a small unit of length equal to one-hundredth of a meter. A centimeter is slightly less than one-half of an inch.

combustion: Combustion is when something ignites or bursts into flame.

compass: A compass is an instrument that shows which direction a person is facing: north, south, east, or west.

compost: Compost is usually plant material (such as leftover food and shredded paper) that breaks down into nutrient-rich material. This nutrient-rich material also occurs in soil (when leaves and grasses rot). Compost can be used to enrich soil.

condensation: Condensation occurs when molecules of water in a vapor state are cooled. If they lose enough energy, they will form a liquid state.

continental drift: Continental drift is Alfred Wegener's geologic theory. He proposed that because the shapes of the continents fit together like a puzzle, it was likely that the continents had been together at one time and later moved to their present locations.

controlled experiment: An experiment in which only one factor is changed and all the other factors remain the same is called a controlled experiment. If experimenters want to see whether one factor is affecting a pattern, they must do a controlled experiment (a fair test).

convection cell: A convection cell is a pattern in which a cold fluid (for example air or water) in one region sinks and warm fluid in another region rises. This creates a circular pattern of motion.

core: The core is the very innermost part of the earth. The core is made up of a liquid outer core and a solid inner core.

Coriolis (core ee OH lis) effect: The Coriolis effect is when something moving in a straight line appears to curve because it is moving above a spinning surface. The apparent motion of an object will depend on whether it is observed from a stationary or a rotating viewpoint. The stationary observer will see the object moving in a straight line when there are no outside forces. An observer on a rotating surface will see the same object moving on a curved path as if it did have an applied force.

correlation: A correlation is a pattern in which two or more things are related or connected to each other. For example, in humans the length of a person's forearm is about the same as the length of his or her foot. This is a correlation.

costs: Costs are the harmful or negative effects of a decision.

crust: The crust is the outer shell of the earth, which mostly consists of hard rock.

cycle: A cycle is a repeating pattern, such as the repeating pattern of daylight and darkness.

data: Data can be things such as measurements, numbers, observations, dates, or times. Data is the plural of the word datum. Because most often we are working with more than one piece of information, we say "data."

data point: A data point is a point on a graph that indicates the observed results.

data table: A data table is a chart that helps a person keep track of observations.

density: The density of an object is its mass divided by its volume. The units could be gm/cm^3, for example.

drought: Drought is a time when no rain or snow falls in an area. A drought may last for months or years.

energy: Energy is the ability to change the motion of an object or its physical state (for example, from a liquid to a gas).

energy of motion: Energy of motion is the energy that an object has because of its motion. It is also called kinetic energy.

energy of position: Energy of position is the energy that something has because of its position. This is also called potential energy.

evaporation: Evaporation occurs when water particles move from a liquid into the air.

evidence: Evidence is information that you obtain using your senses: you can see, hear, smell, taste, or feel evidence.

explanation: An explanation is more than just a yes-or-no answer to a question. When someone proposes an explanation, he or she can justify why it is probably accurate.

factors: Factors are things that influence patterns, so scientists consider factors when they set up experiments.

faults: Faults form when forces within the earth push rock to the point of breaking. These forces may push a broken block of rock up, down, or sideways. Movement along a fault can push one type of rock next to another type of rock.

flood plains: Flood plains are flat areas next to rivers. This area is the first place to be flooded if a river overflows its banks.

folding: Folding occurs when rock layers bend but do not break.

force: A push or a pull that causes something to move or change its speed or direction is called a force.

fossils (FAH suhls): Fossils are the hardened remains or traces of animals or plants that lived long ago.

gram: A gram is a unit of mass.

graph paper: Graph paper is special paper with evenly spaced lines. The lines run from side to side and from top to bottom, forming a grid.

groundwater: Water that moves through the soil and underground is called groundwater.

horizontal axis: The horizontal axis is the line in a graph that runs from left to right.

hot spots: Some places on the earth have a lot of volcanic activity and yet are not near a plate boundary. These are called hot spots. Two examples of places affected by hot spots are the Hawaiian Islands and Yellowstone National Park.

hurricane: A hurricane is a large storm that may form over the warm oceans. The winds are greater than 74 miles per hour. Considerable damage from wind and floods may occur when a hurricane moves onto land.

incinerators: Garbage is burned in furnaces called incinerators.

landfill: A landfill is most often a large pit or hole where people put garbage. The landfill can become so large that it is a mound. In some landfills, called sanitary landfills, layers of garbage are covered with dirt each day to keep the garbage from blowing away.

line graph: When a line connects the data points on a graph, a line graph is formed.

magma: Magma is hot matter (molten rock) beneath the earth's surface. When it reaches the earth's surface, it is called lava.

mantle: The layer beneath the earth's crust that is 10 percent molten and 90 percent solid.

mass: Mass is the measure of the inertia of an object to a change in its motion.

millimeter (mm): A millimeter is a very small unit of length equal to one-thousandth of a meter. A millimeter is smaller than one-eighth of an inch. Millimeter marks are between centimeter marks on a metric ruler.

mountains: Mountains are high places on the earth's crust. They form by volcanic eruption, by folding when plates collide, or by movement along some types of faults.

number scale: A sequence of numbers plotted along a line is called a number scale. The number scale may be vertical or horizontal. If the number scale is on a graph, the numbers usually are read from left to right on the horizontal axis and from bottom to top on the vertical axis.

pattern: A pattern is a collection of things or events that repeat themselves.

pendulum (PEN dyew lum): A pendulum is a system composed of a mass and a supporting string that is free to swing under the action of gravity.

phase: The word *phase* comes from the Greek word phaino, which means "to appear or to bring to light." In this book we talk about the phases of the moon as a pattern that we can see from the earth. A phase is a change that is "brought to light," or acknowledged.

plagiarism (PLAY jer ism): Plagiarism consists of copying what someone else has written and using it as your own work.

plates: The continents are part of plates of rock that make up the entire surface of the earth.

predictions: A prediction is a statement about the future that is based on information. A prediction differs from a guess because a guess is not based on information.

pressure: Pressure is the force that is exerted per unit area.

probability: Statements of probability indicate how likely an event is to occur, but they do not indicate whether the event actually will happen.

quality: The quality of something refers to its degree of excellence or character.

quantity: A quantity is the measured amount of something.

quantity and quality: Quantity and quality are two factors to consider when gathering information. To make accurate predictions based on information, you need enough of the best kind of information.

quote: A quote contains the exact words someone wrote or said, with an acknowledgment of the source.

radar: Radar is a system that uses reflected electromagnetic radiation to determine the location and velocity of something.

recycling: Recycling means that materials repeat a cycle or that people use them more than once.

ridges: Ridges are the places where two plates are moving apart permitting material to move up from below. On earth, most ridges are towering mountain chains on the ocean floor that are as high as 2,400 meters (7,880 feet) and that encircle the earth like seams on a baseball.

round off: To change a mixed number (e.g., 2.7 or 2.5) to the nearest whole number (for example, 3) is called rounding off. The basic rules for rounding off numbers are: any fraction less than 0.5 rounds down, and any fraction from 0.5 and higher rounds up.

San Andreas fault: One example of a transform fault is the San Andreas fault in southern California. When the Pacific and the North American Plates move along this fault, earthquakes occur.

scientific explanation: A scientific explanation is more than just a yes-or-no answer to a question. A scientific explanation explains the cause of a pattern and is based on information. With a scientific explanation, a scientist can explain why he or she thinks that a particular idea is probably accurate.

sum: The total of a group of numbers added together is called a sum.

technology: Technology is a process of designing and building things that solve peoples' problems; it is a way of adapting. Technology can be very simple, like a can or a toothpick, or more complex, like a car or a computer.

test: A test is a series of questions or problems designed to prove whether an explanation is correct.

theory of plate tectonics: This theory proposes that the earth's surface is covered by a set of interlocking plates and that these plates move slowly across the earth's surface.

tornado: A tornado is a violent, highly localized storm that is the result of very unstable atmospheric conditions. Winds hundreds of miles per hour rotate in a characteristic funnel cloud. Tornadoes usually occur with severe thunderstorms.

toxic or hazardous waste: Trash that is potentially harmful to people is called toxic or hazardous waste.

transform faults: Transform faults occur when two plates slide past each other. When this movement occurs, it can produce earthquakes.

trenches: Trenches are the deepest parts of the ocean. At a trench, one edge of a plate sinks beneath another plate.

trend: A trend is a type of pattern in which change occurs in a particular direction across time. One example would be the continual increase in the use of a particular item, such as computers.

vertical axis: The line in a graph that runs up and down is called the vertical axis.

volume: The product of length times width times height for an object. The volume is stated in units cubed (cm^3, for example).

water cycle: The water cycle is the pattern of water movement on the earth, in which water particles move from liquid to vapor and back to liquid again. The water cycle occurs as water moves from lakes or oceans into the clouds, falls as rain or snow, moves through the ground and into creeks and rivers, and rises back into the clouds.

Artists, Photographers, and Photography Suppliers for the Second Edition

Advanced Graphics and Publishing (electronic production and prepress)
Susan Bartel
The Bettmann Archive
Carlye Calvin
Center for Marine Conservation
Corel Corporation
Cukjati Designs
Davis Creative
Carmen Franco-Stephenson
Jan Chatlain Girard
Bruce Hamilton
Janet Huntington-Hammond
Sariya Jarasviroj
Bert Kempers
NASA
NCAR
NOAA
Jacqueline Ott-Rogers
Bill Ogden
PC&F, Inc.
PhotoDisc Corporation
Leah Rachlis—Pizzazz Designs
Brent Sauerhagen
Karelle Scharff
Mark Schoenenberger
Nancy C. Smalls
Smithsonian Institution
Mary Snyder—MS Graphics
Tom Stack and Associates
- M. Bradley
- W. Perry Conway
- A. Duncan
- Jon Feingersh
- Inga Spence
- M. Thomas
- Greg Vaugn

Tony Stone Images
- Elan Sun Star
- Schafer & Hill
- H. Sokol
- R. Wells

Marie Tharp
Linn and Bob Trochim—Animart
USGS
Visuals Unlimited
- Bill Beatty
- D. Cavagnaro
- John D. Cunningham
- Tom Edwards
- Bruce Gaylord
- John Gerlach
- R. Kessel
- Charles Newman
- Mark Newman
- William Palmer
- David L. Pears
- Nada Pecnik
- G. Shih
- Ted Whittenkraus

Dr. Carl Vondra
Yellowstone National Park Service

Advisory Board Members for Initial Development

Elliot Asp, *Littleton Public Schools, Littleton, Colorado*
Randall Backe, *Kansas State University, Manhattan, Kansas*
Pat Barry, *Wilbur Wright Middle School, Milwaukee, Wisconsin*
Bonnie Brunkhorst, *California State University, San Bernardino, California*
Herbert Brunkhorst, *California State University, San Bernardino, California*
H. Mack Clark, *Air Academy District #20, Colorado Springs, Colorado*
Mary Doyen, *Rocky Mountain Center for Health Promotion and Education, Northglenn, Colorado*
Linda Ganatta, *Timberview Middle School, Colorado Springs, Colorado*
April Gardner, *University of Northern Colorado, Greeley, Colorado*
Cynthia Geer, *University of Cincinnati, Cincinnati, Ohio*
Merton Glass, *University of South Florida, Tampa, Florida*
Johnnie P. Hamilton, *Franklin Intermediate School, Chantilly, Virginia*
Debbie Hill, *Eagleview Middle School, Colorado Springs, Colorado*
David Housel, *Oakland Schools, Waterford, Michigan*
Roger Hubley, *Pleasant Run Middle School, Cincinnati, Ohio*
Paul DeHart Hurd, Professor Emeritus, *Stanford University, Palo Alto, California*
Candace Julyan, *Technical Education Research Centers, Cambridge, Massachusetts*
David Kennedy, *State Department of Education, Olympia, Washington*
Joyce Kerce, *W. D. Sugg Middle School, Bradenton, Florida*
Keith Kester, *Colorado College, Colorado Springs, Colorado*
Julie Kropf, *Hollenbeck Middle School, Los Angeles, California*
Thomas Liao, *SUNY, Stony Brook, New York*
Thomas Lord, *Indiana University of Pennsylvania, Indiana, Pennsylvania*
Susan Loucks-Horsley, *The NETWORK, Andover, Massachusetts*
Glenn Markle, *University of Cincinatti, Cincinatti, Ohio*
James McClurg, *University of Wyoming, Laramie, Wyoming*
Francesca Mollura, *Academy of Liberal Arts and Sciences, Kansas City, Missouri*
Cathy Oates, *Challenger Middle School, Colorado Springs, Colorado*
Michael Padilla, *University of Georgia, Athens, Georgia*
Rita Patel-Eng, *SUNY, Stony Brook, New York*
E. Joseph Piel, Professor Emeritus, *SUNY, Stony Brook, New York*
Tracy Posnanski, *University of Wisconsin-Milwaukee, Milwaukee, Wisconsin*
Douglas Reid, *Southridge Middle School, Fontana, California*
Rochelle Rubin, *Instructional Materials Center, Waterford, Michigan*
Charlotte Schartz, *Kingman Elementary School, Kingman, Kansas*
M. Gail Shroyer, *Kansas State University, Manhattan, Kansas*
Elayne Shulman, *Classroom Consortia Media, Metuchen, New York*

Barbara Spector, *University of South Florida, Tampa, Florida*
John Staver, *Kansas State University, Manhattan, Kansas*
John Swaim, *University of Northern Colorado, Greeley, Colorado*
Robert Tinker, *Technical Education Research Centers, Cambridge, Massachusetts*
David Trowbridge, *University of Washington, Seattle, Washington*

Project Advisors and Consultants

William D. Gillan, *IBM, Boca Raton, Florida* (Corporate Advisor for Design Study)
Martin Guttmann, *IBM, Boca Raton, Florida* (Corporate Advisor for Design Study)
Ann Haley-Oliphant, *Mainville, Ohio* (Contributing Author)
Norris Harms, *Arvada, Colorado* (Evaluation)
A. W. Harton, *IBM, Atlanta, Georgia* (Corporate Advisor for Design Study)
James McClurg, *University of Wyoming, Laramie, Wyoming* (Curriculum Development)
Robert Miller, *Science Kit & Boreal Laboratories, Tonawanda, New York* (Safety Consultant)
Ann Primm, *Knoxville, Tennessee* (Contributing Author)
James R. Robinson, *Boulder, Colorado* (History)
M. Gail Shroyer, *Kansas State University, Manhattan, Kansas* (Implementation)
Dave Somers, *Colorado Springs, Colorado* (Editor)
Terry G. Switzer, *Fort Collins, Colorado* (Contributing Author)
Luise Woelflein, *Washington, DC* (Contributing Author)

Reviewers for the Second Edition

Clyde R. Burnett, *Fritz Peak Observatory, Rollinsville, Colorado*
Jerald Harder, *NOAA Aeronomy Laboratory, Boulder, Colorado*
Mark Johnson, *Gustavus Adolphus College, Saint Peter, Minnesota*
Sam Milazzo, *University of Colorado, Colorado Springs, Colorado*
Lynda B. Micikas, *BSCS, Colorado Springs, Colorado*

Contributing Writers for the Second Edition

Clyde R. Burnett, *Fritz Peak Observatory, Rollinsville, Colorado*
Sariya Jarasviroj

Educational Technology

Minds On Science, (1991). Agency for Instructional Technology, Bloomington, Indiana

Program Reviewers, First Edition

Michael R. Abraham, *University of Oklahoma, Norman, Oklahoma* (Science Content, Instructional Model)
Thomas Anderson, *University of Illinois, Champaign-Urbana, Illinois* (Reading)
Albert A. Bartlett, Professor Emeritus, *University of Colorado, Boulder, Colorado* (Science Content)
Clyde R. Burnett, *Fritz Peak Observatory, Rollinsville, Colorado* (Science Content)
Elizabeth Beaver Burnett, *Fritz Peak Observatory, Rollinsville, Colorado* (Science Content)
Kallene Casias, *Turman Elementary School, Colorado Springs, Colorado* (Cooperative Learning)
Audrey Champagne, *SUNY, Albany, New York* (Instructional Model)
Aileen Dickey, *Wildflower Elementary School, Colorado Springs, Colorado* (Cooperative Learning)
Peter Drotman, *Centers for Disease Control, Chamblee, Georgia* (Science Content)
Richard A. Duschl, *University of Pittsburgh, Pittsburgh, Pennsylvania* (Nature of Science, Science Content)
Diane Ebert-May, *Northern Arizona University, Flagstaff, Arizona* (Science Content)
Timothy Falls, *Meadows Elementary School, Novi, Michigan* (Safety)
Robert J. Francis, *GM Hughes Electronics, Los Angeles, California* (Science Content)
Terry Gerbstadt, *KRDO, Channel 13, Colorado Springs, Colorado* (Science Content)
Jerald Harder, *Aeronomy Laboratory, National Oceanic and Atmospheric Administration, Boulder, Colorado* (Science Content)
Henry Heikkinen, *University of Northern Colorado, Greeley, Colorado* (Science Content)
Werner Heim, *Colorado College, Colorado Springs, Colorado* (Science Content)
Jane Heinze-Fry, *Cornell University, Ithaca, New York* (Science Content)
Sheryl Hobbs, *Carmel Middle School, Colorado Springs, Colorado* (Cooperative Learning)
Martin Hudson, *Hughes Aircraft, Denver, Colorado* (Science Content)
Jack Lochhead, *Ventures in Education, New York, New York* (Instructional Model)
James McClurg, *University of Wyoming, Laramie, Wyoming* (Science Content)
Joseph D. McInerney, *BSCS, Colorado Springs, Colorado* (Science Content)
Verjanis Peoples, *Grambling University, Grambling, Louisiana* (Equity)
E. Joseph Piel, Professor Emeritus, *SUNY, Stony Brook, New York* (Science Content)
Belinda Rossiter, *Baylor College of Medicine, Houston, Texas* (Science Content)

Kathleen Roth, *Michigan State University, East Lansing, Michigan* (Instructional Model)

Frank Tallentire, *Aerospace Engineer, Retired, Littleton, Colorado* (Science Content)

Lynn Williams, *University of Oklahoma, Norman, Oklahoma* (Nature of Science)

Other BSCS Staff Contributing to the Project

Cindy Anderson
Debra Hannigan
Michael R. Hannigan
Rose Johnson
Sandy Keller
Joseph D. McInerney
Jean P. Milani
Dee Miller
Dee Nolan
Carolyn O'Steen
Judy Rasmussen
Bruce Thompson
Pam Thompson
Katherine A. Winternitz
M. Jean Young

Field-Test Sites for First Edition Primary Site Centers and Affiliated Schools

California

Almeria Middle School, Fontana, California, 1990–91

Southridge Middle School, Fontana, California, 1990–92

Coordinated by Herbert Brunkhorst (Site Coordinator) and Carol Cyr (Graduate Assistant 1990–91) and Cynthia Peterson (Graduate Assistant, 1991–92) based at California State University, San Bernardino, California.

Colorado

Carmel Middle School, Colorado Springs, Colorado, 1990–92

Challenger Middle School, Colorado Springs, Colorado, 1990–92

Colegio Los Nogales, Bogota, Colombia, South America, 1991–92

The Colorado Springs School, Colorado Springs, Colorado, 1990–92

Desert School, Rock Springs, Wyoming, 1991–92

Eagleview Middle School, Colorado Springs, Colorado, 1990–91

East Junior High School, Rock Springs, Wyoming, 1991–92

Gorman Middle School, Colorado Springs, Colorado, 1990–92

Panorama Middle School, Colorado Springs, Colorado, 1990–92

Smiley Middle School, Denver, Colorado, 1991–92

Timberview Middle School, Colorado Springs, Colorado, 1990–91

White Mountain Junior High School, Rock Springs, Wyoming, 1991–92

Coordinated by BSCS staff based in Colorado Springs, Colorado.

Florida

Clearwater Comprehensive School, Clearwater, Florida, 1990–91

Harllee Middle School, Bradenton, Florida, 1991–92

Lincoln Middle School, Palmetto, Florida, 1991–92

16th Street Middle School, St. Petersburg, Florida, 1990–92

Southside Fundamental School, St. Petersburg, Florida, 1990–92

W. D. Sugg Middle School, Bradenton, Florida, 1990–92

Coordinated by Barbara Spector (Site Coordinator) and Merton Glass (Graduate Assistant) based at University of South Florida, Tampa, Florida.

Kansas/Nebraska

Chapman Middle School, Chapman, Kansas, 1990–92

Dawes Junior High School, Lincoln, Nebraska, 1991–92

East Junior High School, Lincoln, Nebraska, 1991–92

Fort Riley Middle School, Fort Riley, Kansas, 1990–92

Kingman Middle School, Kingman, Kansas, 1990–92

Murdock Elementary School, Kingman, Kansas, 1990–92

Norwich High School, Kingman, Kansas, 1990–92

Norwich Junior High School, Kingman, Kansas 1990–92

Pound Junior High School, Lincoln, Nebraska, 1991–92

Coordinated by John Staver (Site Coordinator) and Randall Backe (Graduate Assistant, 1989–91) and Ronald Krestan (Graduate Assistant, 1991–92) based at Kansas State University, Manhattan, Kansas.

Maine

Tremont School, Mount Desert, Maine, 1990–91

New York

Roy W. Brown Middle School, Bergenfield, New Jersey, 1991–92

Longwood Junior and Senior High School, Middle Island, New York, 1990–91

Longwood Middle School, Middle Island, New York, 1990–91

Mount Sinai Middle School, Mount Sinai, New York, 1991–92

Shoreham-Wading River Middle School, Shoreham, New York, 1990–91

Southampton Intermediate School, Southampton, New York, 1991–92

Coordinated by Thomas Liao (Site Coordinator) and Rita Patel-Eng (Graduate Assistant, 1989–91) and Cynthia Anderson (Graduate Assistant, 1991–92) based at State University of New York, Stony Brook, New York.

Ohio

Dater Junior High, Cincinnati, Ohio, 1990–91

McCord Middle School, Worthington, Ohio, 1991–92

Perry Middle School, Worthington, Ohio, 1991–92
Pleasant Run Middle School, Cincinnati, Ohio, 1990–92
Coordinated by Glenn Markle (Site Coordinator) and Cynthia Geer (Graduate Assistant) based at University of Cincinnati, Cincinnati, Ohio.

Secondary Site Centers and Affiliated Schools

Arizona

Lee Kornegay Junior High School, Miami, Arizona, 1991–92
Tso Ho Tso Middle School, Fort Defiance, Arizona, 1991–92
Williams Middle School, Williams, Arizona, 1991–92
Coordinated by Diane Ebert-May (Site Coordinator) and Alison Graber (Graduate Assistant) based at Northern Arizona University, Flagstaff, Arizona.

California

Hollenbeck Middle School, Los Angeles, California, 1990–91
Coordinated by Andrea Gombar based at Los Angeles Unified School District, Los Angeles, California.

Colorado

Bookcliff Middle School, Grand Junction, Colorado, 1991–92
East Middle School, Grand Junction, Colorado, 1991–92
Fruita Middle School, Grand Junction, Colorado, 1991–92
Orchard Mesa Middle School, Grand Junction, Colorado, 1991–92
Mount Garfield Middle School, Grand Junction, Colorado, 1991–92
West Middle School, Grand Junction, Colorado, 1991–92
Coordinated by Kathleen Kain (Site Coordinator) and Rebecca Johnson (Field–Test Teacher) based at Mesa County Schools, Grand Junction, Colorado.

Michigan

Isaac E. Crary Middle School, Waterford, Michigan, 1990–92
Detroit Country Day School, Birmingham, Michigan, 1990–92
Stevens T. Mason Middle School, Waterford, Michigan, 1990–92
John D. Pierce Middle School, Waterford, Michigan, 1990–92
Coordinated by Rochelle Rubin based at the Instructional Materials Center, Waterford, Michigan, and David Housel based at Waterford Public Schools, Waterford, Michigan.

Missouri

Academy of Arts & Sciences, Kansas City, Missouri, 1990–91
Coordinated by Francesca Mollura based at the Academy of Arts & Sciences, Kansas City, Missouri.

North Carolina

Farmville Middle School, Farmville, North Carolina, 1991–92
Coordinated by Brenda Evans based at the Department of Public Instruction, Raleigh, North Carolina.

Pennsylvania

Davis School at IUP, Indiana, Pennsylvania, 1991–92
Freeport Junior High School, Freeport, Pennsylvania, 1990–92
Milton Hershey School, Hershey, Pennsylvania, 1991–92
North Hills Junior High School, Pittsburgh, Pennsylvania, 1991–92
Coordinated by Thomas Lord (Site Coordinator) and Terry Peard (Assistant) based at Indiana University of Pennsylvania, Indiana, Pennsylvania.

Wisconsin

Lundahl Junior High, Crystal Lake, Illinois, 1991–92
North Junior High, Crystal Lake, Illinois, 1991–92
Richfield Senior High, Richfield, Minnesota, 1991–92
Wilbur Wright Middle School, Milwaukee, Wisconsin, 1990–92
Coordinated by Jean Moon (Site Coordinator, 1989–90) and Craig Berg (Site Coordinator, 1991–92) and Tracy Posnanski (Graduate Assistant) based at University of Wisconsin-Milwaukee, Milwaukee, Wisconsin.

Coordination, Text Design, Electronic Production and Prepress

PC&F, Inc., Hudson, New Hampshire

Public Support

National Science Foundation

Private Support

Science Kit & Boreal Laboratories, Inc., Tonawanda, New York
IBM Educational Systems, Atlanta, Georgia
Kendall/Hunt Publishing Company (art grant)

Index